**More than 150 previously unpublished letters
between Ezra Pound and his wife Dorothy document
his postwar incarceration and indictment for treason—and the writing of his greatest literary work**

EZRA AND DOROTHY POUND

Letters in Captivity, 1945-46
Edited by OMAR POUND and ROBERT SPOO

These fascinati[...]erience of
Ezra Pound's life, when he was m[...] World War
II and indicted for treason. Omar Pound and Robert Spoo have collected and edited the unpublished correspondence between the poet and
his wife, combining it with military and FBI documents, previously
unknown photographs, and an extensive, insightful introduction, to
create the definitive work on this period of Pound's life.

During his incarceration in a U.S. Army detention camp outside Pisa,
Pound was allowed to write only to his wife, so these letters afford a
unique look at a painful yet highly productive period, when Pound wrote
his acclaimed *Pisan Cantos* and worked on his translations of Confucius.
Readers will discover many fresh insights into the sources and contexts
of the *Cantos* and the circumstances of their composition. Here, too, are
many moving passages testifying to Pound's partnership with Dorothy
and her courageous efforts to help him; her experiences no less than his
come to life in this volume. But perhaps the most moving are the harsh
conditions Pound found himself in: at one point, in the Pisan camp, he
was confined for three weeks in an open air cage, until the sixty year old
poet suffered a breakdown and was moved to a tent in the medical compound. The editors connect the anxious lyricism of the *Pisan Cantos* to
these dramatic experiences, as the poet alternated "between savage
indignation and suave serenity." The book also covers Pound's return to
the U. S. and his confinement in a federal mental institution there.

With more than 150 previously unpublished letters and documents,
all authoritatively annotated, this book offers a rare glimpse into the
life and work of one of our greatest poets.

Omar Pound is a translator of Persian and
Arabic poetry and is presently editing let-
ters written during the Indian Mutiny of
1857. He lives in Princeton, New Jersey.
Robert Spoo is Associate Professor of
English at the University of Tulsa and
Editor in Chief of *James Joyce Quarterly*.
He lives in Tulsa.

Literature

**$35.00t, 0-19-510793-4, 352 pp., 54
halftones, 6⅛ x 9¼**

Ezra
and
Dorothy
Pound

Edited and Annotated by

OMAR POUND and ROBERT SPOO

Ezra
and
Dorothy
Pound

LETTERS IN CAPTIVITY, 1945–1946

OXFORD UNIVERSITY PRESS · NEW YORK · 1998

Oxford University Press

Oxford   New York
Athens   Auckland   Bangkok   Bogota   Bombay   Buenos Aires
Calcutta   Cape Town   Dar es Salaam   Delhi   Florence   Hong Kong
Istanbul   Karachi   Kuala Lumpur   Madras   Madrid   Melbourne
Mexico City   Nairobi   Paris   Singapore   Taipei   Tokyo   Toronto   Warsaw

and associated companies in
Berlin   Ibadan

Published by Oxford University Press, Inc.
198 Madison Avenue, New York, New York   10016

Oxford is a registered trademark of Oxford University Press

CIP: ISBN 0–19–510793–4
© 1997 Letters of Ezra Pound by courtesy of Omar S. Pound and Mary de Rachewiltz.
© 1997 Letters of Dorothy Pound and Omar S. Pound by courtesy of Omar S. Pound.
© 1997 Introduction and editorial matter by Omar Pound and Robert Spoo.
© 1997 Writings and photographs of Frank L. Amprim by courtesy of Ruth Amprim.
© 1997 Writings and photographs of Ramon Arrizabalaga by courtesy of Joan Arrizabalaga.
© 1997 Letters and photographs of Arthur V. Moore by courtesy of his daughter, June Castle.
© 1997 Letters and photographs of John L. Steele by courtesy of Gwen Steele.
© 1997 Letter by T. S. Eliot by courtesy of Valerie Eliot.
© 1997 Letters of Julien Cornell by courtesy of J. Martin Cornell.
© 1997 Letters of Basil Bunting by courtesy of Sima Bunting.

1   3   5   7   9   8   6   4   2

Printed in the United States of America on acid-free paper

To the memory of

ARTHUR VALENTINE MOORE
1894–1975

whose loyalty, perseverance, and friendship alleviated much

ACKNOWLEDGEMENTS

IN PREPARING THIS VOLUME, WE HAVE CONSULTED NUMEROUS individuals and institutions and have been impressed to find so many people willing to go beyond their official responsibilities to help us. We are especially grateful for the kind assistance of former officers and men of the U.S. Army Detention Training Center outside Pisa, and of their families, who have with great generosity and patience answered our questions about the camp and provided us with military documents, private correspondence, and photographs. This volume is the richer for their help.

We wish to thank the trustees of the Ezra Pound Literary Property Trust for originally granting permission to publish the letters and writings of Ezra Pound, and for their sustained support of this project.

We acknowledge with gratitude the financial assistance given by the Marguerite Eyer Wilbur Foundation and by the Donald C. Gallup Fellowship in American Literature (Beinecke Library, Yale University).

We wish to thank the following institutions for the use of letters, manuscripts, and books in their collections: Lilly Library, Indiana University; Beinecke Library, Yale University; McFarlin Library Special Collections, University of Tulsa; Houghton Library, Harvard University; Harry Ransom Humanities Research Center, University of Texas at Austin; Burke Library, Hamilton College; Art Institute of Chicago; and the London Guildhall School of Music.

We wish to thank the following persons for permission to use unpublished materials and photographs: Ruth Amprim, Joan Arrizabalaga, June Castle, J. Martin Cornell, Valerie Eliot, Col. and Mrs. Morris J. Lucree, Col. Julien H. Le Page, Homer L. Somers, and John L. and Gwen Steele. If, despite our efforts, we have failed to locate the owners of any copyrighted materials, we hope we will be pardoned. Our special thanks are due to those who have helped in preparing photographs for publication: Andrew Blackwell; Don Breza, Photographic Services, Princeton University; and Aaron Wiethoff.

We also wish to thank Charles Varga for his invaluable help in locating FBI and National Archives records relating to Ezra Pound; Susan White, the United Nations Librarian at Princeton University, for her tireless efforts; Valerie Eliot for searching out letters from Dorothy Pound to T. S. Eliot; Martin J. Heijdra, sinologist at Princeton University, for identifying the Chinese ideograms and providing invaluable scholarly suggestions; and Massimo Bacigalupo who provided details concerning local residents of Rapallo before and after World War II.

We wish to thank the staffs of various national and military archives for their assiduous searches for material—especially the archival section of the Federal Bureau of Investigation and the U.S. Military Academy Library at West Point.

We greatly appreciate the assistance of Ronald Bush, Tim Redman, and Richard Taylor, who read the entire manuscript in draft form and offered much useful advice. Without Elizabeth Pound's meticulous reading of the manuscript, we would have missed numerous fine points; we owe her a considerable debt for her patience and her historian's eye for detail and accuracy.

We are indebted to many others for their assistance, including John Thomas Anderson, S. J. Anglim (Royal Military College, Sandhurst), David Armitage, Marjorie A. Atwood, Jean Auld (University Library, Dundee, Scotland), Jeff Avila, Kevin Barry (Social Science Reference Center, Princeton University), Emily M. Belcher, Thomas Benediktson, Albert Bowman (Registrar, Dundee, Scotland), Sally Burkman, Thomas Sanders Busha, Jr., Richard Caddel, William R. Cagle (Lilly Library, Indiana University), April Caprak, Anne Carson, Effie Chen, Furio Colombo (Italian Cultural Institute, New York), Julien Conway, Michael Cook (Near East Studies, Princeton University), Loris Curtis (McFarlin Library Special Collections, University of Tulsa), Maj. Randal Cross (Light Infantry Museum, Winchester, UK), Michael Davis (Princeton Theological Seminary), Roy Domenico, Scott Donaldson, Mark Epstein, Achilles Fang, David Farley, F. Faulkner, Jr. (San Antonio Public Library), Victor Flach, Ian Flett (Archive and Record Centre, Dundee, Scotland), Peggy Fox (New Directions Publishing Corporation), Donald C. Gallup, Emery George, Mary George (Information Services, Princeton University), Mrs. Floyd N. George, Susan Glover Godlewski (Art Institute of Chicago), David Gordon, Peg Grafeld, John J. Gruesen, Dean Haas (U.S. Military Academy Library, West Point), Bertha-Licia Harvey, John Henneman, Mary

Herring (Interlibrary Loan Services, McFarlin Library, University of Tulsa), Richard G. Hewlett, Malcolm Higgins (Guildhall School of Music and Drama, London), Jean Holliday, Matthew Hull, Sidney F. Huttner (McFarlin Library Special Collections, University of Tulsa), Samuel Hynes, Ian Jack (Cambridge University), Mary Ann Jensen, Sooni Johnson, William Tremont Johnson III, Steve Jones (Beinecke Library, Yale University), William Chester Jordan, William Joyce (Rare Books and Special Collections, Princeton University), Jeffrey H. Kaimowitz (Watkinson Library, Trinity College), Kathy Kane (College of Law Library, University of Tulsa), Doris Kelly, Jame Laughlin, Rosemary Little, A. Walton Litz, Corinna del Greco Lobner, John Logan (Firestone Library, Princeton University), Frank K. Lorenz (Alumni Secretary, Hamilton College), Andy Lupardus (Government Documents, McFarlin Library, University of Tulsa), Robert Margolis, Thomas McDevitt, Susanne McNatt, Cameron McWhirter, Thorp Merriman, Earl Miner, Michael Montgomery, Gene Moore, Paula Morgan (Music Department, Princeton University), Carol Murphy (Information Services, Firestone Library, Princeton University), Paul O'Keeffe (University of Liverpool), Linda Oppenheim, Degna Marconi Paresce, Patti Ponzoli, Orlando Potter, Grace Pound, Oriana D. Pound, Lawrence Rainey, Luciano Rainusso, Peggy Reinhart, Thomas P. Roche, William Salzillo (Hamilton College), Kenneth D. Schlessinger (National Archives, Military Reference Branch, Washington, D.C.), Randy Schneider (State Department Law Library), Vincent Sherry, Ralph Stenstrom (Burke Library, Hamilton College), Saundra Taylor (Lilly Library, Indiana University), Col. Ralph A. Tolve, Dr. Gael Turnbull, Helen Tweddle, Hans van Marle, Alexander Wainwright, Richard Watson (Gleeson Library, University of San Francisco), Patricia C. Willis (Beinecke Library, Yale University), A. E. Woolley, J. Howard Woolmer, Audrey Wright, and Nancy Young (Mudd Library, Princeton University).

Finally, we wish to thank Oxford University Press, our editor, Susan Chang, and her predecessor, Elizabeth Maguire and members of Oxford University Press for their patience, enthusiastic support, and excellent work. We also wish to thank Adam Bohannon for his help with production and design, Susan Ecklund for her copyediting, and Carla Bolte for her text design.

NOTE ON THE TEXT
BY OMAR POUND

ALL KNOWN LETTERS AND WRITTEN MESSAGES BETWEEN Ezra and Dorothy Pound from the time of his capture in May 1945 to her arrival in Washington, D.C., in July 1946 are printed here. Despite the vicissitudes of war and peace, these letters have survived, along with military orders, travel permits, and other documents, many of them carefully preserved by Dorothy. Other documents were provided by former officers and men of the U.S. Army Disciplinary Training Center (DTC) outside Pisa, or were discovered in government or university archives.

We have aimed throughout at a readable and accurate text. While trying to preserve the appearance and flavor of the originals—especially Ezra's idiosyncratic positioning of paragraphs, sentences, and words on the page—we have, when necessary, made modest changes in order to clarify logical sequence within the texts. Numerous factors—including Dorothy's strategies for overcoming wartime paper shortages, Ezra's use of different army typewriters, his longhand additions of afterthoughts and postscripts in the margins of documents, the interpolation of Chinese characters by both Ezra and Dorothy—have made the job of preparing a clear reading text particularly challenging and have required us to make adjustments when transferring such complex documents to the printed page. We have photographically reproduced letters by Ezra and Dorothy at pp. 000 and 000 to give the reader a sense of the originals.

EDITORIAL CLARIFICATIONS AND DATING OF LETTERS

We have regularized the headings and addresses of all letters, while preserving original spacing and significant variations as far as is conveniently possible. Brief editorial clarifications, as well as translations of most foreign words and phrases, are inserted in the text between brackets. Brackets are also used to indicate conjectural dating of letters; evidence for such dating may be found in the notes following the letters. In particular, the first note after each letter contains a concise postal history and physical description of the letter as well as of its envelope, if extant. Dorothy Pound's diary (Lilly Library, Indiana University), with its meticulous record of letters sent and received, was especially useful for determining dates and other details.

We have silently corrected Ezra's typing errors and misspellings of common words, unless they appear to be deliberately playful or in some other way significant. Dorothy's rare spelling mistakes are treated in a similar fashion. Misspellings of names are permitted to stand in the text and are corrected in the notes. Alternative spellings (e.g., marshal/marshall, Genova/Genoa) are also allowed to stand. The original punctuation of the letters remains unchanged, except where it is indecipherable or creates unnecessary ambiguity, in which case we have added punctuation between brackets.

EZRA'S LETTERS AND THE OFFICIAL CENSORS

Each of Ezra's letters sent from the DTC was examined and initialed by an officer charged with censoring sensitive material. We have identified most of these initials. After his transfer to Washington, D.C., Ezra's outgoing mail continued to be scrutinized by officials at the District Jail, Gallinger Hospital, and St. Elizabeths Hospital. So far as we can tell, nothing in his letters was ever deleted or altered by a censor.

CHINESE CHARACTERS

Ezra and Dorothy inserted Chinese characters into many of their letters. Wherever a Chinese character appears in a letter, we have placed beneath the character, in brackets, the corresponding number from Morrison's Chinese-English dictionary, so that the reader may turn to the glossary in Appendix 2 for a concise definition of the ideogram.

CONTENTS

Ezra
and
Dorothy
Pound

INTRODUCTION

BY ROBERT SPOO

IN 1928, FOUR YEARS AFTER HE HAD LEFT PARIS TO MAKE HIS home in Rapallo, Italy, Ezra Pound announced in his short-lived magazine, *The Exile*: "Quite simply: I want a new civilization."[1] Like many of his passionate utterances, this sweeping call for change was addressed primarily to his native America, a land suffering the disgrace, as he saw it, of Prohibition, book censorship, protectionist copyright laws, and a succession of mediocre occupants of the White House. As he became less tolerant of liberal democracies and bureaucratic systems, he grew more enamored of the charismatic fascism of Benito Mussolini, who, he believed, had restored dynamic individualism and action to government. By 1933, Ezra had persuaded himself that the Duce was a continuation of the best political energies of early America: "The heritage of Jefferson, Quincy Adams, old John Adams, Jackson, Van Buren is HERE, NOW *in the peninsula* at the beginning of the fascist second decennio, not in Massachusetts or Delaware."[2] The poet who had labored to "make it new" by reclaiming forgotten literary traditions was now forging a myth that would allow him to connect his present beliefs with his vision of a vanished America. The exile had found his new civilization in a resurgent Italy.

Much of Mussolini's appeal lay in what Ezra took to be his progressive monetary policies. If the Duce's political instincts had made him a modern incarnation of Jeffersonian virtue, his economic intuitions had led him to the sane policies of social credit and the medieval just price, which Ezra had been advocating for years. Although historians have questioned the value and sincerity of Mussolini's innovations, Ezra along with many others during the period was impressed by the fascist plan for corporative assemblies, the battle for wheat and for land reclamation, and the revaluation of currency. In particular, Ezra believed that Italian fascism was committed to breaking the stranglehold of international banking, which he held responsible for the systematic creation of wars as a means to private enrichment. In fact, Mussolini, despite occasional flashes of his early socialism, was far from doing away with the system of capitalism that underpinned his regime, but Ezra's admiration had rendered him uncritical of the man he called "the Boss." By 1933, Ezra could assert that "any thorough judgment of MUSSOLINI will be in a measure an act of faith, it will depend on what you *believe* the man means, what you believe that he wants to accomplish."[3]

Ezra's correspondence and journalism of the 1930s reflect his growing obsession with international usury and with the bankers' conspiracy that he imagined kept it in place. In 1940 he described himself in the *Japan Times & Mail* as "a fanatical monetary reformer or insister on monetary fact, and the known history of money."[4] When America entered the war on the side of Britain at the end of 1941, he found himself cut off from the two nations that he most wanted to educate, and he relied on radio broadcasting as a way of getting past the barrier. He had long urged that parliamentary and congressional sessions be opened to the public through the technology of radio. As early as 1934, he had told Francesco Monotti, an Italian journalist with connections to influential fascists, that he longed "to croon it over the air to the six million little pink toes American bolsheviki, and the back woods heckers who take the American Muck/ury etc/."[5] After repeated requests, Ezra was permitted by the Italian Ministry of Popular Culture to come to Rome for the purpose of making shortwave overseas transmissions. According to his own recollection, he "began broadcasting in person over the Italian Radio about the Summer of 1940" (Document 6). At first he spoke directly over the air, but in time he was asked to record his talks for later transmission. By early 1941, he was cutting records to be played during the *American Hour*, a program of news, comment, and music. For each broadcast he was paid 350 lire.

Listening to these recordings today, one wonders what the propaganda ministry thought it was accomplishing by allowing Ezra on the air; indeed, his performances raised doubts in official Italian circles as to his intentions and even his sanity. American listeners must have been even more puzzled. The typical broadcast was preceded and followed by selections from Italian opera or by outdated American dance music that could hardly have appealed to the new taste for the big band sound of Glenn Miller and Harry James. After a brief introduction by a female announcer, Ezra's voice would slice through the shortwave static, "EUROPE CALLIN', EZRA POUND SPEAKIN'," and he would hold forth for several minutes in stage Yankee or in a weird brogue, rolling his *r*'s in the style he had adopted for reading his poetry. Sometimes he spoke in a measured didactic voice, almost professorial in its suave patience, at other times in a taunting growl that flattened out and trailed away in a manner reminiscent of W. C. Fields.

However various the vocal personae of these talks, the content was persistently Poundian: the history of money, the evils of the gold standard and international finance, the usurocracy's plot to create wars in regular sequence. Although Ezra occasionally devoted a broadcast to literary topics or to a reading of one of his cantos, more often he could be heard denouncing Winston Churchill or Franklin D. Roosevelt along with the conspiracy of powerful Jews that allegedly controlled these politicians, a conspiracy he sometimes called "high kikery." The anti-Semitic invective that had spread through his personal correspondence in the 1930s reached a fever pitch in his broadcasts: "America ought not to be makin' war on Europe, and America knows it. I think it is time the American U.S. citizen studied Mr. Morgenthau's treasury reports, whether or not he is out in front proclaiming the coming of Zion." "You have got to learn a little, at least a little about the history of your allies. About Jew-ruin'd England. About the wreckage of France, wrecked under yidd control. Lousy with kikes." "The Talmud is the one and only begetter of the Bolshevik system." "And as to all visible signs Roosevelt is MORE in the Jew's hands than Wilson was in 1919."[6]

In these talks, Ezra urged Americans to study the causes of war and to realize that their nation should not be fighting Italy and Germany, but, as he would later insist, he never suggested that servicemen revolt or lay down their weapons. "It is one thing to tell troops to desert, another to try to build up political indignation to take effect AFTER the end of hostilities" (Document 7). His efforts had been made in defense of the U. S. Constitution, not in defiance of it. After America entered the war, Ezra's broadcasts were introduced by a statement of his own devising: "Rome Radio, acting in accordance with the fascist policy of intellectual freedom and free expression of opinion by those who are qualified to hold it, has offered Dr. Ezra Pound the use of the microphone twice a week. It is understood that he will not be asked to say anything whatsoever that goes against his conscience, or anything incompatible with his duties as a citizen of the United States of America."[7] In October 1945 he informed his solicitors in London that "FREE SPEECH was preserved precisely where the British Public would least expect it, namely in Italy by a few unknown, I suppose you would call them 'liberals' working inside the Italian framework" (Letter 17).

After the Japanese attack on Pearl Harbor, Ezra's broadcasts took on a new significance for the U.S. Department of Justice, and the Federal Communications Commission carefully monitored and recorded his transmissions. The FBI's investigation of Ezra was intensive and far-flung. The Bureau's files show that dozens of field offices were involved in pursuing leads and conducting interviews. In a memo dated 30 November 1942, FBI Director J. Edgar Hoover said of the treason investigations: "These cases are considered as being of paramount importance, particularly in view of the interest of the President, the office of War Information, and the Department, and should be given immediate and continuous investigative attention until all leads are exhausted."[8] On 25 July 1943, with the Allied forces advancing on Italy from North Africa, Mussolini was dismissed from office by King Vittorio Emanuele III and placed under arrest. Ezra heard the news in Rapallo while listening to the radio; the announcement was made a few minutes after one of his own broadcasts. The following day, a federal grand jury in Washington, D.C., returned treason indictments against Ezra and seven other Americans acting as Axis broadcasters. All except Ezra had been transmitting from Berlin.

With Mussolini imprisoned and his fascist party dissolved, Marshal Pietro Badoglio, newly appointed as head of an Italian nonparty government, entered into peace negotiations with the Allies. On 8 September 1943 an armistice between Italy and the Western powers was announced. German forces still controlled two-thirds of Italy, however, including the industrial north, and Hitler's commandos succeeded in kidnapping Mussolini from his Italian captors. By the end of September the Germans had installed the Duce as nominal head of a new fascist government, the Italian Social Republic, or Salò Republic, on the western shore of Lake Garda. Ezra went to Milan in late 1943 to offer his services to the new propaganda ministry, but the German-run bureaucracy was not to his liking and henceforth his activities were confined chiefly to sending scripts, short items, and slogans to be broadcast by others.

In the final year of the war, Ezra concentrated his energies on disseminating his economic ideas by means of pamphlets issued under the imprint of Casa Editrice delle Edizioni Popolari of Venice, a branch of the Ministry of Popular Culture. In particular he hoped his Italian translations of Confucius might form part of the "education of the members of the administrative divisions,"[9] as he told Alessandro Pavolini, secretary of the fascist party. As early as 1928, Ezra had been recommending that "higher bureaucrats" be made to read Confucius.[10] Now that an Axis defeat seemed inevitable, he was determined to spread the Confucian doctrine of personal, familial, and governmental order through the Italian hierarchy and educational system. If he had failed to persuade America and Britain to see the rightness of his views, at least he might help the Italians to put their house in order.

By May 1944 the Germans had fortified the coastal defenses at Rapallo, and seafront residents were ordered to evacuate their homes. Ezra and his wife, Dorothy, left their apartment of twenty years in Via Marsala and moved in with Olga Rudge, Ezra's companion and mistress, who lived up the hill from Rapallo at Casa 60 in Sant'Ambrogio. The year during which the three dwelled together could not have been a happy one. Dorothy's English reserve and Olga's American impetuosity were not well suited, and each woman was possessive of Ezra in her own way. Dorothy said little of her year in Sant'Ambrogio, but she recorded one telling remark in September 1945 after moving in with Ezra's mother, Isabel, who lived on another hill of Rapallo. Noting that Isabel's octogenarian primness could be trying at times, Dorothy consoled herself with the reflection that "this life is a mild purgatorio compared to the HELL of No. 60."[11]

By 1945 the Italian partisan liberation movement had grown in strength and numbers, and in late April one of its brigades captured Mussolini and several top-ranking fascists near Lake Como. Dorothy's diary for 29 April laconically notes: "giustiziati [executed] Mussolini Benito, Pavolini Alessandro, Mezzasoma, Starace, etc. ecc."[12] By early May 1945, American troops had entered Rapallo and set up headquarters in one of the seafront hotels. On Wednesday, 2 May, Ezra walked down from Sant'Ambrogio and attempted to make some Americans understand that he wanted to be taken to the United States "to give information to the State Dept."[13] No one seemed to understand who he was or what he wanted, so he returned to Sant'Ambrogio and resumed work on an English translation of the commentary of Mencius, one of the four Confucian classics. "At first I puzzled over having missed a cog somewhere," he told Donald Hall in 1960. "I expected to turn myself in and to be asked about what I learned. I did and I wasn't."[14]

The next morning, Thursday, 3 May, while Olga was off shopping and Dorothy was paying her weekly visit to Isabel, two Italian partisans (partigiani) belonging to the Zoagli Group arrived at Casa 60 and ordered Ezra to come with them. "I was working on the Mencius when the Partigiani came to the front door with a tommy-gun," he later said (Letter 17). As he was led out, he slipped a copy of the Confucian text on which he was working and a small Chinese dictionary into his pocket. Descending the hill path with his captors, he stooped to pick up a eucalyptus seed and pocketed it as well, as he recalled in Canto 80: "one eucalyptus pip / from the salita that goes up from Rapallo" (lines 244–45).

He was taken to partisan headquarters in nearby Zoagli. Meanwhile, Olga returned to Sant'Ambrogio and learned that he had been captured. She dashed down the hill and found him in custody in Zoagli. Together they were taken to Chiavari, where the partisan command was located. "I was driven in to the courtyard at Chiavari," Ezra recalled in 1960. "They had been shooting them, and I thought I was finished then and there. Then finally a guy came in and said he was damned if he would hand me over to the Americans unless I wanted to be handed over to them."[15] Ezra insisted on being taken to a U.S. command post, and the partigiani obliged by delivering him to the Allied Military Post at Lavagna. There was a black troop there commanded by white officers, and a colonel provided Ezra and Olga with sandwiches. At about 5:00 P.M. on 3 May they were driven to U.S. Counter Intelligence Corps headquarters in Genoa, arriving around 7:00 P.M. The CIC detachment of the Ninety-second Division had its offices on the sixth floor of 6 Via Fieschi, which it shared with a branch of the Office of Strategic Services (OSS). Italian carabinieri were posted as guards around the clock.

GENOA

Ezra and Olga were kept waiting all night without food or drink in the hall of CIC headquarters. The next day they were moved to another room, which was, according to Olga, "quite comfortable once we had discovered that the cushions of the armchairs & davenport could be used for covering—it was very cold in Genoa & no blankets or even towels. For food we had emergency ration boxes which we found excellent, & the carabinieri on guard heated water for us in tins so we could have bouillon & hot coffee for first time in years!"[16] At about 2:00 P.M. on 4 May, Maj. Frank L. Amprim, the FBI special agent assigned to Ezra's case in Italy, arrived in Genoa from Rome and proceeded to the office of the CIC.

Amprim, a young attorney from Michigan who had been recruited by the FBI, had been on the trail of targeted Italian and Croatian fascists since Mussolini's fall from power in mid-1943. A secret memo from Amprim in Algiers to the Washington Bureau, dated 7 November 1943, shows that he was already investigating Ezra's connections with fascist officials at that date. By June 1944 he had gotten access to the files at Ente Italiano Audizioni Radiofoniche (EIAR), the radio division in Rome where Ezra recorded his broadcasts, and had collected substantial evidence and interviewed employees. In November 1944 he was in the process of unearthing Ezra's broadcast scripts from the files of the Ministry of Popular Culture.[17]

On arriving at CIC headquarters, Amprim at once sought permission from the commanding officer there, Ramon Arrizabalaga, to question the prisoner. In the days that followed, Amprim and Arrizabalaga pooled their patience and ingenuity in interrogating him. A well-known photograph shows Arrizabalaga (not Amprim, as is often claimed) with notebook and pencil in hand, interviewing Ezra on a couch (see photo on p. 000). On the morning of 5 May, Amprim formally began his questioning and continued for five hours, afterward cabling the Bureau: "EZRA POUND IN CUSTODY CIC, NINETY SECOND DIVISION, GENOA. ADMITS VOLUNTARY BROADCASTS FOR PAY. ADVISE DISPOSITION OF SUBJECT. AMPRIM AT GENOA." A related memo stated that Ezra had been assigned a room at the CIC with a comfortable sleeping couch and was being provided Army K rations, coffee and milk, and a means of heating his food.[18]

Amprim had no sooner begun his questioning than Ezra asked if he would help him send a telegram to President Truman offering his services as a peace negotiator with the Japanese. Ezra explained that, as executor of the literary estate of the American Orientalist Ernest Fenollosa, he had the credentials and the knowledge to help the United States conclude a Confucian peace with Japan that would be acceptable to China as well. In addition to requesting the cable, Ezra wrote out the text of a final radio broadcast, which he titled "Ashes of Europe Calling," a somber variation on his customary opening, "Europe Calling." The script is essentially a plea to the victorious United States to show justice to the vanquished Axis nations. Ezra urges that Italy be placed under American management until it can elect a new government on the basis of fairness and honesty. He also hopes that Italy and Germany will not "lose benefit of economic advance." Fearing another Versailles treaty, he implores: "No peace not on justice—not crush germany—not leave hate." Amprim told Ezra that he could neither arrange for a broadcast nor dispatch any cables to Truman, he carefully passed these texts on to Bureau headquarters in Washington (see Documents 3 and 4).

Amprim and Arrizabalaga labored for two days, 6 and 7 May, to extract a formal statement from their prisoner; at least two drafts were produced, then revised and amplified at Ezra's insistence. The resulting text, a six-page "Sworn Statement" (Document 6), is an extremely detailed account of his activities and motives between 1940 and 1945. Not satisfied that the essence of his ideas had been expressed, Ezra composed two additional statements and asked that these be appended: "Outline of Economic Bases of Historic Process" and "Further Points" (Document 7). These texts set forth his fundamental economic and Confucian rationales for broadcasting—"points I have been trying to make during the past 25 years, and which I rashly did NOT stop trying to make, when caught off sides, but in reach of a microphone." The hint of self-criticism continues: "I hope my errors will be considered in relation to the main picture." Mussolini's failure ("Poor old Benito err'd all right") is attributed to his not receiving Ezra's translation of Confucius in time to reform his government in accordance with ancient Chinese wisdom.

Ezra's acknowledgments of error stop short of confession, however: "I do not believe I have betrayed anyone whomsoever." The distinction he implies between error and guilt is crucial to an understanding of his ethical posture in the period following his capture, and it bears comparison with the famously elusive language of "error" and "vanity" in *The Pisan Cantos*, which he began drafting a few weeks later. For Ezra, error must be placed in the context of a life of ethical exertion, balanced by the prevailing rightness and the instinct to act; yet, so precarious are the fortunes of the just man that a single error might destroy the dream of a lifetime. The events of 1945 had forced a sense of enormous tragedy upon Ezra's customary zeal.

Olga Rudge remained at the CIC office while Ezra was being interrogated and later remarked that her four days there were "among the happiest of my life."[19] On 7 May, she was driven back to Sant'Ambrogio by two American officers, probably Amprim and Arrizabalaga. Dorothy jotted in her diary for 7 May: "Olga back 6.30 + 2 USAs."[20] On the same day, Amprim handed Dorothy a note from Ezra authorizing a search of his papers (Letter 2), and proceeded to collect a large quantity of books, letters, and radio scripts. In his memo of 20 May to J. Edgar Hoover, Amprim noted that Dorothy "was very cooperative in finding incriminating evidence against her husband and did not seem to be in the least disturbed when the writer [Amprim] searched the premises at #60 Sant'Ambrogio." Over the next several months, Amprim made further visits to Sant'Ambrogio and Rapallo in quest of evidence.

"When in May 1945 I got back from C.I.C.," Olga wrote, "I found D. with her valises all packed for Baccin [a peasant who worked for Olga] to take down next morning—I said of course *now* stay as long as convenient—'Oh no I can't, the old ladies [*sic*] tenants left the end of the month & I can't leave her in the flat alone.'"[21] With Ezra gone,

Dorothy lost no time in escaping from Sant'Ambrogio and moving in with Ezra's aged mother, Isabel, at Villa Raggio on a hill above Rapallo. Dorothy's brief letters to Ezra during his detention in Genoa mainly concern practical matters and show that she was willing to travel to the United States to be near him, should he be transferred there. "I hope all the time you are getting well fed!" she says in Letter 5.

In a draft letter to T. S. Eliot, dated 19 July 1945, Olga said of Ezra, "I saw him last in Genoa on May 7th. He was in a state of Confucian serenity."[22] The CIC stay was indeed a happy, productive one for Ezra. He had a room with a couch, regular rations, the use of a typewriter, and attentive listeners to educate. Investigators or no, Amprim and Arrizabalaga were actually reading and responding to his ideas, something he had greatly missed during the war years. He grew so comfortable with his hosts at the CIC that on numerous occasions he gave the fascist salute as they entered the room.[23] Amprim was to be trusted, he decided, because he had "expressed himself as convinced that I was telling him the absolute truth [and had] with great care collected far more proof to that effect than I or any private lawyer could have got at" (Letter 17). If the world would not attend to Ezra any other way, perhaps with Amprim's help he could get a hearing once enough evidence had piled up to make the soundness of his views irrefutable.

During his three weeks in Genoa, Ezra made considerable progress on his English translations of Confucius. A well-known photograph taken at the CIC (not at the Pisan detention camp, as captions usually assert) shows him sitting before a typewriter with one of his Confucian pamphlets spread open on the desk (see photo on p. 000). He spoke of this project as his "american version of Kung" (Letter 14) and declared the texts to have been "at the root of the DURABLE chinese dynasties[,] the ONLY basis on which a world order can work." Just as he had hoped to reform the Italian government by exposing its officials to Chinese wisdom, so he felt it his duty now to instruct Americans in the just uses of power. The economic revolution that he had believed the Axis leaders to be on the point of carrying through had migrated, with the Allied victory, to the United States and Britain. Now he must educate the world's new leaders, and he could point to the ashes of Europe as the final lesson of his own Confucian tuition: "I do not know that I would have gotten to the centre of [Confucius's] meaning if I had not been down under the collapse of a regime" (Letter 17).

Ezra was between tasks, trying to regain his balance and direction. He was tormented by the desire to be useful, whether as a member of the diplomatic peace mission to Japan or as a special envoy to the Soviet Union authorized to speak with Stalin in his native Georgian. In October 1945 he wrote Dorothy of his wish to be sent to Rome to help with "an Italo-american amity" (Letter 19). He could not believe that his knowledge of Europe and Italy and his research into the history of money and credit were not going to be made available to Truman, Hugh Dalton, and other leaders of postwar reconstruction. He saw England and America as beginning to turn to economic policies that he had been advocating for twenty years, and he felt painfully left out. "Work in the chaos," he wrote Dorothy, "that is the time to plant sprouts. NOW" (Letter 46).

Ezra's worldview was essentially a static one, a time lag of the mind. Circumstances might change, years elapse, but his stock themes and characters remained the same: villains of international finance, political buffoons and miscreants, and the small countervailing cenacle of serious characters and heroes. Now, under the strain of events, he more than ever dreamed of playing a world-historical role as the sane economist, the Confucian super ambassador. Such grandiosity alternated with admissions that he was utterly without information about current events. He complained often of his "ABSOLUTE ignorance" of America since 1940 and wondered if his broadcasts had done any good at all (Letter 17). He was plagued by doubts that his transmissions had even been heard. "I wonder if anyone listens?" was a question that worried him often during the war;[24] now it returned to nag at him in moments of keen self-doubt.

For all the amenities of the CIC, there must have been an undertow of fear beneath Ezra's energetic mood. Ramon Arrizabalaga believed that Ezra was intensely afraid of falling into the hands of the partigiani and was grateful to be in protective custody at Genoa. News of accused traitors was appearing regularly in the Mediterranean edition of *The Stars and Stripes* in the spring and summer of 1945: "Traitor Pound Reported Captured Near Genoa" (7 May); "Quisling Appeals" (8 May); "Robert Ley Captured" (17 May); "Quisling on Stand, Poses as Lunatic to Save His Scalp" (28 May); "Lord Haw Haw Now Prisoner of British" (30 May); "Pound's Treason Trial to Be Held in America" (31 May); "The Trail of 'Axis Sally' Grows Hot in North Italy" (5 June); "Laval, Busy on His Memoirs, Believed Fearing Lynch Mob" (11 June); "Pétain's Trial Awaited, He'll Be His Own Counsel" (25 June); "Laval Surrenders to Yanks in Linz; En Route to French" (31 July); "Quisling Is Found Guilty of Treason; Gets Firing Squad" (11 September).

Amprim's memos to Bureau headquarters show that he and Arrizabalaga were increasingly anxious to learn what they were to do with their prisoner now that they had finished questioning him. On 21 May Amprim received a phone call from Counter Intelligence, telling him that Ezra would soon be placed "in a military stockade near Pisa," where the Department of Justice wanted him held "pending investigation of his case."[25] Although Amprim felt that he had concluded the bulk of his investigation, authorities in the States insisted that he continue to develop witnesses because the U.S. Constitution requires the testimony of two witnesses to each overt act of treason. Since the only people who had actually seen Ezra record his broadcasts were Italian radio employees who spoke little or no English, Amprim's task was not going to be an easy one. Official memos stated that Ezra was to remain in Italy during the remainder of the investigation, so that he might be available for further interrogation.

On 22 May, orders were cabled to transfer him "without delay under guard to MTOUSA Disciplinary Training Center for confinement pending disposition instructions. Exercise utmost security measures to prevent escape or suicide. No press interviews authorized. Accord no preferential treatment" (Document 1). Arrizabalaga recalled that on 24 May the "5th Army Provost Marshal sent several Jeep loads of MP's to Genova to take him away. It was actually rather a sorry sight to see the big six foot MP's commanded by a Captain relieve Subject [Ezra] of his shoestrings, belt, necktie and clamp a huge pair of handcuffs to one of his wrists, the other end to an MP's wrist and take him away. We had treated him courteously and he couldn't understand it. He said to me, 'I don't understand it.' I said, 'Mr. Pound, you are no longer in my jurisdiction, and I can't help it.' He then said, 'Do they know who I am?' I answered, 'Yes they do.' They took him to Pisa" (Appendix 1).

PISA

At the U.S. Army Disciplinary Training Center (DTC) outside Pisa, a special cell had been prepared for Ezra. The wire mesh of one of the cages there—units known as "death cells," used for holding prisoners awaiting execution at Aversa near Naples—had been reinforced with "air-strip" steel. These exposed cages were situated inside several barriers of barbed wire. Ezra's was at the end of the row, next to the perimeter fence, with a view of the military road beyond the stockade. He arrived at the main gates of the DTC around 1500 hours. According to Robert L. Allen, one of the DTC medical staff, Ezra "thought that his visit would end as soon as a plane was readied at Pisa air-field." He still hoped that his knowledge would prove more important to the government than his supposed guilt.[26]

Ezra was stripped of his civilian clothes, which he had been allowed to wear in Genoa, and issued army fatigues and laceless boots. Unlike other prisoners, he was not permitted to exercise outside his cage and was supplied a pile of blankets to arrange on the cement floor. A tin can served for a toilet. He was allowed to keep his volume of Confucius and the small Chinese dictionary, and was given a regular-issue Bible. One of the guards recalled: "Pound's volume of Confucius was by his side continually, and the prisoner read for hours, or simply sat and combed his ragged beard, watching the Pisa road where passers-by and an occasional white ox were visible."[27] Orders required that he be kept under constant observation; bright lights were trained on his cell at night. He later alluded to the "Gorilla Cage," convinced that he had been put on display for the merriment of all.

Julien Cornell, Ezra's attorney, described the cage experience after interviewing his client in November 1945: "He knew not whether he would rot away in this cage or be taken out and hanged as a traitor. But far worse than these was the thought that his wife and daughter would never know his fate, and would dream, until they reached their own graves, of the agony interred in his. Not far away were the pens in which long term offenders were confined, but all other prisoners were forbidden to speak to Pound, and could not come near him. [. . .] After enduring the tropical sun all day, neither sleep nor rest came with the night—electric lights glared into the poet's cage and burned into his bloodshot eyes."[28] In a DTC mug shot taken on 26 May after he had spent two nights in the cage, Ezra stares into the camera with taut impatience, as if expecting someone to explain the error of this treatment. His eyes already appear to be inflamed by dust and glare (see photo on p. 000).

The Mediterranean Theater's Disciplinary Training Center held U.S. soldiers who had been convicted of crimes. *Yank: The Army Weekly* for 11 November 1945 described the camp as holding thirty-six hundred prisoners on "the dusty, one-half-mile-square tract, three miles north of Pisa." Trainees, as the prisoners were called, had

a last chance to clean up their records and return to honorable status in the Army and then to civilian life. All the prisoners have been court-martialed, dishonorably discharged and sentenced to from five years to life imprisonment. Now they have an opportunity to work out their full sentences by enduring one year of training 14 hours a day, one year of terrible discipline, unbroken regimentation, monotony and constant chewing. Every Saturday, about 150 men make it and "graduate" as full- fledged privates in the Army once more.

Organized at Casablanca in 1943, the MTOUSA center moved to Pisa last Christmas Eve, when the front lines were only 12 miles away. The cadre of 74 officers and 514 EM [enlisted men], under the command of Lt. Col. John L. Steele of St. Johnsbury, Vt., are mostly combat veterans and have been specially trained. The toughest top kick in a regular outfit would blanch at the sternness of a corporal on the DTC staff. The greatest single cause of confinement in the DTC is going AWOL, which has been the undoing of 22 percent of the inmates. Desertion has put 15 percent there; misbehavior before the enemy, murder, rape, larceny and other felonies, 7 percent and disobedience, 5 percent. Officers, of whom there are now three confined in the center, stay confined there pending review of their court- martial decision. They are segregated from the EM, live in pyramidal rather than pup tents, and do not perform work details, but they do not get the courtesy usually shown commissioned officers.[29]

Lieutenant Colonel Steele described the DTC in an undated letter to his family: "I think the army has sunk at least a million dollars into this place, and we don't have any luxuries to speak of either. Our buildings are made of light wood frames with chicken-wire and tar paper for roofs and walls, and the stockade is simply a big barbed wire fence. The prisoners live in pup tents and we live in larger ones. Even so there are countless things that go into a camp like this that one would not ordinarily think of, such as the sewage system, extensive road networks, electric power plant, etc."[30]

After several days of scorching sun and nights of chill air, Ezra was allowed to have a pup tent in his cage, which "quite ingeniously, he pitched in several different ways."[31] With unlimited opportunity to contemplate the natural scene before him, he named one peak of the Carrara mountains "Mount Taishan," after a sacred Chinese mountain, and two other hills the "Breasts of Helen." He told Allen that he spent "hours watching wasps construct a nest and of his fascination with the work of an ant colony." "His daily exercises caused quite a stir. He would engage in imaginary tennis matches, making graceful, looping forehands and backhands. He assumed fencing stances and danced nimbly about the cage, shadow boxing."[32] Yet the camp itself frightened him; the guard towers around its perimeter came to seem, as he put it in *The Pisan Cantos*, "4 giants at the 4 corners." The long line of fence posts resembled "10,000 gibbet-iform posts supporting barbed wire," and prisoners went through their routines "with the shadow of the gibbets attendant." The menace of this prefab hell was intensified by its isolation: "beyond the stockade there is chaos and nothingness."[33]

In mid-June, after complaining to the guards of giddiness and claustrophobia, Ezra received a medical examination. He had been in the cage for three weeks. Two psychiatrists were detailed to study him. Captain Richard W. Finner's 14 June report mentions a "spell" that Ezra had "about a week ago" while sitting in the sun, accompanied by "great difficulty in collecting his thoughts." He was also experiencing "difficulty in concentration" and "easy fatiguability." He had become "afraid of the door and the lock of his enclosure" and worried that he would "forget some messages which he wishes eventually to tell others." The next day Captain Walter H. Baer, the other psychiatrist, warned that, "[d]ue to his age and loss of personality resilience, prolonged exposure in present environment may precipitate a mental breakdown, of which premonitory symptoms are discernible. Early transfer to the United States or to an institution in this theatre with more adequate facilities for care is recommended."[34] An FBI memo of 26 June 1945 from Hoover to Assistant Attorney General Tom Clark echoed Baer's conclusions and added that Major Amprim was recommending Ezra's return to the States "without delay."[35]

The physical strain of confinement must have been the chief cause of Ezra's collapse, along with the prohibition on exercise. At sixty, he was still in the habit of playing tennis or swimming almost daily. Another factor was present, however. Throughout his life Ezra had tended to become excited and irritable whenever he was deprived of means of communication with others, a pattern that may be discerned in his impulsive moves from London and Paris in the 1920s after he had grown impatient with the intellectual life of those cities. It also lay behind the frenzy of his radio talks, which he often said were a strategy for reestablishing contact with colleagues in England and America once the war had severed other forms of communication. Ezra's reaction to incarceration at Pisa and Washington had considerably to do with panic and frustration at being silenced and prevented from assisting in events unfolding in the postwar period.

As a result of the psychiatrists' reports, he was transferred to the medical area and given a pyramidal (eight-man) tent of the type assigned to officer prisoners. "During the first week or so in the Medical Compound he kept to himself in his tent," Allen recalled. "He soon stripped off his Army fatigue clothes and spent the warm summer days comfortably attired only in Army olive drab underwear, a fatigue cap, G.I. shoes and socks. He found an old broom handle that became a tennis racquet, a billiard cue, a rapier, a baseball bat to hit small stones and a stick which he swung out smartly to match his long stride. His constitutionals wore a circular path in the compound grass."[36] Some of the most moving lines in *The Pisan Cantos* describe Ezra's experiences in his tent: "Only shadows enter my tent / as men pass between me and the sunset." "[I]n the drenched tent there is quiet / sered eyes are at rest."[37]

At the time of Ezra's arrival at the camp in May, Lieutenant Colonel Steele was on compassionate leave for a family illness in the States. He returned on 13 June, about the time that Ezra was moved to the medical compound. Steele soon went to inspect his prisoner, who talked at him for two or three hours before he could get an answer to his simple question about additional blankets. Steele recalled that Ezra wanted to discuss only "economics, and the fact that he needed to go straighten out Truman. He thought that this could be done if he could get to Washington. [. . .] He was very animated, and the piercing eyes were just fascinating." After the initial mistake of putting him in the cage, Steele thought, "it worked out pretty well. . . . We did what we could [though] he would still be confined."[38]

Ezra's life in the medical compound began to assume the regularity that he had always needed to be happy and busy. Every evening he reported on sick call to the medical hut to be given footbaths or eyedrops. The medical staff consisted of "four MDs, one dentist, and two clinical psychologists, who performed their duties in prefabricated structures built of plywood, with electrical power supplied by generators."[39] Ezra lectured the staff at the DTC just as he had his interrogators at the CIC, a sign that his energies were returning. He ranted about "the 'dunghill usurers' and 'usuring cutthroats.' Among others, he damned Mussolini ('the crude peasant'), Hitler, FDR, Churchill, and Henry Morgenthau."[40] On 20 August, Steele wrote his mother about Ezra's eccentricity, colorful language, and fixed opinions, and said that he might "stop by for a chat with the old boy" that evening.[41]

Ezra was once again getting work done, a joyous resumption of the creative burst of Genoa. A kindly soldier, "Mr Edwards," provided him with a "table ex packing box" for his tent, and he discovered a copy of *The Pocket Book of Verse* "on the jo-house seat."[42] He had got hold of a pencil and cheap paper, and was at work setting down new cantos, scrawling hastily in defiance of the paper's ruled lines. "Throughout the summer of 1945 Pound was in excellent spirits," noted Allen. "He was granted permission to use the dispensary typewriter in the evening. [. . .] After taps when all trainees were in the tents, Pound worked on his *Cantos* and Chinese translations. The constant clanging and banging of the typewriter, which he punched angrily with his index fingers, were always accompanied by a high-pitched humming sound he made as the carriage raced the bell. He swore well and profusely over typing errors."[43]

Meanwhile, the treason investigation was dragging on. An FBI memo to Amprim dated 25 June 1945 reveals impatience on the part of the authorities in the States: "Discontinue all General Investigation in case and concentrate on development of two witnesses to same overt act. For example, two or more persons who saw Pound make a particular recording on a particular day." As of 7 September Amprim still had not found two witnesses to Ezra's acts of recording his broadcasts. On 21 September the FBI cabled Amprim that the prisoner could not be returned to the United States until witnesses were developed.[44] Earlier in the summer, Brig. Gen. John M. Weir of the War Crimes Office had noted that a Justice official felt "it would be unfortunate to bring Pound back to the United States and then find that he would be needed in Italy for the effective building up of the case."[45]

During these months Dorothy became increasingly worried, for the authorities refused to tell her where her husband was being held. She wrote Ronald Duncan on 15 July 1945 that she had had a brief note from Ezra in late May (Letter 6). "Since when we have had nothing whatever. I do not know whether he is dead or alive—We have written to consuls etc. etc: no go."[46] John Drummond, an English friend of Ezra's who was a lance corporal at HQ Allied Commission in Rome, was a steady source of strength and information to Dorothy and Olga Rudge in this period. Drummond played a particularly valuable role as intermediary between the two women and their interests in Ezra. The tensions between Dorothy and Olga made this a difficult office at times.[47]

At last, on 24 August, Col. Walter A. Hardie, provost marshal general of the Mediterranean Theater of Operations, wrote Dorothy to inform her of Ezra's confinement at the DTC and to instruct her about regulations for visiting. "He is enjoying a good state of health," he added (Document 8). On 18 September, Lt. Col. Ralph A. Tolve, provost marshal, wrote to tell her that she was permitted to correspond with her husband, "subject to usual censorship in effect." "Oh Mao! Glory be!" she wrote Ezra. "I have burnt incense to Apollo several times for help" (Letter 11). Around the same time, an official routing slip, signed by Lieutenant Colonel Steele, was issued to Ezra, indicating that he could now correspond with his wife and receive visits from her (Document 10). In Canto 76, composed earlier that summer, Ezra had grumbled, "O white-chested martin, God damn it, / as no one else will carry a message" (lines 233–34). Now he could depend on messages being carried in the normal way.

His first three letters (Letters 7–9), written between 20 and 23 September, are filled with excited requests and instructions. He is understandably eager for "news of everything" and wants Dorothy to tell various friends to write him. In Letter 9 he enclosed a typed copy of Canto 81, the first of several extracts from the new cantos that he passed on to her. Probably the best known of *The Pisan Cantos*, Canto 81 records a visionary moment that Ezra experienced in the camp when "there came new subtlety of eyes into my tent." The canto also contains the moving "libretto" with its defiant affirmation: "What thou lovest well remains, / the rest is dross" (lines 120, 136–37). Ezra had chosen one of the most lucid and dramatic sections of the new work to pass on to Dorothy, as if to convey in five typed pages the essence of his predicament since May. With amusing understatement he observed that the enclosure was "more human than a dull letter—& in parts mild enough to suit mother" (Letter 9). Dorothy quickly perceived what many critics since have remarked, that these cantos are "the memories that make up yr. person" (Letter 23).

As Ezra's "Note to Base Censor" (Letter 47) explained, *The Pisan Cantos* are a "narrative," the flow of the poet's mind about the heaped wreckage of its dreams. It is a narrative more carefully wrought than is usually supposed. From his tent in the medical compound, the poet lets his memory range over a vast temporal landscape, often back to London in the period before World War I, or what Ezra calls "the sanity of 1912" before the world was given over to wars (Letter 19). Brief references to his three weeks in the cage are all cast neatly in the past tense, jagged stones set in the river's flow. The narrative faithfully traces the metamorphosis of memory and reflection, with events in the camp occasionally impinging and the observed natural world adding the dignity of slow beauty and rhythmic change. While the poem tells the story of Ezra's mind under the collapse of its ideals, he himself is strangely without identity, an Odysseus whose makeshift raft has broken up in the whirlpool of events: "A man on whom the sun has gone down." Months of being held incommunicado had made him feel lost to his loved ones and to the world. "[N]ow there are no more days / οὖτις," declares no-man Odysseus in Canto 80 (lines 212–13).

The Pisan Cantos show the poet alternating between savage indignation and suave serenity. There is a restless darting from stern didacticism to sudden lyric to humorous observation, and back. Thoughts of usury lead to a memory of the "death cells," as if by suppressed syllogism Ezra were laying the blame for his treatment at the door of the Rothschilds. Abrupt juxtapositions of values continually startle the reader. Erotic vision gives way to political anger, which in turn yields to the consolations of nature or the trivialities of camp life. Ezra's letters to Dorothy from the DTC show similar patterns of thought. One particularly bustling, manic letter contains instructions concerning economic reform to be passed on to various people: friends are to be told to assist Hugh Dalton, the new chancellor of the exchequer in Britain, by promoting Social Credit policies. In the midst of these urgings Ezra suddenly breaks off to notice a "[n]ew set of odd noises traced to kat climbin' tent flaps," and then resumes: "Only true democracy is Douglasite, per capita, way out of huge formation of monopolies etc" (Letter 46). The noisy visitor was probably "Ladro the night cat," the DTC feline that steals in and out of the pages of *The Pisan Cantos* with equally little warning.

Ezra wrote Dorothy on 8 October to say that he had "received her first letter this a.m." He also noted that he had done "10 Cantos" (Letter 19). Cantos 74 to 83 represented the Pisan achievement up to that point. Had the sequence halted there, it would have been a very different poem from the one we know. When Ezra read in Dorothy's letter that J. P. Angold, a young English poet whom he admired, had been killed, he was painfully reminded of talented friends who had died in the World War I. The lament that opens Canto 84—"8th October: Si tuit li dolh elh plor / Angold τέθνηκε"—is Ezra's immediate, visceral response to what he had learned. In the draft version of Canto 84, the lines about Angold replace some rather mawkish and tentative verses about Ezra's own imagined death, as if the fiction of a poet's demise, no matter how plausible in the circumstances, had no place beside the reality of war's wastage.

Once Dorothy's letters began arriving at the DTC, they left their mark on the poem in progress—a convergence that makes the most human of *The Cantos* more human still. Canto 84, the last of the sequence, contains several phrases plucked from Dorothy's description, in her 5 October letter, of snow atop the Carrara mountains, which she saw while returning from her first visit to the DTC (see Letter 18n). She had finally managed to reach the camp on 3 October, despite difficulties of transport. "I have seen Ez. for a long hour," she wrote Olga afterward. "An awful journey—but he looks really wonderfully well—in Khaki—with plenty of woollen underneath & huge army boots. [. . .] Food good—his weigh[t] normal once more. His nerves I thought not bad at all. Latterly has been working on Confucius & done some more Cantos. The two officers I met (present at interview) both *very* nice. He has a tent, with view of mountains & 'a mappin terrace' for fresh air."[48] Ezra's reference to "a mappin terrace" was the kind of telegraphic quip that two people who had lived in London before World War I might share. In 1912, Mappin & Webb, the well-known silver and jewelry company, made a handsome donation to the London Zoo for the creation of great stone terraces for the resident bears to roam upon. *In The Pisan Cantos* Ezra imagines himself as a caged panther, but in his conversation with Dorothy he chose a different animal from their shared bestiary.

Ezra wrote Dorothy after the visit that he was "grateful for her heroick voyage" (Letter 16) and obliquely commemorated it in Canto 84: "and as who passed the gorges between sheer cliffs" (line 47). In Letters 18 and 41 she describes her "fantastic journey back"—from Pisa to Viareggio in a car provided by the DTC, thence to Massa on foot and via motorbus in the company of an elderly doctor, by post office van to La Spezia where she rested and ate sandwiches given her at the DTC, from La Spezia to Sestri in a train, and by motorbus into Rapallo. Years later she recalled "all the saga of my two trips to the camp, one in a strange car, the other [on 11 November] in a camion with a New Zealand football team . . . with sandwiches, my first meat for weeks—and how I walked several miles to get home after seeing E.P., with an unknown doctor who took me to his home at Massa Carrara for the night—his antique house devastated by troops—his wife and son so kind—cold soup and hot milk was all the food they had . . . Why and how one survives! Poor E. P."[49]

The letters in this volume reveal the important role that Dorothy played in the long months of Ezra's initial incarcerations—a prelude to the years she would spend by his side in Washington, D.C. She knew instinctively that confinement would make him crave news of the outside world and took pains to write letters that would reassure him that the ordinary life of Rapallo continued, that friends in England and America were thinking of him, and that she herself was quietly but determinedly getting her affairs and his in order. The compassionate practicality of her letters contrasts sharply with the scattered intensity of his own; placed side by side, these letters reveal much about the profound compatibility of two very different people who had known each other since 1909. Dorothy's prudence and calm resolve emerge as a steadying influence on Ezra in this turbulent period of uncertainty.

Although always supportive, Dorothy was not passive, and she made clear her opposition to Ezra's idea of defending himself at the expected trial. He doubted that any attorney would have the background necessary to plead his case: "I favour a defender who has written a life of J. Adams and translated Confucius. Otherwise how CAN he know what it is about?" (Letter 37). John Drummond, T. S. Eliot, and other friends agreed with Dorothy on the matter of legal counsel. Drummond wrote Ezra: "When there is someone out for your blood (as the prosecutor will be—quite irrespective of the fundamental rights or wrongs of your case), and using the law as his weapon, you *must* have someone able to use the same weapon in your defence. It's not as if you were challenged to a duel and could choose your weapons."[50] If Ezra regarded the impending legal proceedings as a kind of duel of honor, Olga Rudge saw them in terms of a potentially successful radio talk. When she was interviewed in the early 1980s, she was still expressing disappointment that he had not been allowed to conduct his own defense: "he spoke beautifully and he had a chance of getting off!"[51] Fortunately, Ezra never did get the chance to appear *pro se*, partly as a result of Dorothy's diligent correspondence with James Laughlin, A. V. Moore, and others who were working to secure proper legal counsel.

By the middle of October, Ezra was beginning to show a restless irritability with his situation. Robert L. Allen noticed that he was depressed in this period: "with no indication of when the occupation of Italy would be terminated, he almost despaired of ever leaving Pisa."[52] His letters contain various hints of impatience, as when he tells Dorothy in Letter 29 that "the time has now come when it wd/ be suitable for you to write to Unkle George, The Hon. G.H.T. [Congressman George Holden Tinkham]," or when he tries in Letter 32 to convince the DTC commandant to release him to Rapallo on parole, an idea he had mentioned to Dorothy when she visited the camp. More than ever he wanted to play a part in the current political scene. "I could be of use NOW in reconstruct[ion]," he tells Dorothy in Letter 44. "In view of the situation in China and Japan," he informs the DTC commandant, "it seems to me that the bottling of my knowledge now amounts to suppression of military information" (Letter 42). A visit from his daughter, Mary Rudge, in the company of Olga on 17 October provided some distraction in this period of anxious waiting.

On 6 November, Attorney General Tom Clark announced at a press conference that five technicians from Rome Radio who had been identified by the FBI as witnesses to Ezra's broadcasts were being flown to the United States to testify. At first Ezra joked about the report and said that no one had seen him broadcast. The technicians "were obviously impostors 'just making the flight to get some decent food.'" But Allen noticed that Ezra's "tone of conversation changed and occasionally he spoke of himself in the past tense. Several times he said, 'If I go down, someone must carry on.'"[53] He continued to add to his growing cantos, but some of the new lines had a brittle, nervous quality not present in the earlier parts. Certain passages, later cut from the poem, brooded on the sacrifice of young artists to war, such as the musician Rudolph Dolmetsch, of whose death Ezra learned during Dorothy's second visit to the DTC on 11 November.

"One evening after taps in the middle of November, Pound was sitting in the dispensary reading Joseph E. Davies' *Mission to Moscow*. The Charge of Quarters sat at the desk next to him. From time to time Pound commented on the book. Suddenly the door opened and two young lieutenants entered. They told Pound that he would be flown to Washington in one hour and to get his personal effects together. They turned and left. Pound handed the book to the C.Q. He asked him to thank all the medical personnel for their kindness. He then walked to the door of the prefab, turned and, with a half-smile, put both hands around his neck to form a noose and jerked up his chin."[54] This was 16 November. A letter to Dorothy that Ezra had begun typing two days earlier breaks off with a sudden pencil scrawl: "Leaving probably Rome. love E" (Letter 50).

Homer Somers, a young officer at the DTC, was sorry to see him go. Many years later he recalled that the poet "sadly removed his fatigues and put on the clothes he arrived in. All the time everyone was kidding and joking with him. I believe at that time he was apprehensive of the future and could only think of the solitude, friendliness and productiveness of the latter part of his stay at the DTC."[55] According to Lt. Col. P. V. Holder's record, Ezra left the DTC in a military jeep in "cold raw" weather at 2030 hours and arrived at Ciampino airport near Rome at 0445 on 17 November (Document 13). He was held in the guardhouse there for a few hours. At 0830, a plane carrying him and the escorting officers left the airport. Ezra had never flown before.

WASHINGTON, D.C.

Ezra's plane landed at Bolling Field, an airstrip on the bank of the Potomac, late on the evening of 18 November 1945. Two plainclothes U.S. marshals took him to an office where he was told his rights before being locked up in the District of Columbia Jail. The next day he was brought before Bolitha J. Laws, chief justice of the District of Columbia District Court, for a preliminary arraignment. Ezra explained that his purpose in broadcasting was "to keep all hell from breaking loose in the world" and asked to be allowed to act as his own counsel. Judge Laws denied the request, saying that the charge was too serious, and overruled Ezra's suggestion that "the court go on asking me questions until it gets what I mean." Afterward, Ezra told reporters that he wanted to learn Georgian, Stalin's native tongue, so that he could confer with the Soviet premier and find out "what's in the back of his mind" (Document 14n). Ezra had not yet given up hope of dispensing Confucian wisdom to world leaders, or, failing that, arguing his case eloquently to a Washington jury. Newspapers quoted him as denying that he had ever supported Mussolini, that "puffed up bubble," or that he had betrayed his country in any way. "If that damn fool idea is still in anybody's head, I want to wipe it out."[56]

Ida and Adah Lee Mapel, elderly friends of Ezra's who lived in Washington, visited him at the District Jail on 20 November and found him "a bit nervous."[57] Julien Cornell, the young Quaker civil liberties lawyer who had agreed to defend him, saw him for two hours the same day and later wrote James Laughlin: "He is very wobbly in his mind and while his talk is entirely rational, he flits from one idea to another and is unable to concentrate even to the extent of answering a single question without immediately wandering off the subject." He added that he had "discussed with him the possibility of pleading insanity as a defense and he has no objection. In fact he told me that the idea had already occurred to him."[58] Cornell planned to argue that Ezra was too shaken mentally by his long incarceration to be able to stand trial.

On 20 November, Ezra wrote his first letter to Dorothy from Washington, describing his plane trip and praising the "marvel of Bermuda" at sunset (Letter 51). His enthusiasm for this vista carried over into verses that he scribbled on the back of a letter in his jail cell. One of the lines pays homage to Baron Shigeru Honjo, a high-ranking Japanese army official and adviser, who, according to newspaper reports, had committed hara-kiri in Tokyo one day after his arrest was ordered by the Allies (see Letter 51n). Ezra's own sense of being a trapped quarry must have been keen during these first days in Washington.

Dorothy learned that Ezra had been flown to the States from her son, Omar, who arrived in Rapallo on 20 November. A private in the U.S. Army of Occupation in Germany, Omar had been told the news at the DTC, where he had gone in the hope of seeing Ezra. On 21 November Dorothy wrote A. V. Moore that "Omar stopped at the camp on his way up from Livorno—but E. P. had gone away two days before."[59] Neither the army nor the U.S. government had bothered to inform her of what was happening to her husband, and in the weeks that followed she continued to be uncertain about his precise whereabouts in Washington. At the DTC Omar was handed several letters that Ezra had not been able to post before he was taken away; these the young private brought with him to Rapallo.

On 24 November, there was a jailbreak at the District Jail during which five inmates escaped from a window in the recreation hall. As a consequence, prisoners were confined to their cells and forbidden exercise. Ezra's mental state suffered from the increased rigor, just as it had during his initial confinement at the DTC. He told Charles Olson that the "jail at first was all right . . . and I wasn't bothered by claustrophobia. But then that break, and they put us in the cells."[60] Ezra wrote Ronald Duncan on 25 November: "All this is marvelous xperience if it dont break me and if the lesion of May cured (I thinks) in Sept. dont bust open under the renewed fatigues."[61] That evening he was moved to a bed in the jail infirmary.

The following day, 26 November, the attorney general announced that a fresh indictment charged Ezra with nineteen overt acts of treasonous broadcasting between 11 September 1942 and 15 May 1943. The next afternoon he was formally arraigned, again before Judge Laws. As instructed by Julien Cornell, he remained mute as Cornell told the court that he lacked sufficient judgment to make any plea and asked that a plea of "not guilty" be entered for him. Cornell further requested that his client be released from the District Jail because he was suffering from claustrophobia and might lose his sanity. Judge Laws ordered that he be transferred to Gallinger Hospital in Washington for examination and observation. The order was carried out on 4 December, and a few days later Ezra wrote Dorothy from Gallinger that he was "[h]aving a rest cure" (Letter 58).

Dorothy, meanwhile, was getting to know Omar, whom she had not seen since 1939. During his ten days in Rapallo, he impressed his mother with his interests in music and psychology, his affable ease with new acquaintances, and, most of all, his earnest desire to help her and Ezra in any way he could. As an army private stationed in Bremen, he had limited means, but he sent Dorothy money when he could and wrote to her regularly. From the time of his visit, Dorothy began to toy with the idea of settling down somewhere with Omar and Ezra, as she hinted in late December: "Omar too wants a home" (Letter 67). In March she returned to the subject: "I'd like to make a home for the two of you—somewhere—Japan?" (Letter 106). "I wish to goodness," she wrote in April, "we could all be in Wash: wasting the latter years of our, anyway, lives in this fashion" (Letter 131). The war had modified Dorothy's attitudes toward domesticity; separation from her husband and her son had made expatriate freedom seem less appealing than ordinary stability.

At Gallinger Hospital, Ezra was examined by four psychiatrists, three of whom were appointed by the government and one by his defense. Dr. Joseph L. Gilbert noted that, although Ezra "remained in bed practically all of the time," he would "move quickly about from the bed to a table nearby to get some paper, book or manuscript," then "as suddenly throw himself on the bed and again assume the reclining position." Dr. Wendell Muncie felt that Ezra was distractible, grandiose, and paranoid. "If you touch on his case and hospitalization," he later testified, "Confucius and these other things seemed to get roped in."[62] Ezra told Dr. Marion King that he was suffering from a "queer sensation in the head as though the upper third of the brain were missing and a fluid level existed at the top of what remained."[63] This account resembles the condition that he had complained of to the DTC psychiatrists and described to Ronald Duncan as "the lesion of May." The four doctors concluded that he was insane and unfit to stand trial. They submitted their unanimous report to Judge Laws, who on 21 December ordered Ezra's transfer to St. Elizabeths Hospital for the Insane, a federal institution, pending a jury hearing on his sanity.

Dorothy was greatly upset by reports of Ezra's condition and confessed to Omar that she had received a "jolt" from Julien Cornell's description of him at the District Jail (Letter 59). She told A. V. Moore that she detected signs of his "sufferings" in the batch of canto extracts that had arrived a few days before.[64] Her worry made her all the more determined to join him in Washington: "I am quite intent on getting over to be with you," she wrote. "Its just silly, my living this life, & so dam [sic] far away from you. I *must see you & be near you*, & you can say so, please, to anybody." She refused to "lug" Ezra's mother along, however; she had enough to manage as it was without being responsible for Isabel, who was well into her eighties, frail, and difficult (Letter 62). She made arrangements for Isabel's accommodation and care with friends in Rapallo.

Ezra was admitted at St. Elizabeths on 21 December 1945 as Case Number 58,102. "Whom God would destroy, he first sends to the bug house," he had once declared over the microphone.[65] He was placed in Howard Hall, a separate penal building—or "forensic pavillion," as it was called—reserved for patients who had been found not guilty by reason of insanity or who had been deemed mentally incompetent and unfit to stand trial. Ezra was a "U.S. prisoner" in the second category, to be brought to trial as soon as he regained his competency. A grim structure surrounded by a dry moat and a high wall, Howard Hall housed its patients in small cells with heavy iron doors. Ezra dubbed it the "hell hole" and the "snake pit." The building has since been pulled down, and a softball field has been laid out in its stead.

Locked in a solitary cell and not allowed to exercise in the walled compound like other prisoners, Ezra began to feel a return of the claustrophobia that had threatened in the District Jail. Psychiatrists' reports from his first months at St. Elizabeths suggest that he was a manageable patient but demanded "extra attention" and special privileges: newspapers, a pint of milk every other day, ice cream at intervals, tub baths. He made the acquaintance of other patients but engaged in only brief conversation with them. When he was denied permission to roam beyond the wall surrounding Howard Hall, he protested that he could not see the "logic" in his incarceration.[66]

To doctors he complained that "[t]hey won't believe me when I tell them the main spring is busted." On 22 December Dr. Edgar Griffin, the admitting psychiatrist, wrote: "He expressed what might be interpreted as delusions of persecution and grandeur. Asked how he accounted for his extreme fatigue, Pound replied in rage and exasperation, 'all of Europe is on my shoulders.'"[67] At the diagnostic admissions conference a few days later, none of the psychiatrists who had examined him felt that he was psychotic.

On 28 December the faithful Ida Mapel visited Ezra again and wrote Dorothy the next day that he "looks better and is much less nervous, than when I saw him the first time. [. . .] His attendants all speak with pleasure of him, they all seem to do everything he wishes" (Letter 84n). But in a letter to his daughter, Mary, written "vers le noel," Ezra recalled the grim prophecy of Tiresias from Canto 47: "first must thou go the road to hell & to the bower of Circe's daughter Proserpine."[68] He was still, as at the DTC, conceiving of himself as a lost Odysseus or a Villon condemned to the gallows. In reality, the law was already beginning to forget him. On 27 December Hoover issued a memo to the FBI Communications Section: "DEPARTMENT HAS AUTHORIZED DISCONTINUANCE OF INVESTIGATION PENDING FURTHER COURT ACTION AS TO POUND'S SANITY. YOU WILL BE ADVISED IF INVESTIGATION DESIRED AT LATER DATE."[69]

Ezra's letters to Dorothy from late December through February are mostly scraps written in a frail, methodically controlled pencil, suggesting that a breakdown had occurred around that time. He came to rely on the poet Charles Olson's visits: "Olson gt comfort," he wrote. "Hope they will let him come back. only solid" (Letter 71). On 4 January 1946 Olson had made the first of several visits to Howard Hall. He had attended Ezra's formal arraignment back in November and thought him then "older and weaker" than he had expected. Now Olson was struck by Ezra's "eagerness and vigor as he came swiftly forward into the waiting room." Yet he also noticed his unsteadiness and the fact that "he can't seem to put down more than one or two sentences." Once again, Ezra mentioned his desire to learn Georgian in order to talk with Stalin.[70] Olson's intelligent conversation and sympathetic listening seemed to rescue him from the brink of collapse; after Olson left, Ezra sagged again. In several of his letters to Dorothy, he weakly urges "patience," as if counseling himself as much as her. "Please everybody write a *LOT* to me & not expect answers," he implores in Letter 73. It was not until April that his letters began to get longer and more vigorous.

When Olson arrived for a third visit on 24 January, Ezra rallied again from fatigue induced by psychiatric questioning. Olson said of the visit that "the only word is gay. Right from the start it was wild and strong. [. . .] He remains on the creative side of him, whole, and as charming and open and warm a human being as I know. Despite all the corruption of his body politic."[71] Ezra told him how much he was enjoying the visits of an old friend from Philadelphia days, Katharine Proctor Saint, who was dedicating herself, rather incongruously, to converting him to faith in Christianity. She had even written J. Edgar Hoover to inquire about having a large-print Bible sent to Ezra.[72] Far from resenting her zeal, Ezra was delighted to see her again and told Olson that her visits "restored" him.[73] In Olson and Saint he found a way to order his thoughts about an America he was forced to study from inside a cell: the young writer symbolized the intellectual potential of a new, unfamiliar country; the elderly proselytizer was a reminder of his preexilic home. The unlikely pair became his chief sustainers in this period.

Ezra was capable of only passive exertions in these first months in Washington and repeatedly told Dorothy, Olga Rudge, and other correspondents that he could not perform strenuous mental tasks such as judging or analyzing. He lost himself in novels, happy to give his mind over to the welcome tug of narrative. He especially admired Ford Madox Ford's World War I tetralogy, *Parade's End*, and began to speak of a nagging sense of having let Ford down (Letter 86n). Olson saw that he was "bothered by a sense of guilt" concerning his old friend who had died in 1939, either for "not having fought for him as a writer or for having attacked him, though he insisted—'no backbiting.'"[74] Arnold Bennett was Ezra's other regret now that his mind was retrospecting freely in captivity; it was as if he was resuming the roll of the dead so poignantly begun in *The*

Pisan Cantos. Bennett's novels were a revelation, he said, "as good as the french—my damn snobbery deprived me of knowin it in 1910." "I go on livin' apologies," he wrote Olga, "1st to Fordie for incomplete recognition [...] & now to Bennett whom @ 25 I deeespised fer his etc."[75] Just as at the DTC after his first breakdown, Ezra's mind was skipping back to the London of 1910, as if stability lay only in that world of congenial ghosts.

On 27 January he wrote Julien Cornell from the "Dungeon": "mental torture. constitution a religion. a world lost. grey mist barrier impassible ignorance absolute anonyme" (Letter 83). Part of his panic stemmed from the fact that postwar conditions had made transatlantic mail sluggish, and he had not had a letter from Dorothy since November. "[I]t is long long long," he wrote her on the same day (Letter 82). He was greatly relieved when her letters began arriving at the end of January and he could expect regular news and gossip from Italy. Dorothy quickly intuited his need for a steady diet of the unspectacular. At the DTC he had been able to study nature as a way of persuading himself that the eternal ordinary persisted despite the madness raging through man's world. During the first months of St. Elizabeths, however, there was no green katydid to offer lessons in sanity, no infant wasp to show that nature's courses ran undisturbed, no sunset to chide the vanity of man-made beauty. Now Ezra lay in Hades' bosom; Tiresias's prophecy of a sorrowful journey and the loss of all companions was proving all too accurate in the poet's case.

Ezra objected when Olga Rudge sent letters airmail, telling her he did not want accelerated communiqués but rather an unbroken flow of chatter from Italy to his cell at Howard Hall. "[A]ir mail hardly does more than change order in series of letters," he explained. "Time bein' non-exist—it aint so much gettin news air-mail quick as gettin' some every so often."[76] Olga's impulsive nature made her want to hasten contact. Now that Dorothy was making progress in her efforts to join Ezra, Olga felt she must look to her interests and exact assurances regarding her place in Ezra's life. His letters attempting to allay her fears show great agitation and must have cost him dearly in this period when his energies were at a low ebb.

Forced by her ferocity into uncharacteristic personal avowals, he told Olga that he would happily join her in Sant'Ambrogio if he had any choice in the matter, but he also made it clear that he was against her coming to Washington.[77] Somewhat disingenuously, he said that he was not urging Dorothy to come either; she was taking that step on her own. In fact, he never contradicted Dorothy's repeated vows to join him and even hinted that he was expecting her. It almost seems that he was inviting Dorothy to come by his silence while putting Olga off with taciturnity broken now and again by explosive protest. Probably he was reluctant to reconstitute the ménage of 1944–1945 in the altered and uncertain circumstances of 1946. It was one thing to dream of the visitation of multiple women at the DTC, another to experience their actual rivalry in the corridors of St. Elizabeths. Olga suspected that Ezra's friends also opposed her coming to the States on the grounds that her uncompromising temperament and her status as his mistress might complicate his chances for freedom.

Dorothy was slowly removing the barriers to her reunion with Ezra. With the help of A. V. Moore and her London solicitors, she took steps to wrest her bank account from the British Custodian of Alien Property, and was making progress as well with the Genoa consulate in getting her passport reissued. Despite the frustrations of sharing Isabel's Villa Raggio apartment and the noise of workmen repairing the bomb-damaged ceilings, she found time to write Ezra and to engage in a prodigious correspondence on his behalf. On Sundays she visited Ma Riess, an old friend in Rapallo, through whom, on 13 January, she met Ezra's daughter, Mary Rudge, noting that she was "a large healthy object [. . .] I expect there's some charm" (Letter 76). Julien Cornell kept Dorothy informed of developments in Ezra's case. On 25 January he wrote reassuringly that "a state which would, no doubt, appear to you to be normal, is defined by the doctors as paranoid in character, to an extent which impairs your husband's judgment of his predicament and renders him unable to properly defend himself."[78]

Ezra's sanity hearing took place, after postponements, on 13 February, during which the four psychiatrists who had earlier examined him testified concerning his mental state. After a few minutes of deliberation, the jury returned a verdict of "unsound mind," and Judge Laws ordered Ezra to be returned to St. Elizabeths. The next day, Albert Deutsch in the New York newspaper *PM* attacked the prosecution's performance, noting its "impressive unfamiliarity with the psychiatric issues at stake and a lackadaisical interest in its political implications. They acted throughout as if they were going through the motions." Deutsch added: "When the verdict of insanity was brought in, [Ezra] jumped up with alacrity and engaged in affable conversation with his young lawyer."[79] When Charles Olson visited Ezra on 14 February, he found him waving newly typed copies of Cantos 74–84, delivered to him that morning by James Laughlin (Letter 94). Ezra had his "bounce back," Olson noted.[80]

It was not long before he was feeling pent up and anxious again. He wrote Dorothy on 21 February: "I long for Pisan paradise./ & the jail was Cherry Bim till 4 blokes climbed out & rest of us then confined to cells—no assembly hall—(Gallinger quiet & human)—oh well" (Letter 99). In contrast to the "hell hole" of St. Elizabeths, the army camp seemed very heaven. "I miss the Pisan paradise like hell," he wrote Homer Somers, one of the DTC officers. "No such congenial surroundings since I landed . . . am very fatigued."[81] His spirits improved in early March when he was allowed into the dry moat surrounding Howard Hall to take exercise with the other patients. He was also cheered by a new blue suit that Caresse Crosby had given him.

Ezra had hoped to make his Confucian translations the basis of a *pro se* defense. Now that this was no longer possible, he was more determined than ever to see them published. "I am god damnd if I write a word till the Confucius is printed," he told Ronald Duncan. "If they cant weigh that they are below the level to which communication is possible."[82] In fact, he was already at work on tentative drafts of the Confucian odes. One psychiatrist noted that Ezra spent "most of his time lying upon his bed in his room, reading a Chinese text and a few slim volumes of poetry, making a few notes on random slips of paper."[83] He was reading the odes "for consolation," he told Dorothy (Letter 90), but he was also testing his old skill at creating English versions of poems in a foreign tongue. Between February and August 1946 he sent a dozen or so drafts of odes to Dorothy and Olga. Often he added a disclaimer doubting the quality of the work: "I dont know about these versions. Too much like magazine po'try?" He need not have worried; as at the DTC, cataclysm had left his lyric gift intact, perhaps had even freed it from distractions. Many of these draft translations are indirect comments on his own plight:

> pheasant in rabbit net,
>
> I, untroubled in youth,
>
> Whom now an hundred nets surround.
>
> Would I sleep long & make no sound.

Or: "shall not homing man tread like a ghost / when he cares most."[84] Where *The Pisan Cantos* had released in Ezra an unaccustomed personal impulse, the Confucian odes gave him a hundred masks with which to brood on his situation.

"Pound. Healthy. Better. His door is open, he now is let into the moat," wrote Olson after a visit on 19 March.[85] As his energies returned, Ezra began, typically, to find projects for everyone. On 20 March he wrote Cornell: "Next point is to get Jas. [Laughlin] to understand need of pub/ing a nucleus of civilization, more organic than a 'Five foot shelf', & the *tooter* the *suiter*."[86] He had already worked out an essential curriculum for Omar: Confucius, Homer, Frobenius. "[G]o *back* to what I once knew," he told the young man, hinting perhaps that his own mind had lost its hold on the Poundian verities, had jumped the track of the true (Letter 97). The idea of playing tutor to world leaders had necessarily receded somewhat, but he could still worry for the young and offer suggestions as to how they might lay a foundation for themselves amid the postwar ruins.

On 31 March Dr. Harold Stevens of St. Elizabeths reported that Ezra began most of his sessions by complaining of fatigue, then gradually became

quite animated in his conversation, bangs the desk, jumps up, raises his voice, becomes flushed and displays evidence of energy, the interview often lasting an hour. At times his speech is fragmentary, although telegraphic in style, resembling the cryptic letters he writes. [. . .] In frequent discourses with him, he is unable to answer some questions because of an alleged partial amnesia which he states developed during his confinement in the "cage" in Italy. [. . .] But when queried about his scurrilous and anti-Semitic broadcasts in Italy, which the interviewer has reviewed, he protests that his memory fails him. On one occasion when he was asked if he wishes to stand trial, he effected [*sic*] an elaborate caricature of fatigue and the interview had to be terminated. [. . .] His views on economics, and especially on money, are unorthodox, but logical and coherent. He is extremely and destructively hypercritical, has praise for very few, vilified Congress, Roosevelt, the State Department, describes Woodrow Wilson as "that constipated jerk with prostatitis," and often punctuates his vituperations with picturesque profanity. For the British, he reserves his most scathing and scatological invectives, attacking the Nation collectively and the English readers individually.[87]

Meanwhile, Dorothy was still struggling with her financial situation. In early April she was forced to sell a gold chain and was down to her last two thousand lire before A. V. Moore got some money through to her (Letter 124). Conditions in Italy made her more eager than ever to embark for America. Rapallo was in the process of repairing substantial bomb damage caused by straying Allied planes that had meant to hit the port of Genoa a dozen miles up the coast. Dorothy remarked that the Italians "are now beginning to understand they've lost the war—the miseria [destitution] & unemployment awful" (Letter 95).

The coming elections made the atmosphere in Rapallo very unpleasant, with roughneck young communists swaggering about and plastering the walls of the town with red posters. On 9 May King Vittorio Emanuele III abdicated in favor of Umberto II, who was himself forced into exile a month later due to a referendum demanding an Italian republic in place of the monarchy. At the end of May, Dorothy wrote Ezra that "this place is vile nowadays avvilita—& vicious—atmosphere most repulsive" (Letter 148). Alluding to Dante, whom she was then rereading, she noted that "this land turns evil—its such a messy bolge" (Letter 149). Postwar Italy had become a degraded place; lacking Ezra and its own wonted dignity, it was no longer *la terra santa* but rather a pocket in Dante's hell, one of many blasted craters in the wreck of Europe. To add to Dorothy's worries, in mid-May Ezra's mother broke her hip in a fall and had to be hospitalized. In one respect Dorothy was relieved, for the accident ended any question of Isabel's accompanying her to America. She could now focus all of her energies on getting passage for herself.

On 25 May Ezra sent Dorothy a few lines of new verse:

> I err'd, I pay, I awaken
> Wasps be not stroked by men
> Nor hawk for wren twice mistaken
> let me not be engulph'd in
> the multitude of my family's calamaties [*sic*],
> nor nest twice on a sand-storm. (Letter 146)

This "Chinese Prayer," as Dorothy called it, encapsulates the ambiguities of self-critique and ethical responsibility that *The Pisan Cantos* write large. Donning one of his Confucian masks, Ezra seems to admit error, but is it error of moral judgment or merely a tactical blunder, the political naif's failure to recognize that the world was too corrupt, too bent on waspish war, even for his ministrations? The allusion to "my family's calamaties" may hint at the difficulties that Ezra now faced in accommodating Dorothy and Olga both, in being a father to children an ocean away, and in dealing with an invalid mother.

Ezra still considered himself "in serious breakdown" as late as April.[88] In early June he wrote Olga that "ANY effort causes gt. fatigue. I don't think you get picture of here.

e.g. Today red letter in that am hand-kuffed to be taken to dental bld.—perfectly comfortable wide leather cuffs. do not cause nervousness after 1st time. NOT that am supposed violent but patients are continually beating up guards & guards therefore prefer etc. (when prisoners tempted by sight of wide open spaces). [. . .] pleasant ride to dental in station wagon—back in vulgar bus. small things make a day." Of conditions at St. Elizabeths he said: "Solitary? Lord, no. 90 in dining room."[89] He was desperate for contact with the outside, as he explained to Mary Barnard on 12 June: "Yes, like p'cards— or any evidence that outer (oltre le mura [beyond the walls]) world exists."[90] Locked up in a cell in an alien America, he felt doubly exiled. At one point in this period, while doodling on a subscription form, he gave his nationality as "paradiso perduto."[91]

At last on 6 June the U.S. Consul General in Genoa issued Dorothy a passport in anticipation of her scheduled 16 June departure on the S.S. *Marine Carp*, a "piroscafo di soccorso," or "relief ship." After a week's delay, the *Marine Carp* sailed from Genoa on 23 June with more than 450 passengers aboard. Dorothy shared a cabin with seven others and ate at a table that seated fourteen. The sea was occasionally rough, but Dorothy was a good sailor and enjoyed the American-style food served by the kitchen. The ship docked in New York on 6 July and was met by James Laughlin. Dorothy sent a telegram to Ezra at 1:57 P.M. and left for Laughlin's home in Norfolk, Connecticut, to spend a day recovering. The following day, 8 July, she met with Julien Cornell at his office in New York, and on 9 July she flew to Washington, D.C., where she stayed temporarily with the Mapel sisters, as arranged.

She made her first visit to Ezra at Howard Hall on Wednesday, 10 July, and was permitted one hour with him as a special concession. They discussed Confucius and family matters. "He seems clear on the subject he has arranged to talk about," she wrote Laughlin. "Says if he can rest 2–3 hrs, one hour is clear to him. It *is* a rotten deal."[92] To Cornell she confessed that she found him "very nervous and jumpy. I believe his wits are really very scattered, and he has difficulty in concentrating for more than a few minutes. During the one hour [the first visit] we spoke mostly of family odds and ends,—on Thursday of his Chinese translating chiefly. [. . .] Today Ezra spoke of my trying to find out what was going on in the outside world. He has newspapers, but naturally hasn't much faith in that kind of news."[93]

So began a routine that would continue for the next twelve years. Early in 1947 Ezra was moved from Howard Hall to the more congenial Center Building, and eventually he was allowed to spend afternoons lounging on the grounds in a canvas chair with

Dorothy beside him. Established in her own room in Washington, Dorothy paid daily visits to St. Elizabeths, conversing with her husband, taking notes and writing letters at his request, and helping him entertain the steady stream of visitors. She knew how important routine and regularity were to his creative life, and as she had done for nearly four decades, she devoted herself to nurturing his talent. Her gifts of patience and quiet fortitude she placed in the service of his more conspicuous gifts. Harry Meacham, who came to know Ezra a year before his release from St. Elizabeths in 1958, once wrote that Dorothy was "a great lady who deserves a book of her own."[94] In a sense, this is that book—the story, written partly in her own words, of Penelope's quest to rejoin her husband, expert in adversity.

NOTES

1 "Desideria," *Exile* 3 (Spring 1928); rpt. in *Ezra Pound's Poetry and Prose Contributions to Periodicals*, ed. Lea Baechler et al. (New York: Garland, 1991), 5:18.

2 *Jefferson and/or Mussolini: L'Idea Statale. Fascism As I Have Seen It* (1935; rpt. New York: Liveright, 1970), p. 12.

3 Ibid., p. 33.

4 "Letter from Rapallo," *Japan Times & Mail*, Tokyo (12 August 1940); rpt. in *Ezra Pound's Poetry and Prose Contributions to Periodicals*, 8:63.

5 EP to Francesco Monotti, 1934, Ezra Pound Papers, Yale Collection of American Literature, Beinecke Library, Yale University.

6 These remarks are found in EP's broadcast scripts for, respectively, 27 April 1943 ("On Retiring"), 4 May 1942 ("Universality"), and 7 December 1941 ("Those Parentheses"), in *"Ezra Pound Speaking": Radio Speeches of World War II*, ed. Leonard W. Doob (Westport, Conn.: Greenwood Press, 1978), pp. 289, 290, 117, 22.

7 *"Ezra Pound Speaking,"* p. xiii.

8 Memorandum issued by FBI Director J. Edgar Hoover, 30 November 1942 (FBI document 100–34099–14). This document and all other FBI materials cited in this volume were obtained under the Freedom of Information Act (5 U.S.C.A. § 552).

9 EP to Alessandro Pavolini, undated, translated from Italian by the FBI (FBI document 100–34099–266). EP's Italian original is in the Ezra Pound Papers at the Beinecke Library.

10 "Bureaucracy the Flail of Jehovah," *Exile* 4 (Autumn 1928); rpt. in *Ezra Pound's Poetry and Prose Contributions to Periodicals*, 5:54.

11 From DP's personal notes, 1945–1946, private collection.

12 DP's diary, 29 April 1945, Lilly Library, Indiana University.

13 Quoted in Julien Cornell, *The Trial of Ezra Pound: A Documented Account of the Treason Case by the Defendant's Lawyer* (London: Faber and Faber, 1966), p. 52.

14 Donald Hall, "Ezra Pound: An Interview," *Paris Review*, No. 28 (Summer-Fall 1962): 45.

15 Ibid.

16 Olga Rudge to James Laughlin, undated letter, 1945 Copybook, Olga Rudge Papers, Beinecke Library, Yale University.

17 FBI memoranda and reports by Special Agent Frank L. Amprim, dated 7 November 1943 (FBI document 100–34099–113), 20 June 1944 (100–34099–130), and 25 November 1944 (100–34099–166).

18 Memorandum by Amprim to J. Edgar Hoover, 20 May 1945 (FBI document 100–34099–185), which quotes the text of Amprim's cable.

19 Olga Rudge to James Laughlin, 11 November 1945, 1945 Copybook, Olga Rudge Papers, Beinecke Library.

20 DP's diary, 7 May 1945, Lilly Library.

21 Olga Rudge to EP, 26 May 1946, private collection.

22 Olga Rudge to T. S. Eliot, 19 July 1945, 1945 Copybook, Olga Rudge Papers, Beinecke Library.

23 Memorandum by Amprim to J. Edgar Hoover, 12 July 1945 (FBI document 100–34099–236).

24 EP to Daniel B. Dodson, 13 September 1941, Ezra Pound Papers, Beinecke Library.

25 Memorandum by Amprim to J. Edgar Hoover, 21 May 1945 (FBI document 100–34099–186).

26 Details of EP's experience in the cage are drawn chiefly from the following: Julien Cornell's affidavit in support of application for bail, dated 27 November 1945 and based on his interview with EP a week earlier, in *The Trial of Ezra Pound*, pp. 20–21; Cornell's notes from the same interview, quoted in Charles Norman, *Ezra Pound*, (1960; rev. ed. New York: Minerva, 1969), pp. 396–97; Robert L. Allen, "The Cage," and David Park Williams, "The Background of *The Pisan Cantos*," both in *A Casebook on Ezra Pound*, ed. William Van O'Connor and Edward Stone (New York: Thomas Y. Crowell, 1959), pp. 33–43.

27 *A Casebook on Ezra Pound*, p. 40.

28 Cornell, *The Trial of Ezra Pound*, p. 20.

29 Sgt. Norbert Hofman, "The Toughest Training Detail in the Army Is Dished Out to Court-martialed GIs at the Disciplinary Training Center Near Pisa," *Yank: The Army Weekly*, 11 November 1945.

30 John L. Steele to his family, undated, private collection.

31 *A Casebook on Ezra Pound*, p. 35.

32 Ibid.

33 These lines are taken from Cantos 74 (line 146), 77 (lines 267, 59), and 80 (line 284), respectively.

34 Quoted in Humphrey Carpenter, *A Serious Character: The Life of Ezra Pound* (Boston: Houghton Mifflin, 1988), pp. 663–64.

35 Confidential memorandum by J. Edgar Hoover to Assistant Attorney General Tom C. Clark, 26 June 1945 (FBI document 100–34099–212).

36 *A Casebook on Ezra Pound*, p. 35.

37 From Cantos 80 (lines 736–37) and 83 (lines 30–31).

38 Quoted in Carpenter, *A Serious Character*, p. 666.

39 This description of the medical staff was provided by Morris J. Lucree in a letter to Omar Pound, 12 April 1994.

40 *A Casebook on Ezra Pound*, p. 36.

41 John L. Steele to his mother, 20 August 1945, private collection.

42 From Cantos 81 (line 67) and 80 (line 663), respectively.

43 *A Casebook on Ezra Pound*, p. 36.

44 FBI memorandum to Amprim, 25 June 1945 (FBI document 100–34099–217); memorandum by Amprim to J. Edgar Hoover, 7 September 1945 (100–34099–288); FBI cablegram to Amprim, 21 September 1945 (100–34099–301).

45 Quoted in Carpenter, *A Serious Character*, p. 690.

46 DP to Ronald Duncan, 15 July 1945, Harry Ransom Humanities Research Center, University of Texas at Austin.

47 For John Drummond's role as intermediary, see in particular his letters to Olga Rudge from July 1945 on, Olga Rudge Papers, Beinecke Library.

48 DP to Olga Rudge, Friday [5 October 1945], Olga Rudge Papers, Beinecke Library.

49 Quoted in Harry M. Meacham, *The Caged Panther: Ezra Pound at St. Elizabeths* (New York: Twayne, 1967), p. 25.

50 John Drummond to EP, 19 October 1945, copy enclosed with Drummond's letter to Olga Rudge of the same date, Olga Rudge Papers, Beinecke Library.

51 From the transcript of an interview with Olga Rudge for a television program on Ezra Pound (*Voices and Visions*), p. 4 (Code #AG).

52 *A Casebook on Ezra Pound*, p. 37.

53 Ibid., pp. 37–38.

54 Ibid., p. 38.

55 Quoted in James Randler, "His Wartime Jailer Laments the Emprisoning [*sic*] of Ezra Pound," *New England (Boston Sunday Globe)*, 21 May 1995: 53.

56 These quotations of EP appeared nationwide in Associated Press and United Press articles on his arrest and arraignment, datelined, variously, 18, 19, and 20 November 1945. Certain details are taken from "Court Delays Trial of Pound in Treason Case," Washington, D.C. *Times-Herald*, 20 November 1945: 6.

57 Ida B. Mapel to DP, 27 November 1945, Lilly Library, Indiana University.

58 Cornell, *The Trial of Ezra Pound*, pp. 13, 14.

59 DP to A. V. Moore, 21 November 1945, private collection.

60 *Charles Olson and Ezra Pound: An Encounter at St. Elizabeths*, ed. Catherine Seelye (New York: Grossman, 1975), p. 37.

61 Quoted in Carpenter, *A Serious Character*, p. 709.

62 Remarks by Drs. Gilbert and Muncie, from their court testimony, are quoted in Cornell, *The Trial of Ezra Pound*, pp. 203, 160.

63 Quoted in Carpenter, *A Serious Character*, p. 720.

64 DP to A. V. Moore, 8 December 1945, private collection.

65 Radio broadcast of 29 January 1942 ("On Resuming"), in *"Ezra Pound Speaking,"* p. 27.

66 Quoted in Carpenter, *A Serious Character*, p. 728.

67 EP's statements to the psychiatrists are quoted in Robert D. Gillman, "Ezra Pound's Rorschach Diagnosis," *Bulletin of the Menninger Clinic* 58 (Summer 1994): 311, 317–18.

68 EP to Mary Rudge, "vers le noel" [Christmas 1945], Olga Rudge Papers, Beinecke Library.

69 Urgent message to Communications Section issued by J. Edgar Hoover, 27 December 1945 (FBI document 100–34099–417).

70 *Charles Olson and Ezra Pound*, pp. 36, 39.

71 Ibid., p. 56.

72 The correspondence between Katharine Proctor Saint and J. Edgar Hoover was preserved by the FBI (documents 100–34099–382 and -383). See also Letters 56 and 61 herein.

73 *Charles Olson and Ezra Pound*, p. 59.

74 Ibid., p. 71.

75 EP to Olga Rudge, letter of 15 and 17 March 1946, Olga Rudge Papers, Beinecke Library.

76 EP to Olga Rudge, letters of 22 March and 30 April 1946, Olga Rudge Papers, Beinecke Library.

77 EP to Olga Rudge, letters of 28 March and 8 April 1946, Olga Rudge Papers, Beinecke Library.

78 Julien Cornell to DP, 25 January 1946, Lilly Library.

79 Quoted in Carpenter, *A Serious Character*, pp. 747, 752.

80 *Charles Olson and Ezra Pound*, p. 72.

81 Quoted in Randler, "His Wartime Jailer," 53.

82 EP to Ronald Duncan, undated, Harry Ransom Humanities Research Center.

83 Quoted in Carpenter, *A Serious Character*, p. 728.

84 EP to Olga Rudge, letters of 9 April, 8–9 April, and 27 June 1946, Olga Rudge Papers, Beinecke Library.

85 *Charles Olson and Ezra Pound*, p. 82.

86 Quoted in Cornell, *The Trial of Ezra Pound*, p. 83.

87 Quoted in Harold Stevens, "Ezra Pound and the Sheltering Arms of St. Elizabeths," unpublished paper, pp. 12–14.

88 EP to Mary Barnard, 9 April 1946, photocopy of D. D. Paige transcription, McFarlin Library Special Collections, University of Tulsa.

89 EP to Olga Rudge, letters of 3 June and 24 May 1946, respectively, Olga Rudge Papers, Beinecke Library.

90 EP to Mary Barnard, 12 June 1946, photocopy of D. D. Paige transcription, McFarlin Library Special Collections.

91 Subscription form enclosed by EP in letter to Olga Rudge, early July 1946, Olga Rudge Papers, Beinecke Library.

92 Quoted in Carpenter, *A Serious Character*, p. 766.

93 DP to Julien Cornell, 14 July 1946, quoted in *The Trial of Ezra Pound*, p. 51.

94 Meacham, *The Caged Panther*, p. 47.

War is the maximum sabotage. The game of inflate

and deflate is played in the whole OF SERIES of

wars, staged one after another.

ÑEzra's supplement to his

Sworn Statement, 8 May 1945

I hope all the time that you are getting well fed!

Dorothy to Ezra, Letter 5

GENOA

1 Notes. In pencil on a legal-size sheet of ruled yellow paper, one side, folded and addressed for hand delivery; no envelope (Lilly).

6 Via Fieschi] Headquarters in Genoa for the Counter Intelligence Corps (CIC) Detachment of the Ninety-second Division, where EP was held from 4 May until 24 May 1945, when he was transferred to the Disciplinary Training Center (DTC) near Pisa. See Ramon Arrizabalaga's memoir (Appendix 1).

Coz] An affectionate nickname for DP, based on the Elizabethan use of "cousin" or "coz."

O.] Olga Rudge (1895-1996), American concert violinist, Vivaldi scholar, and EP's companion for many years. She was born in Youngstown, Ohio, and raised in Europe. From 1916 to 1920 she gave concerts in London, where EP heard and reviewed her playing. They met in Paris in 1923, and EP persuaded George Antheil to compose two violin sonatas for her, which she and Antheil performed in December 1923. A few years later she moved to the hilltop village of Sant'Ambrogio outside Rapallo, to be near EP. She divided her time between homes there and in Venice, and worked at the Accademia Musicale Chigiana in Siena, where she promoted the music of Vivaldi. In the 1930s she helped plan and, with Gerhart Münch and other musicians, took part in concerts that EP sponsored in Rapallo. She and EP had a daughter, Mary Rudge (later Mary de Rachewiltz), in 1925 (see Letter 10n). Olga worked tirelessly to clear EP's name of the treason charge during his incarceration at St. Elizabeths. A late canto fragment pays tribute to her: "Her name was Courage / & is written Olga."

On learning that EP had been captured by *partigiani*, Olga hurried to catch up and accompanied him to Genoa, remaining with him at the office of the CIC for several days before returning by jeep to Sant'Ambrogio. See Introduction.

Gentill. Egr.] "Gentillissima Egregia," an Italian epistolary form meaning "most kind, distinguished."

2 Notes. Handwritten on two sides of ruled paper similar to that used in Letter 1, with an additional sheet of pink paper typed on one side; no record of an envelope. Check marks are placed against many of the items in these pages, and all three pages are initialed "FLA [Frank L. Amprim] Genoa 5-7-45" (FBI documents 100-34099-191 and -192). EP was interrogated at the office of the Counter Intelligence Corps in Genoa by FBI Special Agent Amprim and Ramon Arrizabalaga, special agent in charge (commanding officer) at the CIC. Amprim probably presented Letter 2 on 7 May when he searched No. 60 in Sant'Ambrogio for materials relevant to EP's case. See Arrizabalaga's memoir (Appendix 1) for an account of this visit. DP's diary for 11 May 1945 notes, "Antrim [sic] & friend 11.30-2 to lunch."

scrap book clippings - interviews 1939] During his visit to the United States in 1939, EP offered journalists his views on economics and politics and was quoted in newspapers in New York, Washington, D.C., and elsewhere. His scrapbook covering the visit was taken from Sant'Ambrogio by the *partigiani* who captured him. They turned it over to the CIC in Genoa, and Amprim passed it on to FBI headquarters with a memo to J. Edgar Hoover dated 29 May 1945 (FBI document 100-34099-206).

Mandati] A *mandato* was an order, signed by Italian government officials, directing the treasury of a province to pay a sum of money to an individual. The *mandati* that the Ministry of Popular Culture approved as compensation for EP's radio scripts and broadcasts were of special interest to the FBI because they established a record of payment for services rendered to the Italian government. Amprim recovered dozens of mandato receipts during his search of No. 60 in Sant'Ambrogio on 7 May 1945. Most of these were for 350 lire or multiples of 350 lire—the amount that EP received for a single broadcast.

1 EZRA TO DOROTHY

[Office of the Counter Intelligence Corps]
[6 Via Fieschi]
[Genoa, Italy]
[?4-7 May 1945]

Dear Coz.
    being nicely treated. etc.—
    O. will give details.
            love.
                E.
Gentill. Eg. D. Pound.

2 EZRA TO DOROTHY

[Office of the Counter Intelligence Corps]
[6 Via Fieschi]
[Genoa, Italy]
[7 May 1945]

Dear Coz.
Please give bearer my New York scrap book clippings—interviews 1939 (box foot of my bed)

Mandati of receipts (radio)—sack in wardrobe etc.

————————————

MSS of Radio Discorsi [speeches] = separate package = not in files.
            E.P.

Orientamenti . . .] This list of books and pamphlets deemed important by the investigators, as well as by EP, reflects the range of EP's economic, political, and literary activities in the previous decade or so. In 1944 alone, he published, through Nino Sammartano who directed the Office of Cultural Exchange in Venice, a series of works under the imprint of Casa Editrice delle Edizioni Popolari: *L'America, Roosevelt e le cause della guerra presente* (later translated into English by John Drummond as *America, Roosevelt and the Causes of the Present War; Introduzione alla natura economica degli S.U.A.; Orientamenti* (a gathering of EP's journal articles on money, usury, and politics); *and Jefferson e Mussolini: Studi politici ed economici* (a rewriting by EP in Italian of his Jefferson and/or Mussolini ([1935]). (Most copies of *Orientamenti* and *Jefferson e Mussolini* were destroyed shortly after printing because of their political and economic nature.) In the same year EP saw into print, also through Casa Editrice, Arthur Kitson's *La Storia di un reato*, which contended that a bankers' conspiracy to profit by a return to the gold standard after World War I had set the stage for another world war (see Document 6n).

EP also refers here to two manifestos issued in 1944 and 1945 over the signatures of several Tigullian writers, including EP, G. B. Nassano, Giuseppe Soldato, and Edgardo Rossaro. (The first of these was also printed in *Il Popolo di Alessandria* for 27 February 1944.) Other works by EP listed in Letter 2 are *ABC of Economics* (London, 1933); a broadside questionnaire, *Volitionist Economics* (Rapallo, 1934); *Introductory Text Book* (Rapallo, 1939); *What Is Money For?* (London, 1939); *Oro e lavoro* (Rapallo, 1944; later translated into English by John Drummond as *Gold and Work*). EP also translated *Italy's Policy of Social Economics 1939/1940* (1941), a book by Odon Por, the Hungarian-born economic theorist of Italian fascism (see Letter 107n). EP's Guido Cavalcanti Rime—a scholarly presentation of Cavalcanti's poems with reproductions of manuscripts—was issued after many delays in a patchwork edition in Genoa in 1932.

EP's efforts to spread Confucian enlightenment are also reflected here. With Alberto Luchini, he published *Confucio. Ta S'eu. Dai Gaku. Studio integrale* (Rapallo, 1942), an Italian version (with Chinese text) of the *Testament of Confucius*, the first of the four Chinese classics. Through Casa Editrice of Venice, EP issued a separate edition of this italian translation, minus the Chinese as *Testamento di Confucio* (1944), followed by an Italian version of the second of the four classics, *Chiung Iung. L'Asse che non vacilla* (1945), although the bulk of this edition was burned following the Liberation ("asse" being the Italian word for "axis"). EP culled maxims from various Confucian works and published these in Italian as "Confucio parla" (Confucius speaks) in *Il Popolo di Alessandria* (23 December 1944, 2 January 1945) and "Parla Confucio" in *La Marina Repubblicana* (1 January 1945). At the CIC in Genoa and later at the DTC, EP worked on English translations (for American readers, as he insisted) of the first two Confucian books—the Chung Yung and the Testament—published together by New Directions as *Confucius. The Unwobbling Pivot & The Great Digest* (1947).

Amprim] Frank Lawrence Amprim (1910-1985), born in Donora, Pennsylvania, moved to Detroit in 1920, attended Wayne State University and the University of Michigan Law School. From 1934 to 1942 he practiced law in Wyandotte, Michigan, then worked for the FBI until 1946 in North Africa and parts of Italy, with the acting rank of major (though not actually in the army). From a family (Amprimo) originating in the Piedmont region, he spoke fluent Italian and was assigned by the FBI to Rome, where one of his duties was to find and arrest EP. As special agent in charge of the case, Amprim was responsible for interrogating EP, examining his broadcasts, writings, and private papers, interviewing friends and colleagues, developing witnesses to the alleged acts of treason, and collecting evidence. See also Introduction.

Rossaro] Edgardo Rossaro (1882-1972) lived in Rapallo and did landscape painting and portraiture. His letters to EP show that he believed that the fascist regime in Italy was being undermined by Masons, Jews, and priests (Beinecke). He signed both of the "Tigullio manifestos" that EP mentions in Letter 2.

Parodi] Giorgio Parodi lived in Santa Margherita near Rapallo and corresponded with EP in 1944-1945 about his Confucius translations and other projects (Beinecke). In the summer of 1944 Parodi went to Lecco on Lake Como to be away from the embattled coastal area. While in Lecco in March-April 1945, he used his office in Genoa for routing mail to EP after the postal service had been disrupted by war conditions. As he received copies of EP's *Orientamenti* (1944) and *Chiung Iung. L'Asse che non*

Orientamenti =
Confucio Ta Seu - bilingual.
Asse che non Vacilla.

Jeff. / Muss.
ABC of Economics.
Last[?] letter files.
Storia d'un Reato
Introd all
Roosevelt & Cause della Guerra

Ez.

---

my Trans.
Odon's Italys Econ. Policy—

E.

[separate typed sheet]

I. L Asse che non Vacilla/ one copy for Amprim, one for me. there were several copies/ some in yr/ room, one in mine, at least one in the big shelves; I think, in diningroom/ keep one for yrself; if you can only find two.

2. Ta S'eu / Studio Integrale/ several copies wanted/ they are in package, along with G. Cavalcanti, back of blue cloth screen in dining room. BIG package of heavy paper, on floor.

3. Is there a copy of "Orientamenti" or did the patriots take that? (there were two copies, and Rossaro has another/ Dont waste the ONLY one left: until you can get another via Parodi.)

4. Copies of Causes of War / and of Natura Economica degli S.U.A. one each for me and for Amprim.

5. One copy of the Testamento di Conf/ just to show that there was a 2nd edtn. (I mean the one without the chinese text).

Must be plenty of copies of Roosevelt e Cause / if not, look in yellow wooden suit case in the hall.

Also want several copies of BOTH the Tigullio manifestos/ on big wooden shelves in hall.)

vacilla   (1945)   from   the   publisher,   he   passed   them
on to EP.

3 Notes. In pencil on a sheet of white paper, one side, folded and marked by DP on the back "EP" and (not by DP) "Olando," signifying the Caffe Jolanda in Rapallo which DP and Olga Rudge used as an informal mail drop and message center; no envelope (Lilly). Letter 3 appears to be a reply to Letter 2.

Mao] Used as an affectionate salutation by EP and DP in letters to each other, possibly in imitation of a cat's meow.

No. 12/5] 12/5 Via Marsala in Rapallo, the apartment where EP and DP had lived since 1925, with an open roof terrace overlooking the Gulf of Tigullio. They were ordered to move out in May 1944—as aliens in a prohibited area—when the Germans fortified the coastal defenses in Rapallo; and for the next year EP and DP lived with Olga Rudge at No. 60 in Sant'Ambrogio. Shortly after EP's capture on 3 May, DP left Olga's house and moved in with EP's aged mother at Villa Raggio, subletting 12/5 Via Marsala to Tullio Corradi and his family (see Letter 5). DP retained a "studio" at 12/5, which she used for storing books and artwork. See map of Rapallo (p. 000, graphic artwork).

Isabel] Isabel Weston Pound (1860–1948), EP's mother, whom he once referred to as the "Presbyterian peacock." She and her husband, Homer, retired to Rapallo in 1928 to live near their son. After Homer's death in 1942, she lived in an apartment in Villa Raggio, a house in Sestiere Cerisola up the hill behind Rapallo. She is referred to in these letters as "the old lady," "ma," "mother," "Isabel," and "IWP."

4 Notes. Typed with blue ribbon on a thin sheet of pink paper; no signature. Address at the top of the letter reads: "D. Pound 12/5 Via Marsala or at Villa Raggio; Sestiere Cerisola." No envelope: Letter 4 may have been hand-delivered (Lilly).

~~Six~~ Four copies "Oro e Lavoro" (~~hall shelves or~~ dining room big shelves.

Can you find: <u>What is money for?</u> That also useful here.

ALSO: Introductory Text book / the one leaf affair/ must be lots of copies/ and also a copy of <u>Volitionist Manifesto</u>/ I think in papers in my room.

Am doing american version of l'Asse but forget some of the analyses: so must have at least one copy of my ital trans.

Send me any newspapers you have kept. I mean of the past week.

ESPECIALLY the sheet of Confucio Parla/ proofs printed on one side. AND tooth paste AND the STIFF tooth brush from kitchen. the STIFF one.

3   DOROTHY TO EZRA

[Rapallo, Italy]
May 7. 45.

Mao,
    Dearest.
    Thankful to get news of you & so on.
    I shall now try to proceed with getting No 12/5 in order - Isabel O.K. - & I am going to stay with her - as more convenient -
    Have found everything except perhaps some more mandati.

All my love
D.

43

5 Notes. In black ink on one side of a sheet of white paper; no extant envelope (Lilly).

Washington] In Letter 4 EP mentions the idea of his mother's going to Washington, D.C.

Rocca's] Giovanni Rocca was the landlord of 12/5 Via Marsala, EP and DP's apartment in Rapallo. In May 1945, after moving in with EP's mother at Villa Raggio, DP arranged to sublet 12/5 to Tullio Corradi and worked to get Rocca's furniture, which had been stored at Villa Andraea and other locations in May 1944 when the Germans cleared the coast, restored to 12/5. See also Letter 3n.

Ina's sister] Ina Benatti's sister. The Benatti family looked after Homer and Isabel Pound and worked for EP and DP for many years, before and after World War II. Left homeless, Ina's sister and her family were currently staying in the kitchen end of 12/5 Via Marsala.

Villa Andraea] Paolina ("Pima") Andraea (1873-1953) was married to Corrado Andraea. Mme. Andraea, of German origin, knew Gerhart Hauptmann, Marcel Achard, and other noted residents and visitors in Rapallo. Her hospital stay and other troubles during the recent upheavals in Rapallo are described in Letter 142. Some of EP's books, including the large folio editions of *A Draft of XVI Cantos* (Paris: Three Mountains Press, 1925) and *A Draft of the Cantos 17-27* (London: John Rodker, 1928), had been taken to Villa Andraea for safekeeping and buried by servants in a rubbish heap, later to be rescued by DP. See also Letter 128.

"Carta da Visita"] EP first published *Carta da Visita* in Rome in 1942; it was later translated into English by John Drummond as *A Visiting Card* and published in London in 1952. The work contains brief expositions of EP's ideas on money, credit, usury, stamp scrip, Confucius, Brooks Adams, and Leo Frobenius.

Document 1 Notes. Reprinted from King (55), who had access to a copy of the cable owned by John L. Steele, commanding officer at the DTC when EP was there. "CG MTOUSA": "Commanding General, Mediterranean Theater of Operations, United States Army."

No press interviews] EP had been interviewed at the CIC by Edd Johnson, whose article "Confucius and Kindred Subjects: Pound, Accused of Treason, Calls Hitler Saint, Martyr" appeared in the *Chicago Sun* and the *Philadelphia Record* on 9 May 1945.

[Office of the Counter Intelligence Corps]
[6 Via Fieschi]
[Genoa, Italy]
[8-21 May 1945]

Mao

Ask Isabel if she wants to go back to Washington, later; It might cheer her. No necessity for so doing.

send on yr/ news if any.

5   DOROTHY TO EZRA

Villa Raggio.
Sestiere Cerisola
[Rapallo, Italy]
May 22 '45

Dearest.

I am for the time being staying with yr. Mother. We are getting on all right. She will go to Washington, by airplane, preferably not in the hottest weather—& is making it an excuse to have a new frock. Of course I would go, if such contingency arose.

I am getting Rocca's pots & pans etc back into our flat slowly: I have arranged with Ina's sister, her husband & child to inhabit the kitchen end, temporaryly, as they are homeless: pleasant people & perfectly trustworthy. Am hoping to get an order to get out Rocca's stuff from Villa Andraea; it is under sigillo [seal] & she is v. ill in Verdi hospital.

I found another copy of "Carta da Visita" - & brought down here the Chinese Dictionary.

Very friendly interview with Rocca & daughter. No post or telegraph yet for l'estero [abroad]. I have some shirts etc. packed in your tennis bag should any opportunity occur to carry them.

Yours always

D.

I hope all the time that you are getting well fed! -

DOCUMENT 1   ORDERS TO TRANSFER EZRA POUND

MAY 22, 1945
TO FOR ACTION: CG FIFTH ARMY
               CG REPLACEMENT AND TRAINING COMMAND
SIGNED: CG MTOUSA

American civilian Doctor EZRA LOOMIS POUND reference Fifth Army cable 2006 under federal grand jury indictment for treason.

Transfer without delay under guard to MTOUSA Disciplinary Training Center for confinement pending disposition instructions. Exercise utmost security measures to prevent escape or suicide. No press interviews authorized. Accord no preferential treatment.

DOCUMENT 2   DTC COPY OF TRANSFER ORDERS

Received at PENINSULAR BASE SECTION
                   SIGNAL CENTER
                                23 MAY 1945

: SECRET
: PRIORITY
TO (ACTION)   : CO 6677 DETENTION TRNG COMPANY (OVHD)
(INFORMATION)   : NONE
FROM   : REPCO SIGNED JAYNES
DATE-TIME SIGNED : 231509B
DATE-TIME REC'D : 231919B
REFERENCE NR   : J-12351
CITE   : RCGAP

SECRET. BEING TRANSFERRED TO YOU PENDING DISPOSITION INSTRUCTIONS IS CIVILIAN AMERICAN EZRA LOOMIS POUND WHO FOR TREASON IS INDICTED BY FEDERAL GRAND JURY. PREFERRED TREATMENT WILL NOT BE GIVEN. TAKE UTMOST CARE TO PREVENT SUICIDE OR ESCAPE. INTERVIEWS BY PRESS NOT AUTHORIZED.

FORM # 18-A   CRYPTO /s/ *C Barnes*

CERTIFIED TO BE A TRUE COPY:
[signed]
RALPH A. POLLARA, 1st Lt, Inf
Asst Adj - MTOUSA DTC

6 Notes. Typed with blue ribbon on a thin sheet of pink paper, with the concluding line scrawled in black ink; no signature; no envelope. DP's Villa Raggio address is typed on the reverse of the letter (Lilly). DP noted in her diary for 6 June 1945 that she went to the "AMG [Allied Military Government office in Rapallo] 8.15 found EP's letter of 24th." This was the last time DP had a letter from EP until Letter 7, written in late September 1945.

I may go to Rome] Military orders were issued on 22 May 1945 to transfer EP without delay to the DTC near Pisa. After typing this note to DP and a similar one to Olga Rudge, also beginning "Talk is that I may go to Rome oggi" (OR Papers, Beinecke), EP was handcuffed and driven by armed guards to the DTC. His mention of Rome suggests that he thought he was bound for an airport to be flown to the United States. See also Arrizabalaga's memoir (Appendix I).

Confucio e Mencio] EP was translating the Confucian commentator Mencius at the time he was taken by partigiani on 3 May 1945. He continued this work while at the CIC in Genoa and later at the DTC (see Letter 2n). Lieutenant Colonel Steele, commander at the DTC, wrote his mother on 20 August 1945: "Instead of spending his many spare moments organizing whatever he may think he has for a defense for his case, he spends his time pottering away at a translation of Menghis [Mencius], the Chinese philosopher" (private collection). EP published "Mencius, or the Economist," an abridged translation of the Book of Mencius (the fourth Confucian classic), in *New Iconograph* (Fall 1947). His article "Mang Tsze (The Ethics of Mencius)," containing discussion and quotation, had appeared earlier in *The Criterion* (July 1938).

"Non sto"] "Gotta go now." This and the remark about money for Olga Rudge were hastily scrawled in black ink. In a letter to Olga dated 7 June 1945 DP wrote: "I am enclosing one of the thousand-lire notes that I found in his room after he was taken away. This as you may remember was his money, not mine - We have never had a joint account at Chiavari Bank. Mine is blocked. I will let you know should it be reopened" (OR Papers, Beinecke). In his matching letter to Olga (see note above), EP enclosed two checks for five thousand lire each, drawn on his account at the Bank of Chiavari (OP). Not wishing to receive charity and believing that any extra money should go to helping EP, Olga offered to return the thousand lire note to DP and later gave back the two five-thousand lire checks. EP's anxieties over the financial straits of Olga and Mary Rudge are a continuing theme of these letters.

[Office of the Counter Intelligence Corps
[6 Via Fieschi]
[Genoa, Italy]
Giovedi [Thursday]
24 Mag/ [24 May 1945]

Mao

Talk is that I may go to Rome oggi [today], in which case hope to see you en passant.

Yes, have been perfectly fed, balanced diet etc. for forget how long. Tell Isab/ [Isabel] that I have been doing Confucio e Mencio, for american reader, if any.

That about covers my time. Question of picking up a change of clot[h]ing in Rap/ etc.

Non sto. please see that Olga has enough money.

Documents 3–5 Notes. Special Agent Amprim's memo to FBI Director J. Edgar Hoover, dated 26 May 1945, is document 100–34099–238 in the FBI files. Typed on two pages, it contains Bureau routing notations that are not reproduced here. EP's text "Ashes of Europe Calling"—which must be considered his final radio script, never broadcast—and his statement for Reynolds Packard were included with Amprim's memo as "attachments." Both of these latter documents are now in the Ezra Pound Papers (Beinecke). "Ashes of Europe Calling" is written in pencil by EP on four legal-size sheets of ruled yellow paper similar to that used for Letters I and 2, and the statement for Packard is written on two sheets of the same paper. Both documents were composed at the Office of the Counter Intelligence Corps in Genoa, probably around the time that EP dictated the telegram for President Truman on 5 May 1945 (Document 3), and are marked in pencil "EPB 6–19–45." "EPB" was Elisabeth Prender Buchanan, an attorney who had joined the U.S. Department of Justice in 1930.

FEMOLOSAS] Ernest Francisco Fenollosa (1853–1908), poet and student of Oriental art, graduated first in his class from Harvard and went to Japan in 1878 to teach political economy and philosophy at the Imperial University at Tokyo. When the Tokyo Fine Arts Academy and the Imperial Museum were opened in 1888, he was made manager of both institutions. He studied traditional Japanese art and Noh drama, became a professing Buddhist, and was several times decorated by the emperor of Japan. In 1890 he became curator of the Oriental department of the Boston Museum of Fine Arts. His two-volume work, *Epochs of Chinese and Japanese Art*, was published posthumously in 1912. His widow, Mary McNeill Fenollosa (1865?–1954), who wrote novels under the pen name of Sidney McCall, met EP in London in 1913 and entrusted her husband's literary papers to him. EP told John Quinn in 1917: "All she said was, after she had known me about three weeks, 'You are the only person who can finish this stuff [as] Ernest would have wanted it done. He cared about the poetry not about the philology'" (*Pound/Quinn* 118). From this material EP *edited The Chinese Written Character as a Medium for Poetry*, first published in installments in *The Little Review* in 1919 and later in *Instigations* (1920), and drew matter and inspiration for the poems in *Cathay* (1915) and translations of Japanese Noh plays.

he had met two Japanese] In a letter to Olga Rudge written from "Salo" and postmarked 3 December 1943, EP reported: "Parlato con tre nipponici hieri: avendo in mano 'Le Ode' di Kung. 'lungo e cordiale colloq.'" ["Spoke with three Japanese yesterday, with 'the Odes' of Confucius in my hand. 'Long and friendly chat'"] (OR Papers, Beinecke).

Japan Times] Between December 1939 and October 1940, EP published a dozen articles in the *Japan Times & Mail* and *Japan Times Weekly* of Tokyo, on Noh drama, music, politics, money, international finance, and the war, often under the heading "Letter from Rapallo."

New Age] Alfred Richard Orage (1873–1934), Guild Socialist and author, edited *The New Age* (1907–1922) and the *New English Weekly* (1932–1934) and was one of EP's chief mentors and benefactors. EP met Orage in 1911 and was impressed by his range of interests, and it was through Orage that he later met Major C.H. Douglas, whose Social Credit theory figured prominently in *The New Age* and shaped EP's ideas on money and economics. EP published nearly three hundred articles in *The New Age* between 1911 and 1922, including translations, social commentary, and criticism on literature, art, and music (often under pseudonyms). Among his contributions appearing in serial form were "I Gather the Limbs of Osiris," "Patria Mia," "Pastiche: The Regional," and "Indiscretions." Several months before Orage's death in 1934, EP remarked to John Drummond: "[H]e did more to feed me than anyone else in England, and I wish anybody who esteems my existence wd. pay back whatever they feel is due to its

DOCUMENT 3   MEMO OF FRANK L. AMPRIM
TO J. EDGAR HOOVER

Rome, Italy
May 26, 1945

Director, FBI

Re: Ezra Loomis Pound
Treason

Dear Sir:

When the writer [Amprim] began questioning Ezra Pound on the morning of May 5, 1945, at the Office of the Counter Intelligence Corps, Genoa, Pound immediately requested that the writer send a cable for him to President Truman, explaining that it was "a serious matter and not just an eccentricity." The Subject [EP] dictated the following cable to the writer:

"PRESIDENT TRUMAN, WASHINGTON. BEG YOU CABLE ME MINIMUM TERMS JUST PEACE JAPAN. LET ME NEGOTIATE VIA JAPANESE EMBASSY RECENTLY ACCREDITED ITALIAN SOCIAL REPUBLIC, LAGO DI GARDA. FEMOLOSAS, EXECUTOR AND TRANSLATOR OF CONFUCIUS, CAN WHAT VIOLENCE CANNOT. CHINA ALSO WILL OBEY VOICE OF CONFUCIUS. EZRA POUND."

Pound then went on to explain that he was the "literary executor" of Ernest Femollosas [Fenollosa] who died in 1908, saying that Femollosas had gone to Japan as a professor of economics and had become Imperial Commissioner of Fine Arts for Japan. The Subject stated that he believed he could negotiate a peace between the United States and Japan, because in November of 1943, at Salo, Italy, he had met two Japanese who were from the Japanese Embassy, and they were surprised to learn that he was familiar with Confucius and Femollosas. He advised further that he would appeal not to the Japanese militarists, but to the ancient culture of Japan.

The Subject became very indignant when the writer told him that he could not dispatch such a cable for him. Pound then stated that peace should be negotiated with Japan, allowing her to retain the territory she had conquered.

A manuscript for a radio broadcast entitled "Ashes of Europe Calling" was prepared by Pound and is being submitted herewith [printed below]. The writer advised Pound that he could not arrange for him to make any such broadcast.

Pound then prepared a statement for [blacked-out] which statement is attached

stalvarrdt sustainer. My gate receipts Nov. I, 1914–15, were 42 quid 10 s. and Orage's 4 guineas a month thereafter wuz the SINEWS, by gob the sinooz" (Paige 259).

C. H. Douglas] Clifford Hugh Douglas (1879–1952), an engineer, was manager of the British West-inghouse Company in India. After World War I, during which he was a major in the Royal Flying Corps, he devoted himself to economics and his theory of Social Credit, which holds that public purchasing power will always lag behind available goods and services, with consequences as dire as economic depres-sions and wars, unless governments intervene to supply social credit in the form of a "national divi-dend," thus stimulating consumption and eliminating the need for bank loans and private moneylenders. His theories, expounded in *The New Age* and in his books, *Economic Democracy* and *Credit Power and Democ-racy* (both 1920), had a great impact on EP, who embraced Social Credit as a workable system and pro-moted Douglas in his poetry and prose, reviewing his books *in The Athenaeum, The Little Review,* and elsewhere. Later, EP believed that Hitler and Mussolini were implementing, by fascist decree, measures similar to Douglas's proposals. "Douglas may object that this is not 'democratic' (that is egalitarian)," wrote EP in *What Is Money For?* (1939), "BUT for the monetary scientist or economist the result is the same. The goods are getting distributed" (Cookson 294). For Douglas's A + B theorem, see Letter 17n.

Verona program] In November 1943 the First Congress of the Republican Fascist Party in Verona issued a manifesto denouncing capitalism, along with alleged British intrigues and international plutocracies, and proclaiming the importance of labor to the new fascist state (the Salò Republic). EP admired this document, in particular Mussolini's verbal distinctions: "'alla' non 'della' in il Programma di Verona / the old hand as stylist still holding its cunning" (Canto 78, lines 35–36). Mary de Rachewiltz provides a gloss: "work as basis of money. No right *of* property but *to* property. Work no longer the object but the subject of economy" (*Discretions* 195–96). See also Redman 235ff.

Brest Litovsk] In March 1918 a separate peace treaty was signed by Soviet Russia and the Central Powers at Brest-Litovsk, by which Russia had to give up her Polish, Baltic, and part of her White Russian provinces, as well as other regions, and to recognize the independence of the Ukraine and Finland. Rus-sia was also required to pay three hundred million gold rubles as compensation for the losses suffered by Germans. Treaty negotiations had been delayed by disputes within the Russian party, but Lenin forced through the agreement in order to safeguard the gains of the October Revolution. The treaty was set aside by the armistice and abrogated by the Treaty of Versailles. The "zhamefull beace" of Brest-Litovsk is mentioned in EP's Canto 16 (lines 209–13).

hereto [printed below]. The writer informed the Subject that he could not forward said statement for him.

During the course of various conversations with the Subject, he stated to the writer that he still believes the United States should have stayed out of the war and sold to both the Axis countries and to England and Russia. Pound admitted that he was a correspondent for the *Japan Times* for about five months during 1941. He stated that the last money he had received from outside Italy was a postal money order from the *Japan Times* during 1941. He could not remember the amount or where he had cashed the money order.

The Subject advised that he had become interested in economics when he was writing for the *New Age* of London as an art and music critic. According to the Subject, this was about 1919. Pound said that the articles on economics by

C. H. Douglas began appearing in the newspaper, and that from 1920 to 1930 he had written three reviews on Douglas' social credit.

Very truly yours,

Frank L. Amprim

Special Agent

FLA:rkm
Attachments [as follows]

DOCUMENT 4   EZRA POUND'S DRAFT
FOR A FINAL RADIO BROADCAST

Ashes of Europe Calling

Italy should be under American management until they, the Italians can elect a government, assembly chosen on basis of personal honesty, not on capacity to diddle the other fellow, or on political theory.—No real political training in Italy. The people should vote on the Verona program not as a whole but point by point so as to give the representatives (deputies) *some* idea of what they want—not merely jumble of names of the 57 varieties—

No peace not on justice—not crush germany—not leave hate. The Russian give way @ Brest Litovsk basis of Russias strenght [sic]. Hitler's NOT fighting for Tyrol basis of axis strength. Dont leave irredentas, or a Jugo-Slave Venice, as tinder box for next war— Dont divide Austria from Germany—Germany not today the germany of 1939—If they now have learned NOT to try to get by violence what can ONLY be got by intelligence the war is one won, & the peace should not be lost.

europe so thankful the war is over that hate is dead, for the moment—only injustice can resurrect it.

Todt organization] The German Organisation Todt (OT), headed by Fritz Todt (1891–1942), employed slave labor for the construction of the Westfall (Siegfried Line), airfields, rocket-bomb sites, and submarine bases. Todt was the military engineer who planned the system of *autobahnen* (superhighways) under the Hitler regime and became minister of armaments and munitions, responsible for the functioning of Germany's industrial machine.

Another point -

There are 3 varieties of imperialism -

export of goods, export of capital, export of men. The 1st can be & often is aggressive. The 2nd is ALWAYS corrosive.—only the 3rd is basicly constructive if the men of higher civilization carry it, as Italy did—into North Africa —

Italy must not lose, & germany must not lose benefit of economic advance, advance of economic justice under the land improvement, the rural housing, swamp drainage in short the new deals of the past two decades -

U.S. has great opportunity—the ruin of Art Works is IRReparable, but the U.S. with the great means can in One year do in Italy what Mussolini with small means did in ten.

& you have got the Todt organization to beat—you can do it.—you can do it the american way, & be loved. hungry people grateful for lunch packets & quick to forget. —

Jews—I believe in Palestine for the jews as a ~~symbol of~~ national home & symbol of jewry—not merely as a real estate speculation—zionism against international finance. —

Naturally I want peace with japan. ~~nothing can beat modern~~ modern japanese business vulgarity & ~~aggressive or~~ aggressiveness ~~save~~ can best be beaten by 2500 years of japanese civilization.—at any rate I would welcome that victory—If one cant have it—the ~~best~~ only other alternative ~~is~~ must go by a long & bloody road. —

In the mean time there is Europe, to win or lose.

Packard] Reynolds Packard (1903–1975) was an American journalist who covered wars and revolutions throughout the world during the 1930s and 1940s, first for the United Press and later for the *New York Daily News*. After reporting on the Italian invasion of Ethiopia and Hitler's conquest of Czechoslovakia, he followed the Allied forces from North Africa through Italy. His career, which included service as UP bureau chief in Rome, was marked by flamboyance and colorful reporting. EP, impressed by Packard's insight and candor, sent him short "interviews" on various subjects, including, in 1941, the suggestion that the United States exchange Guam for sound films of Japanese Noh plays (Beinecke). In *Balcony Empire: Fascist Italy at War* (1942), Packard and his wife, Eleanor (d. 1972), who was his partner in news reporting, gave a possibly overdramatized account of EP's visit to their house in Rome on the day of Pearl Harbor.

Kumrad Koba] "Koba," meaning "the bear" or "the indomitable," was a boyhood nickname of Joseph Stalin (1879–1953). EP uses it again in Canto 84. EP thought that if he were allowed to meet with Stalin, he could persuade him of the value of Social Credit and stamp scrip, as he indicates in Canto 74:

> and but one point needed for Stalin
> you need not, i.e. need not take over the means of production;
> money to signify work done, inside a system
> and measured and wanted (lines 43–46)

See also Document 7 and Letter 29.

Senator Cutting] Bronson Cutting (1888–1935) was a cultured, progressive senator from New Mexico whose stands on customs censorship, copyright laws, and federal public assistance measures appealed to EP. EP corresponded with Cutting from 1930 until the senator's untimely death. In November 1930 EP wrote him requesting "a list of the literate members of the senate," and a month later Cutting obliged: "As for 'literacy,' I don't suppose you are interested in people like Moses & Bingham & Dave Reed, who sin against the light. That leaves Borah & Norris & LaFollette & Hiram Johnson & Tydings & Wheeler & Walsh of Montana & I suppose Dwight Morrow, & not much else" (*Pound/Cutting* 38, 40). EP alludes to the "eleven literates" in Cantos 86, 98, and 102, as well as in his prose writings, misnaming the banker and Republican New Jersey senator Dwight Whitney Morrow (1873–1931) "Dwight L. Morrow," as he does here. Harry Truman was not in the senate when Cutting assembled his list.

DOCUMENT 5   STATEMENT BY EZRA POUND
FOR REYNOLDS PACKARD

Packard. A.P. exclusive.

Pound interviewed by A.P.

Stalin has the best mind in Russia. Man I most want to talk to is Kumrad Koba (Stalin) hope to meet him in Georgia (Caucasus Georgia).

Been so cut off, not seen congressional directory since that for 1939—didn't know who was vice president till I heard Truman was President. as far as I recall First time ever heard of Truman was in letter from Senator Cutting. think Trumans name was 2nd or 3rd on list of the eleven literate senators. It's a list that ends up: "and I suppose Dwight L. Morrow.

Ezra Pound

To Packard
Associated Press.
Rome.

————————————

Document 6 Notes. This six-page typed document was sworn to and signed by EP on 7 May 1945 at the CIC office in Genoa. According to FBI document 100–34099–182, EP had signed a first version, with additions and corrections, on 6 May; on 7 May the text was retyped to include these "marginal notations." Document 6 is the retyped text, though it too contains changes in EP's hand, each one initialed by him and an additional paragraph inserted in his hand: "The Casa Editrice [. . .] the radio items." Our text is taken from a negative photostat (Tulsa) that was evidently made by John Edwards from Ramon Arrizabalaga's personal copy of the Sworn Statement (see Appendix 1). Document 6 was previously published with minor differences under the misleading title "Confession," ed. Richard Sieburth, *Paris Review*, no. 128 (1993): 193–206.

RAMON ARRIZABALAGA] Ramon Arrizabalaga (1914–1984), a native of Nevada, was sent to Europe in November 1942 and saw active duty in 1944 in Algeria and Morocco and throughout the Italian campaign, from Naples to Genoa. He was awarded the Bronze Star in Italy by Lt. Gen. Mark Clark on 16 November 1944. (See photo, p. 000.) Being bilingual in Spanish and English, with some knowledge of Basque, French, and Italian, he was placed in Military Intelligence. A first lieutenant, he was commanding officer at the Counter Intelligence Corps (CIC) detachment of the 92nd Infantry Division in Genoa when EP was held there for questioning. The original of the famous photograph of EP being interviewed on a couch by Arrizabalaga (see photo, p. 000) was taken by the U.S. Army Signal Corps and is stamped on the back: "16 May, 1945 Fifth Army, Genoa area, Italy. On the left is Mr. Ramon Arrizabalaga, C.I.C. chief investigator, talking with Ezra Pound, author, radio commentator and advisor to Mussolini." See also Letter 2n and Arrizabalaga's memoir (Appendix I).

FRANK L. AMPRIM] Frank Lawrence Amprim (1910–1985), FBI special agent in charge of EP's case. See Letter 2n.

the opera "Villon"] *Le Testament de Villon*, a one-act opera with a libretto taken from François Villon's poems, was written by EP in the early 1920s with the help of the English musician Agnes Bedford and later of George Antheil. *Villon* carries EP's troubadour passion for the union of words and music into rhythmic composition for voice and instruments. The scene is set in a bordello near a cathedral. "They will hang me possibly as an academic," EP wrote Bedford in 1921, "but scarcely as a dynamitist" (Paige 167). *Villon* premiered in Paris in 1926 and was broadcast by the BBC in 1931.

evacuate my home] See Letters 3n and 5n.

loan of the Littorio] Government bonds. "Littorio" was a synonym for "fascismo," not to be confused with Littoria, a town in central Italy built in the early 1930s on land reclaimed from the Pontine marshes. EP admired Mussolini's drainage project (*la bonifica*), which "made the desert to yield" (Canto 78, line 90).

BENITO MUSSOLINI] EP was granted an audience with Mussolini (1883–1945) on 30 January 1933 (not 1929) in the Palazzo Venezia in Rome. As they spoke, the Duce examined a copy of *A Draft of XXX Cantos* that EP had provided, remarking that it was "divertente" (entertaining, amusing)—a comment celebrated in Canto 41. EP also presented him with a list of the essential points of Social Credit.

GIDO CAVALCANTI] EP published his first translations of *the Sonnets and Ballate of Guido Cavalcanti* in 1912, but it was his Marsano edition of *Guido Cavalcanti Rime* (Genoa, 1932) that he gave to Mussolini. He also sent him *Eleven New Cantos XXXI-XLI* and *Make It New* (both 1934), inscribed to "Duce," as well as other works.

FRANCESCO MONOTTI] Francesco Monotti (1899–1983) was an Italian journalist and art critic who lived in Rome and was associated with many newspapers, reviews, and publishing ventures in the 1930s, including Bibliografia Fascista *and La Vittoria*, the journal of the national association for disabled veterans. He also wrote for *Il Mare*, the Rapallo newspaper. Monotti knew many influential people and tried in 1932 to arrange a meeting between EP and Mussolini and later to help EP get on the radio. In 1940, looking back on his efforts to spread economic enlightenment in Italy, EP noted that Monotti "fu qui il primo a capirmi" ("was the first one here to understand me") (*Poetry and Prose* 8:65). Between 1929 and 1931 Monotti published translations from *How to Read* and other works by EP in *L'Indice*, *La Fiera Letteraria*, and *Belvedere*. In 1929 or 1930 he conducted the interview to which EP refers (quoted

DOCUMENT 6   SWORN STATEMENT BY EZRA POUND

[Office of the Counter Intelligence Corps]
[6 Via Fieschi]
Genoa, Italy
May 7, 1945

I make the following statement to RAMON ARRIZABALAGA and FRANK L. AMPRIM. Ramon Arrizabalaga has identified himself to be an Agent of the Counter Intelligence Corps of the 92nd Division of the United States Army; Frank Amprim has identified himself as a Special Agent of the Federal Bureau of Investigation of the United States of America. No threats or promises of any kind or nature have been made to me by anyone either directly or indirectly, and I have been advised that I do not have to make any Statement if I do not wish to do so. This statement is voluntary. I have been advised also that this statement can be used against me in a court of law.

My full name is EZRA LOOMIS POUND. I am an American citizen. I have never renounced my American citizenship. I was born at Hailey, Idaho, United States, on October 30, 1885. I lived in the United States until 1908, when I moved to London, England, where I lived until 1920, doing free lance writing. From 1920 to 1924, I lived in Paris, France, where I composed the opera "Villon," and wrote art and music reviews. In 1924 I moved to Rapallo, Italy, where I lived until May of 1944, when I was forced by military order to evacuate my home, and I moved to SANTA AMBROGIO 60, which is my present address.

While living in Europe, I had visited Italy often, and after the last war I noticed the Fascist renewal or rejuvenation of the Country. My wife and I subscribed 25000 lire each to the first loan of the Littorio but I cannot remember the date. My purpose was to give Mussolini a "square deal" by pointing out his good work. About 1929, I had an audience with BENITO MUSSOLINI, who knew my book "GIDO [sic] CAVALCANTI," which I had presented to him the year before. He expected me to talk about my book, but I ~~explained my~~ took a very strong economic ~~theories to him~~ questionnaire to him.

About 1929, I granted an interview to one FRANCESCO MONOTTI of the newspaper LAVORO FASCISTA. In this interview I stated that England was dead and the corpses were lying about in the streets; that France was dead but had had the decency to bury the dead; that Italy was the only Country of the three where any vital activity was taking place.

About 1935, ~~I had~~ was published my book "Jefferson and Mussolini." In this book I pointed out that Fascism was Mussolini's "New Deal" for Italy, contrasting his method with Jefferson's.

I finally made contact with the Italian Ministry of Popular Culture at Rome, Italy, during 1939, while visiting Rome. On that occasion I contacted the head of the Italian Ministry of Popular Culture, ALESSANDRO PAVOLINI. I handed him a list of five points. He said he was not as interested in any of the other points as in the fifth point, which was a suggestion that I talk over the Italian Radio to the American people for the purpose of pointing out the fine work which Mussolini had done in Italy.

substantially in Redman 76–77); it was published in 1931 in the Roman daily *Il Lavoro Fascista* and in *Belvedere*. In a 1941 radio talk, EP credited Monotti with alerting him to Enrico Pea's novel, *Moscardino*: "So I read it, and for the first time in your colloquitor's life he wuz tempted to TRANSLATE a novel, and did so" (Doob 7). See also Letter 34n.

LAVORO FASCISTA] EP's article "Le Fonti d'Informazione del Signor Roosevelt," an attack on usury, Churchill's England, and the allegedly tainted sources of FDR's information, was reprinted *Il Lavoro Fascista* (1 April 1941).

"Jefferson and Mussolini"]*Jefferson and/or Mussolini: L'Idea Statale. Fascism As I Have Seen It* (London: Stanley Nott, 1935). See also Letter 2n.

ALESSANDRO PAVOLINI] Alessandro Pavolini (1903–1945) took part in the 1922 march on Rome that brought Mussolini to power. A journalist, he was elected to the Italian Parliament in 1934 and served as a war correspondent in Ethiopia. In 1939 Mussolini named him minister of popular culture and director of government propaganda but dismissed him in February 1943. After the regime's collapse in 1943, Pavolini escaped to Germany and from there helped persuade Mussolini to head the Salò Republic, of which he himself became party secretary. EP wrote him on many subjects: taxes, inflation, usury, Scotus Erigena, Leo Frobenius, Silvio Gesell, and stamp scrip. Pavolini was captured by partigiani and shot at Dongo on 28 April 1945.

Mr INTERLANDI] Telesio Interlandi (b. 1894), a prominent fascist journalist, established the newspaper *Il Tevere* (Rome), the unofficial mouthpiece of Mussolini. He was arrested by Marshal Badoglio in 1943, freed by the Germans, and joined Mussolini at Salò in northern Italy, where he was again active in journalism and in charge of propaganda for invaded territories under the Ministry of Popular Culture.

Mr. PARESCE] Gabriele Paresce (1900–1982), born in Florence, was a journalist for *La Stampa* and the official news agency Stefani, and press attaché at the Italian embassy in London before 1940. Later he was a division head of the inspectorate for radio and television transmissions at the Italian Ministry of Popular Culture. On 18 January 1941 he wrote EP inviting him to prepare a radio script and to come to Rome to record it for transmission to North America and Great Britain (Beinecke). EP worked closely with Paresce, Adriano Ungaro, and Prince Ranieri di San Faustino at "Minculpop," and occasionally visited Paresce and his wife, Degna, the daughter of Guglielmo Marconi, who lived together in the same apartment building in Rome as did Prince Ranieri and his wife. John Drummond's letter to DP of 9 November 1945 indicates that Paresce had told him that he was willing, if called upon, to testify in court on EP's behalf (Lilly). After the war, Paresce was appointed press counselor at the Italian embassy in Washington, D.C. (1949–1960), and later was made Italian ambassador to South Korea.

ENTE ITALIANA AUDIZIONE RADIOFONICHE] Ente Italiano Audizioni Radiofoniche, or EIAR, located at 10 Via Asiago in Rome. "In 1923 Marconi pointed out to Mussolini that there were important political advantages in having a modern radio network in Italy, and in August 1924 the Unione Radiofonica Italiana (URI) was established. Stations were set up in Rome, Milan, and Naples over the next several years, and URI was given a temporary monopoly over broadcasting. In November 1927 Ente Italiano Audizioni Radiofoniche (EIAR) replaced URI. [. . .] The government's control over EIAR's actual program content was exercised through a 'committee of vigilance' [and EIAR later became] a specialized division for radio created within the Ministry of Popular Culture. A persistent problem, however, remained the fact that Italians could freely listen to either Radio Vaticana or to foreign broadcasts to obtain unbiased or noncensored news. [. . .] After Mussolini's fall in 1943, EIAR was reestablished in the Salò Republic but was largely under German control and not very efficient. Mussolini himself wrote many of the texts for the 'Corrispondenza Repubblicana' program of the period, but effective competition was provided by the partisan clandestine radios in the north and the Pietro Badoglio government in the south" (Cannistraro 446).

UNGERO] Adriano Ungaro, an official in the radio section of the Italian Ministry of Popular Culture, was, according to EP, "an Italian liberal" who made the final decision to employ him as a radio broad-

In the Spring of 1940 I was invited to come to Rome to discuss my proposition of broadcasting over the Italian Radio by Mr INTERLANDI and later by Mr. PARESCE, and asked him if I could broadcast to the American and English peoples over the Italian Radio. I was finally allowed to give two broadcasts per week to the United States and one broadcast per week to England. No written contract was entered into.

I began broadcasting in person over the Italian Radio about the Summer of 1940. I constantly fought for more time on the Air in order to get my ideal across to the American and English peoples. At first, for a very brief time, I used to speak directly over the Air, but on one occasion during 1940 I made some remarks at the end of my talk, not in the script, simply a repeat of a main point, and after that incident I was ordered by PARESCE to record my talks on a disk, and this disk would be rebroadcast over the Air.

For the broadcasts made by me either directly or by disc, in my voice, I received three hundred and fifty lire, and for the articles read over the Air by someone else I received three hundred lire. This money was paid to me from the Summer of 1940 to the Summer of 1943 by the Italian Ministry of Popular Culture, which was part of the Italian Fascist Government. The Ministry of Popular Culture would authorize the Italian Accounting Office to send a so called "MANDATO" to me by mail to Rapallo, Italy, where I was living. I would then take the "mandato" to the Italian Tax Office at Rapallo where I would sign a receipt and receive the amount called for in the "mandato."

During 1942 and the first half of 1943, at Rapallo, I would write about twenty or twenty-one radio manuscripts or talks, and then I would go to Rome where I visited the registration room of the ENTE ITALIANA AUDIZIONE RADIOFONICHE [sic] and make disks for rebroadcasts of my talks. I usually remained in Rome about three weeks, making three recordings per day. I made these recordings only after my manuscripts had been approved by Mr. UNGERO, sub-head of the Radio section of the Italian Ministry of Popular Culture. The Italian Ministry of Popular Culture may have copies of the manuscripts used by me in making disks for radio talks.

During 1942 and 1943, I used to make a broadcast by means of disks about three or four times every week. The broadcasts were managed and sponsored by the Ministry of Popular Culture, but went out over the EIAR at Rome. The EIAR was an independent private firm, semi government control.

Some of the aforesaid broadcasts were made in my name. I would come on the Air with the introduction "EUROPE CALLING—EZRA POUND SPEAKING."

During 1942, I invented a fictitious character called "AMERICAN IMPERIALIST." So far as I know I wrote all the broadcasts made under the name "American Imperialist." I think that Prince RANIERI SAN FAUSTINO may have read or announced some of them over the Air.

During 1942 and 1943, I wrote, also, brief items and "wise cracks" for a feature known as "News from Nowhere." This feature was dedicated to ridiculing English news broadcasts.

During 1942 and 1943 some of the recordings I made for the Italian Ministry of Popular Culture were sent to Berlin, Germany, and broadcast over German radio. Only a few were so sent.

Much of my business during 1942 and 1943 with the Italian Ministry of Popular

caster (Carpenter 583). EP's letters to Ungaro of 9 and 12 December 1941, immediately following Pearl Harbor, express his desire to continue broadcasting "so long as I say nothing that can in any way prejudice the results of American military or naval (or navel) action, the armed forces of the U.S.A. or the welfare of my native country" (*Poetry and Prose* 10:251). Ungaro was mentioned in the November 1945 grand jury indictment of EP.

RANIERI SAN FAUSTINO] Prince Ranieri di San Faustino, born ca. 1900, was one of EP's superiors at Rome Radio. They corresponded regularly, and EP received advice and encouragement from him regarding broadcasts and effective propaganda strategies (Beinecke). See also Letter 35.

Marshall BADOGLIO] Pietro Badoglio (1871–1956), Italian field marshal who conquered Ethiopia (1935–1936). For Badoglio's role in Italian affairs after the dismissal of Mussolini in July 1943, see Introduction. EP despised the Badoglio government and coined the verb *badogliare*, "to betray" (Carpenter 626).

FRANKLIN D. ROOSEVELT] After reading *Looking Forward* (1933), in which FDR (1882–1945) discussed the urgent need for U.S. reforms in state land planning, government organization, and taxation, EP wrote to the Paris edition of the *Chicago Tribune* with praise for FDR's remarks on insufficient purchasing power, adding that the president might now proceed to the economic theories of C. H. Douglas (7 May 1933). On 2 May 1933 EP wrote to FDR, offering to dedicate *Jefferson and/or Mussolini* to him (Beinecke). He also sent him an inscribed copy of *ABC of Economics* (1933). Over the next several years, EP wrote letters to Eleanor Roosevelt (1884–1962) and to FDR himself, urging various economic and political ideas (FDR Library, Hyde Park). At first he had cautious hopes for FDR, but later he became convinced that the president was a "hypnotized lunkus" (Doob 344), a tool of warmongers and Jewish international financiers. EP's radio speeches trace a crescendo of abuse hurled at "Franklin D. Frankfurter Jewsfeld."

AMILCARE ROSSI] Amilcare Rossi (b. 1895), fascist bureaucrat and publicist, served in the Ethiopian war. In February 1943 Mussolini appointed him undersecretary for the Presidency of the Council of Ministers.

I walked from Rome] In the chaotic period after Italy's capitulation to the Allies in September 1943, EP decided to leave Rome, where he had been consulting with officials at the Ministry of Popular Culture, and travel north to see his daughter, Mary Rudge, in the peasant village of Gais in the Italian Tyrol. With borrowed rucksack and boots, he walked to Rieti, about fifty miles northwest of Rome, and then rode a series of trains to Gais, where he was reunited with his daughter and explained to her the complications of his domestic life. After a short stay, EP returned to Rapallo. In *Oro e lavoro* (*Gold and Work*) (1944), he memorialized his journey in the form of a Gesellite fable: "On the 10th of September last, I walked down the Via Salaria and into the Republic of Utopia, a quiet country lying eighty years east of Fara Sabina" (Cookson 336).

FERNANDO MEZZASOMA] Fernando Mezzasoma (1907–1945), minister of popular culture in the Salò government. He was fanatically loyal to Mussolini and had confidence in EP, who wrote him frequently on many topics: economics, radio broadcasts, his Italian Cantos (72 and 73), a Tigullio manifesto, publication and diffusion of Confucian texts, an edition of Vivaldi, bus services for the new republic, plans for repairing bomb damage in Rapallo (Beinecke). Mezzasoma was executed by partigiani in late April 1945.

money clause] EP quotes this passage from the U.S. Constitution in his *Introductory Text Book* (1939): "The Congress shall have power; To coin money, regulate the value thereof and of foreign coin and to fix the standards of weights and measures" (Cookson 159). See also Document 7.

my grandfather] Thaddeus Coleman Pound (1832–1914) was born in Elk, Warren County, Pennsylvania. In 1847 he and his family settled in Rock County, Wisconsin, where he began teaching, at the age of fifteen, at Milton Academy in Janesville. In 1856 he moved to Chippewa Falls to work with his brother, Albert, in the lumber business. He was four times elected to the Wisconsin State Assembly

Culture was conducted with ADRIANO UNGERO, sub-head of the Radio Section of the Italian Ministry of Popular Culture.

The last broadcast over the EIAR made in my voice was made on July 25, 1943. I recall the date vividly. I was listening to my talk while at my home in Rapallo. A few minutes after my talk had concluded, there came over the radio the announcement that Mussolini had been over thrown and Marshall BADOGLIO had taken over the Italian Government. I then ceased broadcasting over EIAR because the Badoglio Government "kicked me out." However, between July and September 1943, I sent to Prince RANIERI SAN FAUSTINO of the Italian Ministry of Popular Culture at Rome four or five radio talks under the name of "PIERO MAZDA." He had them read over the EIAR. These talks were similar to my previous talks in which I had attacked President FRANKLIN D. ROOSEVELT and the International Financiers in America and elsewhere who had dragged the United States into the present war. I probably received three hundred lire for each of these talks which I had written under the name of "Piero Mazda."

After Badoglio became head of the Italian Government I went to Rome to see what was going on, about August 1, 1943 and soon returned to Rapallo. I returned to Rome about September 6, 1943, and saw someone whom I believe to have been AMILCARE ROSSI, former Italian Ambassador to the United States, and asked him to talk over EIAR to the American people to ask the American army to cease bombing churches and babies, in Italy. He told me that it would do no good.

On September 10, 1943, I walked from Rome to Rieti and then by train went to the Tyrol, and then to Rapallo.

During the Autumn of 1943, some of the Fascists formed a new Party in Northern Italy, and ALESSANDRO PAVOLINI went to Germany and named himself Secretary of the new Party, which eventually became the Fascist Republican Government. Later I wrote to Pavolini and he invited me to come North if I could get there, and I accepted. At Salo, I could not see Pavolini, but I saw FERNANDO MEZZASOMA, who had become head of the Ministry of Popular Culture in the Republican Fascist Government. Mezzasoma let me go to Milan since I told him that even if Italy fell I must go on with my own economic propaganda, that is, my observance of the money clause in the United States Constitution which my grandfather had fought for in 1878, saying the same things I was saying.

I went to Milan on a cattle truck, and found the Republican Fascist Radio in disorder, with a few honest men wanting a Radio Station and the "wise guys" sabotaging, and none of them being free from German control. The Germans censored all the programs. In Rome I had met one CARL GOEDEL who was in the English section of EIAR during 1942 and 1943. I again met Goedel on this visit to Milan, and one of his officials gave me three thousand lire toward expenses. At Milan I refused to broadcast to American troops and no pressure was put on me. I then returned to Rapallo.

From about May to September of 1944, I sent items to the Republican Fascist Radio at Milano. When I wanted my name known or used, these items were written in the form of an interview with me. However my main work from this time on was writing and advising the CASA EDITRICE EDIZIONE POPOLARE of Venice, which publishing firm printed my version of the CHUNG YUNG of CONFUCIUS and my

(1864–1869), and in 1870 and 1871 he served as lieutenant governor of the state. In 1876, the year he became a Republican congressman, he put through the Chippewa Falls and Western Railway and got legislation through to build a railway line west of Marinette and north of Green Bay, for which achievement the town of Pound was named for him. During his years in Congress he originated bills to aid the American Indians and to promote female suffrage. EP idealized his grandfather and saw in him foreshadowings of his own radical political and economic energies. He took special pride in the paper money that Thaddeus had printed for his Union Lumbering Company, "bearing the promise to 'pay the bearer on demand ... in merchandise or lumber,'" as EP explains in *A Visiting Card* (1942), adding that "T.C.P. had already in 1878 been writing about, or urging among his fellow Congressmen, the same essentials of monetary and statal economics that I am writing about today" (Cookson 325). EP sent FDR a postcard printed with a photograph of his grandfather's scrip, with the message, "Lest you forget the nature of money/ i;e; that it is a ticket" (Carpenter 523).

CARL GOEDEL] Carl Giorgio Goedel, born in Germany in 1892 and raised in Philadelphia, returned to Europe and in 1914 entered the German army to serve as a translator. After the war, he was active in publishing and radio fields. In 1940 he went to Rome and began working for the Ministry of Popular Culture and soon joined its North American section, where until July 1943 he was a translator and news broadcaster. After the Salò Republic was established, Goedel did propaganda work for the Ministry of Popular Culture, operating out of the German embassy in Rome. In late 1943 he was transferred to Milan to head the "Tunis" transmissions beamed at American troops in North Africa. Although he had known EP slightly in Rome in pre-Badoglio days, it was in Milan that their acquaintance deepened, and they discussed EP's role in propaganda. In mid-1944 Goedel moved the program "Jerry's Front Calling" to Fino Mornasco, and EP sent him comments and short news items via the German consulate in Milan. Goedel was arrested by Allied authorities near Trento in 1945 and held for questioning in Milan and Rome. EP recalls his help in Canto 78 and again in Canto 79: "(to Goedel in memoriam) / Sleek head that saved me out of one chaos" (lines 24–25).

CASA EDITRICE EDIZIONE POPOLARE] See Letter 2n.

CHUNG YUNG] Confucius, *The Unwobbling Pivot*. See Letter 2n and Document 7n.

PELLEGRINI] Professor Giampietro Domenico Pellegrini (b. 1899), minister of finance for the Salò Republic. EP, who met with him once to discuss economic matters, refers to his knowledge of government finances in Cantos 74 and 78.

Kitson's "Banker's Conspiracy"] Arthur Kitson (1860–1937), British engineer and inventor, was president of the British Banking and Currency Reform League and a fierce opponent of the gold standard. He started writing on economic questions in 1895 with an emphasis on systems of currency and their effects on society, and later expressed his views in *The New Age*. He was critical of the Cunliffe Committee (1918–1919) for its conclusion that Britain should return to the gold standard, and he believed that there was a secret plot by international bankers and the "usurocracy" to control world finances at the cost of worldwide debt, depression, and war. In 1944, through EP's efforts, Casa Editrice delle Edizioni Popolari of Venice published *La Storia di un reato*, an Italian translation (possibly by Olga Rudge) of *The Story of a Great Crime* (1933), a summary of Kitson's *The Bankers' Conspiracy! which started the world crisis* (1933), and *Industrial Depression, its cause and cure* (1905). The FBI translated *La Storia* back into English during its investigation of EP. See also Letter 2n, Document 11, and Appendix 1n.

Lenin's "Imperialism"] EP's annotated copy of V. I. Lenin's (1870–1924) *Imperialism: The Highest Stage of Capitalism* (New York: International Publishers, 1934, 2nd printing) is at HRHRC. EP admired Lenin as a prose writer and a man of action who could bring order out of Russia's "vague blithering mass of abstraction," as he put it in a four-part article in the *New English Weekly* in 1936 (*Poetry and Prose* 7:70). A year later he declared: "When I say I admire Lenin, I mean it. Italians admire Lenin. Lots of Italians speak well of him" (*Poetry and Prose* 7:246). On 19–20 April 1945 EP reread *Imperialism* and tried to persuade fascist cultural directors Fernando Mezzasoma and Nino Sammartano to add it to a series that was to include works by Marx, Stalin, Kitson, C. H. Douglas, and other writers on economics and money. See also Document 7n.

pamphlets on economic history. I also wrote articles on economics for "rebel papers in smaller towns," which articles were excluded from the larger press.

About September of 1944, I began sending short items to Carl Goedel at Milan. The items sent to Goedel and those sent to the Republican Fascist radio at Milano were along the same lines as my radio talks of 1942 and 1943.

Through the Republican Fascist Accounting Office the Ministry of Popular Culture of the Republican Fascist Government used to send me about eight thousand lire about $80 per month by mail from Venice. The last item I sent to Goedel was about three weeks ago, and there may be a check for me in payment in the mails somewhere between Venice and Rapallo. I never heard any of the items that I sent to Goedel over the Air. The last information was "Goedel uses your stuff in his own way."

The Casa Editrice Edizione Populare was part of the Ministry work, working for the department of Cultural Exchanges (Scambi Culturali). There was no increase in the monthly chque [cheque] because of the radio items.

About a year ago the Republican Fascist Ministry of Popular Culture sent me an employment application to fill out, but I declined to return it. They would keep sending me statements "enclosed is your salary for the month," and I would cross out these words and insert the words "for services rendered." I always accepted the checks which they sent me. These checks were drawn on the Banco di Lavoro of Venice, and I cashed them at the Banca di Chiavari in Rapallo. The last check that I received from the Republican Fascist Ministry of Popular Culture was in March of 1945. I recall that during 1944 I received from the Republican Fascist Ministry of Popular Culture a bonus which raised my monthly pay check to about eleven thousand lire. Early in 1945, I received a ten per cent cut in my monthly pay check because of a general salary cut.

I always sent two copies of my articles to Goedel. One copy I addressed to Carl Goedel at the German Consulate at Milano, and the other I addressed to Carl Goedel at 24 Piazza Castello, Milan, Italy. I suppose that Goedel wanted copies of my work for record and censorship. I did not work for Goedel, but for the Republican Fascist Ministry of Popular Culture.

From about 1929 to July of 1943, I received annually from the Italian Ministry of Communications a Foreign Journalists Railroad Pass at seventy per cent discount for eight trips a year.

I believe that I was justified in continuing to criticize President FRANKLIN D. ROOSEVELT after the United States entered the war in December of 1941.

I admit that during my broadcasts in 1942 and 1943 over EIAR I charged that the International Financiers of New York and elsewhere plotted to "drag" the United States into the present war.

During 1942, I became a member of the Committee for Malta, which had its headquarters in Rome, and which sponsored the independence of Malta. The British Empire was such a "goddam stink." I never was a member of the Fascist Party, but used to give the Fascist salute occasionally.

After the Italian Fascist Government declared War against the United States, I pointed out over EIAR in my radio talks that the United States was getting into a "whale of a debt," and should get out of the War immediately. I was making a test case for the freedom of speech. I think "my talks were giving pain to the *worst* enemies of the U.S.A."

SAMMARTANO] Nino Sammartano (b. 1897) was director of the *publications Il Libro Italiano* and *Il Libro Italiano nel mondo* and professor of pedagogy at the University of Rome. He later became general director of cultural exchange in the Ministry of Popular Culture and, after transferring to Venice, developed the publishing list for Casa Editrice delle Edizioni Popolari, which issued various works and translations by EP, including Confucian texts. See Letter 2n.

"Aesopian language"] Count Mikhail Evgrafovich Saltykov, pseudonym N. Shchedrin (1826–1889), Russian novelist and satirist of radical sympathies, who used the term "Æsopian language" to describe a style with hidden or ambiguous meanings, fashioned so as to disguise dissident political views. He himself knew the need for this, since one of his stories forced him into exile within Russia. Lenin, in his "Preface to the Russian Edition" *of Imperialism: The Highest Stage of Capitalism,* said that he wrote his book in 1916 and made use of "that cursed Aesopian language—to which tsarism compelled all revolutionaries to have recourse whenever they took up their pens to write a 'legal' work" (Lenin 7).

No one ever suggested to me what I should say over the radio during 1942 and 1943 or at any other time. All talks were my own ideas, and I was at no time ever coerced by anyone in anyway either directly or indirectly.

I admit that after December 8, 1941, I suggested in my radio talks that PRESIDENT ROOSEVELT be looked at by a psychiatrist because he seemed to be struggling against some more or less hypnotic influences.

After the Republican Fascist Government was formed in Northern Italy in the Autumn of 1943, I contacted PELLEGRINI who was Minister of Finance, and presented to him my stamp script [sic] plan for financing the new Government. I also suggested to FERNANDO MEZZASOMA, the Minister of Popular Culture that he should place before the people of Italy certain books such as Kitson's "Banker's Conspiracy" and Lenin's "Imperialism." I made the same suggestions to SAMMARTANO, head of the Cultural Exchange Section of the Ministry of Popular Culture.

After Italy declared war against the United States, the Italian Government "froze" my safety deposit box and bank accounts in the Banca di Chiavari in Rapallo, and other accounts but I succeeded in having the safety deposit box at Rapallo released by appealing to the Ministry of Popular Culture and by pointing out that it contained bonds bought by my wife and me when we subscribed to the first Littorio Loan, and that the rest of the contents were almost exclusively Italian Government Loans.

The terms on which I spoke over the radio at all were that I should *not* be asked to say anything contrary to my own conscience or contrary to my duties as an American citizen. This was also broadcast more than once, coupled with a rather forced definition of Fascism, which asserted that this was in accord with the Fascist principle which asserted that there should be free expression of opinion on the part of those qualified to have an opinion. I have at all times opposed certain "gray" zones of the Fascist opportunism by defining Fascism in a way to make it fit my own views. This sort of thing has been called "Esopian language" by so eminent a political force as the late Lenin.

This statement should not be considered separate from a statement which I will write out by myself as to the "main foundations" of my beliefs and the objects of my thirty years of writing [see Document 7].

I am willing to return to the United States to stand trial on the charge of treason against the United States. I will admit the contents of this statement in open Court since this statement is the truth.

I have read the above statement consisting of six typewritten pages, and I have initialed any changes I wished to make, and have initialed the bottom of each page.

[Signed] Ezra Pound

Witnesseth:
Ramon Arrizabalaga, Spec. Agt. in Charge CIC Det [Detachment].
92nd Inf. Div.
Frank Amprim, Special Agent, F.B.I.

Document 7 Notes. EP typed the five-page "Outline of Economic Bases of Historic Process" together with the two-page "Further Points" as supplements to his Sworn Statement (Document 6), at the CIC office in Genoa on 8 May 1945 for the interrogating agents. Our text is taken from EP's personal copy, a typed carbon with pencilled date and corrections on thin sheets of paper, the first and last bearing the printed heading, "Costruzione Nuovo Aeronautico E Marittimo di Genova-Sestri" (OP). A memo from J. Edgar Hoover to Assistant Attorney General Tom C. Clark, dated 29 May 1945, discussed Document 7 (FBI document 100–34099–186). We have silently corrected EP's typing errors except where they seemed significant.

Emperor Ching] Founder of the Shang Dynasty and ruler from 1766 until 1753 B.C., the Emperor Ching (Tching-Tang), renowned for his interest in his people's welfare, is said to have created a written language and to have introduced metalworking in bronze. De Mailla in his *Histoire générale de la Chine* (see below) tells how in 1760 B.C. Ching's principality suffered a great drought and famine, and the emperor ordered that money be coined and distributed to the poor for the purchase of grain. EP regarded this decree as an early example of national dividend and adapted the passage from de Mailla in Canto 53:

> For years no waters came, no rain fell
> > for the Emperor Tching Tang
> grain scarce, prices rising
> so that in 1760 Tching Tang opened the copper mine
> > > (ante Christum)
> made discs with square holes in their middles
> > and gave these to the people
> wherewith they might buy grain
> > > where there was grain
> [lines 59–67]

Charlemagne's fixing of the grain price] In the Capitulary of Frankfurt (794 A.D.), Charlemagne instructed his emissaries "that no man, whether he be cleric or layman, should ever sell corn in time of abundance or in time of scarcity at a greater price than the public level recently decided upon" (H. R. Loyn and John Percival, *The Reign of Charlemagne: Documents on Carolingian Government and Administration* [New York: St. Martin's Press, 1975], pp. 57–58). EP refers to the Capitularies in *Guide to Kulchur* (1938) (47–48, 325). *In What Is Money For?* (1939) he discusses Charlemagne's grain measure and the medieval "canonist doctrine of the just price," adding that both "the Douglas Social Crediters and modern Catholics POSTULATE the JUST PRICE as a necessary part of their systems" (Cookson 292–93).

bracteates] Early medieval coins enlarged in diameter to give greater scope for images but thinned to save silver, often to the thickness of modern tinfoil. They required frequent reminting, with related taxes, and were common throughout the Holy Roman Empire until at least the end of the fourteenth century.

Paterson's prospectus] William Paterson (1658–1719), founder of the Bank of England, whose statement about interest EP repeated often, elevating it to a founding text of usury. In *Oro e lavoro* (*Gold and Work*) (1944) he described the Bank of England as "a felonious combination or, more precisely, a gang of usurers taking sixty per cent interest," and declared, "This war was no whim of Mussolini's, nor of Hitler's. This war is a chapter in the long and bloody tragedy which began with the foundation of the Bank of England in far-away 1694, with the openly declared intention of Paterson's now famous prospectus" (Cookson 337, 343). Two writers on money whom EP admired, Christopher Hollis *in The Two Nations* (1935) and Gorham Munson in *Aladdin's Lamp* (1945), also cite the statement.

"downright iniquity"] This remark by John Adams, made in a letter to Benjamin Rush of 28 August 1811, is cited by EP in Cantos 71, 74, and 88. Jefferson's "pawky comment," from a letter to John Wayles Eppes of 24 June 1813, is quoted in Canto 46 as a counterblast to "hyper-usura" (lines 111–13).

A bank lending ten times] John Adams stated this view in a letter to F. A. Vanderkemp, dated 16 February 1809: "Our medium is depreciated by the multitude of swindling banks, which have emitted bank bills to an immense amount beyond the deposits of gold and silver in their vaults, by which means the price of labor and land and merchandise and produce is doubled, tripled, and quadrupled in many instances.

DOCUMENT 7 EZRA POUND'S SUPPLEMENTS TO HIS SWORN STATEMENT: "OUTLINE OF ECONOMIC BASES OF HISTORIC PROCESS" AND "FURTHER POINTS"

[Office of the Counter Intelligence Corps]
[6 Via Fieschi]
[Genoa, Italy]
8 May 1945

OUTLINE OF ECONOMIC BASES of historic process/

I. In the year 1766 b.C. during time of famine when monopolists were hoarding what grain there was, the Emperor Ching opened a copper mine and coined copper disks with square holes in them. He GAVE these disks to the poor, who could then buy grain where there was grain. This shows clear conception of the distributive nature function of money.

2nd. Item to take into account. The Mediaeval doctrine of the just price (as per Charlemagne's fixing of the grain price in different years) also in lesser degree the precedent of bracteates, or coins that had periodically to be reminted and pay mintage fee.

3. Foundation of the bank (or stank) of England, a private company in Paterson's prospectus stated that "the bank hath profit of the interest on all the moneys that it creates out of nothing." John Adams aptly called this "downright iniquity, robbing the public for private individual's gain." Jefferson alludes to this swindle in his pawky comment "No one has the right to lend money save him who has the money to."
    A bank lending ten times as much as its deposits, lends a good it hasn't got.
    Here you can add my "Introductory Text Book" of 4 chapters, is 4 quotations, one each from J. Adams; Jefferson, Lincoln, and the American Constitution. I trust a copy can accompany this/ If not I will type it out. Elihu Root (once known as "young Elihu") spoke about this leaflet in his address at the Hamilton commencement in 1939 when he, I and Kaltenbourne recd. honorary degrees.

4. The next essential datum is the statement in Lenin's "Imperialism." "Imperialist wars will never cease as long as capitalism stays capitalism. As long as capitalism is capitalism surplus capital will NEVER be used to raise the standard of living of the people inside a country. BUT it will be sent abroad to 'backward countries' to increase the profits of the capitalists." Lenin however presents a false dilemma when he says the only remedy is the nationalization of the means of production. There are alternate remedies, indicated by C. H. Douglas, by Gesell, and by the Constitution of the U.S. IF applied as its authors intended. That is why I wish,—after due LINGUISTIC preparation to meet Stalin.
    You may not care about a formula that would prevent a third world war, but it seems to me that a real agreement on an honest basis would be worth doing a bit of

Every dollar of a bank bill that is issued beyond the quantity of gold and silver in the vaults, represents nothing, and is therefore a cheat upon somebody" (*The Works of John Adams*, 10 vols., ed. Charles Francis Adams, [Boston: Little, Brown, 1850–1856], 9:610).

"Introductory Text Book"] A folded sheet with quotations from John Adams, Jefferson, Lincoln, and the U.S. Constitution concerning money and credit, printed privately in 1939 for distribution by EP to correspondents (reprinted in Cookson 159–60). It also appeared in several magazines and newspapers. See also Document 6 and Letter 2n.

Kaltenbourne] Hans Von Kaltenborn (1878–1965), a well-known radio news commentator. He, Elihu Root, Jr. (see Letter 18n), and EP were awarded honorary degrees at Hamilton College in Clinton, New York, on 12 June 1939. At a luncheon, Kaltenborn spoke against dictatorships and alluded to the "doubtful" alliance between Italy and Germany, whereupon EP challenged him to define his terms. According to Professor George Nesbitt of the Hamilton English department, someone had the presence of mind to end the confrontation by asking the college choir to sing *Carissima*, the college song.

the statement in Lenin's "Imperialism"] This statement appears in chapter 4 ("The Export of Capital") of *Lenin's Imperialism: The Highest Stage of Capitalism* (Lenin 63). EP repeats it in Canto 74: "Never inside the country to raise the standard of living / but always abroad to increase the profits of usurers" (lines 164–65). See also Document 6n.

C. H. Douglas] See Documents 3–5n and Letter 17n.

Gesell] Silvio Gesell (1862–1930) was a German businessman, monetary reformer, and author of *The Natural Economic Order*, published in 1916 in German and printed in English in two volumes by Dr. Hugo Fack (San Antonio, Tex.: Free-Economy Publishing Company, 1934–1936). Gesell proposed the issuance of a stamp scrip not linked to the value of metals; it would serve as a "tax on money," encouraging spending and discouraging hoarding. EP defines stamp scrip *in What Is Money For?* (1939) as "a government note requiring the bearer to affix a stamp worth up to 1 per cent of its face value on the first day of every month. Unless the note carries its proper complement of monthly stamps it is not valid" (Cookson 295). The Austrian community of Wörgl used this system with apparent success and "sent shivers down the backs of all the lice of Europe, Rothschildian and others," according to EP in *A Visiting Card* (1942) (Cookson 314).

Hobson] John Atkinson Hobson (1858–1940), British economist who argued that the capitalist system suffers inherently from overproduction and underconsumption, and drives nations to compete for markets abroad, with war as the consequence. He contributed to the *Nation* (1906–1920) and *The New Age*, and influenced C. H. Douglas (Redman 59–60). Lenin acknowledged that Hobson's *Imperialism* (1902) provided the basis for his own *Imperialism: The Highest Stage of Capitalism* (see Document 6n). Samuel George Hobson, who was an associate of A. R. Orage and other Guild Socialists, wrote *Functional Socialism* (London: Stanley Nott, 1936), which EP owned. EP may be confusing these two Hobsons here.

Orage] A. R. Orage. See Documents 3–5n.

Mr Amprim] See Letter 2n.

the Testament] EP used various titles for this first of the four Chinese (or Confucian) classics, including "The Great Learning," "The Great Digest," "The Adult Study," "Ta Hio," "Ta Hsio," and "Ta S'eu, Studio integrale." He first published it as *Ta Hio, The Great Learning*, "newly rendered into the American language," in Seattle in 1928. The "Unwavering or Unwobbling axis" is one of his variants for the title of the second classic, which he also refers to as "The Standing Fast in the Middle," "Chung Yung, the Unwobbling Pivot," and "Chiung Iung, l'asse che non vacilla." The third and fourth classics are the Analects of Confucius and the Book of Mencius, both of which EP translated. In *Guide to Kulchur* (1938) he remarks that "the Four Books contain answers to all problems of conduct that can arise" (352). See Letters 2n, 6n, 12n, and 46n for details of EP's Confucian translations.

work for. Lenin based his book in great part on Hobson, and I have reason to suppose that this was the same Hobson who said to Orage that he "would like to accept Douglas" (i.e. C. H. Douglas') analysis, but that it would make his own book look so out of date."

Incidentally Mr Amprim has used the word "theories" in ref/ to my position.

I am not interested in theories but in specific historic facts; and in known results of known processes.

SECONDLY.

Whenever a Chinese dynasty has lasted three centuries it has been founded on the principles ascertained by Confucius, i.e. based by him on his collection of historic Documents; and formulated by him in his Testament. Dynasties not so founded have flopped, as have the systems of Mussolini and Hitler. I mean they the other dynasties have flopped in briefer periods. Hence my translations of the Testament, the first, and of the Unwavering or Unwobbling axis, the second of the FOUR chinese classic confucian books.

The actual "testament" is printed as beginning of the Ta S'eu of [or] Great learning. Italian version with chinese text. Earlier translations do NOT sufficiently analyze the ideograms, but treat them as phonetic words. re/ Fenollosa's paper on the nature of the Chinese Written Character.

This brings me to my other desire. Namely the possibility of a peace with Japan, based on Confucian principles, the approach being facilitated by an acquaintance with Fenollosa's work and position in Japan. Where they still carry flowers to his grave.

As ~~translator~~ his literary executor, I have contacts, and means of contact to a different side of Japan. That is not the side of Japan's imitation of modern occident.

A peace in the orient can ONLY be on a Confucian basis. Chiang Kai Chek is probably ready to admit this. The Chinese republic having erred in eliminating confucian teaching, or diminishing it in the schools. My question the other day and the request to be supplied minimum terms on which the U.S. could honourably make peace with Japan, before sacrificing another million lives and immense amounts of money, is not due to my wish to ~~diet~~ determine the geographic borders of any country, but to USE our present advantages to reestablish sane and friendly relations with a nation temporarily off its course.

Japan can surrender to her own best tradition much more comfortably than to force.

Perfect as may be the harmony between the U.S. and Russia It might be tempting providence to have no other strong power to west of us. The Russians are human after all.

I am trying to put things in simple words, and briefly. My conclusions are based on L'Histoire Generale de la Chine, 10 or 12 vols.

translated by de Moiriac de Mailla.

Collected works of John Adams and Jefferson,

Brooks Adams: Law of Civilization and Decay; and "The New Empire"

Lenin's Imperialism.

Cairoli's: Justo Prezzo nel Mediaevo.

etc. further bibliography on demand.

Fenollosa's paper] *The Chinese Written Character as a Medium for Poetry.* See Documents 3–5n.

Chiang Kai Chek] Chiang Kai-shek (1887–1975), Chinese military leader and statesman in constant struggle with the Communists. He led the resistance to Japan (1937–1945) and in 1942 was appointed commander of Allied forces in the China theater of war. He held enormous power as the Nationalist leader and became president of China's National government (1943–19), continuing his presidency in Taiwan after the Communists won control of the Chinese mainland in 1949. EP believed that Chiang's Western-backed government had lost hold of traditional Confucian values and that a war between China and Japan was a perversion of ancient compatibilities. In his radio talks he denounced Chiang's "exotic government imposed in the interests of foreign loan capital" and referred him as "Chiang Kike Chek [. . .] the prize buyer of gold bricks" (Doob 287, 95).

minimum terms] See EP's proposed telegram to President Truman, in Document 3.

L'Histoire Generale de la Chine] *Histoire générale de la Chine* by the French Jesuit Joseph-Anne-Marie de Moyriac de Mailla (1669–1748), was published in Paris in thirteen volumes (1777–1785). The *Histoire* is a translation of a Manchu version of the Chinese history compiled by Chu Hsi (1130–1200), itself a condensation of an earlier work. EP used de Mailla for his China Cantos in *Cantos LII-LXXI* (1940). See also Letter 26.

Collected works of John Adams and Jefferson] EP owned and used for his cantos *The Works of John Adams* (see above), as well as *The Writings of Thomas Jefferson*, 20 vols. (Washington, D.C.: Thomas Jefferson Memorial Association, 1905), which T. S. Eliot had given him.

Law of Civilization and Decay] Brooks Adams (1848–1927), brother of Henry Adams, wrote *Law of Civilization and Decay* (1895; reprinted in 1943 by Alfred Knopf with an introduction by Charles A. Beard), which EP describes in *A Visiting Card* (1942): "His cyclic vision of the West shows us a consecutive struggle against four great rackets, namely the exploitation of the fear of the unknown (black magic, etc.), the exploitation of violence, the exploitation or the monopolisation of cultivable land, and the exploitation of money" (Cookson 307). In his 1943 radio talk "Philology," he noted that Adams had written about "the FLOP of empires consequent on the dislocation or loss of trade routes" (Doob 407). EP's annotated copy of Adams's *The New Empire* (1903), on the new supremacy of America, is at HRHRC. He tried to get Adams's works printed by the Italian fascist government in translation and in English-language editions (Redman 257–59).

Cairoli] Luigi Pasquale Cairoli, author of *Il Giusto prezzo medioevale: Studio di economia politica* (1913), a study of the medieval concept of the just price. In 1936 EP wrote that, although Cairoli showed "no anti-semitism," he concluded that "the Jew was the divulgator of usury, and thereby helped to break down an economy whereof MAN was the centre and to substitute one whereof MERCHANDISE is the centre" (*Poetry and Prose* 7:61).

D. R. Dewey's Financial History] Davis Rich Dewey (1886–1933), economist and professor at the Massachusetts Institute of Technology, published *Financial History of the United States* in 1903 and later revised it. The twelfth edition in the American Citizen Series was published in 1934 and reprinted several times. EP praised Dewey for defining "finance" but regretted that he did not define "money" (*Poetry and Prose* 8:57).

Drummond] John Drummond (b. 1914) received his B.A. from Queens' College, Cambridge, in 1934, and lived in Italy for many years. He began corresponding with EP while still a student and took a keen interest in EP's writings, helping him with selections from his poetry and later translating several of his Italian political and economic works into English. He contributed his own articles on economics to Ronald Duncan's magazine, *Townsman*. During World War II Drummond served in the British army in Algiers and Caserta, and later with the HQ Allied Commission in Rome. He played a crucial role in the months after EP's capture, meeting with FBI Agent Amprim and others in Rome to gain information about EP's health and whereabouts, providing DP and Olga Rudge with news and advice, and acting as an intermediary between the two women and their respective interests in EP. Drummond's extensive cor-

This is the sort of material I have been trying to force into Italy in an attempt to educate the italians in democracy and economics.

A work like D. R. Dewey's Financial History of the U.S. contains many facts, but omits JUST those that would enable the student to understand what it is all about. Naturally it has been a standard work in U.S. universities. And for this reason intelligent students take to athletics. Same conditions pertain in England. for example J. Drummond wrote me from Cambridge re/ an economics course: The professor admitted that it had nothing to do with real life, but said the course could not be altered. I therefore did not take the course.

Education of this kind serves to keep young men out of the labour market for a few years, but it is difficult to see why they shd/ pay for it; or why professors shd/ be paid for f/giving it.

Perhaps I have indicated one or two [of] the points I have been trying to make during the past 25 years, and which I rashly did NOT stop trying to make, when caught off sides, but in reach of a microphone.

At any rate I hope the ^my errors will be considered in relation to the main picture. No one sees everything; but even the lack of a few parts of a motor may damage its working may interfere with its working.

Kaltenbourne and I, in 1939, may EACH have had ~~reasons for~~ fragments of knowledge that would have corrected mistaken views. The exclusion of news from the press, and ~~from~~ of historic fact from the serious reviews does NOT assist the federal government; and the citizen possessed of odd bits of knowledge that might be useful has not only the right but the duty to try to communicate with the competent authorities, even at the risk of seeming excentric or making a fool of himself.

When a Chinese diplomat says to me, of the Chinese and Japanese: These peoples should be like brothers, they read the same books, one has the perception of a diplomacy based on humanity and not merely on swindling. When I without credentials can meet Japanese envoys in the middle of chaos, and talk man to man because I happen to be carrying the third volume of the Confucian anthology, there is an avenue of approach NOT closed by the horrors of jungle warfare.

If I had not handed them a copy of my Studio Integrale (Ta S'eu) I might not believe in my capacity to talk to them as a gun merchant could not.

Life consists in taking the million to one chance when instinct bids, and the stake is worth it, and when it can, in any case do no harm.

If I could bring the slaughter in the Pacific to a sane and speedy end, I should, I believe, have justified my existence.

I understand that the new secretary of state believes in preparing diplomats. No one ever knows enough, and there is NEVER too much knowledge at the disposal of any state minister or of any government.

I have also seen things in Italy ~~that~~ knowledge of which might conceivably be of use at this time.

respondence with EP and DP (Lilly) and Olga Rudge (OR Papers, Beinecke) concerns many facets of the case, from the search for appropriate legal counsel to getting DP's funds released. In July 1945 he told Amprim that he would gladly testify at EP's expected trial.

Japanese envoys] See Documents 3–5n.

new secretary of state] James Francis Byrnes (1879–1972), U.S. secretary of state (1945–1947).

money clause] In the U.S. Constitution. See Document 6n.

Voorhis' bill] Horace Jeremiah (Jerry) Voorhis (1901–1984), Democratic congressman from California from 1937 to 1947, introduced scores of bills ranging from social security measures to national defense acts designed to end war profiteering. He spoke out against the banking system's credit monopoly and urged the government to take ownership of the Federal Reserve banks and issue its own credit, with the object of boosting buying power to the level of goods and services produced. He claimed that without mechanisms for distributing buying power (such as old-age pensions), nations would have to go to war to destroy surplus production. These points were set forth in his remarks in the House of Representatives, 6 June 1938, which began with the same quotation from John Adams that EP used as chapter 1 of his *Introductory Text Book*. EP owned *Dollars and Sense*, a pamphlet version of this speech, and praised Voorhis's bill (H. R. 8080, January 1940) for a national defense fund based on "the real credit of the people [. . .] without recourse to the method of making war loans from the banking system"; "it shows a nice quality of mind in one Congressman," EP quipped (*Poetry and Prose* 8:59). He corresponded with Voorhis (Beinecke) and spoke with him during his visit to the United States in 1939.

Overholser's History of Money] Willis A. Overholser (1901–1995), village attorney for Libertyville, Illinois, for forty-four years, amateur trombonist, and author of *A Short Review and Analysis of the History of Money in the United States with an Introduction to the Current Money Problem* (Libertyville, Ill.: Progress Publishing Concern, 1936). In *A Visiting Card* (1942), EP described him as a "small country lawyer, 'not trained in research,' which means he was not in the pay of usurocratic capital and the monopolists, not dominated by the trusted functionaries of some 'university'—Overholser gives us, in his *History of Money in the United States*, the essential documents" (*Cookson* 310). In 1943 EP noted that Admiral Ubaldo degli Uberti had translated the work but had not yet found a publisher for it (*Poetry and Prose* 8:199).

Kitson's "Banker's Conspiracy"] See Document 6n.

Further Points.

I. That in an age of radio, free speech that does not include freedom to transmit by radio is a hollow sham.

2. That the constitution was being violated, most notably in the money clause/ Not particularly Roosevelt's fault. Probably had been violated ever since the assassination of Lincoln. In any case congress could not impeach the President because congress itself was particeps criminis. Only the citizen who had not consented in the violation was in position to raise the issue.

The vast ignorance of the people and naiveté of the people's representatives was apparent. Note Voorhis' bill, which proposed to pass all the real power [into] hands of an IRRESPONSIBLE committee to be appointed by the president, but to be appointed for seven years, i.e. to survive the presidential term. This under the idea that it was bringing the president's powers back to normal limits.

3. To put it at the mildest: the enormous drain of the peoples' money to buy gold at a price suddenly raised from 21 dollars 60 cents, or thereabouts, to 35 dollars per ounce, and FROM unknown and often foreign sellers, the treasury having no record of its origin, nothing in short but name of last owner or agent.

I take it this idea has by now penetrated some sections of the public, or at least a few minds.

4. The question of ex post facto law might seem to arise. At least so far as I am concerned, I do not YET know at what date the mere use of a radio in foreign territory became a crime. I certainly had no news of its being illegal before the date, whenever it was, that I ~~was~~ heard I was accused of treason.

And I do not believe I have betrayed anyone whomsoever.

Wars are made to make debt. Vide various citations in Overholser's History of Money in the U.S., in Kitson's "Banker's Conspiracy" and in my printed quotation therefrom.

War is the maximum sabotage. The game of inflate and deflate is played in the whole OF SERIES of wars, staged one after another.

It is one thing to tell troops to desert, another to try to build up political indignation to take effect AFTER the end of hostilities. After the last war ONLY those countries where the returned troops came to power managed to effect reforms. And the present promises of the victors follow the wake of the improved distribution, diminution of unemployment etc. achieved by Mussolini and Hitler. Who have been betrayed repeatedly and beyond anything you can read in the school histories. The German love of Hitler, summarized in "He took us off the streets"/ all of which can be separated from the militarism etc.

The question is whether Germany has learned NOT to try to effect by violence what can only be effected by understanding. Certainly I observed a change in german

Beraud's] Henri Béraud (1885–1958), French journalist, political writer, novelist, and winner of the Prix Goncourt. He wrote accounts of his visits to Moscow, Berlin, London, and New York, and in 1929 *published Ce que j'ai vu à Rome* (Paris: Les Editions de France), which he dedicated, with barbed irony, to "M. Benito Mussolini" for encouraging him to write freely of the new regime and then ordering newspapers with serial installments of the book to be seized by border police, thus becoming "the only Italian to whom the truth can still be told" (iii). This theme of power and knowledge continues in chapter 19, where Béraud predicts that the Duce will soon be "not only master of the country, but the only person with responsibilty, and graver still, the only person with information" ("le seul informé") (164). Béraud's wartime writings contained attacks on Britain and on the Free French movement, and he also criticized the Germans. In December 1944, after a controversial trial, a French court condemned him to death for collaborating with the Germans. General de Gaulle commuted the sentence to life with hard labor.

1878, a congressman] EP's grandfather, Thaddeus Coleman Pound. See Document 6n.

Republican program] Probably the Verona Program of the Salò Republic. See Documents 3–5n.

"To hate what people love ..."] From the Confucian Ta Hsio or Testament, which reads in EP's final version: "To love what the people hate, to hate what they love is called doing violence to man's inborn nature. Calamities will come to him who does this (definite physical calamities), the wild grass will grow over his dead body" (*Confucius* 81). In Genoa EP was already at work on the English versions of Confucius that he completed at the DTC.

manners and carriage for the better from the first bouncing exuberance, to the later reasonableness.

All of which takes us "out of the present case."

One comes back to the fundamental question of free speech, VERITABLY free, and the need of assuring the diffusion of useful information, despite ALL editorial controls and control by advertisers.

The most acute criticism of Italy's danger under Mussolini, was Beraud's "The danger not that M. had so much power, but that he would be *le seul informé*, the only man having information."

In America the people get one sort of bunk, and the journalists absorb a sort of second line bunk, which they believe, but which is only one degree less doctored than what is handed out in the newspaper

I may be Rip van Winkle. Perhaps during my separation from american news print (over five years of it) these things have altered.??

War is used to make debt, and debt used to control the national currency. 1878, a congressman trying to keep at least a part of the NON=INTEREST=BEARING national debt in circulation as currency.

Whole subject so bores the public, that it MUST be brought into lime light repeatedly, I mean at ten or 20 year intervals at least. by one device or another.

5. ABSOLUTE inadequacy of the printed financial history of the U.S. for example D. R. Dewey wrote me that no account of activities of foreign financial agents in the U.S. is available. The Republican Nat. Committee had, as I remember it, one typewritten page of such information available in 1939. How in heaven's name CAN there be financial history of the U.S. without an account of foreign agents in the country?

6. As to the sort of advice I gave in Italy, and sent to the Head of the Government, I give one sample. It had to be done as a translation from the Chinese, and is an exact version of the Ta S'eu Cap. 10. v. 16. "To see men of great capacity and be incapable of promoting them; promote them and be incapable of doing it at once, is destiny.

To see dishonest men and be incapable of kicking them out; or to fire them and not manage to send them to the furthest frontiers (i.e. the *confino*) is to err."

Poor old Benito errd all right. I was assured he received first edition of this confucian book, but when his secretary acknowledged the second edition (italian without the chinese text) it was too late. Very much too late. The Republican program; moved we may [say] in the Jeffersonian direction away from dictatorship, was also too late, but interesting as a project.

"To hate what people love is to offend human nature. Calamities will come on him who does so even to doing him physical harm, the wild grass will cover his corpse." Ta S'eu 10/17.

Of course all these last, apparently, scraps, of cantos, are your self, the memories that make up yr. person. Is one then only a bunch of memories? i.e. a bunch of remains of contacts with the other people?

Dorothy to Ezra, Letter 23

You have given me thirty years of peace clear as blue feldspar and I am grateful.

Ezra to Dorothy, Letter 44

PISA

Document 8 Notes. Typed letter, one side (OP). On receiving this letter, DP wrote the provost marshal of the Peninsular Base Section, asking for permission to visit EP at the DTC. She received Document 9 in reply.

DOCUMENT 8

MEDITERRANEAN THEATER OF OPERATIONS
Office of the Provost Marshal General
APO 512   U.S. Army

PWIB 1-641   24 August 1945

Mrs. Dorothy Pound
Villa Raggio
Sestiere Cerisola
Rapallo

Dear Mrs. Pound:

In reply to your letter of 31 July 1945, please be advised that your husband is at present located at the MTOUSA Disciplinary Training Center, A.P.O. 782, c/o post-master, New York City, N.Y., located near Pisa. He is enjoying a good state of health.

If you desire a personal visit with your husband, suggest [sic] a letter be written to Provost Marshal, Peninsular Base Section, A.P.O 782, U.S. Army.

> Very truly yours,
> [signed]
> WALTER A. HARDIE,
> Colonel, CMP,
> Provost Marshal General.

Document 9 Notes. Typed letter, one side (OP). DP noted in her diary that she received this letter on 26 September 1945, one day after she had sent Letter 10 c/o of the provost marshal and two days before she received EP's first letter (Letters 7 and 8, mailed together).

DOCUMENT 9

HEADQUARTERS PENINSULAR BASE SECTION

Office of the Provost Marshal

APO 782

BPSPM   18 September 1945

Mrs. Dorothy Pound
Villa Raggio
Sestiere Cerisola
Rapallo

Dear Mrs. Pound:

1. This letter will constitute your authority to visit your husband, Ezra Pound, at the MTOUSA Disciplinary Training Center, north of Pisa, on Highway #1, subject to the normal rules governing visits to confinees at that installation.

2. Clothing which is the property of your husband may be brought to him.

3. Correspondence between yourself and husband is authorized subject to usual censorship in effect.

4. Arrangements for travel and lodging must be made through whatever channels are available to civilians.

[signed]

RALPH A. TOLVE,

Lt. Col., C.M.P.,

Provost Marshal

Document 10 Notes. Notice of permission for correspondence with and visits from DP, issued to EP at the DTC on 20 September 1945. Typed on an army form, one side, and signed in black ink (OP).

JOHN L. STEELE] Lieutenant Colonel John Lincoln Steele (1911–1994), commandant of the DTC during EP's incarceration there. He allowed EP to have writing materials and reading matter as a precaution against mental relapse. Born in St. Johnsbury, Vermont, Steele studied economics as well as personnel and guidance at Boston University, where he received his B.A. and M.A. in 1934; that summer he went to the University of Heidelberg to complete language requirements for his Ph.D. at Columbia University. He did student teaching and counseling at Boston University and Harvard. Shortly after Pearl Harbor he joined the army and in 1944 was sent to be personnel officer at the DTC in North Africa, where he eventually became commandant and was responsible for transferring the camp and prisoners to Pisa.

On 20 August 1945, Steele wrote his mother from the Pisa DTC:

> [Ezra Pound] is a dreamer if I ever knew one and is absolutely sold on his own ideas. A lot of well known people, to whom he refers by their first names, are "criminally stupid," "bullheaded," etc. Instead of spending his many spare moments organizing whatever he may think he has for a defense for his case, he spends his time pottering away at a translation of Menghis [Mencius], the Chinese philosopher. He still figures on saving the world if he can get enough people to listen to him who also happen to be reasonably bright, by which he means in agreement with him. I think he overestimates his influence considerably. He came out with a typical remark when informed recently that Santayana was now working on an economic treatise. "My God," he said, "you don't mean to tell me I've finally gotten George down from his ivory tower!" I think I'll see how things are going in the stockade tonight, not having done any night prowling for quite a while, so maybe I'll stop by for a chat with the old boy.

In November 1945, Lieutenant Colonel Steele was reassigned and eventually put in charge of all the dependents' schools for military families in Europe and Africa. Major Morris J. Lucree became commandant of the DTC. Steele is mentioned in Canto 78:

> The touch of sadism in the back of his neck
> tinting justice, "Steele that is one awful name."
> sd/ the cheerful reflective nigger (lines 71–73)

See also Introduction.

DOCUMENT 10

ROUTING SLIP

HEADQUARTERS
6677TH DISCIPLINARY TRAINING COMPANY (OVHD)
MTOUSA DISCIPLINARY TRAINING CENTER
APO 782, U.S. Army

File No. _____

SUBJECT: Correspondence _____

Number each memo consecutively. Fill in each column. Initial action and draw one line across the sheet. Pen or pencil may be used. No papers attached to this routing slip may be withdrawn unless specifically directed. _____

No.	Date	From	To	
I	20 Sept 1945	MTOUSA DTC	Ezra Pound	1. Correspondence between Mrs. Pound and yourself, subject to current censorship regulations, has been authorized by the Provost Marshal, Peninsular Base Section, in a letter to Mrs. Pound, dated 18 September 1945. 2. Mrs. Pound has also been authorized to visit you here, subject to regulations of this installation concerning such visits. If Mrs. Pound arrives for a visit, arrangements will be made for you to see her at Post Headquarters, outside the stockade. Our regulations require that an officer of the organization be present during such a visit and limit the time of each visit to approximately one-half hour. [signed] JOHN L. STEELE Lt. Col., Corps of Engineers Commanding

7 Notes. In pencil on two sheets of white paper, one side each, enclosed with Letter 8 in an envelope typed by someone other than EP, postmarked "U.S. Army 9th BPO, Sep 22 1945," and stamped received in Rapallo "27.9.45" (27 September 1945). On the envelope, which is addressed to DP at Villa Raggio, she jotted in pencil: "Two sides alike show beginning of rigidity of sensibility—also lack of imagination" (Lilly).

MTOUSA . . .] Mediterranean Theater of Operations United States Army, Detention Training Center, Army Post Office 782, care of Postmaster, New York. Letters did not actually go via New York. EP tended to vary the order of the address from letter to letter.

Possum] Thomas Stearns Eliot (1888–1965), American-born poet and critic, established a dominant position in modern letters with *The Waste Land* (1922) and his editing of *The Criterion* (1922-1939). In 1948 he received the Nobel Prize in literature and the British Order of Merit. He and EP first met in London in 1914 and remained close friends throughout their lives, despite disagreements over politics, religion, and literature. EP dubbed him "the Possum" and refers to him twice by that name in Canto 74. Eliot's devotion was never more apparent than in his efforts to help EP during the Pisan incarceration and after. By August 1945 he was in constant communication with A. V. Moore, John Drummond, and others concerned with the case, and had contacted Archibald MacLeish. He monitored the situation closely from London and provided DP and Olga Rudge with updates. His letters to EP at the DTC and later at St. Elizabeths in Washington, D.C., combine friendly concern with firm advice to "do exactly what your lawyer tells you to, and only talk when he wants you to talk. It must be a lawyer who is prepared to read all your works and try to understand them. Ez, you are <u>not</u> good at explaining to the simple-minded" (19 October 1945, Lilly). As a director of Faber and Faber, Eliot agreed to publish the new cantos that EP was writing, and he brought out the English edition of *The Pisan Cantos* in 1949. He could not be persuaded to publish EP's Confucian translations, however.

Throughout World War II, Eliot kept in close contact with Omar Pound while the latter was a student at Charterhouse in Surrey, and in 1944 he helped arrange to get Omar out of London and away from the bombings. From 1946 on, when Eliot was in Washington, D.C., he would visit EP and lunch with DP and occasionally with Omar. EP attended the memorial service for Eliot in Westminster Abbey in 1965, with A. V. Moore representing DP and Omar.

Duncan] Ronald Frederick Henry Duncan (1914–1982), Rhodesian-born British poet, playwright, and opera librettist. He was an active member of the Peace Pledge Union and visited Gandhi in India in 1937. On his way back to England he stopped to see EP in Rapallo, later noting that "Ezra taught me more in one day than I had learned in a year at Cambridge" (*All Men Are Islands* [London: Rupert Hart-Davis, 1964], p. 158). With EP's active encouragement, Duncan founded and edited the magazine *Townsman*, to which EP contributed poems, notes, and essays on music, money, and religion between 1938 and 1941. By 1939 Duncan was contributing regularly to magazines and newspapers, and he was registered as a conscientious objector throughout the war. In this period he ran an experimental farm on the border of Devon and Cornwall (on which Omar Pound worked in 1944) and wrote about the experience in *Journal of a Husbandman* (London: Faber and Faber, 1944). His play *This Way to the Tomb* had a successful run in London in 1945–1946; and he helped Benjamin Britten with the libretto for *Peter Grimes* (1945) and wrote the libretto for Britten's *The Rape of Lucretia* (1946). Duncan and his wife, Rose Marie, corresponded regularly with EP and DP during 1945-1946, and Duncan routinely conferred with T. S. Eliot and A. V. Moore about strategies to help EP.

MTOUSA DTC

APO 782, ARMY Local
care of P.M. New York
[ca. 20 September 1945]

O Mao!

If this letter reaches you it is the glad tidings that people can now write to me @ this address. Please tell Olga [Rudge] - and inform Possum, Duncan etc. - a reasonable selection of friends. (mail will be censored -) but at last possible to get news.

Health O.K.

Love to you & mother.

E.

naturally I want news of everything. E.P.

Address writing, from Italy mail is marked ARMY LOCAL - but carries the care P.M. New York - from England or U.S. does not carry inscription ARMY LOCAL.

8 Notes. Typed with black ribbon on a sheet of white paper, one side, with pencil corrections and additions, and marked in black ink at top left: "Censored J. L. Steele Lt. Col. MTOUSA DTC." (EP's letters were routinely read and passed ["censored"] by camp officers, but not edited.) Typed by EP on back of the letter: "Provost's office please supply envelope and send to Mrs Ezra Pound, Villa Raggio, Sestiere Cerisola, RAPALLO." No envelope: Letter 8 was enclosed with Letter 7 (Lilly).

YOU are authorized] See Documents 9 and 10.

"Confucius" "Zone"] Jottings made by EP in the manuscript of *The Pisan Cantos* suggest that he was contemplating a two-part curriculum for the postwar world. The first part, to be titled "One Day's Reading," would contain the four Chinese or Confucian classics (see Document 7n). For the second part, to be called "Zone," EP considered works on history and economics by Leo Frobenius and Karl Marx, as well as texts by Wyndham Lewis and Jean Cocteau (ms pages 42 and 54, Beinecke). EP alludes to this curriculum in the published version of Canto 74: "and with one day's reading a man may have the key in his hands / Lute of Gassir. Hooo Fasa" (lines 92–93). For the African tale of Gassir as recorded by Frobenius, see Letter 123n.

Dalton] Edward Hugh J. N. Dalton (1887–1962) was educated at Cambridge and the London School of Economics, where he studied inequality of income and the principle of inheritance. During World War I he served in the Royal Artillery and was awarded the Italian Medal for Military Valor. In 1924 he was elected Labour MP for the Peckham Division of Camberwell and later for Bishop Auckland. He went on to become undersecretary of state for Foreign Affairs (1929–1931) and minister of economic warfare in the Coalition Government (1940–1942). As president of the Board of Trade (1942–1945), he oversaw wartime clothes rationing and the production of utility goods. When the Labour Party won the postwar general election on the strength of its program for social and economic reconstruction and nationalization of credit, power, and transport, Dalton became chancellor of the exchequer (1945–1947). He was noted for his cheap money policy, lucid budget speeches, and deep voice and attractive wit. In 1914 he married Ruth Fox (1890?–1966)—a childhood friend of DP's—who had her own career in the Labour Party and was chairman of the London County Council parks committee. She and Hugh had met while they were students at the London School of Economics. See also Letters 17, 130n, and 137n.

Monty Norman] Montagu Collet Norman (1871–1950), governor of the Bank of England (1920–1944) who supported the gold standard and gave oral evidence before the Macmillan Committee (1929–1931) that British monetary policy was conducted without concern for its domestic effects. Arthur Kitson, in his book *The Bankers' Conspiracy*, which EP admired, implicated Norman in a plot of international bankers to restore the gold standard at the cost of world war (see Document 6n). In his 1942 radio talk "Destruction," EP said that the usury system "is as old as the gold brick wheeze. The money system practiced by Monty Norman, and by Baruch's fireside cronies is the system of claiming MORE than there is" (Doob 82). EP attacked Norman in his "Alfred Venison" poems in the *New English Weekly* (1934) and mentioned him in Canto 77.

my pencil scribble] Probably Letter 7.

Jas] James Laughlin (1914–1997), American author, founder of New Directions Publishing Corporation, and publisher of many of EP's works, *including The Cantos*. From a wealthy Pittsburgh steel family, Laughlin visited EP in Rapallo while a student at Harvard and found himself enrolled in the "Ezuversity," which he has lovingly described many times. EP suggested that "Jas" start a publishing house for contemporary authors. In 1936 Laughlin founded New Directions, which has published EP, William Carlos Williams, Tennessee Williams, H.D., and many other major writers of the twentieth century. Laughlin played an important part in EP's and DP's lives after reestablishing contact with them in 1945. He not only pledged to publish the cantos and the Confucian translations that EP had produced at the DTC, but also suggested Julien Cornell as legal counsel for EP. Laughlin's 1945–1946 letters to EP, DP, T. S. Eliot, A. V. Moore, and others (Lilly) reveal his active concern and friendship.

MTOUSA DTC

APO 782, U.S. ARMY

<u>Army Local</u>

<u>Italy</u>

20 sept 1945

(underline the army local and then put apparently CO postmaster New York where it does not go,)

Mao

Notice this evening that YOU are authorized to write to me, and to visit me for approx half an hour in presence of officer. God knows how you wd. get here. It is outside Pisa. Unless the ranger or somebody has an auto disponibile [available]. Nothing said about any other people being authorized to write, so you better make a start collecting whatever news you can get, re readiness to publish "Confucius" "Zone," reprints etc, & whatever.

Correspondence subject to censorship, but I don't think anything is barred now that the war is over.

Naturally I have no news except that I am still here and living in a tent and being fed like the army vurry solidly - back to 166 lbs? which is eleven stone something, eleven stone six, proper weight if I dont go above it. At any rate nothing like pre war bulge. Amusing that Hugh Dalton shd be in charge of liquidating Monty Norman's old infamy, and so forth.

I don't know whether they forwarded you my pencil scribble or merely sent you formal notice that the postal service will function.

Naturally am famished for news, personal gossip anything, especially ubicity of everybody.

I dunno how the mail functions to England, however use yr judgement and collect what you can. add Jas, Possum, Duncan, to list, Angold if alive.

Gawd bless you, an love to mother,

E

Possum, Duncan] T. S. Eliot and Ronald Duncan. See Letter 7n.

Angold] John Penrose Angold (1909–1943), a British poet and writer on economics much admired by EP. He wrote for the *New English Weekly, Country Life,* and *Nine,* and published only one volume of poetry, *NYX Apocalyptike* (London: Shakespeare Head Press, 1933), before he was killed on active service in the Royal Air Force in 1943. In 1944 EP worked on an Italian translation of a manuscript by Angold, "Economy of Tyranny," which argued that the agricultural community can never be in debt (Redman 262). In 1952 Peter Russell of London published Angold's *Collected Poems,* with an introduction by Ronald Duncan. EP learned of Angold's death in early October 1945 and opened Canto 84 with a lament for him (see Letter 19). See also Letter 47n.

9 Notes. In pencil on two thin sheets of white paper, one side each; envelope addressed in pencil by EP to DP at Villa Raggio, postmarked "U.S. Army Postal Service 549, Oct 5 1945," and stamped received in Rapallo "9.10.45." The canto extract enclosed by EP may have invited special scrutiny by the army and thus delayed the posting of Letter 9 (Lilly).

a first bit typed] EP enclosed five typed pages, containing Canto 81 in its entirety and the opening lines of Canto 82 to "When the french fishermen hauled him out he." At the DTC, EP composed pencil drafts of cantos on writing pads, then typed the drafts in triplicate on a machine in the medical hut, setting aside portions to be mailed to DP. After reading these, DP would pass them on to Olga Rudge in Sant'Ambrogio, and Olga's daughter, Mary, would prepare multiple copies on Olga's old French Corona (EP's typewriter having been taken away by the investigators). After receiving copies from Olga, DP would dispatch sets to Ronald Duncan, T. S. Eliot, James Laughlin, or others, as EP indicated. Cantos 74–84, which were published as *The Pisan Cantos* by New Directions in 1948 and by Faber and Faber in London in 1949, were awarded the Bollingen Prize for poetry. Canto 81 is the best known of the series, with its libretto refrain, "*Lawes and Jenkyns guard thy rest / Dolmetsch ever be thy guest,*" and the celebrated lines, "What thou lovest well remains, / the rest is dross" (lines 102–03, 136–37). EP's DTC pencil drafts and typescripts of Canto 81 are at Beinecke. See also Letter 22n.

permit for you] See Documents 9 and 10.

Miss Ida] Ida Bigler Mapel (d. 1960) and Adah Lee Mapel (d. ca. 1955) were sisters who had met EP in Spain in 1906 and lived for many years at 3301 P Street N.W., Washington, D.C. EP stayed with them during his visit to the United States in 1939 and expressed his amused admiration in a letter to Wyndham Lewis: "gawd and the angels wd/ NOT impress Miss Ida and Adah Lee is perfectly c[ap]able of continuin' to sip her tea quietly in the midst of a earth quake" (*Pound/Lewis* 216). Ida's letters to EP and DP in 1945–1946 are full of information and moral support, and she kept a close, canny eye on developments in EP's case (Lilly). EP was grateful for the elderly sisters' regular visits in his first months of incarceration in Washington. They brought him chocolate treats and mended his clothes. See also Letter 54n.

can write to you only] Incoming letters were permitted, but at this point EP could write only to DP and to A. V. Moore in London at Shakespear & Parkyn (Letter 17). Toward the end of his DTC stay, he was also allowed to write to his daughter, Mary Rudge.

Ezra Pound
co Prison Officer
MTOUSA DTC
APO 782, US Army
Sunday 22 or 23 Sept.
[23 September 1945]

Mao.

here is a first bit typed - I don't know whether the earlier parts of the ms. are intelligible as haven't read thru 'em yet. Anyhow - more human than a dull letter - & in parts mild enough to suit mother. Send it up hill to be copied. I spose the little typewriter is still there.

There seems to have been some confusion re/ letters. I don't think the permit for you was intended to be exclusive - in any case tell 'em to write. I'll get to the letters sooner if they are here in the Provost's office than if they are in the far interstices of the postal system.

Mao E.

You'll have to find out whether to post at usual Rapallo post office or at U.S. whatever.

If you can get in touch with Miss Ida & find out what has really happened in the U.S. during the last 6 years. address as I remember 3301 P. St. Washington.

Tell Mary & O [Olga] to write. letters probably get thru but for present can write to you only.

10 Notes. In black ink on a sheet of white paper folded double and written on four sides; no extant envelope (Lilly).

Should this reach you] DP sent Letter 10 c/o the Provost Marshal, Peninsular Base Section, one day before she received from the same official a letter of permission to write EP directly (see Document 9). On 6 October 1945, Major William H. May of the office of the provost marshal wrote DP that Letter 10 had been received and forwarded to EP (OP).

those "Memoirs"?] DP may have written "Memories." On the envelope of EP's Letter 14, DP listed items relating to the page numbers of typed cantos she had just received, and added, "Cantos *are* yr. memoirs." She was the first of many readers to notice the profoundly personal quality of *The Pisan Cantos*. EP had already produced an ironic prose memoir, *Indiscretions*, first published serially in *The New Age* in 1920.

Dottoressa] Dr. Elfriede (Antze) Bacigalupo (1888–1973) was born in Bremen. She and her husband, Ruggero Massimo Bacigalupo (1881–1973), a pharmacist, were married in 1911. After taking her Italian medical degree in 1921, she practiced in Rapallo as a pediatrician for the locals and as a family doctor for the foreign colony. EP and his family were among her patients. Elfriede's son, Giuseppe Bacigalupo (b. 1912), known as "Bubi," took a medical degree in Siena in 1938 and had EP's father, Homer, as one of his first patients. After the war he set up and directed a clinic in Rapallo. Giuseppe and his mother were fond of tennis and played with EP in local tournaments. Giuseppe's wife, Frieda Natali (1909–1983), was born in Pennsylvania of Italian parents and met her future husband while on a scholarship to Siena. After they were married, she obtained a degree in pediatrics, started practicing with her mother-in-law, Elfriede, and soon became popular with the local mothers as "the American dottoressa." She visited EP at St. Elizabeths in 1949 and 1957. She and Giuseppe had two boys, Andrea (b. 1949) and Massimo (b. 1947); the latter became a university professor and EP scholar.

No. 12/5] See Letter 3n. For Ina Benatti's sister, see Letter 5n.

heard from Omar] Omar Shakespear Pound (b. 1926), registered at birth in Paris by EP and DP as an American citizen, grew up in England, where DP's mother, Olivia Shakespear, was responsible for him while he was at the Norland Nurseries in London and after 1933 when he went to live in Felpham, Sussex. He attended Charterhouse, near Godalming in Surrey, where Shakespears, Thackerays, and Tuckers had suffered before him. After leaving Charterhouse, Omar went to work in a London hotel as a trainee in hotel management, but in 1944 while living with A. V. Moore and his family, he was in the house when it was badly damaged by a German bomb, and Moore and T. S. Eliot arranged for him to be sent as an evacuee to work on Ronald Duncan's farm. Early in 1945 he volunteered for the U.S. Army, was inducted in the United Kingdom and sent to France for basic infantry training, then to Germany as part of the Army of Occupation. Early in 1946 he attended the Biarritz American University for college-bound GIs and afterward returned to Bremen. He graduated from Hamilton College in 1954 after a year at the London School of Oriental and African Studies and a further scholarship year at the University of Tehran. After receiving his M.A. in Islamic studies from McGill University, he taught in Boston, Morocco, Cambridge (England), and at Princeton University. He is a poet and a translator of Persian and Arabic poetry.

"Magic Flute"] Omar went to Mozart's *Magic Flute* in Paris while on a few days' leave from the army.

Elsie] John Drummond's wife, whom he divorced shortly after World War II, lived in England throughout the war.

a good play] Ronald Duncan's *This Way to the Tomb*, a verse drama cast in the form of a Renaissance masque and antimasque and written in a variety of metrical forms, portrays the meditations and temptations of Saint Anthony and examines the possibility of "desire for no desire" in the modern world. With incidental music by Benjamin Britten, the play opened in October 1945 at the Mercury Theatre in London and ran for 201 performances. T. S. Eliot attended the first night. Faber and Faber published the text in 1946. See also Letter 7n.

Moore] Arthur Valentine Moore (1894–1975), head clerk of Shakespear & Parkyn at No. 8 John Street

Villa Raggio
Cerisola
Rapallo
Sept. 25. 1945.

Dearest.

Should this reach you - - - You may imagine that I am thinking of you all the time: but I do not worry all that time. I only hope captivity is not proving bad for yr. health, & that you are able to work at some writing or other. The moment perhaps for those "Memoirs"? Yr. Ma is always so: v. rheumatic: The Dottoressa has a good prescription for her. I want if possible to get her parked elsehow: but its not easy: I have had to give up No. 12/5, - too many homeless. Ina's [Benatti] sister & husband & child in it now, & I have my own Studio for myself & my own Key. They are the dearest people. Ina my great comfort. I heard from Omar several times - He is happy in the U.S. Army - practising his french - has heard his first opera, "Magic Flute" - Says he wishes to study psychology - Has an idea of Chicago Univ. Social Science Course. I told him several tips - & to keep his eyes open on the folk around him.

Ronnie [Duncan] has married Rosemary, & they have a boy & a girl: She is alas! just now in hospital with T.B. R. [Ronnie] at the B.B.C. I hear from Elsie he has written a good play, approved by T.S.E. [Eliot] - who has written me a letter about Omar - satisfactory. I am also in correspondence with Moore. Nelly died shortly before Uncle Harry: the latter leaves everything to me: Omar transported all the prints etc. to John Street. Of course this can't be settled up until I can get to England to sign etc: etc: Fear this is not possible yet: also they tell me my "citizenship has lapsed." Drummond a true friend. He corresponds with me & with Olga. I believe Mary is here with her mother: Anita came one day with my wool. I keep clear. Ronnie wants to know what verse you have lately written: I wasn't able to give him a v. satisfactory reply - except that you'd been working so much on Kung & Mencius. All yr. M.S.S. still up at No. 60.

The Bubis are helping me to sell some paintings & the samovar, & some small things of my own - prices very high in the market. I have read Novum Organum with great delight - also the Sonnets: some of wh. are very ideogrammatic.

Please have counsel, & don't try to defend yourself:

All my love always D.

Angold was killed

in London, the law office of Henry Hope Shakespear, DP's father. Moore, who began working there in 1907, was preparing for his law exams when World War I broke out. He enlisted in the Royal Bucks Hussars and served in the Machine Gun Corps of the British Egyptian Expeditionary Force; he was wounded in 1917. After the war he married and, no longer having time to prepare for law exams, did not become a solicitor but remained head clerk at Shakespear & Parkyn until he retired in 1958. Moore played a crucial role after EP's arrest in 1945, receiving and dispatching information to all parties concerned, working to release DP's funds in the United Kingdom, and advising EP about legal counsel and other matters. He was in constant communication with T. S. Eliot, John Drummond, Ronald Duncan, James Laughlin, Julien Cornell, Omar Pound, and others.

Nelly] Edith Ellen "Nelly" Tucker (1868?–1941). In 1911 Nelly married Henry Tudor Tucker (1866–1943), Olivia Shakespear's brother and DP's uncle. Nelly's daughter by a previous marriage, Bertha Georgie Hyde-Lees, married W. B. Yeats in 1917.

"citizenship has lapsed."] Owing to bureaucratic muddle or prejudice, DP was told at the U.S. Consulate in Genoa that her U.S. citizenship had lapsed for failure to renew her passport, despite the legal reality that she had inalienably become an American citizen on marrying EP in 1914. See Letters 21a/21b, 26n, 60, 74n, and 77n.

Drummond] John Drummond. See Document 7n.

Mary] Mary Rudge, EP's daughter by Olga Rudge (see Letter 1n), born in 1925 in the Italian Tyrol and raised by a German-speaking peasant family in the mountain village of Gais. There she grew up and gained a knowledge and love of farm life, and had occasional reunions and trips with EP and Olga. During part of World War II she worked in a German military hospital; in 1945–1946 she divided her time between Gais and Sant'Ambrogio, where her mother had remained. She later married Boris Barratti, who took the title and name Prince de Rachewiltz, and they lived in a refurbished Tyrolean castle. Mary de Rachewiltz, who tells of her early life and the events of 1945–1946 in *Discretions*, is one of the foremost translators and scholars of EP.

Anita] Anita lived on the ground floor of No. 60, Olga's house in Sant'Ambrogio. She was present when EP was taken away on 3 May 1945.

what verse you have lately written] DP knew of EP's work on Confucius ("Kung") and Mencius, which he had mentioned in Letter 6 four months earlier, but she was not yet aware of the new cantos that he was writing.

Novum Organum] Francis Bacon, *Novum Organum* (1620). DP wrote Ronald Duncan on 15 September 1945 that this work contained "All the same ideas that EP has been hammering on: le mot juste—the real word" (HRHRC). She later read Bacon's essay "On Usury" (see Letter 70n).

Sonnets] Shakespeare's *Sonnets*. EP refers to them in Letter 86. It is not known which sonnets DP found "very ideogrammatic."

don't try to defend yourself] DP felt strongly that EP should rely on legal counsel, but he wished to defend himself, perhaps in collaboration with an attorney, and Olga Rudge concurred. At his preliminary arraignment in November 1945, EP announced that he wanted to act as his own counsel, but the judge denied his request. See also Introduction, Letter 11, and Document 14n.

Angold] See Letter 8n.

11 Notes. In black ink on a sheet of graph-ruled paper folded double and written on four sides. An envelope most likely belonging with Letter 11 is addressed in black ink by DP to EP at the DTC and postmarked "Rapallo 29.9.45" (Lilly).

Glory be!] DP had just received EP's Letters 7 and 8, enclosed in the same envelope.

Macleish] Archibald MacLeish (1892–1982), Illinois-born poet and playwright, served as Librarian of Congress (1939–1944) and an assistant secretary of state (1944–1945). He was an outspoken champion of free speech and thought, supported FDR's New Deal, and criticized intellectuals for their weak response to fascism. His later verse plays, some written for radio, reflect a concern with social and political issues. In a radio talk of 23 April 1942, EP scolded MacLeish for defending "Roosevelt's gang" and for not doing more to make known "the key facts of American history" (Doob 106, 104). In July 1943 MacLeish sent Ernest Hemingway photostats of some of EP's radio scripts, remarking: "Poor old Ezra! Treason is a little too serious and a little too dignified a crime for a man who has made such an incredible ass of himself, and accomplished so little in the process" (Winnick 315–16). In December 1945 he wrote Julien Cornell, EP's attorney, that the excerpts he had heard seemed "a toadying attempt to please the Fascist government by beastly personal attacks on President Roosevelt, by a recurrent anti-Semitism, and by a misinterpretation of the American people which could only be justified on the ground that Pound knows nothing about them" (Winnick 335). After his arrest, EP hoped to consult with MacLeish (see Letter 17), who was a lawyer by training, but this did not happen. MacLeish helped DP with inquiries about her U.S. passport and citizenship (see Letter 60). In 1956–1958 he was instrumental in getting the treason indictment dismissed and EP released from St. Elizabeths Hospital.

Swabey] Rev. Henry Swabey (1916–1996) went to Wellington School and the University of Durham, where he wrote a thesis entitled "The Church of England and Usury." He became a Church of England vicar in the eastern counties of England and in Canada. In 1935 he began a correspondence with EP about church history and economic matters that continued over many years. In 1936 he visited Rapallo. Swabey, who also wrote regularly to Wyndham Lewis, was a Social Crediter, knew Greek, studied Chinese in later life, and contributed to Ronald Duncan's magazine *Townsman.*

Bedford] Agnes Bedford (1892–1969), a professional piano accompanist, vocal coach, and close friend of EP and Wyndham Lewis from before World War I. She attended the Guildhall School of Music in London, where she won scholarships. EP praised her in *The New Age*, and she helped him with his opera *Villon* and other musical projects in the 1920s. By the end of World War II, arthritis had ended her musical career. After Wyndham Lewis's return to England, she read to him regularly, enabling him, despite his increasing blindness, to write and publish again; he dictated substantial portions of his later books to her. Bedford was also a good friend of DP's.

Transport difficult] DP's diary shows that she began "hunting transport" almost as soon as she learned of EP's whereabouts. Omar Pound also had difficulty getting from Pisa to Rapallo and had to travel in a rickety Italian truck.

Bubis] Giuseppe and Frieda Bacigalupo. See Letter 10.

Being without citizenship] See Letter 10n.

can't be released] During World War II, most U.K. bank accounts of people in Germany, Italy, and Japan were seized and placed in the hands of the Custodian of Enemy Property.

A.M.G.] Allied Military Government (or Governor). The A.M.G. was created jointly by the Allied forces to establish political and military control over Italy. Military officers and men were assigned to civilian affairs to replace the local Italian civil administration.

Nerina] Nerina Pagliettini, Ina Benatti's daughter, looked after the Pounds for many years.

Nassano] Giambattista Nassano (b. 1887) lived in Rapallo and was a signatory to one of the Tigullio manifestos (see Letter 2n). EP sent him one of his Italian translations of Confucius and corresponded

Villa Raggio
Cerisola
Rapallo
28 Sept. 1945.

Oh Mao! Glory be!

I have burnt incense to Apollo several times for help. I have written this p.m. to Moore & Duncan to tell Eliot etc. & given them the address. T.S.E. [Eliot] is in correspondence ~~with~~ for you with Macleish. Drummond is in Rome, & my centre of strength & help. Post to Rome about week or ten days. To England three weeks or a month each way. Am trying to find Swabey.

Angold Killed.

Ronnie [Duncan] working at b.b.c. Broadcasting House W.I. Also I will track down my dear Bedford.

Omar writes quite often: He has heard "the Magic Flute" - he's crazy on music, I gather! He offers to be of any possible help to you - but I don't see anything he could do—He is trying to get leave to come here - about Xmas perhaps. Isabel always worrying me about him - He wrote her, (on my suggestion), an admirable letter full of nothing at all! I have spent considerable time & energy trying to locate a camion [truck] or sommat to lift me to see you. Transport difficult - I know nearly where you are. Also most expensive. The autobus asks 2,000 lire to Pisa.

The Bubis are helping me towards cashing in. I have taken several paintings to sell, & they are to be put up on show at the "in Porto" shop & various other objects. Being without citizenship at the moment, I can't get the necessary "O.K. from Consul in Italy" that I am U.S. citizen etc: without which can't be released.

I got the cash out of the Cassetta [bank box], through kind help of A.M.G. here. He has really been very good to me. Poor devil just down with jaundice.

Yr. ma much as per usual: don't know how much more I can stand. Always full of ideas of what other people should do - based on erroneous or lack-of information.

Nerina is incinta [pregnant] - for about Easter - seems well. Ina a blessing.

All sorts & conditions ask me news of you: quel'uomo li - tanto buono - mai fatto niente di male [such a good man - that one - never did anything wrong] - & so on - really quite touching. Nassano in jug [jail]: they say too good an organizer to be loose.

John's address
S/2157556 L/Cpl.
J. Drummond
H.Q. Allied Commission
Rome.

Elsie [Drummond] is [in] England. wrote me a nice gossipy letter. Elihu Root doesn't undertake yr. kind of case. He strongly recommends one Stryker - of yr. class - Please dont attempt to defend yourself yourself.

Mao D.

Eliot writes me, from 24. Russell Sq. mostly re Omar.

with him on various topics (Beinecke). FBI documents 100–34099–191, –200, and –207 refer to "the Manuel Nassano ice house in Rapallo" where EP had stored letter files and other documents when he was forced to evacuate his Via Marsala apartment in May 1944. On 7 May 1945, the day that EP authorized FBI Agent Amprim to search his papers in Sant'Ambrogio (see Letter 2), he also signed a note to Signora Nassano giving Amprim permission to examine his property at the ice house.

Elihu Root] Elihu Root, Jr. (1881–1967), was a prominent New York corporate lawyer and son of the statesman and Nobelist Elihu Root. He was a graduate of Hamilton College and of Harvard Law School. As a Republican, he was openly critical of FDR's New Deal. In 1939 he and EP received honorary degrees from Hamilton. When EP was arrested in May 1945, he wanted Root to be made aware of the case. In early July 1945 John Drummond wrote to Root informing him of this fact and asking if he would be willing to defend EP. Root replied on 13 July that he was merely an acquaintance of EP's, "not a very sympathetic one," and that he did not "try cases." He suggested Lloyd Stryker, to whom he was related by marriage. (Both letters are in OR Papers, Beinecke.) Lloyd Paul Stryker (1885–1955), a fellow student of EP's at Hamilton, was a celebrated criminal lawyer who defended Alger Hiss at his first perjury trial. He wrote several books, including *Andrew Johnson: A Study in Courage* (1929). See also Document 7 and Letters 18, 19, 33, and 37.

12 Notes. Typed with black ribbon on a sheet of white paper, both sides, with small corrections and initial in pencil; marked "Censored J. L. Steele, Lt. Col. CE, MTOUSA DTC." DP marked the letter in red crayon, "recd Oct 10." No envelope: Letter 12 may have been enclosed with Letter 9, 14, or 15 (Lilly).

Word went to you on the 18th inst] The provost marshal's letter of permission. See Document 9.

wad of canto] Canto 81. See Letter 9.

Rossaro] Edgardo Rossaro. See Letter 2n.

Soldato] Giuseppe "Pep" Soldato was a writer and propaganda official who assisted EP with his Italian translations of Confucius and signed both of the Tigullio manifestos (see Letter 2n). In April 1944 he was assigned to the Regional Military Command Office of Propaganda in Alessandria, northwest of Genoa, and was in close contact with the staff of *Il Popolo di Alessandria*, to which EP contributed many articles and slogans in 1944–1945, often discussing them with Soldato. In November 1944 EP wrote Fernando Mezzasoma, minister of popular culture for the Salò Republic, that Soldato was "an active propagandist" (Heymann 335). At the end of the war Soldato was sought by the partigiani, who ransacked his apartment in Santa Margherita. In late April 1945 he was barricaded with other officials in the military command at Alessandria, which had been virtually abandoned by defending soldiers. He managed to flee to the mountains of Piedmont and remained there for two years with his sister, running a small farm. Getting back in touch with EP in August 1958, he spoke sadly of the "collapse of dreams" and "the wreck of all our lives" (Beinecke). In 1942 he published a volume of poetry, *Città' lasciata.* He gave EP an inscribed copy, which is now at HRHRC.

Faber and New Directions] EP's British and American publishers.

"One day's reading"] EP believed that the four Confucian classics purveyed a comprehensive education in a few pages. See Document 7n and Letter 8n.

the Analects] The "philosophic conversations" of Confucius, one of the four Chinese classics. EP's *Confucius: Digest of the Analects* was published by Giovanni Scheiwiller of Milan in 1937 and reprinted in *Guide to Kulchur* (1938). His complete translation of the *Confucian Analects* appeared in the *Hudson Review* in 1950 and was reprinted by Square $ Series in 1951 and later by New Directions. For the other works by Confucius and Mencius referred to in Letter 12, see Letters 2n, 6n, and Document 7n.

excited on the 14th] 14 September, DP's birthday.

co/ Provost's office
MTOUSA DTC
APO 782, ARMY LOCAL
Esercito americano [U.S. Army]
Italia
28 sept 1945

Mao

Word went to you on the 18th inst that you cd/ write to me at this address. That is I can be written to here. Others can also write. But I can, as yet, only send answer to you.

Haven't heard from you yet, but apparently that is nothing to worry over as mail from Rome takes a week / as from the U.S.A. Also sent you a wad of canto a few days ago. Dont know that it will be passed, as probably unintelligible. Anyhow, I have done 70 or 80 pages. Some of it good, whether intelligible to anyone who hasn't read early parts I don't know. Some of it must be comprehensible. Of course if there is no de facto post, I have lost less time than I had imagined.

Anyhow, do write at least once a week, and dont wait for answers if it means 15 days round trip for letters.

As per earlier / I want all sorts of News. If Faber exists / if ANYthing still exists. Rossaro, Soldato etc. and from London. Both re/ Faber and New Directions. Have you addresses? There wd/ be enough cantos for a volume / I have worked on the Kung. That also a vol/ "One day's reading, the Testament of Confucius." New Great Learning, the Axis, the condensations from the Analects and from Mencius. That cd/ be ready almost as soon as arranged with Faber or with Jas [James Laughlin]/

As per earlier/ I have appetite and am bein' fed thoroughly.

Permit to write due to my gittin excited on the 14th, remembered the date. Mao / - well he hopes she has pleasanter returns of the day Mao/ and love to mother, hope this short note goes thru quicker than a long one might take. will try to send some more cantos when I hear you have got the first lot.

Naturally want to know if Mary [Rudge] has got to Rapallo / is still there, or whatever etc.

love mao
E.

13 Notes. In black ink on a small sheet of graph-ruled paper, both sides; no extant envelope (Lilly).

Dearest Ming] "Ming," from the Chinese, meaning "bright," as in the Ming Dynasty; it also means "enlightened."

Solari's son] Silvio Solari (1886–1945), the Rapallo podestà (chief authority) before World War II, lived in an apartment two floors below EP and DP in Via Marsala. A common name in the area, DP's "Solari" could have been any of several persons. Gio Batta Solari, nicknamed "Baccin" (1875–1959), was a peasant in Sant'Ambrogio who occasionally worked for Olga Rudge. He is mentioned in Cantos 87 and 88.

Majerna's] Edoardo Ruggeri Majerna (1888–1939) and his wife, Giovanna (1898–1956), ran the Albergo-Caffè Rapallo until 1939. Giovanna ran the Caffè Jolanda after that, with the help of their son, Dante Majerna (1913–1990), who married Angela Guarino in 1945. See also Letters 3n and 23n.

Piovanos] Umberto Piovano (1887–1960) and his American wife, Alma Von Vlecher, were longtime residents of Rapallo.

Poor old Kate] Catherine (Kate) Isherwood, born in Lancaster, England, in 1879, was in a German internment camp in Biberach during the latter part of World War II. She had lived in Rapallo before the war and died in Chiavari in 1953. Macerata is a town southwest of Ancona.

Anita] See Letter 10n.

Desenzano] A town on Lago di Garda where EP had stayed in 1911 and which he revisited with DP often in later years.

Lib. Govt. in England] DP means the Labour government led by Clement Attlee, which came into power after World War II when Churchill and the Conservatives were voted out.

Morganthau is out] Henry Morgenthau, Jr. (1891–1967), Secretary of the U.S. Treasury under FDR (1933–1945). In his radio broadcasts and his private correspondence, EP was unrelenting in his attacks on Morgenthau, who he believed was a puppet of international finance. In a letter of 19 July 1940 to Senator Burton K. Wheeler, EP declared, "The great evil is Morgenthau, or the force that keeps it in office" (quoted in Redman 203).

Biddle] Francis Beverley Biddle (1886–1968), U.S. attorney general (1941–1945) and a judge at the Nuremberg trials. Tom Campbell Clark (1899–1977), who had been assistant attorney general in charge of the criminal division, was appointed attorney general in July 1945. Biddle's office had announced the first indictment of EP in July 1943, and Clark's office the second in November 1945. EP's letter to Biddle of 4 August 1943 is printed in Appendix I.

Signora Aramando] Margherita Perino Aramando (1887–1977), whose husband, Mario Lucio Aramando (1887–1953), was a music publisher.

Baci's daughter] Adriana Bacigalupo (b. 1922), daughter of Elfriede and Ruggero Massimo Bacigalupo, married Alberto Tagliaferro (1920–1972), head surgeon at Galliera Hospital in Genoa, on 3 October 1945. See also Letter 10n.

Villa Raggio
Cerisola
Rapallo
Sept 29 1945.

Dearest Ming.

A few items from the outside - or rather less-inside world. Solari's son has returned perfectly well. Sig^a Majerna's eldest got back yesterday - Dante is to be married! His mother not pleased. I met her on salita [hill path]: so very many saluti [greetings] to you, really quite touching. Piovanos gone back a few days ago to U.S.A. on first boat. Poor old Kate returned to Macerata: penniless, but welcomed by all the village. I sent her a little money. Anita finally brought me my wool, spun: the laundry lady washed it in admiration - & also sent deep affectionate messages to you! Her beloved nephew also just turned up at his home in Desenzano. A report that the Lib. Govt. in England speaks of abolishing p-ports - a sort of permanent carta d'identità [identity card] would be used. Morganthau is out - also Biddle. Tom Clark replaces the latter. Do you by the way see newspapers?

Happened yesty on Signora Aramando. She is here alone - He & the maid gone back to work in Milan. She was rather gloomy - I said [what] I was suffering was oppositions: "passera" [it will pass], - was very sweet. I haven't seen Rossaro; no time or strength, & I'm terrified of meeting Olga [Rudge] if I go that way. She was up here once to make an appalling scene: slightly justified. Baci's daughter being married this week.

Love - Mao D

14 Notes. Typed with black ribbon on a sheet of white paper, one side, with pencil corrections, additions, and initial; envelope addressed to DP at Villa Raggio, postmarked "U.S. Army Postal Service 549, Oct 5 1945," and stamped received in Rapallo "9.10.45." DP penciled on back of Letter 14, "recd Oct. 10" (Lilly).

notice sent you on 18th ult.] See Document 9.

one extract from new CANTI] Canto 81. See Letter 9.

Here are two more] EP enclosed two extracts later to be published as part of *The Pisan Cantos* (1948). What he refers to here as "the bit begin[n]ing 'teapot from another hotel'" consisted of five typed pages running from "with a teapot from another hotel" in Canto 74 (line 803) to the end of that canto; all of the brief Canto 75 (minus the printed music later added to the published text); and the opening pages of Canto 76 to "(every bank of discount J. Adams remarked)" (line 163). The second extract, which EP calls "the Leacok bit" and which he sent in duplicate (one copy for Olga Rudge), consisted of three typed pages from the end of Canto 80, beginning with "Oh to be in England now that Winston's out" (line 705) and running to the end of the canto. The "teapot" extract is at Beinecke. Olga Rudge's copy of the "Leacok" extract is also at Beinecke, while DP's copy is at Houghton in the collection bequeathed by Professor Craig La Drière. The first page of DP's copy bears her jotting: "sent dupl to OR." See also Letter 22n.

have done a Decad 74/83] EP had not yet written Canto 84, which opens with the dateline "8th October" and concludes *The Pisan Cantos.* See Letter 19n.

Leacok] Lacock Abbey in Wiltshire, which EP and DP visited in 1920. EP wrote his mother on 30 September 1920: "We went down to Lacock Abbey for four days, 14th century cloisters, charter of Henry III left there in 1225 still in the tower room, etc. Family name Talbot" (Tulsa, Paige). Charles Talbot, a cousin of DP's, had inherited the abbey, which contained a 1225 charter by Henry III confirming for the county of Wiltshire the liberties granted by King John in Magna Carta (1215). EP recalled the visit in the portion of Canto 80 that he sent to DP in Letter 14:

> To watch a while from the tower
> > where dead flies lie thick over the old charter
> forgotten, oh quite forgotten
> but confirming John's first one,
> and still there if you climb over attic rafters. (lines 714–18)

Old Fordie] Ford Madox Ford (1873–1939), British novelist, poet, and editor of the *English Review* in London and later of the *transatlantic review* in Paris. EP met him in 1909 and admired his writing and his writer's philosophy. In 1914 he called Ford "the best critic in England" and praised his "insistence upon clarity and precision, upon the prose tradition; in brief, upon efficient writing—even in verse" (*LE* 371, 377). Ford taught at Olivet College in Michigan in the 1930s and tried, without success, to tempt EP to join the faculty. EP saw Ford for the last time in New York in 1939, a few weeks before he died. In "Ford Madox (Hueffer) Ford; Obit" he wrote: "There passed from us this June a very gallant combatant for those things of the mind and of letters which have been in our time too little prized" (Cookson 461). Ford is best known for his novel *The Good Soldier* (1915) and his World War I tetralogy, *Parade's End* (1924–1928), which EP read at St. Elizabeths (see Letters 86 and 141).

cheap editions] Armed Services Editions. About 123 million copies of 1,322 titles were distributed to U.S. troops overseas. Two books that EP admired were chosen by the Selection Committee: Charles A. Beard's *The Republic* (P–29), about the U.S. Constitution, and Catherine Drinker Bowen's study of Justice Oliver Wendell Holmes and his family, *Yankee from Olympus* (P–32). There were vigorous protests when it was learned that the army had decided to ban these two works under the Soldier Voting Act of 1944, which Senator Robert A. Taft had sponsored out of fear that the armed forces would distribute political propaganda favoring the reelection of FDR. Another of EP's favorites, George Santayana's *Persons and Places,* was vetoed as "dubious as to democracy," in the words of the army reviewer (Cole 6–7).

american version of Kung] Confucius. See Document 7n.

Legge version] James Legge (1815–1897), Scottish missionary to China who became a distinguished sinologist and translator of the Chinese classics. EP sometimes criticized Legge but deferred to him as

co/ Provost's Office.
MTOUSA DTC
APO 782, American army LOCAL
Forze Armate degli S.U.A.
[Armed Forces of the U.S.A.]
Italy
2 Oct. [1945]

Mao.

Still nothing in response to notice sent you on 18th ult. but tales of the slowness of the post increase. IF there is no postal service, I have lost less time by bein here than might seem.

I sent you one extract from new CANTI. Here are two more. I have done a Decad 74/83 (about 80 pages this typescript), which dont seem any worse than the first 70 [cantos]. Heaven knows whether they make sense in bits. Am sending carbon of the Leacok bit, as dont know what typewriter is left up hill, if any. Will send the carbon of the bit begin[n]ing "teapot from another hotel" in my next, so you can pass on that extract also.

Still, naturally, howling for news of everyone.

Old Fordie may have been right re/ american kids learning to write novels, or it may be previous starvation has softened my critical sense. Have read two with pleasure. also cheap editions have come with the war. what else?

I am indubitably being FED. No news here except what goes into my mouth, or goes on in my head.

Have also worked on american version of Kung/ handicapped by having nothing but the Legge version which I am supposed to be correcting, and so forth.

There is a Lynx canto, which I ought to have sent for yr/ birthday, but permission didnt reach me till the 20th anyhow.

love to you and mother, and keep on writin in the hope that the post will move in time.

E.

well: "One very often comes round to old Legge's view, after devious by-paths" (*Classic Anthology* 33n). EP had with him at the DTC Legge's small one-volume edition of *The Four Books* (a bilingual text of the Confucian classics) and a small Chinese-English dictionary published in Shanghai. These items, which he had thrust into a pocket as he was being led off by partigiani on 3 May 1945, were crucial to his work on Confucius at the CIC and the DTC. Heavily annotated by EP, these two volumes are now in the Burke Library at Hamilton College. In Canto 80 he refers to "the title page in old Legge" (line 64).

lynx canto] Canto 79 is filled with images of the lynx, the protector, part of a private feline iconography shared by EP and DP: "O Lynx, my love, my lovely lynx, / Keep watch over my wine pot" (lines 136–37). EP and DP loved cats, and DP did many drawings of felines throughout her life. EP hoped to send this canto extract in time for her birthday on 14 September but did not have permission to write her until 20 September. He mailed the lynx extract in Letter 24

15 Notes. Typed with black ribbon on a sheet of white paper, one side, with pencil corrections and signature; envelope addressed to DP at Villa Raggio, postmarked "U.S. Army Postal Service 549, Oct 5 1945," and stamped received in Rapallo "9.10.45." DP marked the back of the letter in red crayon, "recd 10 Oct" (Lilly).

tolerable journey back] DP had made her first visit to the DTC earlier that day, 3 October 1945. She and EP were permitted approximately an hour together under supervision. See Introduction for DP's 5 October letter to Olga Rudge describing the visit. See also Letters 16 and 18.

Nelly?] DP referred to the death of her aunt Nelly Tucker in Letter 10, but EP has not yet received that letter, and DP evidently did not mention Nelly during her visit. See Letter 19.

MY OWN stuff] EP's radio broadcasts from Rome during the war.

Chung Yung] Confucius, *The Unwobbling Pivot*. See Document 7n.

while this typewrite is free] EP's tent was in the medical area where officer prisoners were quartered. Lieutenant Colonel Steele, who felt that EP's mental health depended on his being able to write and mail out his literary compositions, allowed him the use of a typewriter in the medical hut during off-duty hours.

16 Notes. Typed with black ribbon, on a different machine from Letter 15, on two sheets of white paper, one side each, with pencil corrections and initial; envelope addressed to DP at Villa Raggio, initialed "RAP" (1st Lt. Ralph A. Pollara), postmarked "U.S. Army Postal Service 549, Oct 10 1945," and stamped received in Rapallo "12.10.45." DP penciled on back of page two, "recd 13 Ott.," and marked sections to quote to Ronald Duncan and T. S. Eliot (Lilly).

Bracco] The major mountain pass between La Spezia and Rapallo, inland and almost due east from Moneglia. See map of Italy (p. 000).

Lucca] Allied troops met heavy resistance around Lucca in early September 1944, but by October they had captured the town and were controlling the surrounding area. EP was intensely aware of his geographic environs while incarcerated and registers this awareness often in *The Pisan Cantos*: "The shadow of the tent's peak treads on its corner peg / marking the hour. The moon split, no cloud nearer than Lucca" (Canto 78, lines 219–20).

her heroick voyage] DP's visit to the DTC on 3 October 1945.

Rose Marie's t.b.] Rose Marie Hansom (b. 1916), whom Ronald Duncan married in 1940, had been diagnosed with tuberculosis. She recovered in a sanatorium in England and afterward used the borax treatment that EP prescribed. She did drawings and portraits, exhibited her art, and illustrated several books, including *The Ward* which contained "illustrative poems" by Ronald Duncan (Devon: Rebel Press, 1978). See also Letter 7n.

Tweddell] Dr. Francis Tweddell (1863–1939), a British pediatrician in New York who published papers on alleviating pulmonary tuberculosis through inhalation treatments. EP corresponded with him in the 1930s and urged others, including William Carlos Williams and Benito Mussolini, to support his discoveries. EP discussed Tweddell in "Reorganize Your Dead Universities" (*Delphian Quarterly*, April 1938) and numbered him among the medical "Men against Death" in Canto 113 (line 17).

cure K. took in Paris] Possibly Katherine Mansfield, who was treated for tuberculosis by a Dr. Manoukhin of the Russian colony in Paris, who claimed he could cure her by irradiating her spleen with X rays. She later went to the Gurdjieff Institute near Paris, where she died in 1923.

15 EZRA TO DOROTHY

co/ Provost's Office
MTOUSA DTC
APO 782, ARMY LOCAL
co/ postmaster New York
Forze armate degli S.U.A., Italia
3 Oct. [1945]

Mao

He hopes she having tolerable journey back. As usual one thinks of the essentail [*sic*] last. Glad to see Omar's [Pound] letters - but no mention of Nelly? Still alive or wot?

This will probably reach you weeks after you have written to all and sundry. Do any of 'em know I was sending MY OWN stuff and that I was not taking orders from anyone? The point is essential, or, yes, it is essential. It makes a difference.

Mao

an thazzatt.

Guess we got thru whatever else there was in the course of the p.m. Will now get on with the Confucius Chung Yung, while this typewrite [*sic*] is free.

love to mother, Love, mao

E Pound

16 EZRA TO DOROTHY

co/ Provost's Office
MTOUSA DTC
APO 782
American army LOCAL (underline LOCAL)
co/ postmaster New York
Forze armate degli S.U.A., Italia
4 Oct. 1945

Put on ALL the bloomink address as yet no post has arrived. They say what is posted in Pisa comes quickest.

O Mao

He hopes she didn't get drownded with rain at 3 a.m. or snowed under on the Bracco. Mounts toward what I believe to be Lucca covered with snow this a.m. but seems gone now. He is grateful fer her heroick voyage. Mind vurry slow. Recall some items.

re/ Rose Marie's t.b. Do tell Ronny [Duncan] about Tweddell. Borax finest possible powder sprayed into air in any room, partic. bed room. Some said it wdn't get into lungs deep enough. Tweddell swore it wd/ and CURE. And that fancy $20 dollar a shot cure K. took in Paris was nowt but the borax with a lot of stage setting.

Agnes] Agnes Bedford. See Letter 11n.

Rudy's] Rudolph Dolmetsch (1906–1942) played the harpsichord and viol, and was a composer and conductor of modern music. EP corresponded with him in the late 1930s and tried to get him to play in Rapallo (Beinecke). In October 1945 EP and DP were not yet aware that Dolmetsch had been drowned at sea on a troopship (see Letter 47). EP greatly admired his father, Arnold Dolmetsch (1858–1940), the musical scholar and maker of early instruments, whose skill he had praised in *The New Age* in 1915: "First, I perceived a sound which is undoubtedly derived from the Gods, and then I found myself in a reconstructed century . . . back before Mozart or Purcell, listening to clear music, to tones clear as brown amber. And this music came indifferently out of the harpsichord or the clavichord or out of virginals or out of odd-shaped viols" (*LE* 433). In 1914 EP visited Arnold Dolmetsch at his home in Haslemere in Surrey and commissioned a clavichord from him. He pays tribute to him and other musicians and composers in the famous "libretto" of Canto 81 (or what in Letter 16 he calls "the Dolmetsch verses"). See also Letter 9n.

Whale's brother] Frank Vigor Morley (1899–1980), dubbed "Whale" by EP, was an American who, with T. S. Eliot, was a director of Faber and Faber until 1939 and later vice president of Harcourt, Brace & Co. in New York. A polymath, he wrote books on travel, chess, geometry, and English authors. His brother, Christopher Morley (1890–1957), prolific author, a founder and editor of the *Saturday Review of Literature*, and president of Haverford College (1940–1945), was joint editor of the eleventh edition of Bartlett's *Familiar Quotations* (Boston: Little, Brown, 1937; rpr. 1943). See also Letter 48n.

Old Rhys] Ernest Rhys (1859–1946), cofounder with W. B. Yeats of the Rhymers' Club, first editor of Everyman's Library, and friend of EP in London before World War I. He helped get EP's *The Spirit of Romance* published in 1910 and is recalled in Canto 74: "and old Rhys, Ernest, was a lover of beauty" (line 712).

Le Gallien] Richard Le Gallienne (1866–1947), poet, novelist, and member of the Rhymers' Club.

Art. Symons] Arthur William Symons (1865–1945), poet, critic, and member of the Rhymers' Club. With Aubrey Beardsley he edited *The Savoy*, publishing Yeats, Dowson, and others. His book *The Symbolist Movement in Literature* (1899) helped introduce French symbolism into England and influenced Imagism. EP said of Symons's versions of Verlaine that he produced "the sort of translation that adds and remakes a poem" (*Poetry and Prose* 4:59).

Old Bin Bin died] Laurence Binyon (1869–1943), poet, authority on Oriental art, Keeper of prints and drawings at the British Museum, and translator of Dante. He introduced EP to Wyndham Lewis. In 1933 he published *Dante's Inferno, with a Translation into English Triple Rhyme*, which EP called "the most interesting English version of Dante that I have seen or expect to see" (*LE* 201). EP responded in detail to Binyon's drafts of the *Purgatorio*, saying in 1938 that "there are damned few pieces of writing that I am thankful for. [My] minute comments are no more than noticing a few nutshells left on the tablecloth post convivium" (Paige 318). Binyon's complete translation of the *Divina Commedia* has been available in *The Portable Dante* (Viking Penguin) since 1947. EP recalls "BinBin" in Cantos 80 and 87.

W. H. Davis] William Henry Davies (1871–1940), British poet who spent many years as a tramp and published his *Autobiography of a Super-Tramp* in 1908. The *Georgian Poetry* anthologies (1911–1922) contain some of his best poems. In 1917 in *Poetry* EP praised his lyric robustness, comparing him with the Elizabethans: "There is a resonance and a body of sound in these verses of Davies which I think many vers-librists might envy" (*Poetry and Prose* 2:299).

Chung Yung] EP's typescript of *Chung Yung: The Unwobbling Pivot* bears the dateline "DTC, Pisa 5 Oct 1945" (Beinecke). For works by Confucius, see Document 7n.

Angold] EP had not yet received DP's Letters 10 and 11 informing him of the deaths of the poet J. P. Angold and of DP's aunt Nelly Tucker. She evidently did not mention them during her visit to the DTC on 3 October. See also Letters 8n and 19.

the good Swabey] Henry Swabey. See Letters 11n and 18.

America is full of news about Pencellin [*sic*] drugs, new miracle, for siph/ etc. as usual England resisting medical discovery. Whether it works on t.b. I dunno. also rumor of a streptonasin [*sic*] for t.b. Tell him about the borax anyhow.

Also he [Duncan] wd/ have Agnes address, and I suppose Rudy's, so send on the Dolmetsch verses if you ever get them. They are not so much song as suggestion for harpiscord piece, possibly with a word here or there. Dunno that Rudy can use 'em but they will like 'em at Haslemere.

Whale's brother Chris Morley has reedited Bartlett's familiar quotations, I may have said that/ edition of 1943 chance to check up on mortality. Old Rhys still alive in '43, also Le Gallien (which as it is N. York edtn. of 1943 they may know, and Art. Symons. Ole Bin Bin died in early '43. Shd/ have had time to finish his translation of Dante. am sorry. Also W. H. Davis, quite a while back. I note that Faber exists, and has an american office. You can question the Possum [T. S. Eliot] re/ Confucius - say the Chung Yung is really done for first time and the Gt. Learning completely redone. Title "The Testament of Confucius." these two "books" and extract, clarified of the Analects and the Mencius, That ought to be possible.

I think I got the first slab of the Chung Y rather well done yester e'en. Not sure if the Ta Hio is quite smoothe enough yet, But, anyhow, wd or ought to be publishable, whatever the weather.

Also ask him re cantos ~~71 OR~~ 72 OR 74 to 83. Whether the N.Y. Faber will squabble with Laughlin re/ Cantos. etc. etc. etc.

Oh well, be generous in handing round my address also the suggestion sending from Pisa when possible.

Glad the kid [Omar Pound] seems so cheerful, thank god he hasn't been depressed etc. etc.

Curious silence re Nelly, or is she just dead? Ronny might be able to supply some information re/ whether one did any good or not?? Angold the [*sic*] AND of course the good Swabey after Agnes the names one wants to hear.

Comfort to feel a letter in the hand once again. Kid writes rather a good letter.

O mao. love, and he hopes she didn't git soaked and fruz.

AND that the mails will function.

E.

17 Notes. Typed carbon (marked "copy" by EP in pencil on the first page) on six sheets of white paper, one side each, with pencil corrections and additions, signed in black ink; envelope (unsealed and unstamped) addressed by EP to Shakespear & Parkyn (Lilly). Letter 17, copies of which circulated among EP's friends, is substantially the same text as the one printed in Cornell 7–11.

John St] See Letter 10n.

Brook Adams] Brooks Adams. See Document 7n.

Kitson's] Arthur Kitson. See Document 6n.

investigator for the American Dept. of Justice] FBI Special Agent Frank L. Amprim. See Letter 2n.

McLeish in Washington] Archibald MacLeish. See Letter 11n.

Lloyd Stryker] See Letter 11n. His father, Melancthon Woolsey Stryker (1851–1929), was president of Hamilton College when EP was a student there.

Mr Dalton at the Exchequer] Hugh Dalton. See Letter 8n.

"A plus B" theorem] One of the crucial propositions of Social Credit is Major C. H. Douglas's A + B theorem, where A represents workers' wages and B factory costs. Since both A and B are added into the price of goods produced, the wage earner never has enough purchasing power to buy the goods he helps produce— without, that is, the intervention of banks and moneylenders, or, as Douglas recommended, national dividends to the people (see also Documents 3–5n). EP expounds the A + B theorem in Canto 38:

> A factory
> has also another aspect, which we call the financial aspect
> It gives people the power to buy (wages, dividends
> which are power to buy) but it is also the cause of prices
> or values, financial, I mean financial values
> It pays workers, and pays *for* material.
> What it pays in wages and dividends
> stays fluid, as power to buy, and this power is less,
> per forza, damn blast your intellex, is less
> than the total payments made by the factory
> (as wages, dividends AND payments for raw material
> bank charges, etcetera)
> and all, that is the whole, that is the total
> of these is added into the total of prices
> caused by that factory, any damn factory
> and there is and must be therefore a clog
> and the power to purchase can never
> (under the present system) catch up with
> prices at large,
>   and the light became so bright and so blindin'
> in this layer of paradise
>   that the mind of man was bewildered. (lines 110–31)

only auditors] Natalie Clifford Barney (1876–1972), a wealthy American writer who ran a famous literary salon in Paris, and her companion, the American portrait-painter Romaine Brooks (1870–1970). EP once called Barney "the best thing that ever came out of Dayton Ohio" (*Poetry and Prose* 5:262) and translated her aphorisms on writing and writers for *This Quarter* in 1929. Barney, who spent the war years with Brooks in a villa in the hills above Florence, shared EP's enthusiasm for Mussolini and was in sympathy with fascist politics. In 1940 she passed through Rapallo and left a radio with EP, which he thought a "God damn destructive and dispersive devil of an invention. But got to be faced" (Paige 342). Her letters from 1941 to 1943 show that she listened regularly to EP's radio broadcasts. On 14 July 1941 she wrote him: "Glad to have heard you over 'Radio' saturday night last—and at last for we have often tried in vain! This time it was clear & good" (Beinecke). EP recalls her in Cantos 80 and 84. See also Letter 99.

Roger Baldwin] Roger Nash Baldwin (1884–1981), one of the founders of the American Civil Liberties Union (ACLU).

co Provost's Office
MTOUSA DTC
APO 782
American U.S.A. Army in Italy
5 Oct 1945

(some say letters shd/ also be marked co Postmaster New York but yours of 24 Sept. to the Provost Marshal was addressed simply to Peninsular Base Section APO 782 U.S. Army

Shakespear & Parkyn
8 John Street, London. Bedford Row W.C.I.

Gentlemen

I am very glad to get your letter of the 7th ult. received on the 24th. which is the first that has reached me from the outer world, though Dorothy was permitted to visit me two days ago and brought the good news of Omar. I am very much pleased with his independence and initiative in all ways.

Also glad to observe from your stationary [sic] that John St has not been bombed out of existence.

I am not sure that your advice is given in full knowledge of certain essential facts of my case.

For example, I was not sending axis propaganda but my own, the nucleus of which was in Brook[s] Adams' works 40 years ago, in Kitson's published works 25 years ago, and in my own pre-war publications.

This was sent and stated to be sent at least over the medium wave, on various occasions, with the preface.

On the principle of free expression of opinion on the part of those qualified to have an opinion, Dr Pound has been granted the freedom of our microphone twice a week. He will not be asked to say anything contrary to his conscience or contrary to his duties as an American citizen. Twice was extended to more times. Those conditions were faithfully observed by the Rome radio. I was never asked to say anything.

The investigator for the American Dept. of Justice expressed himself as convinced that I was telling him the absolute truth months ago, and has since with great care collected far more proof to that effect than I or any private lawyer could have got at.

My instinct all along has been to leave the whole matter to the U.S. Dept. of Justice. The good faith of whose agent I have had no reason to doubt.

I do not know how this will strike you, but the fantastic conditions in Italy have been such that someone who has come here and examined the facts can probably form an opinion more easily than anyone, however perspicacious at a distance.

I had hoped to see Mr. Mc Leish in Washington in May while he was still in the State Dept.

You see there are elements in the case far more interesting than my personal wellfare.

Cantos on the Chinese Dynasties] Cantos 52−61 in *Cantos LII-LXXI* (1940).

Confucius started as market inspector] This echoes the opening of EP's "Note" to his translation of Confucius's *Ta Hsio: The Great Digest* (The Testament), on which he was working at this time, as the dateline at the end of the text shows: "D.T.C., Pisa; 5 October-5 November, 1945" (*Confucius* 19, 89). For the works by Confucius and Mencius mentioned in Letter 17, see Letters 2n, 6n, 12n, 16n, and Document 7n.

I have very cordial recollections of Lloyd Stryker, he is now I believe one of the best known big lawyers in the U.S. whose fees are far far beyond anything I could pay.

40 years ago, about 1905, when his father was President of Hamilton College, Lloyd and I must have been among his prominent headaches, Lloyd in the home, and I in the classroom.

BUT I should much prefer to see Mr McLeish before deciding on so important a step as NOT speaking on my own behalf.

I believe McLeish himself is a lawyer, and in any case he can write to me at this address. If he writes as my lawyer I would certainly be permitted to answer him as I am now answering you.

My most complete fog, my difficulty is my ABSOLUTE ignorance of what had happened in The U.S.A. and in England from 1940 to 1945.

With Mr Dalton at the Exchequer, with the Labour Party not only "in" but also OUT of what to me always appeared to be its obscurantism

I mean, with the public ownership of the Bank put first on its program

a great deal of what you probably consider my moonshine (if you ever considered it at all) must now be made open to the British public.

All over the place what were 20 years ago considered heresies of my friends are now admitted as fact.

The "A plus B" theorem of Maj C. H. Douglas is tacitly accepted in all proposals for government spending.

The public has learned a great deal, but it still has the right to know MORE.

If that be over my dead body so much the worse both for me and for the public.

BUT the suppression of historic fact has NOT been useful, it neither helped to preserve peace nor to carry on the war.

Given the present tension, no one is more ready than I to admit that certain facts should perhaps not be dragged into the limelight at this moment.

BUT that does not apply to other facts that are simply ignored.

I mean that the men in charge both of England and the U.S.A. seem still unaware of them. And that after 25 years of study I can no longer be treated as a whimsical child in these matters.

I am sorry to take up so much space, but I cannot tell from your letter whether you have had enough information to see clearly.

The agent of the Dept. of Justice started by saying that they proposed to consider my past 30 years work

I do not know whether Mr Stryker would be prepared for such labour, and without it, I do not know how he could tell the Court what the case is about.

The picture painted by propaganda has been such, that I do not know whether you can conceive that FREE SPEECH was preserved precisely where the British Public would least expect it, namely in Italy by a few unknown, I suppose you would call them "liberals" working inside the Italian frame work.

I do not think it is an occasion for great skill in presenting a case so much as for great patience in making clear the bearing of known and knowable facts.

Which facts, I ~~do not think you~~ am not sure whether yet grasp[ed], if you will pardon a rather flat statement.

What I am in absolute ignorance of is; whether anyone actually heard my broadcasts; whether they did any good, by which I mean whether they in any way contributed to the better understanding of certain economic fundamentals. Which better understanding is definitely shown now in public pronouncements in England and the U.S.A.

(As C. H. Douglas used to say after the other war: "If they dont do it now, they will have to do it after the next one.")

I do not know whether the public HEARD, or if hearing they understood one single word of my talks.

The only auditors I know of were foreigners in Florence. Plus whatever education one could insert in Berlin. Yes, the RE-education of Europe

Any enlightenment on that point that you can give me, I would be most grateful to receive.

And, of course, seeing that "my program" is going through all over the place, I can not know that those who are putting it through are in any way conscious of my existence, or that they would be pleased to know that I had been on their side of the battle for enlightenment.

Don't gasp. I know it will take time for this strange view to get through the probable mist of prejudice that has been raised by the jingo press.

But a great deal that could in 1938 only be printed in outcast periodicals of small circulation, is now in print and will increasingly be printed in the more general press.

I want very much to know the source or reason for your opinion that I should not address the Court.

Is it due to your not knowing what I actually said on the air?

///

I will send a copy of this letter in 2 days time and if you receive both copies you can send one to Mr McLeish. If you receive only one copy, would you please have it copied and send him ~~your~~ a copy?

It seems to me he might also communicate with Roger Baldwin of the Civil Liberties ~~League (or association)~~ Union as the question of Freedom of speech on the air, together with other constitutional points should interest them.

Emphaticly I want to see Mr McLeish and have been given to understand that it would be possible once I were in the U.S.A.

BUT the simplest plan would be for him to write to me as my lawyer (if I am correct in supposing that he is a lawyer) at any rate he has known my work for 20 years and has some concept of what I have been driving at . . . . . . am not in the least sure that LL Stryker has, or could have.«LSI»

////

Can Omar do anything toward getting his mother's passport put in order.? There seems to be some circumlocution re/ the formalities.

Have I a balance at Faber and Fabers that could be sent to Dorothy pending the release of her own funds.?

Also can you ask Mr Eliot whether Faber will be ready to print another volume of Cantos? or at any rate "The Testament of Confucius"

There is a new translation of the Ta S'eu; and the first proper translation of the Chung Yung, plus an abridgement of the analects and of Mencius.

18 Notes. In black ink on two small sheets of ruled green writing paper, both sides; no extant envelope (Lilly).

elderly doctor] Dr. Mario Casonato lived in Massa, between Viareggio and La Spezia. The Allies had occupied Massa on 10 April 1945. The Italian partigiani occupied La Spezia on 20 April, and four days later a task force of Allied tanks and infantry entered the town without opposition. The first leg of DP's journey back, from Pisa to Viareggio, was in a car provided by the DTC.

yr. big G. Cav.] *Guido Cavalcanti Rime* (1932). See Letter 2n and Document 6n.

Corradi's] The Tullio Corradi family was currently subletting 12/5 Via Marsala, EP and DP's former apartment in Rapallo. See Letters 3n and 5n.

Stryker for yr. defence] For Lloyd Stryker and Elihu Root, Jr., see Letter 11n.

Carrara <u>splendid</u>] The mountains above Carrara, a small town near Massa, famous for its marble. The Allies occupied it on 11 April 1945, in tandem with well-organized partigiani, and once La Spezia and Carrara were secured, the way was cleared for the final drive to Genoa. DP's remarks about her journey in this letter, which EP received on 15 October (see Letter 26), were condensed and fitted into his evolving Canto 84, the last of *The Pisan Cantos*:

He may understand from the Cantos on the Chinese Dynasties, that this text of Confucius, having been at the root of the DURABLE chinese dynasties is the ONLY basis on which a world order can work.

The Chinese Empire during its great periods offering the ONLY working model (and have served REPEATEDLY as proof of being a working model) that can possibly serve in the present situation.

This may sound a large order, but we have come through a very large war. And someone has got to use Adult intelligence in dealing with the world problem.

Confucius started as market inspector, and rose to be Prime Minister AND resigned. He gave more thought to the problem of vast administration than any simple high-brow philosopher.

I do not know that I would have gotten to the centre of his meaning if I had not been down under the collapse of a regime.

But at any rate the work is serious. I mean the translation. Both the First and Second book have been published here. I mean my italian translation of the Ta S'eu with the chinese text facing it / and my italian version of the Chung Yung. I was working on the Mencius when the Partigiani came to the front door with a tommy-gun.

Another point you may not know, i.e. that I was not fleeing from justice.

You may still be under innumerable misapprehensions. I dont want to extend the present letter indefinitely.

sincerely yours

Ezra Pound

18 DOROTHY TO EZRA

> Villa Raggio
> Cerisola
> Rapallo
> Friday. Oct 5 or 6. 1945.
> [5 October 1945]

Dearest.

Oh! Mao! but I was glad to see you: & looking pretty well too. I had a fantastic journey back - left you Wed. pm got here after 10.pm Thursday. I spent the night at the home of an elderly doctor with whom I walked miles - no conveyance, quite dark - we got into Massa after 8.pm & I slept like a log in a stanzina [small room] off his wife's room. I am to send him yr. big G. Cav. some time when post things are easier. I did Spezia - Sestri in the "Train" - filthy smoke, no glass, no light. (6. ocl. p.m.) The two huge sandwiches saved my life! I am staying with Corradi's until tomorrow, as I was too tired to go back & cook & talk etc. etc. If you should ever get here, come straight to them - they will feed & look after you. I will leave my Key with them: & they know about our ringing <u>three times</u>.

To get yr. conto corrente [current account] unblocked a mass of papers to fill in - & Asti seemed dubious - under the circs:

                Incense to Apollo
                          Carrara
                                    snow on the marble
        snow-white
                against stone-white
        on the mountain
        and as who passed the gorges between sheer cliffs
        as it might be by, is it the Garonne?
                          (lines 41–48)

"Incense to Apollo" comes from the opening of DP's letter of 28 September 1945 (Letter 11).

Bedford] Agnes Bedford wrote DP from Essex on 20 September 1945 (Lilly). See also Letter 11n.

A. V. Moore] See Letter 10n.

Parkyn's wife dead] Joseph Atherton Parkyn was senior partner at Shakespear & Parkyn and a coexecutor of Olivia Shakespear's will. He died in 1948.

Bride] EP first met Bride Scratton (1882–1964) in London about 1910. With his help, her writings appeared in *The Dial*, *The Criterion*, and the *transatlantic review*. In 1923 Bill Bird of Three Mountains Press issued *England*, a collection of her prose sketches, under her maiden name, B.M.G.-Adams. In that same year, her husband sued for divorce, naming EP as corespondent. Biographers differ as to the nature of their relationship. In later years Scratton lived in Cambridge and worked as a guide to the city's historical and architectural monuments. The letter from her that DP mentions is dated 4 September 1945 (Lilly).

19 Notes. Typed with black ribbon on two sheets of white paper, one side each, with pencil corrections, additions, and initial; envelope addressed to DP at Villa Raggio, initialed "RAP" (1st Lt. Ralph A. Pollara), postmarked "U.S. Army Postal Service 549, Oct 11 1945," and stamped received in Rapallo "13.10.45." DP marked sections of the letter in pencil to quote to T. S. Eliot, John Drummond, and Olga Rudge (Lilly).

her first letter] Letter 10, dated 25 September 1945.

Heart-break re / Angold] News of the poet J. P. Angold's death, contained in DP's Letter 10, which arrived on 8 October, prompted EP to compose the dirge that opens the published version of Canto 84, the eleventh and last of *The Pisan Cantos*:

        8th October:
                Si tuit li dolh elh plor
                        Angold τσέθνηκε]

See also Letter 8n.

TWO more of her letters] Letters 11 and 13, dated 28 and 29 September 1945.

notice took from 18th to 25th] The provost marshal's notice of permission for DP (Document 9).

John St.] See Letter 10n.

ole Bunk] Family nickname for Henry ("Harry") Tudor Tucker, Nelly Tucker's husband and DP's maternal uncle. See Letter 10n.

Basil] Basil Bunting (1900–1985), Quaker poet from Northumberland, admired by EP for his musical lines and colorful precision. He was imprisoned in 1918 as a conscientious objector. After three terms at the London School of Economics, he went to Paris where he helped Ford Madox Ford on the *transatlantic review* and met EP in the summer of 1923. He spent long periods in Rapallo (1924, 1929–1933), where he worked as a cargo sailor, met Louis Zukofsky, learned Persian, and wrote poetry, of which EP selected nearly fifty pages for the *Active Anthology* (1933). He is best known for his extended lyric sequence, *Briggflatts* (1966). During World War II Bunting saw many fronts in the Royal Air Force, worked aboard a converted yacht protecting convoys in the North Sea, served in Italy and Tripoli, and attained the rank of squadron leader. He was sent to Persia as an interpreter, became an officer in Political Intelligence and later vice-consul at Isfahan, and enjoyed riding and hunting with the nomadic

A letter from [Henry] Swabey awaiting me. Married - daughter 2 yrs. living in Essex. I have given him yr. address - but question of time.

Have written John Dr. [Drummond] that I've seen you. Naturally sent off letter to Olga [Rudge] first thing this am. I shall get into an awful row for having clean forgotten to ask you if you'd have Stryker for yr. defence - He was in yr. class. Elihu Root suggested him, saying he was suitable to this particular job. I will write the letters we discussed tomorrow - when my head has stopped buzzing.

My saluti [greetings] to the two militaries I met: they were good to me - their names escape me.

Please keep steady - & go on with poem, & get all the warm clothing you can! Carrara splendid - it snowed the night I was in Massa & the tops were snow-white, next a.m., as against stone-white - a real relief to see anything so lovely - all day lovely.

A word from our beloved Bedford. Always in Essex: her old mother ½ dotty - I will send her Swabey's address. A. V. Moore forwards me one of his from Omar: & tells me they are charging me income tax 10s/- in £. Parkyn's wife dead.

Dearest. I'm told things don't look too bad for you. So keep going - Yours D

also a short letter from Bride: to whom I had written referring her to S. & Parkyn for news of you, change of add. in Cambridge.

19 EZRA TO DOROTHY

> MTOUSA DTC
> APO 782
> U.S. Army LOCAL
> co. postmaster New York,
> 8 Oct [1945]

O Mao

He was GLAD to get her first letter this a.m. Heart-break re/ Angold, but couldn't have, and didn't, expect much else. He was the best oak, and the few poems the best granite of that generation up to 1938. Ronnie [Duncan] should collect 'em/ mayn't be more than 16 pages, mostly old New English Weekly, I suppose, and the Possum [Eliot] shd/ do a couple of pages of preface, cd/ take off from my two lines, if he needs moral support.

after lunch TWO more of her letters. Thus the notice took from 18th to 25th, a week to reach you, and yr/ last of the 29th, only 9 days to get here. Then later one from Olga and one from Mary [Rudge]. One from Shaks. & Parkyn came a few days ago. So John St. hasn't been bombed to nothing.

Mystery of Nelly explained/ did pore ole Bunk know she had died? Swabey heard from via Olga, so only Basil to hear from and what ole Wyndham has been at in the U.S.A.

SHE keep on burnin' incense. Thank mother for her note. She would like the food here, but I don't suppose they wd/ exchange me fer her, and she wdn't appreciate the beauties of tent life. Vurry fine, but she probably wdn't find it wholly etc. .

mountain tribes. He and the Pounds were out of touch during the war but reestablished contact in 1946. Bunting is mentioned several times in *The Pisan Cantos*: "and in this war were Joe Gould, Bunting and cummings / as against thickness and fatness" (Canto 74, lines 241–42).

ole Wyndham] Percy Wyndham Lewis (1882–1957), writer, painter, editor of *BLAST*, and leading Vorticist in London, where he and EP met in 1909. He was an artillery officer in World War I and served as an artist for the Canadian War Records project. EP admired his novel *Tarr*, first published in the *Egoist* (1916–1917), *and The Apes of God* (1930), which satirized Bloomsbury culture and added to Lewis's reputation as "The Enemy." His early admiration for Adolf Hitler, recorded in *Hitler* (1931), gave way to disillusionment in *The Hitler Cult* (1939). His oil portraits and drawings of EP, T. S. Eliot, Edith Sitwell, and James Joyce are famous. He was in the United States and Canada throughout World War II and returned to London in 1945, nearly blind, to write some of his major works. Omar Pound took him to Ireland in 1951 after he had become totally blind. In "D'Artagnan Twenty Years After" (1937), EP wrote that Lewis's writing is "radically inimitable in that it can only come from a think-organism in action, a mind actually initiating concepts" (Cookson 455).

Ron's play] Ronald Duncan's *This Way to the Tomb* (1946). See Letter 7n.

passports] During World War I the United States and most European countries adopted passport and visa requirements. Under President Wilson, the Passport Control Act was passed in 1918 and extended after the war. EP railed against these regulations in letters to the Paris editions of the *New York Herald* and the *Chicago Tribune* in the 1920s and 1930s. He wrote Senator Cutting in 1931: "The god damned spirit of obstruction came in with Woodie Wilsi's rough necks" (*Pound/Cutting* 29–31).

Old Sraffa] Angelo Sraffa (1865–1937), a citizen of Rapallo who was a scholar of commercial law and bankruptcy at the University of Milan and a founder of the Università Commerciale Luigi Bocconi in Milan, where at his invitation EP gave ten lectures on economics and American history in March 1933. Among Sraffa's many publications was *Sul progetto di legge per la repressione dell'usura* (On a draft of legislation for suppressing usury) (1901). EP corresponded with him in the 1930s (Beinecke) and mentioned him to Senator Cutting (*Pound/Cutting* 58, 60). Angelo's son, Piero Sraffa (1898–1983), was a political economist who taught at Cambridge University and produced a multivolume edition of the works of David Ricardo. One of DP's address books from the 1920s lists Piero at King's College, Cambridge.

Paresce] Gabriele Paresce was willing to testify for EP. His mother, Lydia Ignatoff, was Russian. See Document 6n.

Paolilo] F. Paolillo, private secretary to the general manager of Banca d'Italia in Rome, corresponded with EP in 1943 about banking matters and stamp scrip, which he deemed impracticable (Beinecke). EP sent him a copy of his *Confucio. Ta S'eu* (1942).

Badoglio] Pietro Badoglio. See Document 6n.

Santiana] George Santayana (1863–1952), Spanish-born American philosopher, novelist, and poet who taught at Harvard for many years before moving to Italy. EP sought him out there in the late 1930s to discuss philosophy, money, and the Chinese ideogram, and tried to enlist him in a collaborative book project with T. S. Eliot on a curriculum for the ideal university. Santayana said that EP reminded him of old friends "who were spasmodic rebels, but decent by tradition, emulators of Thoreau, full of scraps of culture but lost, lost, lost in the intellectual world" (quoted in Stock 372). EP wrote Eliot: "Never met anyone who seems to me to fake less. In fact, I gave him a clean bill" (Paige 334). Santayana's magnum opus was his philosophical series, *Realms of Being* (1927–1940), of which *The Realm of Spirit* (1940) was the final volume. Concerned with essence, matter, truth, and spirit, the work attempts to reconcile the dictates of humanity and its animal faith with the ultimate flux of reality. In his radio talk for 26 June 1943, "Materialism," EP said: "I occasionally plunge into the work to calm my heated mind. I mean when I am not up to Confucius or Mencius" (Doob 354). EP refers to Santayana in Cantos 80 and 81.

Chung Yung] Confucius, *The Unwobbling Pivot*. See Document 7n.

Cap. Seitz] Capt. Raymond H. Seitz, Jr., provost office manager at the DTC. EP includes him in a list of camp names in Canto 80 (line 684).

Morrison] Robert Morrison (1782–1834), missionary, sinologist, and compiler of *A Dictionary of the Chinese Language*, the first volume of which was published in Macao in 1815. For many years EP and DP

Can't say Angold was necessarily loss to literature as wasn't sure that he would go on writing, but the few poems all the better for not being full of intended spread.

Possum ought ALSO to print a vol/ of Basil. I reread 'em, as you know, this spring, and they hold. They are the best of that decade, or that 20 years. Then the few pages of Angold.

Glad re Ron's play.

No, Omar can't do anything about me, but he could I think be quite firm re/ yr passport. If the Labour Govt. quashes passports, that is another return to the sanity of 1912, and have I yelled for it since 1920. well, yes. Good local reputation might be of use, if there were anyone there who had any influence. Old Sraffa would have been the man.

The kid [Omar Pound] writes a good letter. I am pleased with him on all counts.

Drummond might look up Paresce, who is in govt. and knows that the formula went "nothing against conscience or duties as american citizen." In fact he signed it. IF he chose to say that he wanted me to work on an Italo-american amity, which they NOW want, and reconstruction, they might get me down to Rome. He, Paresce, would never think of it himself, but has enough open mindedness - russian mother, mind OPEN, but dont usually shut. John [Drummond] cd. guide him. Also Paolilo, private secretary to someone near top, once of Banca d'Italia, and then at the Ministero delle Finanze, under Badoglio govt. Drummond shd/ try to find him if he is still afloat. The fact that my economics passed thru those august portals may surprise etc. etc.

Drummond shd/ also see Santiana, who is [in] a nun's convent whose ubicity can be ascertained at Grand Hotel/ also re/ return of that copy of his "World of Spirit"

For Ronnie, you can say the Chung Yung, I think in shape, & 10 Cantos. The new Ta S'eu almost in shape, four or five characters, that I want to check. Can do it here if Cap. Seitz gets my Italian version out of "Supply," otherwise may send you the ideograms to Hook up in Morrison. That l gets in the way of the o key. I shant bother to correct all the slips.

She go on writin, now that the post seems to function. Too bad old Solari couldn't wait for the boy. Naturally Ma Maj. not pleased re/ Dante, greet Kate and Rosaro. Any news of pore ole "Pep" Soldato?

Yes Lloyd S. son of olde Prexy Stryker, he and I alone resisting the old gheezer, and bein his chief headaches back in 1905. Melancthon Woolsey Stryker to get the Prex's full name.

Any details re/ Angold? or Nelly?

Keep on burnin incense.

Love Mao. E.

return greetings to all etc.

Please tell Olga that I am not yet allowed to write. Ask her and Mary to go on writing to me. There is no specific limit to that, save not wanting to wear out the officers who have to look at incoming mail. A blessed comfort to get letters. Glad Mary has come back. Slocum the other voice to be heard. A good deal of the acid due to misunderstanding / ignorance of the conditions under which, or over which "nothing against conscience or duties as citizen." If they will just go on writing. I have noted all contents of their letters. Trying to keep weight down, now at lb. 173, but nicely distributed, not all on the stomach.

used and annotated the copy that DP had bought in London around 1914. She had it rebound in Italy in five volumes and in the 1960s donated it to the Burke Library at Hamilton College. She had started learning Chinese on her own around 1901 before meeting EP in 1909.

old Solari] See Letter 13n.

Ma Maj] Ma Majerna. See Letter 13n.

Kate] Kate Isherwood. See Letter 13n.

Rosaro] Edgardo Rossaro. See Letters 2n and 12n.

"Pep" Soldato] Giuseppe Soldato. See Letters 2n and 12n.

olde Prexy Stryker] Melancthon Woolsey Stryker. See Letter 17n. "Prex" was nineteenth-century slang for college president.

Slocum] John Jermain Slocum (1914–1997) was James Laughlin's classmate and close friend at Harvard and president of the *Harvard Advocate* (1936), which had published EP's Canto 38 in 1934. In the summer of 1935 Slocum traveled in Austria and Italy with EP, Olga Rudge, and Laughlin. He hosted EP in New York during his 1939 visit, and for a time acted as his literary agent. In 1940, when Wyndham Lewis was in the United States, Slocum provided him with loans, housing, and literary and artistic contacts. During the war he worked as press secretary to Mayor Fiorello LaGuardia of New York before enlisting in the Air Force and being assigned to public information posts. In 1950 he was recruited by the U.S. Information Agency and posted to Frankfurt. He and Herbert Cahoon published *A Bibliography of James Joyce* in 1953.

20 Notes. In black ink on a sheet of graph-ruled paper folded double and written on three sides; no extant envelope (Lilly).

one from me] Letter 18.

letter from Olga] A draft of Olga Rudge's letter to DP, dated 8 October, is in Olga's copybook for 1945 (OR Papers, Beinecke).

Sigᵉ. Nassano] See Letter 11n.

Yr. ma's money] Isabel Pound's widow's pension from the U.S. Mint in Philadelphia, where her husband, Homer, had been an assayer from 11 June 1889 until he retired on 27 June 1928.

supervising in the kitchens] Omar Pound was a guard supervising German marine bakers in a U.S. Army POW camp in France. He has commented: "They taught us how to do German Marine drill with our own rifles—which were, in any case, unloaded."

That was a useful piece of work!] Omar's training in a hotel kitchen in London.

Villa Raggio
Cerisola
Rapallo.
Tuesday Oct 9. 1945.

Dearest.

I wonder if you recd one from me, which I wrote at once on my return? I spent two days at Via Marsala, recovering. They [the Corradis] are so good to me - fed me at once etc: I had a long journey home, two days - at least I mean one night on the way - at Massa. Carrara splendid!

Just had a letter from Olga asking information on various points of journey—re letters arriving—and of course first & foremost was it yr. intention to conduct yr. own defence. (I am v. much against that.) She says she has no intention of leaving until something more definite is known about yr. movements but is ready to do so at short notice - Also Mary [Rudge] is with her. She, O.R., has written you. Get leave to write direct to her if you can. It would be easier for me.

I visited Sigᵃ. Nassano. She is better - He is still in [jail], has got rheumatism - but they are allowed to send food & to write. Ina [Benatti] wanted to know all about you: she is a comfort.

Do let me know whether you will accept [Lloyd] Stryker. We can manage the cash side, one way or another. I feel sure you'd better let some one used to the job, defend you. I have written [John] Drummond & [A. V.] Moore that I've seen you - & have written the letters we discussed. Yr. ma's money for Oct. is coming. I think of you perpetually; & since I have seen you, you are with me all the time: This is a great relief.

Moore tells me Omar is supervising in the kitchens where he is! That was a useful piece of work!

Come if possible - otherwise I'll try for Nov - other things being equal.

Always yours

D.

21a Notes. *Typed with black ribbon on a sheet of white paper, one side, with pencil additions, corrections, and initial. The enclosed separate page, headed "TEXT OF CONFUCIUS," is a typed carbon copy, with everything from "Mao" on added by EP in pencil. Envelope addressed to DP at Villa Raggio, initialed "RAP" (1st Lt. Ralph A. Pollara), postmarked "U.S. Army Postal Service 549, Oct 11 1945," and stamped received in Rapallo "13.10.45." DP noted in pencil on the letter that she sent Mary Rudge the query about* The Odyssey, *and jotted ideograms and definitions on the front and back of the enclosed page, preparatory to composing Letters 28, 30, and 31 (q.v.) (Lilly).*

Morrison] See Letter 19n.

"Ta Seu"] Confucius, *Ta Hsio: The Great Digest.* See Document 7n.

Odes] The Odes (Chi-King or Shih-ching) are a collection of 305 songs traditionally thought to have been assembled by Confucius, who considered them required reading for any intelligent, cultured person. EP's translations of the Odes, which he worked on soon after arriving in Washington, D.C., were published in 1954 by Harvard University Press *as The Classic Anthology Defined by Confucius.*

epithet used for swineherd . . .] Eumaios, Odysseus's faithful swineherd, is introduced in Book 14 of *The Odyssey* and is repeatedly addressed by the narrator as [Εὔμαυβῶτα], "swineherd Eumaios." EP may also be recalling a related epithet for Eumaios, [δῖον ὑφορβόνδ], "noble swineherd" (Book 14, line 3). References to a female swineherd ("la pastorella dei suini") occur in EP's Cantos 76 and 84, and Greek words similar to those he cites appear in *The Pisan Cantos* drafts (Beinecke). Elpenor, a companion of Odysseus, died after a drunken fall from the house of the witch Circe. In Book 11 of *The Odyssey,* which recounts the Nekuia, or interview with the spirits of Hades, the ghost of Elpenor accosts Odysseus and begs him to bury his body and set up a tomb inscribed with the words "A man of no fortune, and with a name to come." EP first used this rendering of the line, [ἀνδρὸς δυστήνοιο καὶ ἐσσομένοισι πυθέσθαι (Book 11, line 76), in Canto I with its Anglo-Saxon-tinged translation from Book 11, and he repeats the phrase in various forms in Cantos 74 and 80. See also Letter 35.

co Provost's Office
MTOUSA DTC
APO 782, U.S. Army ARMY LOCAL
co P.O. New York
9 Oct 1945

Mao

re/ passport, probably quickest wd be to write to Genova, on the line

As mother of son in american army, (give Omar's [Pound] number etc.) who did not wait to be conscripted but volunteered, now in France, etc.

I should be glad if you can get my passport in order without unnecessary delay, so that I can get money from England, urgently needed for current expenses AND to support my U.S. American mother in law, seeing that the rise in prices renders what you send her now in lire insufficient for the comfort of a semi invalid of her age.

Mao. also can you look up the ideograms on next page in Morrison. They got me my "Ta Seu" and the Odes out of "supply" today, but shd/ like Morrison on those 3 ideograms also,

love, Mao

E

When you next send on note to Mary will you ask her to write me giving epithet used for swineherd at Odysseus model pig farm, I think it is [Οεας εεος τυλησς] also the correct greek line about Elpenor, I think it is in the Nekuia, book.

"man of no fortune and with a name to come."

Odyssey XI I think.

TEXT OF CONFUCIUS] This heading and the scrap of text that follows it—"The great digest (grinding the grain in the head)"—differ from EP's final version of the opening of *Ta Hsio: The Great Digest*, completed at the DTC: "The great learning (adult study, grinding the corn in the head's mortar to fit it for use)" (*Confucius* 27).

Legge] See Letter 14n.

The great digest (grinding the grain in the head)

Mao. can you look up what Morrison gives as difference between these two ideograms

and

[3818]   [3810]

seems to be

word & <u>constant</u>   mouth & constant.

(also idea of wind circulating in a closed space??) mouth & constant.

Legge admits Trouble - as the Ta Seu & Chi King dont agree -

Chi K. gives simply forget:

[11632]

in place of the first one -

whether a negative is left out - or simply a case of reversable meaning am not sure.

There is also

= Legge takes as forget

[1084?]

2lb Notes. Typed draft or variant of Letter 2la with additional remarks, including pencil corrections and cancellations, and evidently enclosed with Letter 2la (Lilly).

McLeish] Archibald MacLeish. See Letter 11n.

Roger Baldwin] See Letter 17n.

22 Notes. In black ink on a small sheet of ruled light green paper, both sides, and on a separate scrap of white paper, both sides; no extant envelope (Lilly).

letter this a.m. to you] Probably Letter 20.

Your three come now] Letters 9, 12, 14, and 15. Letter 12 was most likely enclosed with one of the others.

Dickie] Ruth Ethel Dickie (1876–1956) was head nurse (1911–1913) and later matron (1913–1933) at the Norland Institute in London, which trained nannies and cared for young children up to the age of seven whose parents lived abroad. Omar Pound was boarded there until 1933, when he went to live with Mrs. Dickie and her only daughter, Mary, in Felpham, Sussex. Hilda Doolittle's daughter, Perdita, was at the Norland a few years before. Mary Dickie (b. 1910) taught art, painting, and weaving. Ruth Dickie's letters to A. V. Moore in 1945–1946 show that she disapproved strongly of EP and questioned his sanity (Lilly).

duplicate piece to Casa 60.] An extra copy of the "Oh to be in England" (or "Leacock") extract from Canto 80 which EP wanted passed on to Olga Rudge in Sant'Ambrogio. See Letter 14n.

god—sinagogue] DP responds to the typed canto extracts that she received in EP's Letters 9 and 14. The lines, "each one in the name of his god / So that in the synagogue in Gibraltar," occur in Canto 76 (lines 68–69), as does "Teofile's bricabrac Cocteau's bricabrac" (line 49). "Pull down yr. vanity, & the having acted" refers to the conclusion of Canto 81:

co Provost's Office,
MTOUSA DTC
APO 782, U.S. Army ARMY LOCAL
co P.M. New York
[?9 October 1945]

Mao

Re pass port, probably quickest is to write to Genova/ "AS mother of a son in the U.S. Army (give Omar's number etc.) I trust you will accelerate putting my passport in order, so that I can get money from england, needed urgently for current expenses AND to maintain my mother in law, I.W.P. american, as the present prices render lire you send her inadequate for comfort at her age." DONT lay off any of the other measures you were to take about it, you can improve the phrasing, ~~but stiffish?? Isabel~~ might even edit it. oh yes, son in american army, who did not wait to be conscripted but volunteered, now in army of ~~oc?~~ France etc. I request that you manage to get my passport in order without unnecessary delay, (guess that is better phrase) so that I can get my money from england/ current exp/ and american mother in law etc.

Did I suggest that McLeish be asked about Roger Baldwin of Civil Liberties Union (Isabel may have ideas on Civ. etc.) Mebbe leave it.

Will you look up the two, or even the 3 ideograms on next sheet. Wrote yesterday, so won't burden office with long letter to look thru.

love Mao E

When you next send on anything to Mary, send this slip.

I want the epithet used for swineherd at Odysseus model pig farm. Think it was theos [οεος οεος συβολκος] also the correct greek form of line re/ Elpenor, must be in the Nekuia? man of no fortune and with a name to come.

22 DOROTHY TO EZRA

Villa Raggio
Cerisola
Rapallo
Wed p.m., 10 Oct 45

Dearest.

I posted a letter this a.m. to you. Your three come now. I am writing Moore on the point that you were sending yr. own stuff - I think its v. important. Also to Drummond: & telling Moore to let TSE. [Eliot] know, & telling him of stuff ready to be printed.

Please be very plain & explicit in such matters to me. You'll probably get letters from me written before I saw you, with news of various people. Nelly [Tucker] dead, Angold dead - Parkyn's old wife aged 85 - dead.

I had written various letters as soon as I got back. Charming word from Swabey, in Essex. News from Agnes [Bedford], from Dickie. Moore sent on one from OP [Omar Pound]. I am being charged income-tax at 10/- in £.

Pull down thy vanity,
I say pull down.
But to have done instead of not doing
this is not vanity (lines 166–69)

The page numbers that DP mentions are from EP's two extracts beginning "with a teapot from another hotel" (117, 119, 122, 124, 127) and "Oh to be in England now that Winston's out" (231, 233, 237). (See Letters 9n and 14n.) What struck her as irregular page numbering was the result of EP's practice of keying his typescript pages to the manuscript pagination: since each typed page contained between two and four manuscript pages, the typescript pagination appears to skip (Beinecke and Houghton).

no lynx canto yet] See Letters 14n and 24n.

23 Notes. In black ink on a sheet of graph-ruled paper folded double and written on four sides; no extant envelope (Lilly).

Yrs to hand of Oct. 4.] Letter 16.

fantastic journey back] From the DTC to Rapallo. See Introduction and Letter 18.

Ronnie re. t.b.] Ronald Duncan's wife, Rose Marie, was suffering from tuberculosis. See Letter 16n.

Munson] On 17 October 1945, Capt. Leigh J. Monson issued Allied Military Government permit no. 889470, "Movement of Civilians," for DP to travel from Rapallo to Genova.

the 117. pages etc.] The typed canto extracts that DP had received from EP. See Letters 9n, 14n, and 22n. DP and Olga Rudge used the Caffè Jolanda, run by the Majerna family, as a mail drop and message center. See Letters 3n and 13n.

Rudy] Rudolph Dolmetsch. See Letter 16n.

Bremen Port Command] Omar was assigned to the Town Major's office, Headquarters Command, Bremen Port Command, an American section of the British zone of occupation in West Germany, where he dealt mainly with housing for German civilians and transient foreign officers (British, French, and Russian).

duplicating his letter] A duplicate copy of the provost marshal's letter of permission, which DP had requested, reached DP on 13 October. See Document 9.

painter friend] Edgardo Rossaro, whom DP visited on 11 October 1945. See Letter 2n.

The other & his sister] Giuseppe Soldato. See Letter 12n.

Haven't yet had time to read yr. Cantos. Am sending duplicate piece to Casa 60. at once.

Mao!

D.

Later. Escaped to bed early & read yr. Cantos. I find much that is lovely: I find a lot that, on one reading, I can't hitch together - I don't like the sound of - god - sinagogue - most uncomfortable. Of course my poor mind hasn't been thinking along such lines these last 2 – 3 years! & it takes me Time to get back there.

Ma! [well!] am I thankful you've done some more! What seems to come from more recent experience is v. interesting. No lynx canto yet. Theophile en français. Pull down yr. vanity, & the having acted - good. I have recd pages numbered 31, 33, 37. and 117, 19, 22, 24, 27 - & ~~the~~ in duplicate ~~of~~ "Oh to be in England——" Mary Dickie writes many landmarks in London are gone.

Always

D.

Key to my studio with the Corradis at 12/5.

Enclosed letter from [Giuseppe] Soldato - recd in Aug

23 DOROTHY TO EZRA

Villa Raggio
Cerisola
Rapallo
Oct. 13 1945.

Oh! Mao!

Yrs to hand of Oct. 4. Hope you will have recd from me by now.

I had a somewhat fantastic journey back here: the snow was also on Carrara mts - most magnificent - I spent that night in Massa - of wh. more anon. There's now a terain [sic] at 6.p.m. from La Spezia as far as Sestri - & thence to Genova by a waiting autobus. My! but I was tired! but so exhilarated by having seen you - Hope I had good effect on you! I have written Ronnie re. t.b. borax. I was hunting the new Governor this a.m. (who was out - an American this time - name of Munson - with a Russian jewess as inter- preter - I rather liked her.) & ran into Olga [Rudge]: but had very short talk - I had just left the 117. pages etc. at Dante's [caffè] for her to copy. When I have clear copies of the three lots you have sent me, I shall proceed by degrees to send them to Eng. I have heard from Agnes [Bedford]. Another letter today from Ida [Mapel]. She says my first to her was censored - I can't imagine what! & she hears censorship is now lifted. . . She has had a consultation, "& learn what I can about procedure. Now that the Japs are on the run we all feel more sure of things." I will [write] her again presently - wrote after I'd seen you. I will connect up with Rudy, in time. Yrs via Agnes.

The kid [Omar Pound] has a new address: Bremen port Command: so I don't see any chance of seeing him - I'm sorry: I'm curious.

24 Notes. Typed with black ribbon on a thin sheet of white paper, one side, with pencil additions, corrections, and initial. *EP included a carbon copy of this letter on heavier white paper, with minor additions and corrections, and marked in ink, "Censored JS" (Lt. Col. John Steele). On the carbon copy, DP red-penciled sections to quote to correspondents and marked the back, "attended to 31st Oct." Envelope addressed to DP at Villa Raggio, postmarked "U.S. Army Postal Service 549, Oct 24 1945," and marked by DP in black ink, "recd Oct 31st." We have integrated the two versions in our text of the letter (Lilly).*

birthday "lynx" canto] EP enclosed five typed, pencil-revised pages containing the latter part of Canto 79 and the first page of Canto 80. The extract begins, "2 cups for three altars. Tellus [γέα] feconda" (Canto 79, line 117), and ends, "Do they sell such old brass still in 'Las Américas'" (Canto 80, line 31). These pages, accompanied by a small rectangle of Italian cardboard with DP's note, "birthday S.14 '45," are now at the Houghton Library in the collection bequeathed by Professor Craig La Drière. For a description of the "lynx canto," see Letter 14n.

Beard's] Charles Austin Beard (1874–1948) taught history and politics at Columbia University (1904–1917) and wrote several studies of American history that EP admired, including *An Economic Interpretation of the Constitution* (1913) and *The Republic: Conversations on Fundamentals* (1943), which appeared in Armed Services Edition P-29. See also Letters 14n and 26.

cheap books] Armed Services editions. See Letter 14n.

howling for my blood] In a letter to EP of 4 September 1945, Laughlin said that EP would be disappointed in the attitude of some of his friends in the United States (Lilly).

Chinese and Adams cantos i.e. 52–71] Cantos *LII-LXXI* (1940), on the Chinese dynasties and the life and thought of John Adams.

Pearl Buck] Pearl S. Buck (1892–1973), American novelist and missionary to China. Her portrayal of China, as in *The Good Earth* (1931), contributed to understanding between cultures, and she received the

Am still hoping you may turn up some time. We always have pasta & some Green pea army soup in the house - & at the moment we gorge on sweet potatoes.

Nelly [Tucker] died shortly before Harry [Tucker] - hence no mention - Charming word from Swabey. I have answered & given him yr. address - but time, time; so long the posts.

Angold dead - I don't know how or when.

I am getting stupider as I get older. Of course all these last, apparently, scraps, of cantos, are your self, the memories that make up yr. person. Is one then only a bunch of memories? i.e. a bunch of remains of contacts with the other people? Gawd - but it might be a reason for making the other people's memories contain something pleasant, from oneself.

I am enclosing a letter from Omar to A.V.M. [Moore]. The latter, faithful man, has sent on several to me, written to himself: its v.g of him.

Have pondered yr. cantos. Will now get them typed at No. 60 - via Dante's [caffè] so they should be safe.

Always yours

D.

Dont know if its in yr. province to thank the Pr. Marshall from me for duplicating his letter. I am sorry I troubled him - again - post was so very long.

I visited our painter friend - most depressed. The other & his sister safe & well.

Enclosed scribble from Omar.

24 EZRA TO DOROTHY

Co Provost's Office
MTOUSA DTC
APO 782, U.S. Army, Army LOCAL
co Post Master New York
14 Oct. 1945

Mao

Still no news that you got back to Rapallo O.K. Am sending with this your birthday "lynx" canto. Dont know that others have reached you. You better keep this copy, not transmit yet awhile.

Have just read half of Chas A. Beard's "The Republic" ought to be in the U.S. required reading for all capable of understanding it. Also now that reading matter exists AMG [Allied Military Government] might possibly let you have some, army edition of "Time" etc. for mother. Apparently there is some of this reading matter available and AT LAST cheap books as I have been wailing for for past 30 years.

Will you express to Jas [Laughlin] my admiration for Beard. Tell him to go on writing to me (give him this address) say his letter a bit too vague to be of use. I mean thank him. Tell him I wd/ love to know WHICH of my "firends" [sic] are howling for my blood. No resentment. I am merely interested to know how much ANYONE has actually heard, what they have understood. Did it do any good? Thank him for advice. Say I

1938 Nobel Prize in literature. EP thought highly of her and corresponded with her before and after World War II.

W. E. Woodward] William E. Woodward (1874–1950), American journalist, historian, and biographer. EP admired two of his books, *George Washington: The Image and the Man* (1926) and *A New American History* (1936), which he praised in the *New English Weekly* in 1937 as a "consecutive story of America written with to-day's consciousness," exposing much "that our public enemies and your (English) public enemies would like to keep hidden" (*Poetry and Prose* 7:130, 132). Woodward also wrote *Tom Paine: America's Godfather, 1737–1809* (1945) and an autobiography, *The Gift of Life* (1947). He served on various business advisory boards during FDR's first term in office and corresponded with EP in the 1930s about economics, Social Credit, and FDR.

Claude Bowers] Claude Gernade Bowers (1878–1958), American journalist, historian, and ambassador to Spain (1933–1939) and Chile (1939–1953). EP read his articles in the *New York World* and urged him in 1928 to advocate "abolition of passport IDIOCY, visas etc. and generally kicking the bureaucracy back into its kennel" (Lilly). Of Bowers's several historical studies, EP praised *Jefferson and Hamilton: The Struggle for Democracy in America* (1925) and often cited *The Tragic Era: The Revolution After Lincoln* (1929), a reassessment of Andrew Johnson and Republican Radical opposition during the Reconstruction. EP mentions Bowers in Cantos 81 and 86.

his legal friend] Probably Julien Cornell, the New York attorney whom Laughlin suggested as EP's defense counsel in his letter to EP of 4 September 1945 (Lilly). See Letter 33.

a plus b theorem] See Letter 17n and Documents 3–5n.

25 Notes. In black ink on a sheet of graph-ruled paper folded double and written on four sides; no extant envelope (Lilly).

Two, 8th & 9th Oct:] Letters 19 and 21a/21b.

three lots of cantos] The extracts enclosed in Letters 9 and 14 (q.v.).

John St.] No. 8 John Street, the offices of Shakespear & Parkyn, suffered some war damage, but the surrounding area (High Holborn and Gray's Inn Road) was badly bombed.

Tami] Tami Koumé, Japanese abstract painter who lived in Paris in the 1920s and was killed in the 1923 Tokyo earthquake. EP discussed Noh drama with him and organized a show of his paintings in Paris. EP's translation of *Ta Hsio: The Great Digest*, completed at the DTC, ends with an epigraph derived from Koumé—"We are at the crisis point of the world" (*Confucius* 89)—and it may be this sentiment to which DP refers here. EP recalls "Tami's dream," a painting that hung in Olga Rudge's house in Venice, in Canto 76 (line 308).

Laval] Pierre Laval (1883–1945), French politician who served twice as premier in the 1930s and later advocated Franco-German cooperation. During World War II the Vichy government was established by Marshal Pétain to control the part of France not occupied by the Germans, but by 1942, when Laval had full dictatorial powers, Vichy had become virtually a tool of Germany. Laval defended himself eloquently at his treason trial but was sentenced to death on 9 October and executed on 15 October 1945. Vidkun Quisling (1887–1945) assisted the German conquest of Norway and was premier under German occupation (1940, 1942–1945). He was condemned to death in Oslo for high treason on 10 September and shot on 24 October 1945. In a 1941 radio talk EP defended Quisling's right to safeguard Norway's "INTERNAL affairs" and to promote "Autarchy for Norway, and co-operation BY Norway and foreign states" (Doob, 403, 404). EP refers to "Vidkun" in Canto 84 (line 79), and to Laval and Pétain in Canto 76: "L. P. gli onesti" (the honest or honorable ones) (line 245).

E. M. Gray] Ezio Maria Gray (1885–1969), a journalist, was one of the founders of the Italian Nationalist Association in 1910 and was on the Fascist Grand Council (1925–1926). He was also a radio commentator and directed the Milan paper, *Gazzetta del Popolo*, during the Salò Republic. Condemned to death after the war, he received amnesty and later was active in neo-fascist politics.

Ld. Strabolgi] Lord Strabolgi (Joseph Montague Kenworthy) (1886–1953), lieutenant commander in the Royal Navy and Opposition Chief Whip in the House of Lords (1938–1942). He wrote books on military history and naval strategy, including *The Conquest of Italy* (1944).

want the Chinese and Adams cantos i.e. 52–71 sent to a few <u>adults</u>. (he can charge it to me) namely Chas. Beard; Pearl Buck, W. E. Woodward, Claude Bowers also his legal friend. To see if any of 'em grasp the constitutional points. Let him tell Beard I admire "The Republic." Whether ANY of 'em can conceive that I have learned anything in the past thirty years or the past five or six.

Whether he, Jas, realises AT ALL that all but two items of my program are now official and orthodox in England or in the U.S. or in Both. One point on which I am not intemperate and the other not yet time for. The Douglas a plus b theorem tacitly accepted as basis of all public spending etc. etc. Get him off the subject of me personally onto the larger issues.

If there is any money due on royalties let him send it to you or to Olga [Rudge], or let him lend on my security. Of course it is Miss Ida's [Mapel] opinion I want MOST and HER account of what really has occurred in the U.S. since 1940 or 1939.

love Mao E.

Jas' address is New Directions, etc.

25 DOROTHY TO EZRA

> Villa Raggio
> Cerisola
> Rapallo
> Oct: 15. 1945.

Oh Mao.

Two, 8th & 9th Oct: from you this a.m. I have written to Olga [Rudge], who now has yr. copies of three lots of cantos sent to me. I am asking her to make copies for me to keep here, & another to send away—Ronnie [Duncan] or somebody. I guess they must be pretty good as the old Lady's [Isabel Pound] comment at lunch was that she was much disappointed in them: "after five months undisturbed (sic!) I expected something more valuable" & was most grumpy & childish - I didn't argue! Moore says there is much damage in the neighbourhood of John St. I fully expected NO house at all. I daren't write direct to Mary [Rudge]: unless you specify - I wish you would: it might be convenient but I am afraid of contaminating her.

I am considering who here would be of use as witnessing to yr. always excellent civic behaviour - All sorts of odds & ends ask most tenderly after you. Today the youngish woman with vegetables in the market: calling you il poeta. We had a long talk. Her husband in, on v. inadequate. Pep [Giuseppe Soldato] is safe somewhere with the sister. Our painter friend [Edgardo Rossaro] dreadfully depressed - but has not been in trouble so far. They seemed most pleased to see me. Will you let me write to Moore that you'll take [Lloyd] Stryker? or are you allowed to write to Moore as the solicitor? I dont believe in yr. trying to defend yrself, yourself - You always have such a rush of ideas & go off so far to the edge - trying everybody's patience and exhausting them!

Did I say Omar now has address Bremen port command. I am sorry as I shan't see him now - & he will be losing his french again. I have written him to write U.S. Embassy

Anthony Salle] Anthony Joseph Salle (b. 1895), bacteriologist who did key research on leprosy in Hawaii and elsewhere and taught at the University of California at Los Angeles.

the Ch. Characters] The Chinese characters that EP inquires about in Letter 21a/21b.

Swabey's letter] Possibly Henry Swabey's letter to DP of 31 August 1945, received by her on 5 October (Lilly).

26 Notes. Typed with black ribbon on two sheets of white paper, one side each, with pencil additions, corrections, and initial; marked on the first page "Censored JS" (Lt. Col. John Steele). DP marked three sections in red crayon to quote to A. V. Moore. Envelope addressed to DP at Villa Raggio, postmarked "U.S. Army Postal Service 549, Oct 24 1945," and marked by DP in black ink, "recd 31 Ott" (Lilly).

yrs of 6th.] Letter 18.

Bracco] See Letter 16n.

Jas has other suggestion] Julien Cornell as defense counsel for EP. See Letters 24n and 33.

Douglas] Major C. H. Douglas. See Documents 3–5n.

Jeff Mark] Jeffrey Mark (b. 1898), British author of *The Modern Idolatry, being an analysis of usury & the pathology of debt* (1934) and *Analysis of Usury, with Proposals for the Abolition of Debt* (1935). EP admired both works, and his annotated copy of the latter is at HRHRC. A composer of music on Scottish themes, Mark was also involved with *Prosperity* (London), which printed an early version of EP's Canto 45 ("With Usura") in February 1936. Mark agreed with most of Silvio Gesell's ideas but found the Social Credit scheme of Major Douglas to be doctrinaire and based on fallacy, as he noted in letters to EP in the 1930s (Beinecke).

Chambers-Hunter] William Keith Abercrombie Jopp Chambers-Hunter (1893–1958) fought with the Seaforth Highlanders during World War I and lost an arm in 1916. The British Colonial Office sent him to West Africa to help run plantations taken from the Germans in the Cameroons. He later returned to Scotland and became an active member of the British Union of Fascists in Aberdeen. In 1939 he published *The British Union and Social Credit*, which praised the theories of Major C. H. Douglas. He resigned from the BUF because they would not fully endorse Douglas's proposals.

Johnnie Hargrave] John Gordon Hargrave (1894–1982), an English Quaker, served in the Royal Army Medical Corps at Gallipoli, was invalided out in 1916, and returned to work as a cartoonist and an art manager of a publishing firm. Later, he became a dynamic leader of the Social Credit Party of Great Britain (earlier called the Green Shirt Movement for Social Credit) and was an economic adviser to the government of Alberta (1936–1937) when it was experimenting with Social Credit. Hargrave broke with Douglas in 1938. EP owned a copy (now at HRHRC) of his novel *Summer Time Ends* (1935), and

London expressing his astonishment at my situation etc. etc. I have written McLeish also. I have written to the Chase [National Bank] simply telling 'em to send me money - on a chance—Anyway I have promises of 5,000 lire from three people, (none of them rich) which would keep us going for three months barring accidents. I feel like Tami, something must turn up. Are you allowed to receive newspaper clippings from me? Italian. There's the arrangements re Bank of Eng. Laval condemned to death: Quisling also. Eng. mines to be nationalized 1. July '46. E. M. Gray has 20. years.

Ld. Strabolgi proposes to make Palestine into a Brit. Dominion. USA war industries will not be demobilized. One Anthony Salle, Univ. Calif. has a cure for t.b. It can be extracted from the air. The Univ. popolare frequently has a notice in papers of lectures -

I'll try to deal with the Ch. Characters - It will take me a little while - to find time & strength together.

Yes. there is a lot here & there about U.S.A.'s friendship for Italy, & helping her. Well well.

I can't write a better hand, sorry, censor - & can't type.

Love always D.

Am enclosing Swabey's letter to me, have kept his address.

26 EZRA TO DOROTHY

co Provost's Office
MTOUSA DTC
APO 782, U.S. Army LOCAL
15 Oct [1945]

Mao

yrs of 6th. Glad to know you weren't fruz in snow on Bracco. But there are lacunae in yr/ account. Did you walk from Viareggio to Massa, and from Sestri to Rap? tunnels full of smoke? etc. She expatiate and explicitify.

Wrote Moore to do nothing about [Lloyd] Stryker / certainly nothing of that sort in haste. Jas has other suggestion etc. etc.

I mostly want to know if anyone heard? understood? if it did any good, and if so if anyone knows it did any good? Go on writing. What about Douglas, Jeff Mark, Chambers-Hunter? Johnnie Hargrave? if any?

Glad you are payin income tax, indicates existence of income. Tell Moore acc [according to] Chas A. Beard "The Republic" you cannot be deprived of yr citizenship save on grounds of having obtained same by fraud, which you certainly didn't.

Mary's [Rudge] of the 7th and Olga's [Rudge] to hand. Will you tell Mary, or send this slip.

I lost a filling sat/ a/m/ which was promptly replaced by efficient dental dept. in the P.M. But this a.m. broke glasses, thank God not my reading glasses. They are sending for new pair tomorrow, but not sure how long etc. to get 'em. So that if you or Mary do come here again, (and November trip wd/ be no joke) ANYhow, bring all of my

thought it "an *absolute record* of the state of English mind in our time" and a "treatment of live economics" (*Poetry and Prose* 6:344; 7:26). They corresponded for years, but Hargrave grew impatient with EP's enthusiasm for Mussolini and his tolerance of Oswald Mosley and the British Union of Fascists. After World War II, he published a weekly Social Credit Party newsletter, *The Message from Hargrave*, which EP received at St. Elizabeths. Gorham Munson describes Hargrave's life and activities in *Aladdin's Lamp* (1945).

Beard "The Republic"] In Chapter 10 of *The Republic: Conversations on Fundamentals* (1943) Charles Beard notes: "The right of citizenship is a constitutional right by birth. Congress cannot deprive anyone of that right. Nor can any executive official, by mere decree, deprive any American citizen, even a naturalized citizen, of citizenship. Persons who hold that right by birth in the United States cannot be deprived of it by any action short of a constitutional amendment" (137). See also Letters 14n and 24n.

Amprim] FBI Special Agent Frank L. Amprim. See Letter 2n.

donation to Congressional Library] Unidentified.

Histoire de la Chine] See Document 7n.

ONE line about currency] In chapter 20, "The Republic in the World of Nations," of Beard's *The Republic*: "But all the democracies have new deals or managed economies of one kind or another. If any government keeps control over its own currency, it will, in practice, more or less manage its economy and foreign trade" (323; p. 425 of Armed Services Edition P-29).In Canto 84 EP mentions Beard's book and its "one line" about "the currency" (lines 32–34).

Dalton's reform] Hugh Dalton, chancellor of the exchequer in the British Labour government. See Letter 8n.

Gesell scrip] See Document 7n.

a plus b theorem] See Letter 17n.

Hilaire] Hilaire Hiler (1896–1966), American painter in Paris in the 1920s, where he ran The Jockey, a nightclub popular with artists and writers, which he decorated with Wild West and Mexican themes. In 1929 EP wrote that the quality of Hiler's art arose "from one of those quite simple operations that often count as the act of genius" (*Poetry and Prose* 5:190) and thought him superior to most English and American painters. Hiler was an authority on color techniques and the history of costume; in 1939 he published, with his father, Meyer Hiler, a *Bibliography of Costume*. At the DTC EP had just read a *Time* magazine review (1 October 1945) of a volume issued by New Directions, *Why Abstract?* (1945), containing comments on modern art by Hiler, Henry Miller, and William Saroyan. The reviewer quipped, "Like so many of his kind, Abstractionist Hilaire Hiler (rhymes with kill-care smiler) writes more understandably than he paints" (74).

glasses that can be found. Dont worry, it is the reading glasses that matter, and they will probably get me at least plain sphericals for distance etc. G.I. (meaning govt. issue).

For Mary [in margin]. I doubt if the new cantos are the best, but lets hope they are no worse than the first 71. Lemme know if any of 'em have arrived.

No there is nothing to collect. Amprim will attend to all manuscripts etc. Nothing more heard about donation to Congressional Library. I made that proposal before I knew that Archie [MacLeish] was no longer librarian, and I reckon it is burried. At any rate have heard nothing about it.

You might say you came when you got chance car, and wrote as soon as you got back.

At any rate DONT try to send any files or books etc. to the U.S.A. that is ALL Amprim's affair. Thank God M. [Mary Rudge] is at St. Ambrogio.

The new Cantos are simpler in parts, there is a certain amount of new technique but good only in so far as no one will see it. The Histoire de la Chine is a lacuna in most occidental heads, even Beard's. "The Republic" is his most readable book, and a lot of work has been done. It is up to date (1943) ONE line about currency, along about page 426.

Dalton's reform mild enough, but that is sane. No one wants it violent, and it SHOULD make possible the publication of a lot of sane material. All the credit cranks etc ought to enter Labour Party and maintain current.

Really now nothing to add except that Doug. [C. H. Douglas] dividends would take ~~nationals~~ most of the government spending out of politics. And that Gesell scrip, at 12 per cent annual is a way to deal with debt and taxes. a plus b theorem is accepted tacitly all over the place. In short one can pretty well retire from that squabble.

Keep on writing.

E.

——————   ——————   ——————   ——————   ——————

P.S.

Mao anyhow, you have no political opinions, and mine being fer the constitution are not subversive. (This to Moore) I meant to type this so you cd/ tear off the bit for Mary, guess you can manage that anyhow. love to Mother

love, mao

E.

Hilaire has done a new book, naturally critics use old joke about its being better than his painting «LSI»

27 Notes. Typed with black ribbon on one side of a torn scrap of white paper initialed in ink, "J.S." (Lt. Col. John Steele), and marked by DP in black ink, "attended to 31st." No envelope: Letter 27 was probably enclosed with Letter 26 (Lilly).

Geoffrey Mark's head] Jeffrey Mark. See Letter 26n.

Brooks Adams] See Document 7n.

Kitson] Arthur Kitson. See Document 6n.

28 Notes. In black ink on a sheet of graph-ruled paper folded double and written on four sides; no extant envelope (Lilly).

two Chinese Characters] DP replies here to EP's queries about Chinese characters in Letter 21a/21b.

new A.M.G.] Capt. Leigh J. Monson, the local Allied Military officer in charge of civilian affairs, replaced Major C. Robinson, who had been helpful to DP and Olga Rudge after EP's capture in May 1945. See also Letters 11n and 23n.

Moss] Herman Moskovitz (b. 1896), born in New York City, served in World War I and later changed his name to Moss. After working in various parts of Europe, he had commercial assignments at the U.S. consulates in Genoa and Rome until Italy entered the war in 1941. In November 1944 he was reassigned on temporary duty to the consulate in Rome, and in May 1945 he was appointed vice-consul at the U.S. consulate general's office in Genoa, in anticipation of their reopening. In October 1945 he was reassigned to Geneva, Switzerland.

Conrad] Joseph Conrad's *The Shadow-Line: A Confession* (1917), Armed Services edition J-273.

"Reckon with the River"] A novel, published in 1941 and issued also as Armed Services edition Q-30, by "Clark McMeekin," the nom de plume of two writers from Louisville, Kentucky, Dorothy Park Clark (1899–1983) and Isabel McLennan McMeekin (1895–1973), who wrote several books together. Set in 1805, *Reckon With the River* tells the story of a New York State family that moves to a riverboat on the Ohio River to hunt for Spanish treasure.

Ginbà] Unidentified.

poems in duplicate] The canto extracts that EP enclosed in Letters 9 and 14 (q.v.).

Laval] Pierre Laval. See Letter 25n.

27 EZRA TO DOROTHY

> co Provost's Office
> MTOUSA DTC
> APO 782, U.S. Army Local
> Oct 16 [1945] to [*sic*]

Mao

No harm if Swabey or John [Drummond] cd get into Geoffry Mark's head the fact that I was given freedom of microphone and took it with condition that I shd not be asked to say anything contrary to my conscience or to my duties as an american citizen, and I never was, asked nor did.

Seem still to be people who don't know that. AND it makes a difference. Also the nature of what was transmitted etc. Brooks Adams, Kitson, etc, NOT axis propaganda.

28 DOROTHY TO EZRA

> Villa Raggio
> Cerisola
> Rapallo.
> Oct. 17. [and 18] 1945.

Dearest Mao.

Well! well! I have been able to find the two Chinese Characters for you. Thought I should have quite forgotten how to look up the dictionary - enclosed on separate sheet.

I introduced myself today to new A.M.G. who is a pukker [proper] American - white-haired & lean, & with a slow manner; & one can also draw a slow smile. He has given me a pass to go on a lorry to Genova to see if I can find Moss re my passport. He says there will be a lot more isolationists after this war - a most charming personality - that the wife should not be penalized. . .

Am reading a Conrad I don't know "The Shadow Line" -memoirs of his first command v.g. In the army books ed. we had a ~~good~~ long work on "Reckon with the River" - quite an enlightening tale of the behaviour of an old family & the River - The ed. seems to have a few readable works listed.

Am now tired, <u>and</u> the electric cooker wall-connection is bust, so I've had to cook below & run up & down a dozen times - the new nuora [daughter-in-law], Ginhà, is most kind to me - & we often use her oven for potatoes etc:

Yours D.

No. 60. [Olga and Mary Rudge] have sent me the poems in duplicate, neatly copied. I am sending to Ronnie [Duncan].

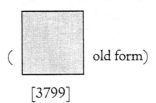

(old form)

[3799]

[3810]

Heuen.
Loud clamorous noise
high words. clamour of grief
& lamentation - incessant weeping of
children.

[3818]

Heuen. fallacious.
false. irregular. noisy
clamourous.

seuen
[9019]

a house or covering, in which winds revolve
& cause to circulate the material
principles in nature. / spread out, expand,
spread out, expand, promulgate
promulg[at]e [?], proclaim to, declare,
summon - a high degree of intelligence.

wang.
[11632]

I don't find anything saying "constant" -
from heart & run-away.
forget. be lost. disregarded
mind absent. escape fr. memory.

I can't at present find the Legge "forget" at all.

Other, Eng., portion of Dict. is at 12/5 [Via Marsala]. I will one day look up

    { constant
    { forget

P.S. Thursday a.m. [18 October]

cooker working on another presa - meno male [outlet - fortunately]. So Laval is gone the way of all flesh. Have joined the local co-operativa - one pays in 200. lire a share - & can buy potatoes, fruit, cheese, farina [flour], at less than the black market price - though always above the tessera [ration-card] price. Elfriede [Bacigalupo] recommended it - & others.

D.

29 Notes. Typed with black ribbon on a thin sheet of white paper, on two different typewriters, the change occurring after "absolute truth"; additions, corrections, and initial in pencil; marked in black ink, "Censored JS" (Lt. Col. John Steele). On the back DP jotted in black ink, "attended to 31st." Envelope addressed to DP at Villa Raggio, postmarked "U.S. Army Postal Service 549, Oct 24 1945," and marked by DP in black ink, "recd Oct 31st." No enclosure has come to light (Lilly).

Unkle George] George Holden Tinkham (1870–1956), big-game hunter, world traveler, and Republican representative from Massachusetts to the Sixty-fourth and thirteen succeeding Congresses (1915–1943). He was noted for his staunch isolationism, defense of blacks' rights, opposition to Prohibition, and, of special importance to EP, a belief that the British Foreign Office and international finance were influencing FDR's foreign policy. EP carried on a massive correspondence with him, and Tinkham visited EP in Europe in 1936; their travels together are recalled in *The Pisan Cantos*. At one point, EP hoped that "Uncle George" would take him on as his private secretary. In 1939 EP saw him during his visit to the United States and told reporters that Tinkham should be nominated for president. EP wrote Katue Kitasono in 1937: "He IS the America I was born in, and that may have disappeared entirely by now" (Redman 176).

death cells] A group of single observation cages so named at the DTC, although former officers and men report that the camp had no facilities for executing prisoners and that those condemned to death were sent to the U.S camp at Averso, outside Naples. EP recalls his reinforced wire cage in Canto 83:

> Nor can who has passed a month in the death cells
> believe in capital punishment
> No man who has passed a month in the death cells
> believes in cages for beasts (lines 64–67)

four months incommunicado] From 24 May to 20 September 1945.

Confucius] For works by Confucius, see Document 7n.

Stalin] Joseph Stalin. See Documents 3–5n and 7. Early in his stay at St. Elizabeths, EP asked Omar Pound to buy him a Georgian grammar, hoping he would have a chance to speak to Stalin in his own language.

Mary and Olga just been in] On John Drummond's advice, Olga Rudge applied to the provost marshal in early October 1945 for permission for Mary Rudge to visit the DTC. Permission was granted, and Olga traveled with Mary to the camp on 17 October and was allowed in also. According to her draft letter to Drummond of 19 October, they were given 2 1/2 hours with EP (OR Papers, Beinecke). In EP's pencil draft of Canto 84, the line "out of all this beauty something must come" (line 71), is followed by the jotting "17 Oct. O & M" (ms page 293, Beinecke).

Jane McLane] Jane McLean (b. 1914), daughter of Alan and Flo McLean, who ran an agency for real estate, insurance, and travel, with offices in New York and Rapallo. Alan's letters to EP show that he was interested in Social Credit and shared EP's views on international finance (Beinecke). In early June 1945 Jane passed through Rapallo and saw, separately, DP and Olga Rudge, who hoped that she and her family could help EP. See also Letter 121.

Chambers-Hunter] See Letter 26n.

Hargrave] John Hargrave. See Letter 26n.

[MTOUSA DTC]
APO 782
17 Oct [1945]

Mao

I think the time has now come when it wd/ be suitable for you to write to Unkle George, The Hon. G.H.T. House of Representatives Office Building Washington D.C. "please forward" Saying that you know I did not want to disturb him or to have him disturbed but that I wd/ certainly be glad for him to know the conditions under which I broadcast if he don't know it already, namely being given freedom of microphone, and accepting on condition that I be not asked to say anything against conscience or against my duties as american citizen. Which conditions were observed all my talks my OWN, backbone of 'em Brooks Adams and other similar matter.

That what has "occurred" namely month in death cells and four months incommunicado happened AFTER Dept of Justice knew this, after their investigator [Frank L. Amprim] had said he was convinced I was telling absolute truth and that they had nothing on which to hold me, and had been thru all of dossier, bank accounts etc. Then tell him about yr passport, stating that you understand nothing of american politics etc., but are mother of son in army, not conscripted but volunteer before being required age. Write clearly.

(enclosed) Say that I have been working on Confucius / that he might like to see the corner stone, (as in new version of Great Learning) and that the second of the Confucian books Chung Yung now really done for first time, and that world order on any other basis is no go, simply wont work. Also that someone who "knows what it is about" ought to be able to talk to Stalin in his OWN language namely Georgian, that I would have done it given the chance. What is the use talking to such a man thru an interpreter.

These two points as my opinion, not yours.

Mary and Olga just been in/ that accounts for change of typewriter in middle of this note. also for not needing to add messages for them. Apparently Jane McLane been thru Rap. [Rapallo] etc.

Love to mother. am rejoicing in new suit, the latest in herringbone twill, TWO piece, as change from coveralls, also a lot of winter wool issued this a.m.

Did I ask in my last about Chambers-Hunter, Douglas, Hargrave. Think I did,

O mao.

Love E

30 Notes. In black ink on a torn scrap of white paper, both sides; no extant envelope (Lilly).

"constant"] See EP's Letter 21a/21b.

witnesses] Under the U.S. Constitution, the Department of Justice was required to produce two witnesses to each overt act of treason. FBI Agent Amprim had great difficulty in locating pairs of Italian radio employees who had observed EP broadcast and understood enough English to testify credibly concerning his remarks. Nevertheless, seven witnesses were flown to the United States in November and put up in first-class hotels at government expense; they were returned to Italy when the treason trial did not materialize.

Mary] For Mary Rudge's visit to the DTC, see Letter 29n.

31 Notes. In black ink on a sheet of graph-ruled paper, one side. On both sides EP penciled tiny Chinese characters and the following numbers, perhaps page numbers from his small Chinese-English dictionary: 138, 142, 166, 181, 192, 195, 198, 207, 213, 226, 257, 339, 372, 408. He also wrote "?echoing chamber" beneath DP's phrase "+ words." No envelope: DP hoped to get Olga Rudge to carry this letter on her visit to the DTC, unaware that Olga had already made the trip on 17 October. In Letter 35 DP tells EP that she is "sending on the letter that I didn't get to her in time to take" (Lilly).

already posted contents] Letters 28 and 30.

Villa Raggio
Cerisola
Rapallo
Oct 18 45

Just hunted up "constant"

chang.
constant. usual.
frequently
manifest.
[310]   display always.

The A.M.G. [Allied military governor] says he's seen a notice that you are off shortly to U.S.A. to Wash: & witnesses. Hoping this may reach you - & that Mary is going to see you.

Yrs always

D.

as from Via Marsala.

Villa Raggio
Cerisola
Rapallo
Oct 18. 1945

Dearest.

Just had a note from Olga, who will carry this if I am not too late. I have already posted contents - yesterday & today a.m.

constant.   chang.   manifest. display always.
constant. usual.
frequently.

[310]

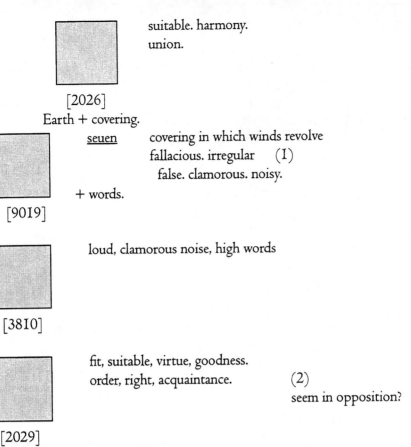

suitable. harmony.
union.

[2026]

Earth + covering.

seuen   covering in which winds revolve
         fallacious. irregular   (1)
              false. clamorous. noisy.

+ words.

[9019]

loud, clamorous noise, high words

[3810]

fit, suitable, virtue, goodness.
order, right, acquaintance.   (2)
                                     seem in opposition?

[2029]

heart & run away.
forget.

[11632]

I haven't yet been able to trace the other which you say Legge gives as 'forget.' Late p.m. to catch Olga early tomorrow.

Yours always

Love

D.

32 Notes. Typed carbon copy on a sheet of white paper, one side; no extant envelope (*OP*). It is not known whether the original ribbon copy of this letter, typed by EP for Major Lucree, who replaced Lieutenant Colonel Steele as commandant of the DTC, was ever sent. Lucree did not have a copy when contacted in 1994, nor could he recall receiving one. See Letter 42, which he did receive. The prior draft of Letter 32 is undated and typed on a sheet of white paper, one side, with no signature (*OP*).

parole] In her letter to Olga Rudge of 5 October 1945, written just after seeing EP, DP said that he "has applied for leave on parole" (OR Papers, Beinecke).

Chas Beard's current vol] *The Republic.* See Letters 14n, 24n, and 26n.

their investigator] FBI Special Agent Frank L. Amprim. See Letter 2n.

To the Officer Commanding   D.T.C. Pisa
Major Lucree   18 Oct 1945

In consideration of the facts now in possession of the Department of Justice; the war being over; the Constitution of the United States being what it is it appears to me that I might seriously request to be sent to Rapallo on parole.

I think you will find that the prison officers are ready to believe that if I gave my word I would keep it.

Apart from character I cannot conceive that a man of my position would be ass enough to try to do his work or expect to have it published were he a fugitive from justice.

It does not make sense. And it would be about as difficult for me to escape from Rapallo, known as I am in that region, as it would to escape from here.

I am not asking to walk into the petty tyranny of minor, irresponsible and anonymous consular officers. I should have to have papers in order, and should also appreciate any steps that can be taken to free my family and friends for [sic] annoyance and delay (of the kind that began after the first world war)

I do not know how much of the case is known to you, but the facts can be placed at your disposal. I may say that any foolishness on my part now would mean throwing away 20 or 30 years work, if that means anything.

very truly yours
[unsigned]

[Prior draft of the preceding letter]
    OC, Lucree

The war being over it seems to me that I might properly request to be sent to Rapallo on parole for the following reasons.

I. The nature of the facts now in possession of the dept. of J.

2. Various constitutional guarantees, which anyone can estimate from Chas Beard's current vol the Repub. if they have not got them in mind without that refresher. ~~Ex post facto~~ The prohibition of ex post facto laws, the ~~habeas corpus~~ and bills of attainder, among other more familiar ~~features~~,

The plain common sense fact that the Prison Officers probably believe that my word will be good, after having had five or six months in which to observe the character of the prisoner.

The fact that I am not ass enough to try a get away from Rapallo, any more than from

33 Notes. In black ink on a small sheet of white paper, both sides; envelope addressed to EP at the DTC, postmarked Rapallo "20.10.45," and stamped received at the Base Post Office "27 OC 45." Enclosure: prescription for EP's glasses, made out by Dr. Mario Corrado of Genoa in March 1943 (Lilly).

letter from John] On 12 October 1945, John Drummond wrote separately to EP and DP, strongly endorsing James Laughlin's recommendation of Julien Cornell as defense counsel. In Laughlin's opinion, Lloyd Stryker, whom Elihu Root, Jr., had suggested, was inappropriate for EP, since he had acquired a reputation for defending "murderers and the like," as Laughlin put it in a letter to A. V. Moore of 30 September 1945, a copy of which Drummond included with his letter to DP. (All these letters are at Lilly.)

Cornell] Julien D. Cornell (1910-1994), EP's defense attorney, graduated from Swarthmore and Yale Law School. A Quaker with a strong interest in civil liberties, he was special counsel to the ACLU in New York on conscientious objectors (1941-1950) and published *The Conscientious Objector and the Law* (1943) and *Conscience and the State* (1944). In 1947 New Directions published his *New World Primer*. Cornell is author of the invaluable work *The Trial of Ezra Pound: A Documented Account of the Treason Case by the Defendant's Lawyer* (1966). He did legal work for the Pounds after 1945-1946, pursuing a writ of habeas corpus and challenging the legality of EP's continued incarceration (until DP asked him to withdraw the appeal in 1948), handling certain intellectual property and estate matters, and dealing with literary infringements.

the Chinese Characters] EP requested the ideograms in Letter 21a/21b, and DP replied in Letters 28, 30, and 31.

the one for Rudy] Canto 81, which EP sent in Letter 9 and asked DP to copy and forward to Rudolph Dolmetsch (see also Letter 16n). The "two pieces of cantos" that Olga and Mary Rudge retyped were the two extracts that EP sent in Letter 14. EP had sent DP's "lynx" extract (from Canto 79) in Letter 24, but she did not receive it until the end of October (see Letters 40 and 41).

Ferrari] A local bank manager.

here. At my age, with my habits, the nonsense of tr of supposing that an author can publish his works while a fugitive from justice or go on with his work,

It just doesn't make sense,

I dont request release merely to fall under petty tyranny of minor, irresponsible and anonymous consular officers.

I shd/ have to have papers in order, and be assured that my friends and relatives wd. be free from minor annoyance and circumlocution.

Would mean throwing away 20 or 30 years work and just doesn't sense [sic].

the belief expressed by their investigator that
I have told him the absolute truth from the beginning
backed up by a quantity of evidence collected by him.
I think you will find that prison officers would expect me
to keep my word if I gave it that is if I were sent to Rap.
I would be there when wanted.

apart from character now
I believe known to various officers in the D.T.C.
seeing how easy it wd be to trace me/

33 DOROTHY TO EZRA

Villa Raggio
Cerisola
Rapallo
p.m. Oct 19 1945.

Dearest.
Just recd a letter from John [Drummond], enclosing a copy of one from Jas [Laugh-lin]. I gather the latter has written you direct: He has found one Cornell 15. William St. N.Y. who seems to be a much more suitable man than Prexy's son [Stryker] - A Quaker, a man of the highest refinement & character. Jas. has known him for some three years & has every confidence in his integrity & good judgement. I think Jas is making himself useful. I wrote out the Chinese Characters you wanted last night, & hope Olga [Rudge] may take them down. I had already sent them by post the day before. She has made clear copies of two pieces of cantos, but not yet the one for Rudy.

No lynx has ever turned up.

Much love oh Mao

D.

New [Allied military] Governor here helping me to open the [bank] box to cut coupons - Ferrari seemed hopeful.

34 *Notes. Typed with black ribbon on a V-mail form on two different typewriters, corresponding to the two dates; pencil additions, corrections, and initial; marked in black ink, "PJW" (1st. Lt. Patrick Joseph White). The form is addressed to DP at Villa Raggio, postmarked "U.S. Army Postal Service 549, Oct 28 1945," and marked by DP in black ink, "recd Nov. 3" (Lilly).*

OUT correspondence rationed] Lieutenant Colonel Steele recalled in 1992 that those in charge of EP knew that his imprisonment was a sensitive political issue and therefore acted in typical army fashion "to protect their butts."

good sense from John] John Drummond wrote several letters to EP in October 1945, urging him to abandon the idea of defending himself and to accept legal counsel (Lilly).

kumrad cummings] Edward Estlin Cummings (1894-1962), American poet, novelist, and painter, called "kumrad" by EP because of his visit to Russia in the 1930s. He served as a volunteer ambulance driver in World War I, was interned in a French concentration camp due to administrative stupidity, and recorded the experience in his novel *The Enormous Room* (1922). He and EP met in Paris in the early 1920s, and EP included his work in *Profile* (1932) and *Active Anthology* (1933). Cummings's visit to Russia resulted in *Eimi* (1933), which EP ranked with Joyce's *Ulysses* and Wyndham Lewis's *The Apes of God*. His many volumes of poetry, including *1 x 1* (1944), combine verbal wit with biting satire on bureaucracy and convention. In his 1942 radio talk "E. E. Cummings Examined," EP told Americans that "your Mr. Cummings is a very great writer, I tell you he follows H. James, and Thoreau, and Whitman. I tell you he is the most intelligent man in America" (Doob 141). In 1945 Cummings gave EP's attorney a check for $1,000 toward legal expenses, saying that the money came from a painting he had sold. Cummings and his wife, Marion, visited EP at St. Elizabeths on several occasions.

Bride's] Bride Scratton. See Letter 18n.

Benchley nonsense] *20,000 Leagues Under the Sea or David Copperfield* (1928; Armed Services Edition M-4), by the American humorist Robert Benchley (1889-1945). In his chapter "The Typical New Yorker," Benchley discusses and quotes from Ford Madox Ford's *New York Is Not America* (1927).

old 'Bib'] Joseph Darling Ibbotson (1869-1952), known as "Bib," taught EP Anglo-Saxon at Hamilton College. He was the college librarian from 1911 to 1936. When Omar Pound decided to go to Hamilton, Ibbotson introduced him to the campus and the dean of admissions. Samuel Hopkins Adams (1871-1958), a graduate of Hamilton College, published over forty books, including *Canal Town* (1944), a historical novel about building the Erie Canal, of which Armed Services Edition R-40 was an abridged version. In the foreword, Adams thanks Ibbotson, "whose scholarly editing has saved me from embarrassing errors." Adams helped bring about the Federal Food and Drug Act (1906) through his articles in *Collier's* exposing patent medicine frauds.

Pea] Enrico Pea (1881-1958), Italian novelist. Working closely with Pea in 1941, EP translated the first volume, *Moscardino* (1922), of his four-volume novel, *Il romanzo di Moscardino*, and published it in James Laughlin's annual, *New Directions* 15, in 1955. The section EP translated depicts a household of lunatic brothers and various sensational incidents. Pea is mentioned in Canto 80. See also Document 6n.

Criterion] For T. S. Eliot's magazine, *The Criterion*, and Ronald Duncan's *Townsman*, see Letter 7n.

ONLY legal advice] DP's father, Henry Hope Shakespear, was a solicitor. DP wrote A. V. Moore on 18 November 1945 that EP's reference was to "a badly broken literary contract & H.H.S. told him that a man will 'rue the day when he starts litigation' if I remember rightly" (OP).

Moss] Herman Moss, U.S. vice-consul in Genoa. See Letter 28n.

"The Republic"] Charles A. Beard's *The Republic*. See Letters 14n, 24n, and 26n.

April 1914] EP and DP were married in London in April 1914, whereupon DP automatically became an American citizen.

co Provost's Office
DTC
APO 782, U.S. Army Local
[Italy]
[19 and 23 October 1945]

19 Oct. Mao: Henceforth my OUT correspondence rationed and Cantos must go via base censor. More good sense from John [Drummond] but I want more information before taking any steps, and probably will not take 'em. If you can get an opinion from the kumrad Cummings, 4 Patchin Place New York. It would be at least interesting. John's handwriting so like Bride's that I thought his letter was from her. Ref/ to Fordie in some Benchley nonsense, and acknowledgement to old 'Bib' in preface to Sam. H. Adams's "Canal Town" rather charming novel as far as I have got, and so far "pleasant" enough for mother. Dunno if some fever scenes or painful events mightn't follow. These cheap books for the troops OUGHT to be useful as publishing habit. Am giving Mary [Rudge] carte blanche to get the Pea or anything else published if Faber or Jas [Laughlin] have the nerve. I thought I had made it clear to Olga [Rudge] months ago, but she asked me to make it still clearer etc. Why dont Faber publish Townsman, as the Criterion is dead? Leaving Ronnie to edit it.

23 Oct. Hell/ second half of that novel not fit for the old lady; charming heroine and beeyewteeful sentiments wasted. You can calm Moore by saying I am following the best and I think ONLY legal advice your father ever gave me, I cert will not rush in precipitate to follow first bit of advice from someone who knows NOTHING about what it is all about. You can help me most by getting yr/ own affairs in order. Moss can scarcely refuse you a letter stating you were REGISTERED at consulate as U.S. citizen between certain dates. Send that to Moore plus statement that the AUTHORITATIVE Chas Beard states in recent book "The Republic" that you can not be deprived on any ground save that of having got it on false pretenses, which you cert did NOT. Also give date, April 1914. Jas sends better suggestion, but NOT GOOD ENOUGH. Oh, mao. Pleasant feeling day/ possibly the thaw, or rise in temperature. Go on writing, you haven't given DETAIL of yr home voyage. Apparently shelter at Red X. in Pisa, so you cd/ start north in a.m. if you come again, but do consider the weather, etc.

will now close. The only rationing is of MY outgoing letters, not on those to me. love to mother. Go on burning incense. Moore to DO nothing yet about me save answer my questions if or when he can.

E.

35 Notes. In black ink on a small sheet of ruled light green paper, both sides; no extant envelope. Enclosure: a small slip of white paper with two Greek phrases from The Odyssey, *copied in Mary Rudge's pencil and DP's pen, as requested by EP in Letter 21a/21b (Lilly).*

from Olga] Olga and Mary Rudge had visited EP at the DTC on 17 October.

sending on the letter] Letter 31.

Dolmetsch canto] Canto 81. See Letters 9n and 16n.

Basil & Angold] Basil Bunting and J. P. Angold. See Letters 8n and 19n.

her brother] Elfriede (Antze) Bacigalupo's two brothers lived in Bremen, where Omar was stationed.

Ranieri's] Prince Ranieri di San Faustino. On 16 October 1945 Ranieri wrote to DP from Rome with suggestions for clearing up her U.S. citizenship (Lilly). See also Document 6n.

Newsweek] *Newsweek* for 1 October 1945: "The treason trial of Ezra Pound, expatriate American poet, will begin in the District of Columbia Federal Court within a month. Pound, who made several hundred propaganda broadcasts from Rome during the war, and a number of Italian witnesses will be flown to the U.S. in a military plane. New and considerably stronger indictments than those returned against him in July 1943 have been prepared" (21).

nothing from you since 13th] Letters 19 and 21a/21b.

36 Notes. In black ink on two small sheets of ruled light green paper, both sides; no extant envelope (OP).

Lloyds] The Law Courts branch of Lloyds Bank in London wrote DP on 10 October 1945 that "within the next few days, I hope to be able to remit to you the sum of £30 and to send you a similar amount during the months of November and December," and that "we have been able to credit your son's account with £100 for the half year ending the 31st December next" (OP).

good wishes for Oct. 30th] EP's sixtieth birthday.

her brothers] Elfriede (Antze) Bacigalupo's brothers. See Letter 35n.

Paolo Zappa] Paolo Zappa (b. 1899), journalist and author, was special Paris correspondent for the Turin newspaper *La Stampa* during the 1930s. His articles on the corrupt influence of gun makers in France appeared anonymously in *La Stampa* in 1932 and were collected under the title *I mercanti di cannoni* (Milan: Corbaccio, 1932). EP urged the importance of this exposé in the *Chicago Tribune*, the *New English Weekly*, and *Il Mare*. In 1938 in *Townsman* EP published a satirical poem, "M. POM-POM," that concluded: "To sell the god damn'd frogs / A few more canon" (*Poetry and Prose* 7:296). Administrative director of *La Stampa* during the Salò Republic, Zappa was arrested after the war and charged with denouncing his antifascist employees to the Germans. He was able to prove that he had written no political articles after 25 July 1943 and had protected members of his staff from political arrest. He was acquitted in May 1946. See also Letter 148.

35 DOROTHY TO EZRA

> Villa Raggio
> Cerisola
> Rapallo
> Oct 22. 1945.

Dearest Ming.

I have had the scrappiest of notes from Olga, saying there was nothing new, except that you had heard from John [Drummond]. I am sending on the letter that I didn't get to her in time to take. Its a repeat of the Chinese. Rain today, at last: & I am wondering how you will get on if, when, its wet & cold. I have now the clear copy of the Dolmetsch canto & am sending to Ronnie [Duncan], for Agnes [Bedford] & Rudy [Dolmetsch]. I wrote Possum [T. S. Eliot] about Basil & Angold. I am enclosing the Greek swineherd & other quote: wh. I have copied & am keeping in case of need in future.

This p.m. I expect Elfriede [Bacigalupo] - we hope to combine now that the Kid [Omar Pound] is in Bremen, some introduction to her brother & get also some news. Ranieri's a brick: but all he elicited was the same story of seeing the people in Genova. Have you seen Newsweek for Oct. 1st? I have had nothing from you since 13th. I am wondering whether you have been allowed to write to Shakespear-&-Parkyn - It should be allowed, to write to yr. solicitor, & always is, I understand.

Ina [Benatti] has just sent us some little cakes - I had taken her a bundle of odds & ends. I am knitting myself a pair of winter stockings with some of that famous wool! In somma [after all], the unimportant continues. Always yours D.

36 DOROTHY TO EZRA

> Villa Raggio
> Cerisola
> Rapallo.
> Oct. 24. 1945.

Dearest Mao.

Today I received a lot of mail: from Moore, John [Drummond] & Lloyds, all saying that they are hoping to forward me money shortly. So let's hope that may settle itself a bit.

And before I forget: all my good wishes for Oct. 30th. & Apollo help us all.

A very long letter from Omar from Bremerhaven - & three of his to A.V.M. [Moore], which the latter so nobly sends on to me. In good health, & evidently has had several from me - He sends a quaint psychological account of his own temperament for me to judge him on: he seems to take v. strongly after his parents! Several points I can explain to him - He still hopes to get leave. He is saving some money out of his allowance: it goes into some kind of army ~~bank~~ deposit & gets 4%, & can be withdrawn wherever he happens to be. He speaks of trying to get educated, when he has done his army job: wonders about London Univ: but I think we could do more for him in a com-

37 Notes. Typed with black ribbon on a V-mail form, with minor pencil corrections; unidentified censor's initials; incomplete postmark. The form is addressed to DP at Villa Raggio, who marked it in pencil, "recd Oct. 7th," an error for "Nov. 7th." Folded and enclosed within the form were two brief messages typed by EP on sheets of white paper: a carbon copy of the 30 October portion; and a carbon message for Mary Rudge, commenting on poems she had sent EP and asking her to greet various people in Sant'Ambrogio (Lilly).

Root] Elihu Root, Jr. See Document 7 and Letter 11n.

"refinement"] Writing to A. V. Moore on 30 September 1945, James Laughlin noted that Julien Cornell was, among other things, a man of the "highest refinement" (Lilly). See Letter 33.

him and Hope] Omar and his maternal grandfather, Henry Hope Shakespear. EP knew Hope in London before World War I.

"Introductory Text Book"] See Documents 6n and 7n and Letter 2n.

H. A. Fack] Dr. Hugo Robert Fack (1885-1954), physician and promoter of the ideas of Silvio Gesell, served in the German army in World War I, was captured, and spent much of the war in a British internment camp. In 1923 he emigrated to the United States and founded the original Gesell group in New York. He was naturalized in San Antonio, Texas, in 1931, where he ran a natural health school and rest home and the Free Economy Publishing Company, which issued works by Gesell and others. He was

fortable home of our own? I don't want to send on his letter at present - It might miss you, & I haven't digested it yet. He works at clerkly job in orderly room & the ~~pos~~ mail dept etc. etc. He says he's hopeless at business of any kind. "I have ambitions to organize Concerts & to have a hand in some musical subjects, although I am unable to play anything except the old recorder." He sends me a poem, wh. he is v. proud of!

> Can I frame in heavy style
> The trials by man of blood & bile
> Amidst aethereal wandr'ings
> I plan the World - but no theme clings.
> I disappear, & do not wait
> The trials of love, or the lusts of Fate.

He seems a pretty queer product! with qualities.

I have just been down to Elfriede, to read her some of the bits abt Germany - She has had a telegram this a.m. from Denmark, saying her brothers are both alive, & the house still standing. News items: Paolo Zappa, alla corte d'assise [at the Assize Courts] - but it doesn't say what for. Truman trying to get military service of two (?) years in U.S.A. A little piece saying to the effect that—(here my head suddenly went blank - !) oh yes! all war industries to be kept on as at present - as far as I made out. I shall soon begin to wish for reincarnation, to make up for all this wasted life, & get back one's own, so to speak. Old Lady [Isabel] pretty boring: & just doesn't "think much of" my best porri [leek] soup - or my minestroni. She might I suppose be much worse! Is there any question of my going to U.S. for you? Isabel would come too - an <u>awful</u> thought.

dearest Ming

Yours   D.

37 EZRA TO DOROTHY

co Provost's Office
DTC
APO 782, U.S Army LOCAL
Italy
[24, 25, and 30 October 1945]

Started 24 Oct. to be mailed after 28th. as am rationed, on output.

Mao/

The egregious Omar has hit the nail plumb bang re counsel in asking "What KIND of a man will he be"? Root suggested a tough one, Jas [Laughlin] pathetically insists on the "refinement" of his candidate. Tell Omar I am sorry I am rationed on sending letters but compliment him on that query. Now have both him and Hope lined

investigated by the FBI for allegedly writing letters supporting Hitler's economic policies, and efforts were made in 1942 to revoke his citizenship. For years Fack published a Gesellite organ, *The Way Out*; in 1946 he was still in San Antonio running a monthly paper called *Freedom and Plenty*, dedicated, as its banner proclaimed, to "Advocating the Application of the Science of Neo-Economics based on the teachings of the South-American businessman and economic thinker, Silvio Gesell, for the establishment of The Natural Economic Order (N.E.O.) permitting Scientific Constitutional Government and the realization of True Democracy." Fack, who corresponded with EP over many years, wrote him and DP several times in 1945-1946 to offer money, food, and moral support. For Silvio Gesell, see Document 7n.

"Ida"] DP's mention of "Ida" (Ida B. Mapel) in Letter 23 put EP in mind of Ida Lillian (Pound) Busha (1858-1949), eldest daughter of Albert Coleman Pound (1831-1913), brother of Thaddeus Coleman Pound (1832-1914), EP's grandfather. She married Charles Thomas Busha, Sr. (1858-1930) in 1885. Their son, Charles Thomas Busha, Jr. (1890-1956), served in World War I as a captain, married Harriet Sanders of Montana, and later practiced law in Washington, D.C., where he defended Indian territorial claims. See also Letter 47n and Pound family chart (p. 000). For Ida B. and Adah Lee Mapel, see letter 9n.

Gerhart?] Gerhart Münch (b. 1907?), German pianist, arranger, and composer, who visited Rapallo in the 1930s and performed in the Tigullian concerts arranged by EP. His wife's name was Vera. EP greatly admired his "La canzone de li ucelli [*sic*]" (Song of the Birds), an arrangement for violin and piano of Francesco da Milano's sixteenth-century lute adaptation of Clément Janequin's choral arrangement of a song possibly by the troubadour, Arnaut Daniel. EP, who believed that the sound of birds persisted through all these adaptations, declared in *Guide to Kulchur*: "One of the rights of masterwork is the right of rebirth and recurrence" (250). He reproduced the music for the violin part in *Townsman* (January 1938) and in Canto 75.

yr/ visit] DP's visit to the DTC on 3 October.

G.I. spectacles] See Letter 26.

Viola] Viola Jordan, née Baxter. EP first met her around 1905 when he was a student at Hamilton College and visited her family in Utica, New York. She later married and lived with her husband and children in Tenafly, New Jersey. EP enjoyed her cheerful, gossipy letters, and he and DP corresponded with her all through the St. Elizabeths period.

Bacon] Francis (Frank) Sherman Bacon (1877-1941), an insurance broker originally from Bridgeport, Connecticut, who had worked for a sugar company in Cuba (1898-1910). EP saw him in New York City in 1910, and again in Paris in 1922. When Bacon married in 1928, he and his wife, Alice, went to Rapallo for their honeymoon. EP visited him in Greenwich, Connecticut, in 1939. Much of Canto 12 is devoted to "Baldy" Bacon's business exploits and urban buccaneering. Alice (Miller) Bacon was born in Montevideo, Uruguay, in 1903, and in her early years lived for a time in the Weston boardinghouse in New York. She wrote DP on 6 November 1946 that she had recently remarried and was running her late husband Frank's business (Lilly). See also Letter 54.

yr letters a gt/ comfort] DP's Letters 28 and 30, which included ideograms. It is possible that by the time EP reached the end of his letter (the 30 October entry) he had also received DP's Letter 33. Her Letter 31, containing more ideograms, was mailed after a delay and may not yet have reached EP.

Ruth] For Ruth and Hugh Dalton, see Letter 8n.

up. Charming letter from Moore today. Tell Omar I favour a defender who has written a life of J. Adams and translated Confucius. Otherwise how CAN he know what it is about? I never suggested that Root take case, but wanted him to be aware of it. Also cd/ witness as his speech at Hamilton commencement was based on my "Introductory Text Book" and he can hardly have forgotten it. As a corporation lawyer he wd/ probably never get a client again if he touched it, at least not of his present lot. H. A. Fack, S. Antonio Tex. shd/ be told of the amount of Gesellite propaganda I have printed since he lost touch with me. Had to think what you meant by "Ida" (Homer's cousin etc). Adah Lee is Adah Lee but her big sister is "Miss Ida." (these nuances) Elfriede's [Bacigalupo] brother is or was chess champ. in Bremen. Cd Omar dig out Vera and Gerhart? I imagine Vera will have contacted U.S. consul etc. re above, Moore said Omar wd like to hear from me, hence my apology. But tell him I am much pleased with him. Make no mistake yr/ visit cert/ did me worlds of good. Only worry as to its being too hard a trip under present conditions. Magnificent pr/ G.I. spectacles arrived some days ago, so no worry for you on that score.

25th/ What a brute one is and the way one forgets people's existence. Do write pore old Viola, Mrs V. B. Jordan 192 Jefferson Rd/ Tenafly N.Y. [sic] that I have survived one month death cells, four month solitary, that you have finally seen me and that I am recovered mentally and physically. Also state conditions under which I broadcast in case by chance she don't know. Same to Bacon better to Mr AND Mrs in case Frank has crocked up, F. S. Bacon, 80 Maiden Lane New York City, unless you have Greenwich add? Conn. Address. Conn Connecticut. I think it was North Rd. You may get fairly queer reply from Viola, to overtop Isabel's wildest/ but she will be on the job as to sending coffee or anything else as soon as transport exists. Not her fault we didn't [get] coffee for years AND years.

30 Oct. Mao yr letters a gt/ comfort. Thanks for ideograms. My memory was O.K. I wonder if even John [Drummond] realizes that economic thought has moved on during the past 5 years, not only inside my head. Brain wave Friday to ask you to write Ruth to tell Hugh [Dalton], etc, then paused. BUT, not "ideas" plain historic fact IGNORED probably because they simply do not KNOW.

I could help. for moment enough to say that I hope all the credit cranks etc. will come in and help him, as I do not think his job is easy. Dont know if it [is] old age, but I begin to wait to state definite plan, until I am asked, if that will ever be. Wonder if John [Drummond] has been able to read any of my recent stuff. Finis, .ilit [limit?] of communique, love E.

38 Notes. In black ink on two small sheets, one white (written on both sides), the other light green and ruled (written on one side); envelope addressed to EP at the DTC, postmarked Rapallo "27.10.45," and marked in blue pencil by a U.S. censor (Lilly).

No yaller dog] DP plays on a term of abuse that EP used in his polemical writings to mean cowardly or dishonest. In his 1942 radio talk "Indecision," he declared: "That yaller hound Dawg Franklin Roosevelt was complainin' the other day about 'indecision' or people favorin' indecision. I trust there is nothin' Undecided about my position" (Doob 84). DP's poem may have been written earlier than the rest of Letter 38, at some point after her 3 October visit to the DTC, which it describes.

Ming Mao, bright-haired one] For "Ming," see Letter 13n; for "Mao," Letter 3n.

Nerina] Nerina Pagliettini, Ina Benatti's daughter. See Letters 5n and 11n.

Hy. Adams' Democracy] Possibly *Democracy: An American Novel* by Henry Adams (1838-1918), published anonymously in 1880, which tells of two sisters who move to Washington, D.C., to observe political life. Their encounters with intrigue, corruption, and the lust for power are vividly portrayed. "Old Granite" is thought to represent President Rutherford B. Hayes. But see Letter 39 for a different Adams work that DP was reading.

Wallace] Edgar Wallace (1875-1932), British writer of detective stories and thrillers, admired by EP for his fertile imagination, narrative pacing, and colorful underworld argot. His first famous thriller, *The Four Just Men*, appeared in 1905. Other works, such as *The Brigand* (1927), comment on financial corruption. Shortly before his death, he was working on the screenplay of *King Kong* (1933). EP told Ronald Duncan: "Edgar Wallace knew a thing or two about flow. Don't under-estimate writers who've got flow" (Duncan, *All Men Are Islands* [London: Rupert Hart-Davis, 1964], p. 160)

[Rapallo]
[27 October 1945]

No yaller dog.
Black huts
dark tents behind,
Levelled & arid flatness -
Camp EM Tousa
Disciplinary Training Centre.
A great draught pushed from the heavy mountains
Sweeping over the walks.
all washed out   }
curtained   }
obliterated   } by the quick clasp
and sudden glow of intimacy
Ourselves joined again
After five months of half-life.
Ming Mao, bright-haired one.

For five days I was undivided from you
Smoothing your wrist & ankle -
        Apollo
        O Apollo
        accept the olibanum
        look after your own.

Oh Mao!

About midnight, scribbling, it seemed passable - just - Now I don't think it has much value, except perhaps as a letter! Hoping its not an annoyance —

Oct 27.

Still no letters from you. Tons of water, mercifully. Nerina losing her figure, but so radiance [*sic*] & brilliant - I have just begun Hy. Adams' Democracy: I never read it before. Yr. ma reads Hardy, in desperation: but cant distinguish it from a novel qualunque [any old novel] that we had. Prefers it, pas pour le bon motif [not for the right reason] to a good Wallace she had asked for! She's trying hard to educate me. I never try to do the same to her. Tells me the tea grows stronger if you let it stand — — Its very tiring mentally living with a perpetual stream of clichés: almost unbelieveable. I said the overcooked carrots were 'nasty.' "I don't like yr. word" - in her primmest. Is it a strong word in her age of American?

Well. well.

Wishing you well.

I shall try to see you again after Nov. 3. if I can get assurance you are still there.

Always yours D.

39 Notes. In black ink on a sheet of white paper folded double and written on four sides; envelope addressed to EP at the DTC, postmarked Rapallo "30.10.45," and marked in blue pencil by a U.S. censor (Lilly).

Tuesday his birthday] EP turned sixty on 30 October 1945.

no letters from you since 15th] Letters 19 and 21a/21b.

Sir Alexander Flaming] Sir Alexander Fleming (1881-1955), Scottish bacteriologist who shared the 1945 Nobel Prize in physiology and medicine for his discovery and development of penicillin in 1928.

Ley] Robert Ley (1890-1945), German political leader who headed the Labor Front from 1933. He committed suicide while awaiting trial as a war criminal at Nuremberg.

Quisling shot] Vidkun Quisling. See Letter 25n.

Winnie] Winston Churchill (1874-1965) resigned as British Prime Minister in July 1945 when the Labour Party came to power. During the week of October 25 the Belgians announced that when Churchill visited their country on 15 November he would receive the Freedom of the City of Antwerp and an honorary degree from Brussels University. He also received other honors and attended various official ceremonies. EP expressed his unqualified disgust for Churchill in *The Cantos*, radio talks, and elsewhere.

That lynx] DP's "lynx" extract (from Canto 79), which EP had sent in Letter 24. See Letters 40 and 41.

Adams Democratic dogma] *The Degradation of the Democratic Dogma* (1919; New York: Harper & Row, 1969) consists of three essays by Henry Adams—"The Tendency of History" (1894), "A Letter to Teachers of American History" (1910), and "The Rule of Phase Applied to History" (1908)—which analyze the historical process in terms of physical laws such as energy and entropy. The volume was assembled posthumously by Henry's brother, Brooks Adams, who added an essay on the Adams family and Henry's mathematical predictions of events. He notes that Henry "in 1912 named the year 1917 as the date at which a probably revolutionary acceleration of thought would take place, and in fact in that year America was drawn into the war by the resistless attraction of the British economic system" (114). Brooks also describes the disenchantment with democracy felt by his grandfather, John Quincy Adams, at the end of his beleaguered presidency (1828), and concludes: "Men are not swayed by words but by impinging forces, and by suffering. Christ taught that we should love our enemies. To compete successfully the flesh decrees that we must kill them. And the flesh prevails" (86). In 1930 EP criticized Henry's attempts in *Degradation* to discover "an analogy outside history: ie., in astronomy, before he had exhausted the study of relations inside his subject (history) itself" (*Poetry and Prose* 5:230).

Edie's pole] Edie M. Wood, one of DP's Shakespear cousins, lived much of her life in Hampshire.

a friend of Hess] Eugen Haas was a lecturer in German at the University of Genoa before World War II and, with EP and Basil Bunting, was on the "foreign affairs" staff of the literary supplement of *Il Mare*, the Rapallo newspaper. He also served with Bunting on a committee (1933) that arranged concerts in Rapallo. His friend was Aurelio Marasà, who in this period hoped to publish works by EP and to circulate manifestos in his behalf. His letters to EP and DP from 1949 to 1950 talk of plans for a bilingual English-Italian edition of *The Cantos* (Lilly).

Paresce] Gabriele Paresce. See Document 6n and Letter 19.

Cocteau] Jean Cocteau (1889-1963), French avant-garde poet, novelist, critic, dramatist, and filmmaker, whom EP met in Paris in 1921. EP admired him as a brilliant thinker and talker, an accomplished poet, and one of the few geniuses he had known. He had high praise for Cocteau's adaptations of Greek drama, particularly his *Antigone*. In "Jean Cocteau Sociologist" (1935) EP declared: "Cocteau has the freest mind, and the purest, in Europe" (Cookson 435). Cocteau is mentioned several times in *The Pisan Cantos*. See also Letter 40n.

Gide] André Gide (1869-1951), French author and intellectual, awarded the 1947 Nobel Prize in literature. EP's opinion of him may be gathered from his remarks in *Guide to Kulchur* on the French literary scene after World War I: "The war had thrown up a few stuffed monkeys, third rate gallic effigies, cranks who hadn't even the excuse of being British to account for their holding the tosh of Manchester they emitted, the bunk of a Romain Rolland, the vacuity of a Gide" (88).

Villa Raggio
Cerisola
Rapallo
Sunday Oct 28 1945

Oh Mao.

Tuesday his birthday: well, anyway he's accomplished a good few jobs! & wasted precious little time. I have had no letters from you since 15th: don't know how the hitch occurs.

Items of news:-

Nobel Prize 1945 for medicine goes to Sir Alexander Flaming discoverer of penicillina.

Ley has committed suicide.

Quisling shot.

Winnie has been invited to Belgium where he will receive the honorary citizenship of <u>Anvers</u> & Brussels.

Do write me a word about penicillina. You mentioned it before - (for Ronnie [Duncan]) but I have never seen anything in the papers. [∴] conclude its for syphylis? All foreigners to register, & get their carta d'identità [identity card] stamped: I have my c.d.'d - tomorrow will go to municipio [town hall].

That lynx has been devoured by the P. office - I'm sorry. Yr. ma went prowling out yesty by herself, unknown to me, & of course fell down, merciful heavens, unhurt. I've told her over & over again she must take a stick if she moves about. I have also warned her that if she damages herself, I am quite unable to nurse her - She wd have to go to hospital.

Am enjoying Adams' Democratic Dogma immensely: it is surprising <u>how</u> people can foresee so clearly, & so near the time, too. He foresaw the war for 1917 instead of 1914 - "Men are not swayed by words but by impinging forces, & by suffering."

Saw Nerina yesty. Oh, I told you - She had seen yr. daughter [Mary Rudge] in the street - recognized her by likeness round the nose & mouth to Isabel, & her legs resembling Olga's. She had her hair all loose on her shoulders - no puritan-peasant 'braids' any more! I do hope the child can <u>think</u>, & not only imitate others. Elfriede [Bacigalupo] agreed with me that that is ~~the~~ a gt. characteristic of U.S.A. females: their good memories, & their imitative faculty: Edie's pole noted it years ago in teaching music.

Later. Here arrived a friend of Hess. I have left his name up at V. Raggio. He is going to undertake a manifesto ~~for~~ in your favour - printing in a vol. & each person saying you are a poet, & they <u>need you</u> - He is hunting a few important names - Several we have gone through - (Marasa or some such name -) I have lent him some vols. of yours to quote from - He knows about Paresce. He has published Cocteau, Gide, Eluard, - & will publish anything you like to give him.

I mentioned some more Kung. Also there is some Cantos? not published, that Maria transl.? and her Hardy.

Eluard] Paul Eluard (1895-1952), pseudonym of Eugène Emile Paul Grindel, French poet and leader in the Surrealist movement. During World War II he was active in the anti-German resistance.

Maria transl.?] Mary de Rachewiltz recalls that in the early 1940s EP started her on translating into Italian Thomas Hardy's *Under the Greenwood Tree* as well as his own cantos (*Discretions* 149ff.).

40 Notes. In black ink on a sheet of white paper folded double and written on three sides, with postscript in pencil; no extant envelope (Lilly).

Marasà] For Aurelio Marasà and Eugen Haas, see Letter 39n.

Cocteau ...] Jean Cocteau's poem sequence *Plain-chant* (1923) and his novel *Les Enfants terribles* (1929). See also Letter 39n.

Gerhardt & Vera] The Münchs. See Letter 37n.

Kitasono] Katue Kitasono (1902-1978), whom EP nicknamed "Kit Kat," was a Japanese poet who founded the literary magazine *Vou* in Tokyo in 1935. He was noted in Japan for his translations of French poets and published translations of EP's prose and poetry in *Vou* and *Tsukue*. In the first issue of Ronald Duncan's *Townsman* in January 1938, EP praised Kitasono and the Vou Club: "I know that nowhere in Europe is there any such vortex of poetic alertness. Tokio takes over, where Paris stopped" (*Poetry and Prose* 7:296). The same issue included poems by Kitasono and his colleagues translated into English. EP corresponded with Kitasono about Confucius, the ideogram, poetry, and other topics.

Scheiwiller] Giovanni Scheiwiller (1889-1965) worked for the Milan publishing firm of Ulrico Hoepli but also published limited editions on his own. EP described him affectionately as "employee, publisher and messenger boy" (Paige 220) and told Louis Zukofsky that he was a "good guy/ ought to be NNNNcouraged" (*Pound/Zuk* 126). Scheiwiller admired EP's work and in 1932 brought out his poetry anthology, *Profile*. In 1937 he issued EP's *Confucius: Digest of the Analects* under his imprint, "Insegna del Pesce d'Oro." In later years Scheiwiller's son, Vanni, also published works by EP.

Pea] Enrico Pea. See Letter 34n.

big Cavalcanti] See Document 6n and Letter 2n.

Miss Clerke] Florence Clerk (1870-1952), English resident of Rapallo and friend of Father Desmond Chute. Unlike several other British residents, she was not interned during the war.

Riverendo] Father Desmond Macready Chute (1895-1962), born in Bristol, England, studied at the Slade School of Art, and was Eric Gill's close friend and apprentice in stonecutting. In 1918 Chute, Gill, and several others were invested as novices in the Third Order of Saint Dominic and established a guild of Christian craftsmen in Ditchling. Chute left to study for the Roman Catholic priesthood in 1921, and Gill engraved a woodblock for his ordination, which took place at Downside Abbey in September 1927. Chute moved to Rapallo in 1923 on account of his health, became fluent in Italian, and produced engravings and drawings, including portraits of EP, Gerhart Münch, and W. B. Yeats. A musician, he helped EP to organize Rapallo concerts and occasionally reviewed them for *Il Mare*. In 1942 he was interned as an invalid enemy alien in the hospital of Bobbio, the abbey founded by Saint Columban, where he studied the history of the abbey, helped with the sick and wounded, and taught plainsong to the young. He spent his last years in Rapallo; EP and Olga Rudge attended his funeral. Mary de Rachewiltz describes the eccentric appearance and talents of this "accomplished and honest dilettante" in *Discretions* (147-49). See also Letter 72n.

three letters from you + lynx] Letter 24, enclosing DP's "lynx" extract (from Canto 79), and Letters 26 and 29. Letter 27, on a scrap of paper, may have been enclosed with Letter 26.

He is writing - or has written McLeish & T.S.E. [Eliot]. It has been his quite recently re-meeting Hess that has stirred him up. Two months in his head, this idea -

I gave him yr. address. He is up at Excelsior [hotel] for the winter. I gave him a large Kung: & have lent him such as I have down here to quote from. The question is <u>time</u>.

Further anon.

Yours D

40 DOROTHY TO EZRA

Villa Raggio
Cerisola
Rapallo
Oct 30 1945

Oh Mao.

His birthday - Pouring torrents, after three years drought. Marasa Aurelio has been up again. He is on the job that he has in mind for a manifesto by artists etc, that the young ones need you & yr. work.

Haas is his friend & is coming to see me soon. I am doing my best, to forward any ideas that may turn to action in yr. favour: naturally politics don't enter. He has a publishing 'house' in Genova - Has done a de Luxe Cocteau "Plain chants" in french & Les E. Terribles amongst others. He says he'll ~~do~~ publish anything you want.

He has a fairly heavy jaw bone: very nervous & quick, light brown eyes - dark straight hair, a trifle jap: this last. He reads English easily but can't speak it. I suppose there are newrich or oldusury in the show: haven't yet discovered.

I had thought of a manifesto in yr. favour, very short, to be signed by anybody in Rap. [Rapallo] but one of yr. most humble acquaintance veto'd it! saying that anyone wishing, could always say that I had bribed for signatures: a very canny remark.

I am writing Omar to find news of Gerhardt & Vera. I have given the names to Marasa as important, of Rudy [Dolmetsch] & Gerhardt & Kitasono as pure artists, also Scheiwiller, & Pea, both whom he knows well. He might be able to sell the big Cavalcanti? but I am waiting not to mix things: & to see how much froth there is or what sticking power. I am inclined favourably.

Here - cooking etc.

and so goodnight
Oh Mao!
Yours ever D.

I hear Miss Clerke & the Riverendo are both back.

PS. Tuesday [Wednesday?] am. recd. three letters from you + lynx. am attending to all matters today D

41 Notes. In black ink on a sheet of graph-ruled paper folded double and written on four sides, with an additional smaller white sheet written on one side. An envelope likely belonging with this letter is addressed to EP at the DTC, postmarked Rapallo "3.11.45," and marked in blue pencil by a U.S. censor (Lilly).

Three from you] See Letter 40n for these letters.

his first night] Ronald Duncan's play *This Way to the Tomb.* See Letters 7n and 10n.

T.S. has also written you] In his letter to EP of 19 October 1945, Eliot discussed Faber and Faber's willingness to publish the new cantos, their reluctance to take on Confucius, the wisdom of retaining good legal counsel, and other matters (Lilly).

G.H.T.] Congressman George Holden Tinkham. See Letter 29n.

kaki] Japanese persimmon, which puts DP in mind of army "khaki" and EP's mention of a "new suit" in Letter 29.

Delmar's grave] Frederic Sefton Delmer (1865-1936), Australian lecturer in English at Berlin University. During World War I he remained in Berlin with his wife and family until interned briefly, went to Britain in May 1917, and later returned to Berlin and earned a living as a correspondent for English newspapers. He retired to Rapallo in 1928. His son, Denis Sefton Delmer (1904-1979), was a distinguished journalist who interviewed Hitler in Munich and worked as a radio propaganda broadcaster for the British during the war.

letters are 14, 15, and 17th Oct.] EP's Letters 24, 26, 29. See also Letter 40n.

anatomic (sic) bomb] The United States dropped the first atomic bomb on Hiroshima on 6 August 1945, the second on Nagasaki on 9 August.

"a hypothetical, primitive opossum"] "Possum" was EP's nickname for T. S. Eliot. Henry Adams in *The Degradation of the Democratic Dogma* (1919; New York: Harper & Row, 1969) discusses the views of Darwinians and anthropologists on the origin of humans: "All this fumbling for an ancestry that should have been self-evident, was sufficiently disconcerting to historians who cared little what kind of a pedigree was given them, but greatly wanted to be sure of it; and who found themselves embarrassed with a primitive man,—or probably a variety of primitive men,—running back without intermediate links to a hypothetical, primitive, eocene lemur, whom no one but a trained palaeontologist could distinguish from a hypothetical, primitive opossum, or weasel or squirrel or any other small form of what is commonly known as vermin" (172-73).

Cary & Georgina] Cary (Fraser) Marshall (1896-1979), British resident in Rapallo from 1927, and Georgina, her daughter, born in Lausanne in 1928.

nice quantity of lynxes.] EP had sent the extract from Canto 79, with its incantatory lines on the lynx, in Letter 24. DP comments on "Lynx, beware of these vine-thorns" (line 230) and on the concluding line of the canto, "O puma, sacred to Hermes, Cimbica servant of Helios." In "Hudson: Poet Strayed into Science" (1920) EP alluded to the South American "puma, Chimbica, friend of man, the most loyal of wildcats" (Cookson 431). "Simba" is Swahili, not Arabic, for "lion."

thought is the degradation of action] In *The Degradation of the Democratic Dogma,* Henry Adams discusses materialist conceptions of the mind: "By the majority of physiologists, Thought seems to be regarded—at present—as a more or less degraded Act,—an enfeebled function of Will" (203).

Bunny] Ronald Duncan's sister.

poor thing] The old nursery rhyme:

> The north wind doth blow,
> And we shall have snow,
> And what will poor robin do then?
> Poor thing!
> He'll sit in a barn,
> To keep himself warm,
> And hide his head under his wing.
> Poor thing!

Villa Raggio
Cerisola
Rapallo
p.m. Oct 31 1945

Dearest Mao.

As I went out early this am, I found yesterday's mail in the letter-box - Three from you, one from Possum [Eliot], one from Ronnie [Duncan]. The latter had seen the former at his first night - ie. Ronnie's. Ronnie has written direct to you & they are both so glad there are some more Cantos. T.S. has also written you. He had written [Archibald] Macleish re my citizenship - so that will about coincide with my own letter to Macleish.

This afternoon I wrote to Miss Ida [Mapel], to Jas [Laughlin], to [A. V.] Moore, and very carefully to G.H.T. & added a few words to a letter I had just finished to John Dr. [Drummond]. I am thankful to know that there is a dentist for you. I will hunt up lenses tomorrow, & have asked Olga [Rudge] to do so too - I am hoping to manage a visit somehow - but the Gov [Allied military governor]: is absent - the telegraph was drowned yesterday, & not yet working: awful floods in Genova - & elsewhere as the ground is so dry, it doesn't absorb.

Great distress here below, as the dawg swallowed a bone wh. has lacerated his insides! He is better today! We are gathering kaki, wh. word reminds me of yr. noo soote - I hoped there would be some more woollies for you - Will read Lynx properly this evening quietly in bed. Glad it wasn't quite dead & buried in the P. Off. Am continuing to enjoy Democratic Dogma. Did I tell you - yr. ma managed to get down to the cemetary ten days ago. it is in quite neat order - & I tidied up poor old Delmar's grave, while she rested. All souls & saints tomorrow. Yr. words for G.H.T. gave me a new point of view altogether - Yr. letters are 14, 15, and 17th Oct.

In re my journey back. I walked with an elderly Doctor from Viareggio for 3 or 4 Km - I don't really know: then we took 24. lire's worth of corriere [motorbus], then we walked, in dark starlight another good piece - & another, 50. lire's corriere to Massa: from Sestri there are 3. motor buses waiting for the train, which go on to Genova. But the Dr. fussed & talked for an hour next a.m. to get me onto the post office van for La Spezia - I sat on the [sea] front at La Sp. for about three hours & eat [sic] my camp sandwiches - got home after 10.pm, & stayed at 12/5 for two days to recover! I just hadn't the strength to do spese [shopping] & cook & all the talk talk talk. By the way: yr ma had an idea: Was S. & Gomorrah destroyed by an anatomic (sic) bomb?

D. Dogma made me laugh - "a hypothetical, primitive opossum." Did I write a while ago, that I heard Marshal was still alive: the eldest girl, with him in Eng: married to the navy. Cary & Georgina in U.S.A. in a bad way, as the Spaniard deserted her & married a female: all this from his ex major-domo -

Thank you for such a nice quantity of lynxes. Do you remember starting off the black leopards down the High St? I wondered about <u>thorns</u> on a <u>vine</u>? unless you don't mean a grape-vine. In english 'vine' is hardly used except for grape. Any other is a "creeper" - & never with the word grape attached - May I spell "Cimbica" with an S? 'Simba' is lion in Arabic. In the Br. Adams, also an entertaining idea, new to me, that

Document 11 Notes. This typed memo (FBI document 100-34099-348) contains various Bureau notations and blacked-out lines which do not affect the text and which we have not reproduced. "SAC" means Special Agent in Charge.

two enclosed documents] *Testamento di Confucio*, translated into Italian by EP and Alberto Luchini (Venice, 1944) (see Letter 2n); and Arthur Kitson's *La Storia di un reato* (Venice, 1944), a summary of Kitson's theory about a bankers' conspiracy, which Olga Rudge may have translated into Italian (see Document 6n). The FBI's English translations of *Testamento* and *La Storia* ran to fifteen and twelve typed pages, respectively, which the Philadelphia office forwarded to Hoover in quintuplicate, along with the original texts, on 21 November 1945 (FBI document 100-34099-369). EP had finished his own English translation of *Testamento* at the DTC about two weeks earlier (see Letter 46n).

F. L. Amprim] FBI Special Agent Frank Lawrence Amprim. See Letter 2n.

thought is the degradation of action - I am taking a quiet afternoon (festa - saints & souls) & knitting my stockings - & so that accounts for these scraps. Shall write to Ronnie [Duncan] soon & ask if Bunny can't send a word about his 'first night.' One is most interested then in the rapidist deterioration of the race!? We must be both good specimens - You for thought; me, lack of action. I suppose the lynxes leave a good smell, by crushing the thyme mint & ma[r]joram with their paws. They probably smell good themselves on the open mountain -

Later. Good night. Its getting colder - Poor mao. do then poor thing.

Always yours D.

DOCUMENT II MEMO FROM FBI DIRECTOR, J. EDGAR HOOVER

TO: SAC, Philadelphia   October 31, 1945
FROM: John Edgar Hoover - Director, Federal Bureau of
            Investigation
SUBJECT: DR. EZRA POUND
            Treason

It is anticipated that this subject [EP] will be brought back to this country from Italy within the next few weeks for the purpose of standing trial. Inasmuch as the Bureau is in possession of a large volume of Italian material that has been written by Pound and whereas the Bureau has a limited number of Italian translators, it is desired that you arrange for Special Agent [blacked out] to handle the translation of the two enclosed documents. It will be noted that one document entitled "Testamento di Confucio" was acquired by Special Agent F. L. Amprim and was initialed by him on July 5, 1945 and August 7, 1945. The second pamphlet "La Storia Di Un Reato" was acquired by Amprim August 7, 1945.

It is essential that these translations be prepared expeditiously and with great care in view of their probable use in evidence at the trial of this case. Special Agent [blacked out] should be prepared to testify to his translations.

It is further desired that the original documents and five copies of the translation be returned to the Bureau to the attention of Five IS as soon as possible.

Enclosure

42 Notes. Typed with black ribbon on a V-mail form; Chinese ideograms and signature in black ink. The same series of Chinese ideograms appears in Canto 77 and is glossed by EP there: "not / one's own / spirit / and / sacrifice / is / flattery / bi gosh," or, "To sacrifice to a spirit not one's own is flattery (sycophancy)." This Confucian motto also appears in Book 2 of EP's version of The Analects (Confucius 201). Letter 42 is printed by courtesy of Morris J. Lucree (private collection). A draft of Letter 42, also typed with black ribbon on a V-mail form and dated 3 November 1945, contains the same text with minor differences of wording and without the Chinese characters (OP).

Lucree] Major Morris J. Lucree (b. 1920) replaced Lieutenant Colonel Steele as commandant of the DTC. Lucree was promoted to lieutenant colonel on 7 November 1945, and the camp he commanded deactivated in November 1947. In 1950 the camp was still being used, mostly for Central European displaced persons, its rows of tents bearing the original DTC numbers; but in August 1994 Col. Julien Le Page, a former DTC officer, photographed the area, which was arable land again and had been planted with crops.

China and Japan] During the war the United States had been concerned with gaining allies against the Japanese, irrespective of the internal struggle between Chinese Nationalist forces under Chiang Kai-shek and those of the Chinese Communists under Mao Tse-tung. While the Japanese still occupied substantial portions of greater China and the Communists were taking control in many regions, the United States continued to recognize the Nationalists as the legitimate government of all China, despite constant friction between the American government and the Nationalists. Russian moves toward the end of the war into areas of north China from which the Japanese were retreating, together with abortive attempts by the Nationalists to thwart these Soviet advances, created a far more complex situation than EP could have known at the time.

43 Notes. In black ink on two small sheets of ruled light green paper, both sides; envelope addressed to EP at the DTC, postmarked Rapallo "5.11.45," and marked in blue pencil by a U.S. censor (Lilly).

Monti's portrait] Rolando Monti (1906–1991) did a large oil painting of EP striding through Rapallo and an oil portrait of Homer Pound (ca. 1933). Monti had been greatly distressed by the Allied bombing of Rapallo and was grateful to EP for his kindness to his mother and sister. See also Letter 151n.

Old lady] Ida Lillian (Pound) Busha. See Letter 37n and Pound family chart (p. 000).

Waldorf] The Waldorf Hotel in central London, where, prior to enlisting, Omar had worked in the kitchens and at the reception desk, training to be a hotelier.

Hutchins] Robert M. Hutchins (1899–1977), president of the University of Chicago (1929–1945), chancellor (1945–1951). He wrote extensively on education.

Willis Overholser] Willis A. Overholser, the historian of money, was also a lawyer. See Document 7n. Henry Swabey wrote DP on 23 October 1946 that he had mentioned Overholser to A. V. Moore as a possible attorney for EP (Lilly).

Ron's play good] Duncan's This Way to the Tomb. See Letters 7n and 10n.

the Kumrad] E. E. Cummings. See Letter 34n.

piante grasse] Literally, "fat plants," an idiomatic form for succulent plants that retain moisture and require little care.

42 EZRA POUND TO MAJOR LUCREE

<<REPLACE TEXT WITH PHOTO T/K>>

DTC.
APO 782
3 Nov. 1945

To Major Lucree O.C.
In view of the situation in China and
Japan, it seems to me that the bottling of
my knowledge now amounts to suppression of
military information. It has, I think, been
that all along but I was too absorbed in the
economic and political and world-state aspects
to consider my data from the military angle.
In view of which I trust I am in order in asking an interview, at your convenience, re/
something properly "in the line of duty."

very truly yours

[signed] Ezra Pound

43 DOROTHY TO EZRA

Villa Raggio
Cerisola
Rapallo.
Nov. 4. 1945.

Dearest Mao.

I am greatly hoping to see you before you get this - but anyway here goes. [Aurelio] Marasà (Arabs in 800 in Sicily) & [Eugen] Haas came this a.m. The latter very large & sober & businesslike. They are setting up publishing together: at least Haas is joining M. They are full of friendship & kindness - They have a good list of names - & I sent em up to No. 60. [Olga Rudge] to get a photo of Monti's portrait, which M. [Marasà] likes so much, & also some addresses I have not got.

Yr. Ma today had a letter from Montana: very long, very thankful for yr. Ma's letter: saying they can't understand what its all about, but worried about you & loyal to you. Asks me to write - Old lady still alive, but quite muddled up about people, plays snatches on the piano & roams around. Wish I could see Ezra when he comes to the States. I am writing her at once - I shall be as clear as I can & hope it will get through, post & heads.

Another charming letter from Omar - He has given over his savings to Moore for

171

44 Notes. Typed with black ribbon on a V-mail form, with minor pencil corrections and initial; marked in black ink, "pjw" (1st Lt. Patrick Joseph White), postmarked "U.S. Army Postal Service 549, Nov 8 1945," with DP's penciled note "visited N. 11th," referring to her second visit to the DTC on 11 November (Lilly).

another batch of ms] See Letter 45. EP had sent the "lynx" extract (from Canto 79) in Letter 24.

peace clear as blue feldspar] Cf. Canto 83:

> in the drenched tent there is quiet
> sered eyes are at rest
> the rain beat as with colour of feldspar
> blue as the flying fish off Zoagli (lines 30–33)

Kirk's head] Alexander Comstock Kirk (1888–1979) served with the U.S. Peace Delegation in Paris in 1918–1919 and later in various diplomatic posts throughout the world, including Rome. He was a close friend of one of Mussolini's mistresses and through her came to know almost everyone in his inner circle. Kirk was appointed U.S. representative with rank of ambassador on the Advisory Council for Italy, in March 1944. In December 1944 he was confirmed as Ambassador Extraordinary and Plenipotentiary to Italy. See also Document 14n.

Lydia] Lydia Ranieri, the American wife of Prince Ranieri di San Faustino. They later divorced. See also Document 6n.

Paolilo] See Letter 19n.

Ungaro] Adriano Ungaro. See Document 6n.

kid's poem] DP's Letter 36 quotes lines from one of Omar's poems.

"succinct"] T. S. Eliot in his letter to EP of 19 October 1945 had said, "I will try to make it succinct." He spoke of his willingness to publish EP's new cantos but drew the line there: "The demand for Chinese wisdom is not so great; and I find no enthusiasm for it amongst my colleagues" (Lilly).

crisis point of the world"] A remark attributed to Tami Koumé. See Letter 25n.

Douglas dividends] See Documents 3–5n and Letter 17n.

me - saying its my money in the first place - I believe that child is a good 'un, much concerned about you. He's working on accommodation at H.Q. [Bremen] & his Waldorf months are standing him in good stead. T.S.E. [Eliot] had written him, saying Chicago has a good man at head, Hutchins, a prominent figure in educational world today: but he suggests OP. had better get a more general Education before specializing (psychology) - & Omar sees that point - I should think myself an U.S.A., or any, univ. would be waste of time——?

Letter from Swabey who has informed A.V.M. [Moore] that he believes Willis Overholser is a lawyer - He reports Ron's play, good. I've written Bunny [Duncan] for news of it.

R-Marie [Duncan] to be cured by April. it was about time - Have written to the Kumrad: am trying out Mr. Moss! but I don't expect any help from that quarter.

I have just been to cemetary - All Saints - & planted two nice clumps of piante grasse - Its all in order. Burnt some olibanum here. A little sun, after floods.

> Yours always D.
>
> thinking of you: were you dry?

44 EZRA TO DOROTHY

> co Provost's Office
> MTOUSA DTC
> APO 782, U.S. Army Local
> Italy
> 4 Nov. Sunday [1945]

Dearest Mao:

I dont know whether yr/ birthday Lynx canto went direct or via base censor. Am sending another batch of ms/via Base Censor this evening. You have given me thirty years of peace clear as blue feldspar and I am grateful. It is important that [Prince] Ranieri remember the formula under which I broadcast "nothing contrary to conscience or duty as american citizen." And that he get it into Kirk's head or of anybody else at embassy that I was engaged in teaching 'em history, U.S. History, Adams, Jefferson, points in Constitution. Better address letter to both him and Lydia in case he is out of Rome. If he is still on speaking terms with [Gabriele] Paresce he cd/ see that Paresce helps. Paresce OUGHT to remember as he signed the formula, but he is so wafty, and cert has a lot to bother him. He COULD understand, in fact understand is what he can do, that I could be of use NOW in reconstruct[ion], that I always did work for intercommunication and understanding. If they would LOOK FORWARD as well as backward. Also Paolilo [i]f you can find his address, would know that I worked as scientist trying to get an experimental science discussed by the MOST QUALIFIED and that I was not tied to any administration, as per continuing my non party and non political work after the fall of Muss. educational, scientific, necessary for ANY government to

Wheeler] Burton Kendall Wheeler (1882–1975), Montana senator who had a long career as an isolationist. Elected as a Democrat to the U.S. Senate in 1922, he was an unsuccessful candidate for vice president on the Progressive Party ticket in 1924 and continued to serve in the Senate until 1947. EP visited him in Washington, D.C., in 1939 and quotes him on FDR at the opening of Canto 100: "Has packed the Supreme Court / so they will declare anything he does constitutional."

News of Nancy?] Nancy Cunard (1896–1965), English poet and publisher, born into a wealthy shipping family. She first met EP in London in 1915 and later received helpful poetry criticism from him. In 1928 she purchased the types and press that William Bird had used for Three Mountains Press in Paris and established the Hours Press there, publishing Richard Aldington, Louis Aragon, Samuel Beckett, George Moore, and others. The Hours Press issued EP's *A Draft of XXX Cantos* in 1930. EP also contributed to her *Negro Anthology* (1934). Cunard became deeply involved in the politics of the Spanish civil war, wrote about it for several newspapers, and in 1937 published *Authors Take Sides on the Spanish War*, the results of a questionnaire she had distributed. EP, who had replied that "Spain is an emotional luxury to a gang of sap-headed dilettantes," was put down as "Neutral?" After the liberation, she returned to her home in Normandy to find that it had been destroyed by Germans who had stayed in it. On learning that EP was trying to contact her, she wrote him on 11 June 1946, recalling what he had once meant to her and deploring his recent activities: "Every single thing you reviled and blasted in your first XXX Cantos was happening in Italy in a modern form around you—corruption, oppression, murder, plus the added vulgarity of Fascism" (Scott 81). EP calls out to her in Canto 80, "Nancy where art thou?" (line 582), and mentions her black companion, Henry Crowder, in Canto 84.

Wyndham] See Letter 19n.

Nancy Cox] Nancy Cox-McCormack (1885–1967), sculptor, born Nannie May Cox in Nashville, Tennessee. She married Mark McCormack in 1904, divorced him in 1907, and went on to study art in St. Louis and later in Chicago, where she earned a reputation as a portrait sculptor and came to know various writers associated with *Poetry* magazine. She met EP and DP soon after arriving in Paris in mid-1921 and through them encountered Brancusi, Picabia, and other artists. In late 1921 she executed a life mask of EP (Beinecke), photos of which he wanted printed in *The Little Review* as his "death mask," although the editors refused to play along with the hoax. Cox-McCormack also did a small portrait bust of EP (Poetry Collection, SUNY Buffalo). Early in 1922 she moved to Italy, where she witnessed the March on Rome and admired Mussolini's skill and creativity as a leader. Through Italian friends she met the Duce in May 1923 and did the first portrait bust of him, which required ten sittings to complete. Although by 1931 she was disaffected with the regime, her initial enthusiasm led her to write the preface for the English translation of Mussolini's *My Diary* (1925). EP acquired much of his early knowledge of Mussolini through Cox-McCormack, and in 1923–1924 he wrote her often to express his growing interest in the regime and to ask her to convey messages and requests to the Duce. Eventually she returned to the United States to pursue a career as a portrait sculptor but was hampered by illness. In 1939 she married Charles T. Cushman. She wrote DP and EP often in the years following World War II (Lilly) and visited St. Elizabeths in 1951. Cox-McCormack is the author of a volume of travel memoirs, *Pleasant Days in Spain* (1927). (Cox-McCormack's memoirs of EP are published as "Ezra Pound in the Paris Years," ed. Lawrence Rainey, *Sewanee Review* 102 [January-March 1994], 93–112).

KNOW. He understood O.K. when he said that I stood for "only the little good there was in it." He might also have news of clavicord etc. As to Radio I don't know who apart from Ran [Ranieri], Paresce and Ungaro had any real knowledge of the nature of the actual texts written by me and broadcast, or who could swear first hand as to their authorship. Certain outsiders knew, of course.

The kid's poem is in sound versification. Both the young turnin' to verse. Mary's [Rudge] rather japanese in tone.

Tell Mother you noted the family style in her letter i.e. allusiveness to matters not in the mind of the general reader, but what she is driving at is sound enough, though I don't expect you gather that from her text. Thank her for it. The letter was O.K. Tell Possum not to be "succinct." I starve for news, and his normal style will be a treat for whatever officer is on censor duty the day his epistles arrive. Whether anyone but Ronie [Duncan] or Swabey can rise to the perception that I could be of USE, now. To Hugh [Dalton], to almost anyone, re both econ, loans, etc. as well as the Confucius, gawd knows. Tell Possum the Confucius is TOPICAL, it is not dead archaeology, "We are damn well at the crisis point of the world," and [C. H.] Douglas dividends wd/ take govt. spending out of politics, to the annoyance of course of certain politicos. Hugh [Dalton] seems to be goin' ahead. More power to his elbow. I see Wheeler is emergin again, re/ Railways, which is along line of bill he had on his desk when I last saw him. No harm in letting him know that I etc.

News of Nancy? etc. I keep thinking of the inhabitants of the planet. Wyndham is back in London. NO. NOT Nancy Cox. but also of her while one is at it.

Mao. love E. and love to Mother

45 Notes. Letter 45 is typed with black ribbon on a sheet of white paper, one side, with pencil signature; legal-size War Department envelope addressed to DP at Villa Raggio, initialed by "pjw" (1st Lt. Patrick Joseph White), and marked by DP in pencil, "recd 4 Dec '45" (Lilly). The "Note to Base Censor," enclosed to allay official suspicion regarding the canto extracts contained in Letter 45, is a typed carbon copy on a single sheet of heavier white paper, one side (Beinecke).

another batch of Canto ms] In addition to the "Note to Base Censor," EP enclosed twenty-nine typed pages from Cantos 74, 76, and 77. The portion from Canto 74 ran from "The suave eyes, quiet, not scornful" (line 12) to "Yaou chose Shun to longevity" (line 586), and from "The Muses are daughters of memory" (line 718) to "in 1912 explaining its mysteries to the piccolo" (line 802). The other portion picked up in Canto 76 and ran from "from the wreckage of Europe, ego scriptor" (line 209) to the end of the canto, and included all of Canto 77 through "for Wanjina has lost his mouth" (line 304) (Beinecke). Between 4 December, when she received these pages, and 19–20 December, when she mailed off the last of the retyped copies to James Laughlin and T. S. Eliot, DP devoted part of nearly every day to copying Chinese characters onto the pages typed by Mary Rudge, who put in the Greek phrases.

"mi-hine eyes hev"] From Canto 80 (line 202), not included among the canto material in Letter 45.

via BASE CENSOR
co Provost's Office
MTOUSA DTC
APO 782, U.S. Army Local, Italy
[4 November 1945, evening]

Dear D/

Herewith another batch of Canto ms/
sent via the Base Censor as per recent decision.

Ezra Pound

[Separate enclosure]

E.Pound

NOTE TO BASE CENSOR

The Cantos contain nothing in the nature of cypher or intended obscurity. The present Cantos do, naturally, contain a number of allusions and "recalls" to matter in the earlier 71 cantos already published, and many of these cannot be made clear (briefly) to readers unacquainted with the earlier parts of the poem.

There is also an extreme condensation in the quotations, for example

"Mine eyes have" (given as "mi-hine eyes hev") refers to the Battle Hymn of the Republic as heard from the loud speaker. There is not time or place in the narrative to give the further remarks on seeing the glory of the lord.

In like manner citations from Homer or Aeschylus or Confucius are brief, and serve to remind the ready reader that we were not born yesterday.

The Chinese ideograms are mainly translated, or commented in the english text. At any rate they contain nothing seditious.

The form of the poem and main progress is conditioned by its own inner shape, but the life of the D.T.C. passing OUTSIDE the scheme cannot but impinge, or break into the main flow. The proper names given are mostly those of men on sick call seen passing my tent. A very brief allusion to further study in names, that is, I am interested to note the prevalence of early american names, either of whites of the old tradition (most of the early presidents for example) or of descendents of slaves who took the names of their masters. Interesting in contrast to the relative scarcity of melting-pot names.

46 Notes. Typed with black ribbon on a V-mail form, with pencil additions and corrections; postmarked "U.S. Army Postal Service 549, Nov 14 1945." EP enclosed a carbon copy of this letter on thin white paper, omitting the section running from "Wyndham is back in London" to "one large slice bread an jam" (Lilly).

Thanks for ideograms] Possibly those in DP's Letter 31.

Unc. George] Congressman George H. Tinkham. See Letter 29n.

Sam Prior] Samuel Frazier Pryor, Jr. (b. 1898), a New York City business executive who lived in Greenwich, Connecticut, served on the Republican National Committee, and was in charge of Wendell Willkie's eastern headquarters in the 1940 presidential campaign. In his 1943 radio talk "To Explain," EP said that he had conversed "with Mr. Sam Pryor, and with young Elihu [Root], and a few other lights of the party" during his 1939 visit to the United States (Doob 248). In 1939 EP wrote Pryor directly and through Frank Bacon, who probably had introduced them (Beinecke). Wendell Lewis Willkie (1892–1944), American industrialist and political leader, was Republican candidate for president in 1940. He worked (1942–1944) to liberalize the Republican Party, mainly attacking isolationism. EP heaped colorful abuse on him at every opportunity, including radio talks: "that Trojan Horse (with apologies to the equine race) Mr. Willkie" (Doob 250). He is mentioned in Canto 77.

Douglas dividend] See Documents 3–5n and Letter 17n.

Gesell] Silvio Gesell. See Document 7n.

D. Lasser] David Lasser, *Private Monopoly: The Enemy at Home* (New York: Harper & Brothers, 1945).

P. Bottome] Phyllis Bottome (1884–1963), novelist and lecturer of Anglo-American parentage, published *From the Life* (Faber and Faber, 1944), containing chapters on Alfred Adler, Max Beerbohm, EP, and others. The chapter on EP covers Bottome's encounters with him in London before World War I and in 1935 on a short visit to Rapallo: "He helped to release any, and every, artist, young or old, whom he came across, from any shackles that prevented the strength of their artistic impulses" (74). See also Letter 136.

Jas Hilton] James Hilton (1900–1954), British author of the novels *Lost Horizon* (1933) and *Goodbye, Mr. Chips* (1934), published *Random Harvest* in 1941, about a man who has suffered memory loss. He wrote mystery stories and other novels under the pen name Glen Trevor.

Fuller] Maj. Gen. J. F. C. Fuller (1878–1966) participated in the Boer War and made important contributions to the strategic use of tanks during World War I. He later wrote extensively on military history and the science of war, supported Oswald Mosley's politics, and early in World War II agreed to sponsor Ronald Duncan as a conscientious objector. EP, who described Fuller as "England's anti-bureaucrat No. 1" (*Poetry and Prose* 7:237), corresponded with him for many years.

Wörgl] An Austrian town that attempted a form of Gesellite stamp scrip before World War II. EP says in *A Visiting Card* (1942): "All went well until an ill-starred Wörgl note was presented at the counter of an Innsbruck bank. It was noticed, all right—no doubt about that! The judaic-plutocratic monopoly had been infringed. Threats, fulminations, anathema!" (Cookson 314). John Hollis Bankhead, Jr. (1872–1946), who was elected to three terms as a Democratic senator from Alabama, proposed a form of stamp scrip in a 1933 bill, which EP attacks in *A Visiting Card*: "the stamps were to be affixed at the insane rate of two cents per week, equal to an interest of 104 per cent per annum. Incomprehension of the principle of the just price could not have been carried to absurder lengths" (Cookson 314). EP talked to Bankhead on his 1939 visit to Washington, D.C., and records the senator's comments about FDR in Canto 84:

> "an' doan you think he chop an' change all the time
> stubborn az a mule, sah, stubborn as a MULE,
> got th' eastern idea about money" (lines 6–8)

new "Ta S'eu"] EP completed translations of *Ta Hsio: The Great Digest* (the Testament of Confucius) and *Chung Yung: The Unwobbling Pivot* at the DTC and mailed the typescript of approximately sixty pages, with a covering letter dated 9 November 1945, to A. V. Moore in London. Moore received the typescript on 14 January 1946 and passed it on to T. S. Eliot. EP's letter read in part: "Herewith the 'Testament of Confucius.' It concerns you as it is an integral part of my defence. I trust Mr Eliot will see daylight in

co/ Provost's Office
MTOUSA DTC
APO 782, U.S. Army Local
Italy
Th/8 Nov. [1945]

Mao.

Thanks for ideograms. Go on writing. Better write again to Unc. George. Tell him date of that cheque. Ask if he had any more fun with treasury after my second letter; or date of his last from me. Say I will kid pants off Sam Prior if I ever see him again for fallin for W. Milky. Ask if he knows any way save Douglas dividend to take govt. spending out of politics, or than Gesell @ 1% MONTHLY to deal with debt. AND if he has any advice for me? You state yr own belief etc. re my probity. And repeat first letter in case he hasn't got it. Formula under which I [broad]cast etc. D. Lasser has writ a book on "monopoly the enemy." Not strange, BUT Harper has published it, which is a step forward. Also write P. Bottome asking about the Lasser book etc. and get her news. Ronnie [Duncan] shd/ look up Jas Hilton whose "Random Harvest" mentions money ONCE. These novelists OUGHT to go further, But Hilton not bad. Also Possum [Eliot] shd see Fuller. Let everybody write to me OFTEN. Oh yes, ask Unc G. if he has ever got round to writing that history he once thought of; say I might supply a few data ancient and modern. Ask everyone the same 2 questions re/ Douglas dividends and the Wörgl money at 1% MONTHLY, no Bankhead nonsense of 2% per week.

Wyndham [Lewis] is back in London. Awfully sorry about poor Bunny (Ronnie's) [Duncan]. Great dissipation yester, up till taps typing new "Ta S'eu," will try to send to Moore. Young 2/3 cat rather scary and stupid, necessitates puttin' toothbrush where it can't use it, otherwise hasn't ruin'd ought save one large slice bread an jam. Has Omar learned to drive? Can anyone realize that Gesellite thought has progressed since 1939/? Get Swabey to write Fack, Fack to realize that I have published a LOT of Gesellite propaganda. Also TIME to pay Douglas dividends in stamp scrip @ 1% monthly. John [Drummond] cd/ translate Oro e Lavoro? but all of 'em ought to work with Hugh [Dalton] not against him. Hargrave? get their minds off the past and look at present situation. Work in the chaos, that is the time to plant sprouts. NOW. And they should write TO each other. New set of odd noises traced to kat climbin' tent flaps. Only true democracy is Douglasite, per capita, way out of huge formation of monopolies etc. as it is fashion to attack fascism, let 'em attack it BECAUSE it did not divide per capita but to monopolies. It is also the ONE way to preserve their beloved "individual enterprise" if they cd/ ever come to understand it. The people having the purchasing power wd/ then CHOOSE which Boulder Dam or Highway they wanted to spend their cash on. etc.

Love to you and mother. Mary [Rudge] seems to find djeeps to travel in. No, dont send me clippings in foreign languages, but WRITE frequently and see that everybody else keeps on doing it.

Love E.

this connection. [. . .] You might remind Eliot that he once expressed a desire to know 'what Mr Pound believes.' I have put in a good deal of time formulating the answer" (OP). See also Document 7n.

Hugo Fack] See Letter 37n.

John cd / translate Oro e Lavoro?] See Letter 2n.

Hargrave] John Hargrave. See Letter 26n.

Boulder dam] At the Nevada-Arizona line in the Colorado River. The Boulder Canyon Project Act was signed into law by President Coolidge in 1928. President Roosevelt dedicated the dam in 1935, and in 1947 it was officially renamed the Hoover Dam.

clippings in foreign languages] DP had asked EP if he was allowed newspaper clippings in Letter 25.

47 Notes. In black ink on a sheet of graph-ruled paper folded double and written on four sides, with an additional half sheet of the same paper written on both sides; no extant envelope. On the first page EP penciled, "rd [received] 7 Jan" (Lilly).

Mistral] Gabriela Mistral (1889–1957), Chilean poet and educator who received the 1945 Nobel Prize in literature. She served in diplomatic posts, the League of Nations, and the United Nations.

Paresce shot] In an interview in 1997, Gabriele Paresce's widow, Degna Marconi Paresce, said that her husband had not been shot or wounded in 1945, nor could she think of any relative who had been. For Gabriele Paresce, see Document 6n.

Rudy killed] Agnes Bedford wrote DP on 28 October 1945 that Rudolph Dolmetsch had been killed at sea (Lilly). DP must have conveyed this news to EP during her 11 November visit to the DTC, for an unused passage in EP's pencil draft of Canto 84, datelined "11 Nov. D[orothy]," laments the deaths of young artists in both world wars: "Gaudier & Hulme in that one / young Dolmetsch & Angold in this one" (ms pages 306–7, Beinecke). The French sculptor Henri Gaudier-Brzeska was killed in action in France in 1915; the English poet and philosopher T. E. Hulme, in Flanders in 1917. For Angold and Dolmetsch, see Letters 8n and 16n.

'Ida'] Ida Lillian (Pound) Busha. See Letter 37n and Pound family chart (p. 000). Beulah Patterson (1886–1979) was a granddaughter of Albert Pound. Her brother, Charles Thomas Busha, Jr., was a lawyer in Washington, D.C. During the St. Elizabeths period, Beulah wrote to DP from Big Timber, Montana, with news of Pound relatives. Her husband was Ernest Riley Patterson (1886–1943).

Vinson bill] Frederick Moore Vinson (1890–1953), U.S. congressman from Kentucky (1923–1929; 1931–1938), secretary of the Treasury (1945–1946), chief justice of the United States (1946–1953). An expert on tax and fiscal matters, Vinson voted in favor of labor measures and a sound tax program. In 1936 he introduced a veterans' bonus bill that was intended in part to save the U.S. Treasury a billion dollars; EP agreed with the American radio orator Father Charles Edward Coughlin that this bill would merely enrich private banks: "Vinson proposing $2.200 million for veterans, and $1.700 million for bankers" (*Poetry and Prose* 7:32). As a legislator, Vinson was best known for his part in crafting the Revenue Act of 1938, designed to impose levies on undistributed business profits and capital gains and to raise more than five billion dollars in new taxes. The final bill, which was a compromise between Vinson's version and a greatly amended Senate bill, was passed in the House in May 1938, to the satisfaction of business proponents and New Deal liberals.

Enormous Room] DP had just received E. E. Cummings's letter of 10 September 1945, addressed to EP in Rapallo for lack of "the slightest clue to your now both distinguished and notorious whereabouts" (*Pound/Cummings* 166). Cummings hints at a parallel between EP's predicament and the one he had undergone and later described in *The Enormous Room* (1922). See also Letter 34n.

I wrote you from 12/5] Letter 49, written on 13 November. DP began Letter 47 on 9 November at Villa Raggio but had not finished it when she left to make her second and last visit to EP at the DTC on 11 November. When she returned to Villa Raggio, she found the unfinished letter and added to it on 18

> Villa Raggio
> Cerisola.
> Rapallo.
> 9 and 18 November 1945]

Dearest Mao.

begun: Nov. 9. 1945. Such a gorgeous day, & I'm so depressed! I spent a profitless morning trying to get convèyance to visit you. I believe they lied to me as to where the 'bus stops—and when I got back worn out, of course I had to cook the lunch - and so on. There are however three swallows sitting on the wire outside my window - & on one of the really chilly wet days, when I went to empty the rubbish, I saw the guineapig sitting firmly on the back of the Rabbit! A letter from E.E.C. [Cummings] airmail two months, today: crossing mine sent a few days ago. I hope to be able to bring it: if not, I'll post it on presently.

Also from A.V.M. [Moore] airmail - 29th to 9th - enclosing two from Omar to him. Omar seems to have a vague hope of getting here in Dec.

Items: Nobel lit. prize given to a female, Mistral, Chilean.

Paresce shot, reason unknown, and another dreadful heartbreak. Rudy killed. This from Agnes, also no details.

I haven't mentioned 'Ida' only Miss-Ida [Mapel] - It must have been in a letter from yr. Ma. All those Montana girls married, except youngest. Three sons in-law fighting - & I think Beulah said seven nephews in the forces. Her husband died in ten minutes of clot to heart.

Olga [Rudge] says you want Vinson bill. She can't find it. I will look at 12/5. but can't remember what it may be like? EEC. by the way; here's hoping you've enjoyed your Enormous Room as much as the undersigned did his. His present address Silver Lake, New Hampshire.

Here I paid you a visit. Nov 11th - this Nov. 18th. I wrote you from 12/5 as soon as I got back, telling of my journey home. this letter was up here.

Letters from John [Drummond] & Omar: both saying they hope to be along almost at once! John goes to Casa 60 [Olga Rudge].

Sent on to Ronnie [Duncan] the bits of canto - "Teapot" & "Zeus." I shall send the rest soon. He wants to print some in a broadsheet - I have written also to the Possum [Eliot] - saying Confucius in [*sic*] the next important from yr. pt. of view & that M.S.S. has gone to Moore. Letters from poor old Louisa: very faithful, from R-Marie [Duncan] herself, much touched by our concern abt her t.b. which she says is slight & better - & sends you much love & thanks: children with Bunny [Duncan]. Consulate as per usual. Yr. letter to Vice Con. [Herman] Moss recd. Records show you were for a number of years included in the registration of your husband as an Am. Citizen. Last time yr. husband registered . . . Oct 23 '39. - approved valid until Oct 23 '41. This office ceased to ~~be~~ operate July 41. Signed Lester Schnare.

I have copied it in full for Moore: & repeated the Beard to him. Marasà two days ago: I spoke of the Kung: what M.S.S. could I give him? have you duplicate? He has written Faber for yr. works in general. Wants Cultch or extracts; is hoping he may see

November. On 14 November DP wrote A. V. Moore that she had visited EP "for about an hour. His health seemed good. He had had a greatcoat issued to him: had a tooth stopped & his broken glasses replaced. We talked mostly of publications, etc. He said he had sent on the Confucius to you, as part of his defence. How long can they keep a man shut away, without trial. Its now over six months" (OP).

"Teapot" & "Zeus"] Two extracts that DP had received from EP, one beginning "with a teapot from another hotel" (from Cantos 74, 75, and 76), the other, "Zeus lies in Ceres' bosom" (Canto 81). See Letters 9 and 14.

Louisa] Louisa Crook was the housemaid of DP's parents. EP was acquainted with her before World War I and saw her again during his visit to London in 1938.

Schnare] Lester L. Schnare (1884–1955), born in Mondovi, Wisconsin, attended George Washington University. He was a law clerk for the U.S. Bureau of Immigration (1912–1915) and joined the U.S. Foreign Service in 1916. Until 1920 he served mostly in China and Japan; later he served in Colombia, Germany, Italy, Burma, India, and Iran. In 1944 he was appointed U.S. consul general in Rome where he served until April 1945. When the U.S. consular office in Genoa was reopened in May 1945, he was consul general there until he retired in November 1947. See also Letter 77n.

Cultch] *Guide to Kulchur* (1938).

transl. of first cantos] By Mary Rudge. See Letter 39n.

little vol. of Kitson] Probably Arthur Kitson's *La Storia di un reato*. See Document 6n.

heap of MacLeish] Unidentified.

Yrs. of Nov. 4th] Letter 44.

Omar's poem] DP quoted from a poem by Omar in Letter 36.

that cheque] See Letter 46.

Pell] Arthur Pell, president of Liveright Publishing Corporation, which had been printing *Personae: The Collected Poems of Ezra Pound*, then in its sixth impression, since 1926. In his letter to DP of 17 September 1945 (Lilly), James Laughlin said that he wished to acquire *Personae* from Liveright, and, with legal help from Julien Cornell, he was able to do this in 1946. In 1949 New Directions published a new offset edition.

Jas: own poems] James Laughlin, *Some Natural Things* (Norfolk, Conn.: New Directions, 1945).

Bill] William Carlos Williams (1883–1963), poet, novelist, and essayist, first met EP in 1902 at the University of Pennsylvania where they were students. Although their friendship was often stormy, EP dedicated *Ripostes* (1912) to him, got Elkin Mathews to publish Williams's volume, *The Tempers* (1913), and printed Williams's work in little magazines and anthologies. Williams espoused Social Credit but disagreed sharply with EP over Mussolini and fascism, yet he never ceased to admire EP as a poet. EP praised Williams for his "unhurried contemplation" and his "integrity" as a writer. He saw him as "a man hurling himself at an indomitable chaos, and yanking and hauling as much of it as possible into some sort of order (or beauty), aware of it both as chaos and as potential" (*LE* 396). When Williams died, EP sent his widow a telegram: "I shall never find another poet friend like him" (Mariani 768). James Laughlin carried on a lively correspondence with Williams and published many of his works with New Directions.

Slocum] John Slocum. See Letter 19n.

a poem in a letter from me?] DP's poem "No yaller dog" in Letter 38.

you to discuss these literary questions. I told him of transl. of first cantos: I did not say by whom. There came back amongst several letters (ages ago) the little vol. of Kitson that was to be translated. I don't think Marasà will touch that sort of thing. He says a whole heap of Macleish is being published in Milano - in English I think he said. I'm not quite sure - . Macleish is ~~gone~~ Communist he tells me. Marasà uses pseudonym Hegedus - He has taken a house of 18. vani [rooms] - & hopes to make an artistic centre - etc: etc: I am not swallowing it quite all: but I believe he admires you & will do yr. writings.

Yr. Ma delighted you approved her letter! I have got some books for her from A.M.G. [Allied Military Government] library: mostly a rotten lot. Yrs. of Nov 4th recd two days ago. I have answered Ranieri's letter to me re Consulate - etc: & told him you were trying to educate the b   s. I told you Paresce was shot.

So glad Omar's poem meets approval! I will write again to Ruth [Dalton] with pleasure (I wrote re my money affairs). What exactly could I say though. That you wished Hugh [Dalton] luck & that you would be only too glad to help him. I can't exactly say he'd damn well better take yr. advice on such subjects! - I am hunting up that cheque as soon as I have strength. This bright cold weather I feel better - Am also writing again to Miss Ida [Mapel] with various items of your intentions to try to help yr. bloody compatriots.

Long chat from Jas [Laughlin]: he says a report in the papers, no trial owing to insufficiency of evidence. If there's any necessity for raising funds. . . . Harvard Library is v. anxious to acquire coll. of letters. . . . They have all Possum's [Eliot] stuff, Hy. James etc. etc. their attitude is v. sympathetic - also some royalties accrued. . . Pell - a prime bastard. . . we must try to get the stuff away from him. . . I have all plates of cantos & hope to bring out complete vol. as soon as things quiet down a little. Do books get through?—Jas's own book of pomes. He sees Bill [William Carlos Williams], Slocum desk officer in Wash. during war . . . pretty plump & has three children: I have two but am not plump.

By the way. I forgot to ask when I was with you: "they" wouldn't take me as hostage for a week? - & let you have a holiday? I could paint those mountains all day! Carrara always splendid - as I returned. I'd come like a shot. Did you get a poem in a letter from me?

Always yours D.

48 notes. *Typed with black ribbon on a V-mail form, with pencil additions, corrections, and initial; marked "P" (Lt. Ralph A. Pollara) and postmarked "U.S. Army Postal Service 549, Nov 16 1945." DP marked the form in pencil, "recd 22," and added "Nov. 24" next to EP's request that she write Mary Burd (Lilly).*

Mary Bird] Mary Burd, formerly a social worker, was, after 1920, a leader in the Delphian Society of Chicago, a women's club with thousands of chapters throughout the country, "organized in the interests of higher education, personal improvement and social progress," as its letterhead declared. Burd served as general supervisor of educational activities and editor of the *Delphian Quarterly*, to which EP contributed articles on money, education, and other topics from 1936 to 1940. A lively correspondence began after Burd read *ABC of Economics* in 1934, and in 1939 she challenged EP to set forth the merits of totalitarianism for the readers of the *Delphian*. "I am NOT an enthusiast for dictatorships," he replied. "That is sheer perversion and willful misunderstanding on your part" (Beinecke).

Overholser] Willis A. Overholser. See Document 7n and Letter 43n.

Ta S'eu and Chung Yung] *Ta Hsio: The Great Digest* and *Chung Yung: The Unwobbling Pivot*. See Document 7n and Letter 46n.

that 1/2 hour] DP's second visit to the DTC on 11 November. She wrote A. V. Moore that she had "about an hour" with EP (see Letter 47n).

Weaver] Harriet Shaw Weaver (1876–1961), a distinguished English Quaker who helped finance and edit Dora Marsden's *The Egoist*, which, through EP's influence, serialized James Joyce's *A Portrait of the Artist as a Young Man* and Wyndham Lewis's *Tarr*, and published many articles by EP between 1914 and 1919. Weaver was also Joyce's faithful, long-suffering patron.

Nott] Stanley Charles Nott (b. 1902), English founder and manager of the *New English Weekly*, publisher of Social Credit works as well as EP's *Alfred Venison's Poems* (1935), *Social Credit: An Impact* (1935), and *Jefferson and/or Mussolini* (1935), which EP claimed forty publishers had refused. In an undated letter (1946?) written from Chelsea, Nott told EP that his publishing business had gone broke just before the war (Lilly).

Angold] See Letter 8n.

Basil] Basil Bunting. See Letter 19n.

The Bells and M. Boddy] Louise F. Bell (Mrs. Thomas S. Bell) was head of the Pasadena chapter of Social Crediters; Manchester Boddy was head of the Los Angeles chapter. Both were on the advisory board of the Social Credit Association of California, a state in which experimental economics and monetary reform had a strong following. A journalist and author, Boddy (d. 1967) was associated with the *Los Angeles Daily News* from 1925 to 1952, first as its editor and general manager, then as editor and publisher. He unsuccessfully challenged Helen Gahagan Douglas for the Democratic senatorial nomination in 1950. Louise F. Bell, who was acquainted with Major Douglas and John Hargrave, met EP in Rapallo in 1935. She also knew California Congressman Jerry Voorhis and sent EP his pamphlet, *Dollars and Sense* (see Document 7n). In the 1930s EP urged Bell to persuade Boddy to write attacks on banks and politicians (Beinecke). Bell wrote DP on 5 September 1946 that DP's letter of November 1945 had not reached her until April. She also recalled EP's irritation that she had no influence with "Mr. Boddy of the L.A. Daily News" (Lilly).

Jeff Mark] Jeffrey Mark. See Letter 26n.

Webster] John Webster (1580?-1625?), English dramatist admired by T.S. Eliot who incorporated Webster allusions into *The Waste Land* and "Whispers of Immortality." The passage that EP quotes appears in Bartlett's *Familiar Quotations* (see Letter 16n) under the heading "*Honorable Employment*"; it is taken from Romelio's speech in the opening scene of *The Devil's Law Case* (1623).

Rodker] John Rodker (1894–1955), English author, translator from French, and owner of the Ovid Press in London, which printed T. S. Eliot, Wyndham Lewis, Edward Wadsworth, and others. He published EP's *Hugh Selwyn Mauberley* (1920) and *A Draft of the Cantos 17–27* (1928). EP issued Rodker's prose experiment, *Adolphe 1920*, in installments in *The Exile* (1927–1928), judging it "a definite contribution to letters; in that perhaps minor, but certainly far from negligible form whose ideogram has been composed by Longus, Prevost, Benjamin Constant" (*Poetry and Prose* 4:378). An appreciation in the *Lon-*

co Provost's Office
MTOUSA DTC
APO 782, American Army Local
Italy
[10 and 11 November 1945]

Starting 10 Nov. Glad she aint been drowned. She write to Mary Bird of the Delphian, telling her the facts, and suggesting that contents of discorsi [radio talks] shd/ be known to her before she believes wild rumour. Also tell her to read Brooks Adams, Kitson, Overholser, giving titles of books.

Handed in the finished Confucius Ta S'eu and Chung Yung today, hope they reach Moore sometime. Swabey and Ron [Duncan] shd/ warm up the Possum [Eliot] as Faber seemed to want Cantos, and be stupid re the Confucius.

Sunday [11 November] O MAOO that ½ hour VERY short, and place much emptier since she left. Weaver, Nott, Ronnie to publish what Faber wont/ Kung, Angold, Basil. If you cant get money at start cd/ at least encourage 'em by prospect. Weaver to look after Basil, she got nowt else to do and both quakers. Possum might realize I know a gt/ deal more chinese now than 6 years ago. The Bells and M. Boddy to know how much Gesell I put over during the chaos. Swabey to realize need of [C. H.] Douglas (as DEMOCRACY, and taking government spending out of politics) and Gesell. He shd/ keep in touch with Jeff Mark, see whether Doug is sulking, and write me once a week. Also let [Hugo] Fack know. Never such need of Doug and Gesell as now. Bit of Webster that Tom omitted (found in Morleys edtn. Bartlett) "never to be out of action The soul was never put into the body Which has so many rare & curious pieces Of mathematical motion, to stand still." It starts "Chiefest action never to be etc. out of etc." Contact even Rodker re printing. But not try to mix him with the Weaver, Ron, Nott lot. OMAR to get Frobenius "Erlebte Erdteile" for his psychology and nearly everything else. Was in 7 small vols. Heine the easiest german to read if he is starting the language. Apart those two I dunno that he needs to bother about much else in that lingo. Swabey also cd. find Chambers-Hunter and any other survivors, tell 'em all I want LOTS of news AND detail. All Stella's circle cd/ be useful. Send out copies of Introductory Text Book in all your letters. Mary [Rudge] will send you a packet. Will also ask her to get you some addresses. Text book dates at least from 1937 possibly from '36 or '35. Forgot to ask you for Ida's [Mapel or Busha] letter. I dont know WHY Faber cant make contract direct. He NEVER gets off mark till Larry moves him. Whether Moore or Ronnie [Duncan] cd/ TACTFULLY ascertain if someone gets a rebate (inside the firm of Fab) or whether Fab simply cant circulate his books UNLess an agent gets 10% I dunno If it is merely question of the 10% Moore might as well have it as Larry. 8 John St. [Shakespear & Parkyn] cd. serve as address to Shxp. and Duncan publishers and Weaver go there twice a week to get the mail ??? etc.

O Mao he was pleased to see her, and now feelin a bit elegiac. Love to mother. Gladys Hines might know Basil's address. Dont give those blokes [Eugen Haas and

don Times for 11 October 1955 quoted EP as saying that Rodker had "more invention and guts" than many of his contemporaries (11). See also Letter 145n.

"Erlebte Erdteile"] Leo Frobenius (1873–1938), German anthropologist, explorer, and author of *Erlebte Erdteile: Ergebnis eines deutschen Forscherlebens* in seven volumes (1925–1929). EP was deeply influenced by Frobenius's work on African tribal cultures, arts and myths, and by his concept of *paideuma*, which EP defined in 1936 as "implying a tangle of ideas, mental habits, predispositions which make the mind of an era" (*Poetry and Prose* 7:77), and later as "the gristly roots of ideas that are in action" (*Guide to Kulchur* 58). EP met Frobenius and corresponded with his research institute in Frankfurt. See also Letter 123n.

Heine] The German poet Heinrich Heine (1797–1856). EP admired him and published "Translations from Heine" in *Canzoni* (1911).

Chambers-Hunter] See Letter 26n.

Stella's circle] Stella Bowen (1893–1947), born in Australia, went to London in 1914 and became a student of Walter Sickert at the Westminster School of Art. She came to know EP, DP, Wyndham Lewis, T. S. Eliot, May Sinclair, and much of artistic and literary London. She also met Ford Madox Ford, with whom she lived from 1919 to 1928, first in Sussex and later in France; their daughter Julia was born in 1920. Bowen traveled with EP and DP in Italy for three weeks in 1923, studying art in the local churches. She produced many paintings and portraits over the years and wrote *Drawn from Life: Reminiscences* (1941).

Introductory Text Book] See Documents 6n and 7n and Letter 2n.

Larry] Laurence Edward Pollinger (1898–1976), EP's literary agent in London. He worked for the Curtis Brown agency but in 1933 began his own business, Pearn, Pollinger & Higham Ltd. "Pol," as EP called him, established rapport with key American publishing houses, including New Directions and Simon & Schuster.

Gladys Hines] Gladys Hynes (1888–1958), born in India, studied art under Frank Brangwyn in London and during World War I lived on the Cornish coast, later returning to London. She received sculpture commissions from Roman Catholic churches and designed the initials for the folio edition of EP's *A Draft of the Cantos 17–27* (1928).

49 Notes. In black ink on two small sheets of light green paper, both sides; envelope addressed to EP at the DTC, post-marked "Rapallo 13.11.45," and stamped "Return To Sender" because EP was no longer at the DTC when this letter arrived (Lilly).

"les prunes"] Unidentified. Possibly an incident during the tour EP, DP, and T. S. Eliot took together in France in 1919.

Ch. Written Character] *The Chinese Written Characer as a Medium for Poetry.* See Documents 3–5n.

that cheque] See Letter 46.

Aurelio Marasà] ALL the Cantos at once, time enough for the vol 52/71 when they have really got the first vols into print, i.e. set up in proofs. And the Kung to take precedence if possible. The 4th vol. [*Cantos LII-LXXI*] can be ordered NOW from London, (three copies at least) and they cd. have one WHEN it arrives. Mao, love E.

49 DOROTHY TO EZRA

Via Marsala 12/5.
[Rapallo]
Tuesday
[13 November 1945]

Oh Mao!

I was very thankful to see you once more. Of course there was lots there wasn't time for - but never mind. I started to walk to Viareggio - after about 2.k. I hailed a rattle-trap marked "La Spezia" & to my astonishment the old man stopped! So I got to La Sp. that p.m. after a very jolty journey in time to miss the evening train home. The old man drove well, but part of the road is awful, & the benches were worse! A pleasant albergo [hotel] pointed out to me, nr. Station where I slept well - I found a trattoria close by - where I fell in about 7.pm and had a perfectly delicious spaghetti al burro - & mark you, a great lump of butter, & cheese, an excellent green salad, & a very pleasant dry white wine, for 80 lire - not so bad - Here it would cost double - Next a.m. I missed the auto-bus to Genova, by not having inquired the previous night: but boarded the train, a merce [thank heavens!], with cattle trucks for goyim - 11.40 - expecting to get to Sestri about 3. ocl or so: not at all - I got in 6.30. Reminded me of "les prunes" in France that year - but there was an auto for G. [Genova] & I got home before 9. ocl - & was I tired!

So I stayed in bed late this a.m. & am staying here until Thursday. I just <u>can't</u> do the spese [shopping] & go up and cook & talk, & talk & cook—I am getting attached to Spezia! Market fine - & its a handsome old town - & a change of food is so refreshing. I was too groggy to get down to the seafront.

I am buying, <u>when, as soon as</u>, my money comes, off Corradi, a magnificent leather jacket. He wants to sell it - being out of a job - & it will do for any of us three! Its a tremendous reddish brown, & he has polished it all up for me. My dearly beloved furkin [small snow-leopard stole] will go inside well. Excuse writing: its turned suddenly terribly cold & my studio is a draught. C. [Corradi] has been sent a sort of thick celofane for the windowpanes: which he is at the moment working on for the kitchen. We shall see if it resists.

Am writing Marasà re Cantos + translation as far as it goes & for the T-hio & Chung Yung; have you a second carbon copy to give him? I am insisting a little on Ch. Written Character for their Problème du Style series. I will hunt up that cheque when I am back at V. Raggio & write Unkel George [Tinkham].

Well well Good Luck.

What are you working on now? My alb. [albergo] in Spezia has two perfect smooth white Katz.

Yours always D.

50 Notes. Typed with black ribbon on a V-mail form, on two different typewriters, the change occurring with "Naturally disagree with Possum." The letter breaks off halfway, and the final words are scrawled in pencil. There is no postmark because, as DP noted in pencil on the form, it was "brought me by Omar from D.T.C. Nov. 20 '45." Omar arrived at the DTC, on leave from Bremen, to find that EP had been flown to Washington. Lieutenant Pollara handed this letter to him (Lilly).

Ronnie's rather terrible Husbandman book] Ronald Duncan's *Journal of a Husbandman* (London: Faber and Faber, 1944), about the experimental communal farm that Duncan began just before World War II and why it failed.

Cocteau] See Letters 39n and 40n.

That without auto-suggestion . . .] EP jotted these same lines at the end of his pencil draft of Canto 84, beneath the notation "not in Cantos.—14? Nov" (ms page 308, Beinecke). An adjacent jotting reads: "Black boy says 'Ah doan want to miss[?] that psychiatrist." EP's aversion to Freud and psychiatry was reinforced by interviews with staff doctors at the DTC and later at St. Elizabeths Hospital. An idea similar to that expressed in EP's lines is found in a quotation from Nietzsche's *Ecce Homo* in the copy of Bartlett's that EP had at the DTC: "All prejudices may be traced back to the intestines" (1198).

Joe E. Davies] Joseph Edward Davies (1876–1958), Wisconsin-born corporation tax and antitrust lawyer who in 1915 became chairman of the Federal Trade Commission and, ex officio, a member of Bernard Baruch's War Industries Board. He served as U.S. ambassador to the Soviet Union (1936–1938), with the major task of negotiating repayment of American loans after the Soviet Union refused to recognize loan obligations incurred by former Russian governments. His *Mission to Moscow* (1941), which became a best-seller, is described on the title page: "A record of confidential dispatches to the State Department, official and personal correspondence, current diary and journal entries, including notes and comment up to October, 1941." Sober and informed, Davies's account covers many topics, including U.S. concerns about the market being flooded with Soviet gold, and shows him to be a farsighted diplomat trying to prevent a European conflict. EP was reading this book at the DTC when ordered to pack for his jeep escort to Rome, thence to be flown to Washington, D.C. An unused passage in EP's pencil draft of Canto 84 includes the lines "it might have been avoided / if Joe Davies had gone to Berlin / instead of Moscow" (ms page 307, Beinecke).

Thank Ida] Ida B. Mapel wrote EP on 5 November 1945 of an auto accident that she and her sister Adah Lee had been in. They came through "with the God given number of arms and legs that we previously owned" (Lilly). See also Letter 9n.

Cumming's letter] See Letter 47.

Leaving probably Rome] On 5 November 1945 the Office of the Judge Advocate General, War Crimes Office, had cabled the commanding general, U.S. Army Forces, MTO, Caserta, Italy:

> Number: WAR 81164
> For Theater Judge Advocate from SERVJAG
> The Department of Justice shortly will ask for return to the United States of Ezra Pound, 14 November probable target date. We will give you about 3 days notice of date for Pound's arrival here. Legal jurisdiction requires that plane returning prisoner land at Bolling Field in the District of Columbia and not at National Airport or other airports in the United States. Arrangements to be made here for relinquishing Pound to Federal Bureau of Investigation upon arrival at Bolling Field. Advise this office of designation of plane and time of departure of 6 Italian witnesses in Ezra Pound case. End.

On 15 November 1945 the same office cabled Caserta again:

> Number: WAR 83408
> From SERVJAG
> Return of Ezra Pound is subject. Secretary of War directs that ATC pick up Pound on highest priority on regular flight leaving Rome 17 November and arriving U.S. 19 November. Pound is to be transported under military guards until relinquishment to federal authorities in U.S. Most important that first landing of plane must be at Bolling Field in District of Columbia and no other. Advise ATC to communicate their headquarters Washington of plane designation and probable time of arrival at Bolling Field. Request immediate reply. End.

(Both cables are in the National Archives, Record Group 153 Judge Advocate General [Army], War Crimes Branch.)

co Provost's Office
MTOUSA DTC
APO 782, U.S. Army local
Italy
[14 and ?16 November 1945]

14 Nov. Mao/

LONG and very cheering letter from Omar, just what I needed also first page of an essay "logical mask of implicit servility" must be rather good for the circumjacent huns. O.K. his going Chicago university. I spose it will do no harm for him to see a psychiatrist if it amuses him, so long as never the same one twice. Nor often, not to degenerate into "I liked confession" the advantage of conversation with friends being that one has to create their willingness to listen. Tell him I cant send back his typescript, but to go on/ objective description of his friends might be good exercise. He has quoted Kung unconsciously. Tell him most of my answers to him will be in next edtn if it ever reaches Moore and gets printed. Ronnie's [Duncan] rather terrible Husbandman book has come, so book post functions and you can get copies Cantos 52-71 for whats his name [Aurelio Marasà] (or if Faber run out, THEY can get copies from Jas [Laughlin] without delaying to write you. If the bloke HAS printed Cocteau the company is good. Right start. The More Omar learns of straight medical diagnosis the better psychiatrist he will make/ less danger of mixing psyc/ and plain medical cases// That without auto-suggestion/ Have found the soul inside the great intestine/Or consciousness that dark and turgid river/ upwelling from a clogged Platonic liver/ As to SEEING a psycho, he better go on writing to me and Ronnie [Duncan]. Naturally disagree with Possum [Eliot], Om will git enuff generl kulchr from my woiks and friends, and what he cd/ git in a university wd/ be merely dilutation to the 1/1000th. Better something definite. If he can learn russian now as well as german, O.K. plus. Reading Jo E. Davies "Mission to Moscow" 1000 pities he didn't go to Berlin or Rome, cd/ have staved off war. Thank Ida for letter and thanks she escaped auto-smash. DONT FORGET to send me DATE of that Cheque. Cumming's letter a comfort.

Leaving probably Rome. love E

Document 12 Notes. Orders typed on one side of a sheet of paper. Published by courtesy of Morris J. Lucree (private collection).

Col. Holder] For Colonel Holder and others mentioned in these orders, see Document 13.

LIEUTENANT COLONEL LUCREE] See Letter 42n.

DOCUMENT 12 TRAVEL ORDERS FOR EZRA POUND'S ESCORT TO ROME

HEADQUARTERS
6677TH DISCIPLINARY TRAINING COMPANY (PROV)
MTOUSA DISCIPLINARY TRAINING CENTER
APO #782

16 November 1945

201 — RICHARDSON, Grieg V. R. (O)
DUHIG, Edgar R. (O)

SUBJECT : Travel Orders.
To : Capt. Greig V. R. Richardson, 0 463 274, Infantry,
2nd Lt., Edgar R. Duhig, 01 050 239, Infantry,
6677th Disciplinary Training Company (Prov)
APO #782, U.S. Army.

I. You will escort Ezra Loomis Pound, American civilian, to Rome, Italy, arriving thereat no later than 17 November 1945. He is to be delivered to the office of Col. Gravis at the Ciampino Airport at Rome. In the event that Col. Gravis is not there, he should be contacted at the Hasler Hotel, telephone Rome Exchange 66524. After reporting to this office at the Airport you are to hold the prisoner until you are relieved by one of the following officers:

Col. Holder
Col. Donaghey
Capt. Manus

(Auth: Tp Com. Col. Barrett-Col. Wolfe, 16 November 1945.)

2. Upon completion of this duty you will return to proper station. Travel by Govt M/T is atzd. TDN.

BY ORDER OF LIEUTENANT COLONEL LUCREE:

[signed]
RALPH A. POLLARA,
1st Lt., Infantry,
Asst. Adjutant.

DISTRIBUTION:
2 – CG, MTOUSA
2 – CG, PBS
2 – SJA, MTOUSA
2 – SJA, PBS
2 – PM, PBS
2 – Col. Gravis
2 – Each Officer
2 – File

"Suddenly, Pound sprang up and, looking down at
the tremendous sunlit sea, became, on his first
ocean crossing by air, ecstatic, like a bird let out of
a cage, like a man pulled out of a deep, dark hole.
He paced the aisles declaiming in poetic rhapsody."

French official aboard Ezra's plane (quoted in Seelye 119)

EN ROUTE

Document 13 Notes. Lieutenant Colonel Holder's record of the trip from Rome and his affidavit are typed carbon copies on legal-size paper, two pages and three pages, respectively, in the National Archives, Record Group 153 Judge Advocate General (Army), War Crimes Branch. Holder's record has been printed in partial form in various books about EP, and the affidavit was included virtually entire, with minor differences from our text, in Ben D. Kimpel and T. C. Duncan Eaves, "More on Pound's Prison Experience," American Literature 53 (November 1981): 475–76. See also Document 12.

AGWAR Signal W-83408 dated 16 November arrived at MTOUSA the same date. Since all at the JA [judge advocate] office felt that it would come in on that date we were all more or less alerted. I left the office about 1600 hours to sort out kit etc. About 1830 hours Col. Barratt called me at the mess and told me to be ready to leave that night and to meet him at the JA office at 2000 hours. Lt. Colonel Donaghy came in about 2030 hours and we waited the issuance of orders for him and Capt. Manus. (My orders had been issued as of the 14th.) Capt. Manus was at 7th PD and some difficulty was experienced in reaching him by phone. However he arrived and we left by staff car for Rome about 2230 hours, arriving at 0200 hours, 17 November. I called Col. Gravis CO Champino [Ciampino] airport immediately upon arrival. He told me that in accordance with a phone call from Col. Barratt everything was arranged and that we were to report back at the airport at 0700 hours. He arranged accommodation at the Hassler Hotel for us and arranged a car for 0630 hours to take us to the airport.

Capt. Manus went to bed and Donaghy and I decided that we had better check on arrangements. We phoned Col. Huntzinger PM of Rome who told us that he had heard nothing of the arrival of Pound and that his section had made no arrangements for his (Pound's) reception or custody until the plane might leave. He promised to tie up all loose ends immediately. Thereafter we called the MP's and the duty officer at the airport and were told that although they had not been alerted there were personnel on duty at all times who could take care of any situation that might arise. We then called the Disciplinary Training Center at Pisa and were told that Pound with escort had left for Rome at 2030 hours by Jeep. It was a cold raw night. By this time it was approximately 0400 hours, so I decided to go to the airport. Donaghy went to bed for a few hours.

Pound arrived at Champino airport at 0445 hours and was detained in the guard house with escort. At 0630 I went to the traffic office to check on the readiness of plane, priorities, tickets, etc. I was told that we were leaving at 0800 hours for Marseilles, Lisbon, Santa Maria (Azores), Bermuda and Washington. Col. Donaghy and Capt. Manus arrived at the airport at 0700 hours. We picked up Pound and all had breakfast, changed our money, weighed in and were on the plane at 0800. Traffic officers had arranged that we have the first three rows of seats in the front of the plane, i.e. twelve seats, so that no one would sit in the immediate vicinity of Pound but his escorting officers. This seating arrangement was carried out throughout the trip and proved to be extremely satisfactory.

We took off at 0830 hours and headed North. The pilot told me that at the last moment orders had been changed and we were routed through Prague, Brussels, Bovington (England), Greenland, Newfoundland. Arrived at Prague approximately 1330 hours. The plane had no lunch baskets on board and there were no facilities for feeding at Prague. After an hours wait, to no purpose that I could see, we took off again for Brussels, arriving at approximately 1700 hours. The wait there, also, was to no purpose that I could discern. No petrol was taken on and we were not permitted to leave the vicinity of the aircraft to go to the lunch counter, which was some distance away. We

took off in about forty-five minutes and arrived at Bovington approximately 1830 hours (GMT). There we had an ample dinner, the first food since 0600 hours (GMT). Mr. Pound was suffering acutely from hunger and was extremely nervous.

There was considerable uncertainty at this point as to our next move. One source stated that we were to wait four hours to see whether the weather cleared over Stephensville (Nfld), if it didn't we were to go to the Azores and see what the situation was from there. The uncertainty of the situation concerned me no little, so I went to operations and after some argument and flaunting of orders, copies of signals etc. induced them to order our immediate departure for the Azores.

We arrived at Santa Maria airport approximately 0300 hours on the 18th. First we were told that No. 4 engine had to be checked and our departure would be delayed until 0600 hours. Then we were told that Stephensville (Nfld) was closed in and we would not leave before 1000 hours, if then. Having some knowledge of North Atlantic weather conditions my concern grew to the extent that I took issue with traffic officers. Finally I flatly refused to go to Stephensville at any time and requested that the first ship enroute to US by way of Bermuda be off loaded sufficiently to accommodate our party. In the meantime Pound under the escort of Col. Donaghy and Capt. Manus had retired to the Stockade to shower and rest.

A plane arrived from Paris at 0700 and two passengers were disembarked. I requested that ATC make the same arrangements as previously, that is, that we occupy the first twelve seats in the aircraft. I learned later that the French Ambassador, his wife and two Colonels had been obliged to move their seats.

We took off at 0830 hours (GMT) and arrived at Bermuda at 2100 hours (GMT) or 1700 hours Atlantic time. Here we found, for the first time, that the CO of the airport was on hand. A special building was reserved for us and we were fed an excellent dinner there. Here, also, there seemed to be some appreciation of the importance and emergency of our mission and everything was done to expedite matters. We were airborn at 1830 Atlantic time and arrived without further mishap at Bolling Field approximately 2230 hours Eastern time, 18 November.

I should point out that junior officers enroute probably did the best they could for us and, in one or two instances, exceeded their authority. I had the impression that from the time we left Rome to our arrival in Bermuda no particular importance was attached to our mission, other than that created by ourselves. That, however, may be entirely erroneous.

Possibly my disinclination to go to Newfoundland was prompted by excessive caution and had we followed normal routine we would have arrived in good time.

The first part of the trip was in aircraft 9115 and from the Azores to Bolling Field in number 9123.

Since no log was kept, all times of arrival and departure are approximate and as I remember them.

[signed]

P. V. Holder

Lt. Colonel

19 November 1945

AFFIDAVIT

DISTRICT OF COLUMBIA
City of Washington

I, P. V. Holder 0–901582, Lieutenant Colonel, Air Corps, Judge Advocate Section, MTOUSA, U.S. Army, being duly sworn, depose and say:

I was one of the three escorting officers who accompanied Ezra Pound, a civilian, departing from Rome, Italy at 0830 hours, 17 November 1945 and arriving at Bolling Field at 2230 hours, 18 November 1945. During the trip Pound conversed freely with all three of the escorting officers. Since he was not charged by Army authorities for any crime that we knew of, we were disinclined to interrogate him or to conduct any conversation which might have the appearance of interrogation. Pound, as is known, is an extremely well educated man with a wide divergence of knowledge and interest. His hobbies are the translating of ancient documents such as Pluto [*sic*] and Confucius. The bulk of our conversation was carried on concerning these matters. He explained in detail the sources of his knowledge and the means by which his translations were accomplished. Also he is a keen economist, although in my opinion his arguments are not entirely sound. In so far as his attitude toward the United States is concerned I got the impression that he was anxious to impress upon us his loyalty and his desire to be considered as an American who was trying to help America rather than hinder her. He is distinctly anti-Jewish and anti-Communistic. He denies that he is pro-Fascist and pro-Nazi. He made statements that he considers Hitler a mountebank and thought that Mussolini was much the better man of the two. Among the heads of the American Government he considers Mr. Morgenthau [former Treasury secretary] a dishonest man and stated that he knew approximately forty instances where the finances of the United State were used to improve the position of Jews in Europe or America. The only one he disclosed to us was the transaction involving the purchase of gold from other nations. He stated that he had proof that four billion dollars of the amount expended for the purchase of gold abroad, was diverted to the profit of individuals, most of them international Jews. He stated that in his opinion the raising of the price of gold from appoximately twenty one dollars ($21.00) per ounce to thirty-five dollars ($35.00) per ounce was not only unnecessary but was devised primarily to enable individuals in the United States and abroad to profit by the transaction. Pound believes that President Roosevelt was a morally dishonest man who had no scruples about dragging the United States into war or about using his office to enable his friends to profit.

Pound endeavored to interest me in securing for him interviews with G-2 Section of the War Department on the grounds that through his contacts in Japan and China he is in possession of information which is of much more importance to the United States than his trial as a traitor.

He discussed his visit to the United States in 1939 and stated that there were many Americans with whom he talked at that time who understood his views and who would be willing to testify that at that time there was nothing traitorous in his ideas and he wanted me to contact one or two of them and ask that they visit him. I did not make any record of their names since I did not want to become involved in his case. I sug-

gested to him that he employ an attorney whose duty it would be to make such contacts for him. He stated that there was no attorney in the United States that he knew of who had sufficient information or knowledge of his works and studies. He states that his whole defense was based upon the fact that his mental capacity and studies placed him in a sphere above that of ordinary mortals and that it would require a "superman" to conduct his defense. He stated that he proposes to conduct his own defense. My impressions of Mr. Pound were that he is an intellectual "crack pot" who could correct all the economic ills of the world and who resented the fact that ordinary mortals were not sufficiently intelligent to understand his aims and motives.

P. V. HOLDER
[unsigned]
Lt. Colonel, 0–901582

Subscribed and sworn to before me this twentieth day of November 1945, at Washington, District of Columbia.

[unsigned]
JOHN F. RICHTER
Lt. Colonel, JADG

he wd like to write her a letter,

she feels very close ce soir.

Ezra to Dorothy, Letter 89

"How is it far if you think of it"

Dorothy to Ezra, Letter 114

WASHINGTON D.C.

arraigned Nov. 19] An Associated Press article datelined Washington, November 19, and titled "Wallace's Help at Trial Sought by Ezra Pound" described EP's preliminary arraignment: "Ezra Pound, poet, indicted for treason, said in District Court today he wanted Secretary of Commerce Henry A. Wallace and Archibald MacLeish to testify for him at his trial. Appearing for a preliminary arraignment, the sixty-year-old Idaho-born poet [. . .] told Judge Bolitha J. Laws he talked to Mr. Wallace and Mr. MacLeish when he came here in 1939. He said his purpose then was 'to keep hell from breaking loose in the world.' Mr. MacLeish is a former Librarian of Congress and Assistant Secretary of State. Pound, one-time Paris dandy, appeared tired and dishevelled in court. [. . .] Declaring he had only $23, Pound asked to act as his own counsel, but Judge Laws told him the charge was too serious for that. Pound then agreed to have the court appoint an attorney for him and Judge Laws set Nov. 27 for a formal arraignment. Talking with reporters later, Pound declared he wanted to learn Georgian, Stalin's native tongue. He then would go to Russia, he said, on behalf of the United States and confer with the Russian leader. He said he wished to 'see what's in the back of his mind.' Pound denied he ever supported Mussolini and gave this description of the late Italian dictator: 'A puffed-up bubble.' Mussolini was unimportant, he said, 'just a figure selected by higher forces.' On his arrival here last night, Pound denied he had betrayed his country in war-time broadcasts from Rome. He told reporters 'if that damn fool idea is still in anybody's head, I want to wipe it out.'"

Stars & Stripes] *The Stars and Stripes* (Mediterranean edition) for 28 November 1945 carried an Associated Press article datelined Washington, November 27, and titled "Ezra Pound Indicted on Treason Charge": "Attorney General Tom Clark announced yesterday that Ezra Pound had been indicted for high treason on charges of broadcasting from Italy during the war. Clark said the indictment charged 19 overt acts of treason, citing dates between September 11, 1942, and May 15, 1943, on which Pound allegedly made recordings in Rome studios for subsequent propaganda broadcasts over Rome radio. Seven Italians, who claimed to have seen Pound make anti-Allied broadcasts from Rome and Milan, flew here voluntarily two weeks ago to testify before the Federal Grand Jury which returned the indictment. The announcement said the indictment charged Pound with receiving payments from Italy for his services and that he 'admitted each and every one of these acts for the purpose of and with intent to adhere to and give aid and comfort to the Kingdom of Italy'" (5). On 4 November, American Ambassador Kirk in Italy (see Letter 44n) had cabled the secretary of state: "Seven witnesses for Ezra Pound trial should reach United States November 9" (National Archives, Record Group 153 Judge Advocate General [Army], War Crimes Branch).

DP refers specifically to *The Stars and Stripes* (Mediterranean edition) for 29 November 1945, which ran an article datelined Washington, November 28, and headed "'He's Less a Traitor Than a Fool,' Fellow Poet Says of Ezra Pound," by Cpl. Sid Kline, staff correspondent. It began: "Ezra Pound, bearded expatriate American poet who became a bush-league 'Lord Haw-Haw' for Mussolini, is safely lodged in the District of Columbia jail now while lively controversies continue on what should be done with him." Kline went on to cite opinions of Conrad Aiken and F. O. Matthiessen and to quote snippets from EP's broadcasts—all of which he had found in the newspaper *PM* (see below). He also mentioned "a most sympathetic story about Pound" by columnist John O'Donnell (see below). Kline concluded: "It's a cinch that tickets for Pound's trial will be at a premium." An Acme wirephoto of EP in the custody of two U.S. marshals accompanied the article. DP noticed EP's handcuffed wrist at the edge of the picture and remarked to A. V. Moore in a letter of 8 December 1945: "a slip of the camera (or not?) shows another hand, extremely close to his right - they take no chances" (OP).

Aiken] The New York newspaper *PM* for 25 November 1945 printed an article titled "The Case for and Against Ezra Pound," compiled and edited by Charles Norman. The piece included a sketch of EP's life, excerpts from his radio talks, and comments by E. E. Cummings, William Carlos Williams, Karl Shapiro, and other noted literary figures. Conrad Potter Aiken (1889–1973), poet, critic, and fiction writer, was quoted as saying that EP "is less traitor than fool" and that "we must all see to it that justice should be done to him also as poet." In the same article, Francis Otto Matthiessen (1902–1950), professor of literature and history at Harvard University, gave an account of EP's poetic development and interest in economics, commenting that "one must never forget his important role in the poetic renaissance of 30 years ago. That importance may finally have consisted more in his critical stimulus and instigation than in his own work, although he was hailed as a master craftsman by no less than both Yeats and

[n.d.]
[Rapallo]

arraigned Nov. 19. just after being returned from Italy.

Stars & Stripes - Nov 29 - 45.

Cpl. Sid Kline. Washington 28 Nov.

Aiken. less a traitor than a fool
F. O. Matthiessen - important rôle in poetic renaissance 30. yrs ago

John O'Donnell N.Y. Daily News most sym. [sympathetic] story.

Nov 28 (AP) pleaded innocent - taken to an institution for mental observation.

Eliot." He added that EP was "a tragic instance of the consequence resulting from the gulf between poet and audience." (The article is reprinted in *Poetry and Prose* 8:254–64.)

John O'Donnell] John O'Donnell wrote about EP several times in his Washington column, "Capitol Stuff." On 28 November 1945 the *New York Daily News* printed his interview with EP at the District Jail, in which EP described the books in his cell, chiefly those he had had at the DTC, as having kept him "from going completely crazy" during his months of confinement. On 27 November O'Donnell published a longer interview with EP under the dateline, Washington, D.C., November 26 (the article to which Cpl. Sid Kline refers, above). While not entirely sympathetic, he gave a balanced account of EP's career and economic views, quoting him on Brooks Adams and Lenin. O'Donnell was at times harshly critical of Franklin D. Roosevelt. His column for 22 November 1946 on the Pearl Harbor investigations, which EP preserved, referred to "the one-man, all-out ignorance and mental arrogance" of FDR (Burke).

Nov 28 (AP)] EP was formally arraigned on 27 November 1945, again before Judge Laws. An AP article, datelined Washington, November 27, described the event: "Unkempt and clad in G.I. hand-me-downs, [EP] stood mute today during arraignment before a Federal district court here, shuffling from one foot to the other while a defense attorney requested that he be released from the District of Columbia jail because he suffers claustrophobia and may lose his sanity if he remains imprisoned. Chief Justice Bolitha Laws remanded Pound to Gallinger Hospital for examination. The defense attorney, Julien Cornell, of New York, said Pound lacked sufficient judgment at present to make any plea before the court, and asked Justice Laws to enter a plea of 'not guilty' for him."

51 Notes. In pencil on the body and flaps of a V-mail form, marked in black ink by the D.C. Jail censor, folded and mailed in a regular letter envelope addressed (not by EP) to DP at Villa Raggio, postmarked "Washington, D.C. Nov 20 1945," and stamped received in Rapallo "19.1.46." DP marked the form in pencil, "recd January 20 '46" (Lilly).

She got to Pisa just in time] DP had managed a second visit to Pisa on 11 November, a few days before EP was flown to the United States. See Letters 47–49.

deadly tired on arrival] On 16 November EP was driven by jeep to Ciampino airport outside Rome, then flown to Washington, D.C., where he arrived on Sunday, 18 November 1945. For details of the trip, see Document 13.

Azores, & marvel of Bermuda] EP's delight in this vista carried over into lines of verse that he penciled on the back of a letter from H. L. Mencken, dated 19 November 1945, which he received at the District Jail (Beinecke):

> ~~the~~ a sea of cloud above les Athores.
> the suns flame in the propellers -
> & ~~under sunset, the blue of Bermuda~~
> > ~~Ber~~
>
> Bermuda in
> > feldspar, an emerald.
> under ~~the~~ sunset.
> as in the cave of Tiberius.
> > thus Bermuda.
> To Shigeru Honjo. homage

Baron Shigeru Honjo (1876–1945), former commander of the Japanese Kwantung Army and adviser to the New Asia Movement of the Imperial Rule Assistance Association, was sought as a war criminal by Allied occupation authorities. On 20 November 1945, one day after his arrest had been ordered, he committed hara-kiri in Tokyo. His death was widely reported in the United States "Cave of Tiberius" may refer to one of the grottos on Capri that are famous for their brilliant water-reflected colors.

Beebe's hole] Off Bermuda, where Charles William Beebe (1877–1962) made his descent in a bathysphere on 15 August 1934.

District of Columbia Jail
200 19th St. S.E.
Washington D.C. U.S.A.
20 Nov. [1945]

Oh Mao:

She got to Pisa just in time. marvelous trip - deadly tired on arrival as djeep'd all night to Roma before 4 engine flight. Venice visible. Prague, cloud ceiling made skip Frankfurt. Brussles, London, Azores, & marvel of Bermuda just in time 10 minutes of daylight on splendour, water as blue grotto, & greens & yellow etc. - Beebe's hole etc. french ambassadore & nine on board, but not of the party, so to speak.

This cell modernist with fine high mess hall below & four story windows, enormous high sala [hall] under the cliff dwellings. heaven knows when mail to Pisa will arrive here.

have seen various journalists, best photo ever had done by A.P. I think - or, et quant aux types [what sorts]!! more of that anon. hope to write again tomorrow. Love to mother. E

cell warmed + good ventilation

best photo ever had done] Wirephotos of EP in the custody of U.S. marshals shortly after his arrival in Washington appeared in newspapers around the world in late November 1945. Bespectacled and wearing a dark broad-brimmed hat, a greatcoat and scarf thrown over his U.S. Army fatigue shirt, and carrying a valise and walking stick, EP looks by turns cheerful, chatty, and intent, but always impressive, in these pictures. One shot, taken on 19 November after his preliminary arraignment and published in papers the next day, shows him without glasses, his hat clutched at his side, his coat slung cloakwise over a shoulder, and his eyes looking sternly past the camera.

52 Notes. In black ink on a half sheet of graph-ruled paper folded double and written on two sides; envelope addressed to the provost marshal at the DTC, postmarked Rapallo "22.11.45," and marked with blue pencil by a U.S. censor. Letter 52 was enclosed with Letter 53 (Lilly).

53 Notes. In black ink on a small sheet of light green paper, both sides, and enclosed with Letter 52 (Lilly).

Lloyd's] Lloyds Bank in London, where DP had an account.

Omar came mostly by air] On 8 November 1945, Omar wrote A. V. Moore from Bremen airport: "I am waiting for the weather to change so I can fly to Paris, en route for Rome - then to Rapallo" (OP). He flew to Marseilles via Paris, and from Marseilles to Naples he went on a small boat crowded with returning Italian POWs. A bad storm at sea delayed his arrival in Naples by two or three days, so he just missed seeing EP at the DTC, who had by then been taken to Rome en route to Washington.

Nov 10. & 14th] Letters 48 and 50.

telegraphed Moore] Cable sent to A. V. Moore on 22 November 1945 from Rapallo, received in London on 24 November: "PLEASE ARRANGE BRIEF CORNELL FOR DEFENCE SUBJECT HIS VISITING AND OBTAINING CONCURRENCE FROM POUND IN WASHINGTON STOP OMAR DRUMMOND HERE = DOROTHY POUND" (private collection of James Laughlin).

52 DOROTHY TO PROVOST MARSHAL

Villa Raggio
Cerisola.
Rapallo.
Nov. 22 1945

To Provost Marshal DTC.

Dear Sir.
    My son Omar Pound tells me that my husband Ezra, has left the D.T.C. for Washington - This leaves me without any means of communication with him. Is it possible for you to forward the enclosed few words to him? I should be most grateful if you are in the position to do this. Chiefly that he may know the boy is with me & called at the Camp on his way up here.

Sincerely

Dorothy Pound

53 DOROTHY TO EZRA

Villa Raggio
Cerisola
Rapallo
Nov 22 1945.

Dearest.
    Omar arrived full of beans two days ago. He called at the D.T.C. on his way up - found you had left two days before. John Drummond also here, brought me cash, and today I got money banked here from Lloyd's - so that is off my mind. Omar came mostly by air - I have had two letter[s] from you - Nov 10. & 14th & am writing to several people in the next few days - Also interesting letter (copy from Moore) to Macleish re citizenship. The latter is by now in London I believe. John, Omar and I telegraphed Moore to send [Julien] Cornell to see you if possible, & Jas [Laughlin] is being useful.
    This may or not reach you. Have nothing else very special.

Always yours

D.

54 Notes. In pencil on two smallish gray sheets of paper, one side each, stamped, "D.C. JAIL, CENSORED, Nov 26 1945, BY MB"; matching gray envelope addressed to DP at Villa Raggio, and signed under the flap, "Ezra Pound Cell 216"; postmarked "Washington D.C. Nov 26 1945," and stamped received in Rapallo "18.12.45." DP jotted in ink on back of page two, "recd D 19 & ansd" (Lilly).

Cornell has been in twice] Julien Cornell's first visit to EP was for two hours on the morning of 20 November. The next day he wrote James Laughlin: "I found the poor devil in a rather desperate condition. He is very wobbly in his mind" (Cornell 13). See also Introduction and Letter 33n.

Mapels had called] Ida B. Mapel and her sister, Adah Lee, visited EP for the first time on 20 November 1945. Ida wrote EP on 21 November to offer to get him a suit of clothes, adding: "It was wonderful to see you and you were wonderful in the good old way of the great past. An epoch completely finished. We must look to the future" (Beinecke). She wrote DP on 27 November: "Ezra stood the trip over very well—seemed a bit nervous" (Lilly). EP recalled the visit in Canto 95: "Miss Ida by the bars in the jail house" (line 63). For the Mapels, see Letter 9n.

Mencken] Henry Louis Mencken (1880–1956), Baltimore author and editor whom EP considered an acute critic of the American scene. He was famous as coeditor of *The Smart Set* (1914–1923), founder and editor of *American Mercury* (1925–1933), and author of *The American Language*, first published in 1919 and later expanded. EP corresponded with him for many years, contributed to *The Smart Set*, and helped James Joyce publish stories in the same magazine. Mencken wrote EP on 19 November and again on 26 November 1945 to offer books and moral support (Beinecke), and later visited him at St. Elizabeths. EP mentions him in Canto 81. See also Letters 51n and 126n.

Purrade] "Life's Just a Passing Purrade to Terminal's Cats," a newspaper clipping about mascot cats at the Grand Central railway terminal in Washington, D.C., featuring a photo of Judy the cat at the cigar counter (Burke).

Frank Bacon] "Baldy" Bacon died in 1941. See Letter 37n.

ED. Wallace angle] Edgar Wallace. See Letter 38n.

cherry Bim] "Ciribiribin," a tune said to be based on an old Neapolitan song, was popularized by the Harry James orchestra in 1939 and by other performers. Omar Pound recalls it as part of the repertoire of piped music in army mess halls in 1945–1946.

Antheil] George Antheil (1900–1959), American avant-garde composer whom EP met in Paris in 1923, actively promoted, and discussed in *Antheil and the Treatise on Harmony* (1924). Though he wrote more conventionally scored music, Antheil is chiefly remembered for his *Ballet mécanique*, which premiered in Paris in 1926 with a cacophonous instrumentation that included eight pianos and two airplane propellers. He called his autobiography *The Bad Boy of Music* (1945). See also Letter 1n.

55 Notes. In black ink on a half sheet of graph-ruled paper, both sides; envelope addressed to EP "c/o Governor Columbia Prison, Washington, D.C."; redirected in another hand to "St. Elizabeths Hosp. West Side"; stamped received in Washington "Jan 25 1946" (Lilly).

Ma Riess] Lucy Mabel Pigott Riess (1864–1953), born in Barnsley, Yorkshire, studied in Germany, where she married Max Riess (b. 1869), a scholar of late medieval German poetry. Widowed, she moved to Rapallo and was known as "Mother May," a name given her by Oskar Kokoschka, who visited her there in the 1930s. James Laughlin stayed with her when he visited EP in Rapallo before World War II.

District Jail
Washington D.C.
CB1 (i.e. Cell Block)
cell 216
24 Nov. [1945]

Mao:

Cornell has been in twice & I like him & he will attend to technicalities - I take it - Thanks for yr. instructions to Moore.

I said the Mapels had called & Mencken written. - best headline is a new one "Life just a passing Purrade for terminal cats." - Pore ole Frank Bacon is dead, as I rather anticipated - tho' naturally hoped otherwise - but I thought he was shaky at the top. - Jas. [Laughlin] is @ bedside of possibly dying father in law - The local comforts are weak chess (not had time for that in years) & a buffet or something that supplies ice cream &, I hear, peanut butter etc. on 3 days notice before hand. -

Pazienza! Miss Ida [Mapel] also wanting to buy me shirts etc.

Ed. Wallace angle. Cherry Bim serving the meals etc.

Love to mother & hope you are gettin fed - wrote Viola [Jordan] to send you Barrington Hall coffee - as thought note from me might reach her before yrs. if you had sent one.

Antheil still advertised as the bad boy of music. - yester snows.

Love E.

Villa Raggio
Cerisola.
Rapallo
Nov 24 1945

Dearest.

Should this reach you . . . Omar with me for ten days - The greatest possible comfort & support: full of filial piety towards both of us. He called at the camp [DTC] on his way here - missed you by two days - great disappointment. John [Drummond] also arrived the same day, bringing me some money: & next day Lloyd's first installment safely banked. Moore forwards me copy of a letter from a friend re citizenship: valuable & interesting.

She was greatly interested in literature and the fine arts, and was a close friend of Desmond Chute. At the end of the war, Mary Rudge worked for her occasionally, and Olga Rudge used her apartment to teach in. She is buried in the Protestant cemetery in Rapallo near Homer Pound.

Harry's Dürers] Henry Tudor Tucker, Olivia Shakespear's brother, had a collection of engravings by Albrecht Dürer.

Mrs Bell] See Letter 48n.

Mary Burd] See letter 48n.

Elfriede's brothers] Dr. Elfriede Bacigalupo's two brothers lived in Bremen, where Omar was stationed.

56 Notes. In pencil on a smallish sheet of gray paper, one side, with postscript on reverse, and stamped by the D.C. Jail censor; matching gray envelope signed by EP under the flap and addressed to DP at Villa Raggio; postmark illegible (Lilly). DP mentioned receiving Letter 56 in her diary for 4 January 1946.

Infirmary] Several days earlier, EP had been moved to the District Jail's infirmary.

Am giving Cornell his head] On 26 November 1945 EP was formally reindicted for nineteen overt acts of treason. He appeared in federal district court for his arraignment on 27 November and, on Julien Cornell's instructions, stood mute and did not enter a plea, with the result that a plea of not guilty was entered for him. Cornell then moved that EP was suffering from mental illness and that, unless he was transferred from jail to a hospital, he would not recover sufficently to be able to stand trial. Judge Bolitha J. Laws ordered that EP be removed to Gallinger Hospital or a similar institution for psychiatric examination and treatment. See also Document 14n.

K. Proctor Saint] Katharine Wright Proctor married Lawrence Bradford Saint in 1910; they had eight children. EP and his mother had known her many years before. In 1945–1946, Katharine Proctor Saint wrote to EP and visited him in Washington to witness to him and convert him to faith in Jesus Christ. Earlier in November 1945 she had written FBI Director J. Edgar Hoover to find out how she might get a large-print Bible to EP (FBI documents 100–34099–382 and -383). See also Introduction and Letters 61n, 110, 118n, and 128.

Omar & I had tea with old Mrs. Riess - we talked of Dürer & Holbein, & had a Haydn symphony & a big Bach chorale on the gramophone. The child [Omar] is <u>very</u> musical & has most distinct ideas about Harry's Dürers etc. etc. & is learning lots rapidly. Ina [Benatti] loves him. Ma Riess such a comfort & so loyal to you. I have written Mrs Bell. Miss Ida [Mapel] (more than once) & to Mary Burd. MacLeish in London. John [Drummond] gone home for a month.

Yr. mother much as usual - We lunched at 12. via Marsala with the Corradis - & today go to Elfriede's.

Laundry woman, Dante [Majerna] & all such, telling me to be of good cheer - as you've done nothing wrong, & have always been so good to everybody: & all hope to see you soon. Omar saw Elfriede's brothers before he left - They remembered tennis with you.

Yours always

D.

56 EZRA TO DOROTHY

Infirmary
District Jail
Wash. DC.
29 Nov [1945]

Mao

Am giving Cornell his head. I like him. am moved to better ventilation. good letter from [Hugo] Fack. Viola [Jordan] may send you coffee - seems some muddle in her mind as to sending it to me.

Patience - send me date of that stopped cheque - Jenkintown [Bank] don't remember it (at least not yet). Hope you got home O.K. from Pisa.

love to mother

love E

Tell ma K. Proctor Saint is offering me special edition of the scriptures - first communique in 35 years.

57 Notes. In black ink on a half sheet of graph-ruled paper, both sides (Lilly). Omar was unsuccessful in forwarding this letter to EP, and DP enclosed it with Letter 79.

Lance Corporal] British equivalent of private first class (U.S.).

I have written you] Letters 53 and 55.

Nassano] Giambattista Nassano. See Letter 11n.

Dr. Gulizia] Mario Gulizia (1902–1970), a local doctor. DP wrote A. V. Moore on 2 December 1945: "Yesterday two witnesses: 1.) Dr. Gulizia visiting us (not professionally) said he knew quite well that EP. was nonpolitical & interested in finance-economic question & that he certainly hadn't made any fortune over the radio. 2.) 'I love my country, but I hate the government' (Roosevelt) 'I would never change my nationality'" (OP).

OP. goes off] Omar returned to Bremen via Pisa on an ambulance carrying a South African soldier who groaned in pain at every bump in the appalling road. DP notes in her diary for 30 November: "Up 6 a.m. down with Omar 7.15 abt 7.45 Red X going to Livorno - wet - snowy."

58 Notes. In pencil on a thin sheet of white paper with a U.S. Great Seal watermark, one side; gray envelope signed by EP under the flap and addressed to DP at Villa Raggio; postmarked "Washington, D.C. Dec 10 1945" (Lilly). DP mentioned receiving Letter 58 in her diary for 15 January 1946.

Gallinger Hospital] Pursuant to the 27 November ruling of Judge Laws, EP was transferred from the District Jail to Gallinger Municipal Hospital on 4 December. There he was given a physical checkup and, between 4 and 13 December, was examined by four psychiatrists, three of them appointed by the prosecution and one by the defense. They concluded that EP was insane and unfit to stand trial and submitted their unanimous report to Judge Laws, who on 21 December ordered EP's transfer to St. Elizabeths Hospital for the Insane, pending a jury hearing on his sanity.

Life of Gallatin] Henry Adams (1838–1918) wrote *The Life of Albert Gallatin* (1879). Gallatin (1761–1849) was a Swiss-born American financier, statesman, and secretary of the Treasury (1801–1814), presiding over the nation's change in financial policy from Federalist to Jeffersonian principles. EP mentions Gallatin in Cantos 31, 34, 41, and 71, and spoke of him in his radio talks: "whether that kike was honest, or merely clever, I leave to men who can get hold of Henry's Life of Albert Gallatin and ulterior documents" (Doob 121). See also Letter 76

Villa Raggio
Cerisola
Rapallo
Nov 29. 1945.

Dearest.

Omar may be able to get this forwarded - I have no address. He has been the great-est comfort to me during these ten days. His tastes seem to lie about Chaucer, Dürer, Bach - with much cheerfulness. He & Ina [Benatti] got on well & she gave him a cook-ing lesson! He cooked several dishes for me. We visited Elfriede [Bacigalupo] more than once, & he liked her immensely: he's very quick to get the person. "What on <u>earth</u> is that coming?!" meeting Desmond [Chute] on the garden path - looking moreso than usual - but liked him - He has you much in & on his mind. Doesn't see how I can stand the old woman [Isabel]. John [Drummond] has gone to London on leave. He & Omar same rank - Lance Corporal. I have written you that I have received some money from my bank - all O.K. for a while now.

Nassano finally free again. I saw his daughter. Dr. Gulizia says you always worked hard & certainly never made large sums of money - & Mrs. Majerna recalled to me how you had said to her you would never change yr. nationality, as you loved yr. country -

I have quoted these to A.V.M. [Moore].

This is p.m. as OP. goes off cockcrow tomorrow -

Always Yours

D -

58 EZRA TO DOROTHY

Gallinger Hospital
19th & B. st.
Washington D.C.
East Building N.E.
8 Dec [1945]

Mao -

Having a rest cure.

[Julien] Cornell has brought me Hen. Adams Life of Gallatin - etc.

Mao   E

Have patience. & Xmas wishes & Love to mother.

59 Notes. In black ink on a large sheet of paper folded double and written on two sides; no extant envelope (OP).

Cornell's re EP's state of health] Julien Cornell's letter of 21 November 1945 to James Laughlin, quoted in Letter 54n. The letter, which Cornell copied to A. V. Moore, is printed in full in Cornell 13–15.

Unkle George] Congressman George H. Tinkham. See Letter 29n.

Cantos also arr:] The new canto material that EP had sent DP via the Base Censor in Letter 45 arrived on 4 December 1945.

60 Notes. In black ink on two sheets of paper folded double and written on alternate sides; envelope addressed to EP "c/o Gallinger Hospital"; redirected in another hand to "St Elizabeth Hosp"; postmarked "Rapallo 13.12.45" and stamped by the Italian censor (Lilly).

I wrote twice] Letters 55 and perhaps 57.

Mr. Cornell's report] On 29 November 1945 Julien Cornell sent a lengthy report to A. V. Moore on EP's health and the progress of his case. Moore in turn sent a copy to DP, which arrived on 12 December. In part the report reads: "While he is able to converse extensively about literary and political matters, he appears to have great difficulty in concentrating upon his case and he appears to be unable to exercise any judgment whatever regarding the impending trial. Because of his lack of ability to exercise any judgment and also because of his mental exhaustion, I considered him unable to plead to the indictment and requested the court that he be permitted to stand mute. [. . .] I told the court that in my opinion Mr. Pound was on the verge of a second mental collapse, and that his sanity, if not his life, required that he be immediately removed from the prison and placed in a hospital for observation and treatment" (Lilly). The report is printed in full in Cornell 25–27.

59 DOROTHY TO OMAR POUND

Villa Raggio
Rap. [Rapallo]
Dec. 8 1945

Dearest Omar.

A letter from A.V.M. [Moore] enclosing copy of Cornell's re EP's state of health & A.V.M.'s cable to Cornell. I have written the latter a word, asking if he can give dad some little messages from me. A.V.M. says don't worry. I am trying not to. The letter gave me an awful jolt. I telegraphed A.V.M. that I was prepared to go to the States, if permission is given - to apply for you also - & to let me have some instructions on how to get there. I can't see any possible way at the moment! I should prefer air, of course. I am only hoping that things aren't so bad as the report - & am trusting A.V.M.

Did you get to London? no news from you yet.

Bitterly cold here, excuse handwriting. I told you the cable to Unkle George was returned - no address left. Second lot of money from Lloyd's arrived safely. Have told Moore.

Your MUM.

Cantos also arr [arrived]: am v. busy copying Chinese Characters clearly.

60 DOROTHY TO EZRA

Villa Raggio
Cerisola
Rapallo.
Dec 13 1945

Dearest.

Hoping this may fetch-up ... I wrote twice c/o Gov. of District of Columbia Prison - - & have sent messages of our welfare through friends. I received Mr. Cornell's report to A.V.M. [Moore] yesterday: I hope you may be in somewhat less vile conditions now. I have wired to A.V.M. & written Cornell to see you into a sanatorium for a rest & relaxation. . . . I shall try to come over: if Moore gets me permission. I hear the Miss Mapels visited you in Wash: thank heaven for that.

I got the bunch of Cantos via Base Censor: No. 60 [Olga and Mary Rudge] is typing the copies & putting in Greek - after wh. I am inserting Chinese Characters in legible manner - (but not for printing). They then go on to Possum [Eliot] and Laughlin. I hear the new version of Kung, & Cantos, are safe in U.S.A. but I am sending Cantos to Jas [Laughlin] because of the Chinese.

the Miss Mapels visited you] Their first visit, on 20 November 1945, as Ida reported in her letter to DP of 27 November (see Letter 54n).

cantos via Base censor] See Letters 45n and 59n.

MacLeish] Archibald MacLeish wrote to the Passport Division of the State Department to inquire about DP's citizenship and reported what he had learned in a letter to her dated 26 November 1945, received by DP on 12 December (Lilly).

copies of Introductory T. BK] EP's *Introductory Text Book* (1939). See Documents 6n and 7n and Letter 2n.

61 Notes. In pencil on a thin sheet of white paper with U.S. Great Seal watermark, one side, with final postscript on reverse; marked "O.K." and initialed in purple ink in an unknown hand; envelope with printed Gallinger Municipal Hospital return address, signed by EP under the flap, addressed to DP at Villa Raggio, postmarked "Washington, D.C. Dec 20 1945," and stamped received in Rapallo "19.1.[46]." DP marked the letter in pencil, "recd Jan. 20 46" (Lilly).

Mr. McGrath] Unidentified. EP referred to some of the hospital guards and attendants as his "guardian angels."

"Weston's george Inn"] Isabel's maiden name was Weston. EP's Aunt Frank (Frances Weston) ran a board-inghouse at 24 East 47th Street in New York at the turn of the century.

Bill Bird] William Augustus Bird IV (1889–1963), born in Buffalo, New York, attended Trinity College (Connecticut) and the Sorbonne, and served in the American Ambulance Corps during World War I. In 1921–1922 while working as Paris correspondent for the *New York Herald Tribune*, he founded Three Mountains Press, which published EP's folio edition of *A Draft of XVI. Cantos* (1925) and drawings by DP in a collection of short stories by B. C. Windeler, as well as important works by Ernest Hemingway, William Carlos Williams, Gertrude Stein, and others. Bird visited EP in Washington, D.C., in December 1945 and recalled the meeting in a letter to DP of 12 November 1946: "he appeared rather disillusioned about Musso[lini]. Ez said that when the end came in Italy he had been trying for some time to get to Moscow, where he hoped to persuade 'Uncle Joe' [Stalin] that the American Constitution was a superior instrument to the Soviet Constitution. [. . .] I only had about 15 minutes with him. I tried to keep the conversation off his 'case' and talk about personal matters, but he kept going back to the Constitution, etc. etc." (Lilly).

stained glass rose window] Lawrence Bradford Saint (1885–1961) was an international artist in stained glass who did work for many churches, including Washington Cathedral where he directed a special glass studio from 1928 to 1935. He completed the north transept rose window, "The Last Judgment," in 1932. It measured twenty-six feet in diameter and contained about nine thousand separate pieces of glass. For his wife, Katharine Proctor Saint, see Letter 56n.

Shelling] Felix E. Schelling (1858–1945) died on 15 December. He had been professor of english literature at the University of Pennsylvania (1893–1929), where EP studied under him.

MacLeish writes that I can't lose my citizenship - nor can it "lapse." I have written State Dept that I have no intention of letting it "lapse." & that I want a new pport . . . A.V.M. has already done this for me: but a letter from me is perhaps wise as evidence . . . . Omar's ten days here a great relief & comfort: I feel him very reliable & most kind & thoughtful. He has, I gave him, a lot of names & addresses in U.S.A. should there be any need. I am so hoping you will be allowed to see some friends - that would help you a deal.

Ina [Benatti] so sweet to me. Yr. Ma taking it all pretty well. She's very grumpy lately: but its been beastly cold.

I am sending copies of Introductory T. BK in all letters. Any sign of life from Uncle G. [George H. Tinkham]?

I have enjoyed working on the Ch. so much! I have found all of them: thank goodness you marked the dictionary!

I will write again quite soon to this address. . .

Always yours

D.

61 EZRA TO DOROTHY

Gallinger Hospital

[Washington, D.C.]

16 Dec [1945]

O MAO

Very wearing. Have patience. Old Katharine [Proctor Saint] with 5th son (or child) out of 8; strong in the Lord, hove in to save soul, complete with bible − but thanks to my irish guardian angel Mr. McGrath (his presence of mind) she did send excellent box of chocolate covered biscuit later − labled "Weston's george Inn" − hotel keepin' evidently inveterate in the family even to unknown branches.

Bill Bird over at marshal's office other day − I didn't know him till he told me who he was. Katharine is Mrs L. Saint + reprod of his stained glass rose window in cathedral here − really fine − something to replace devastations. − Doc. Shelling (Shakspearian etc. scholar) just dead @ age 87. mother will remember even if you dont locate. Last saw him by door Brit Museum reading room. −

Love E.

no mail yet come from Italy. D.T.C. probably without forwarding address.

Love. E

just read minor odes VII I̶V̶ − 74. marvelous. Bill [Bird] says Guy Hickok is in Rome with UNRA. Tell [John] Drummond

minor odes VII ~~IV~~ – 7 4.] Poem IV of Book 7 of the "Elegantiae, or Smaller Odes" in *The Classic Anthology Defined by Confucius,* part of which reads in EP's translation:

> Hot axle, I drove, drove
> to my love
> > hasting,
> neither food nor drink
> > tasting.
> I thought of her inwit,
> No friends with me
> > feasting.
> Pheasant finds home
> in flat forest,
> My heart a nest
> in her thought
> > resting. (133)

If EP's notation, "VII – 4," refers instead to Poem VII of Book 4, then it is the poem that begins, "Abacus against high cloud, crag over crag, Mount South / to echo with cry on cry" (103–4).

Guy Hickok] Guy Carleton Hickok (1888–1951), born in Mecca, Ohio, joined the «MDUL»Brooklyn Eagle«MDNM» and became head of its Paris bureau in 1918. A friend of Ernest Hemingway, he was disgusted with the superficial materialism of America in the 1920s and published a satirical travelogue, "Or Those Synthetic States," in the first issue of EP's magazine, *The Exile* (1927). After returning to the United States in 1933, Hickok joined the McClure Syndicate, worked for *The Literary Digest* and *Newsweek,* directed international shortwave broadcasting for the National Broadcasting Company, and was radio chief for the coordinator of inter-american affairs. During World War II he served as information chief in southeastern Europe for the United Nations Relief and Rehabilitation Administration (UNRRA), created in 1943 to provide social-welfare services to war-ravaged nations and to help resettle displaced persons and refugees.

62 Notes. In black ink on four sheets of paper, one side each; envelope addressed to EP in Gallinger Hospital, postmarked "Rapallo 20.12.45," stamped by the Italian censor, and redirected in an unknown hand to "St Elizabeth Hosp." (Lilly).

Base Censor MSS] See Letters 45n and 59n. The page numbers of EP's typescripts would appear erratic to anyone unfamiliar with his system of pagination. Also, there were gaps in the sequences that he sent.

Basil's arabic] Basil Bunting had written "Firdausi" (not "Allah") in Persian script on his door in Rapallo. EP wished to reproduce this script in Canto 77 between the lines, "If Basil sing of Shah Nameh, and wrote / ~~Firdush~~ on his door" (lines 284–86). Bunting sent the script in a letter to DP of 27 November 1946, adding, "it is as near as I can make it from memory to the lettering used on the oldest tiles in buildings of the Seljuk dynasty, which began about 1050—half a century after Firdausi died" (Lilly). Firdausi (ca. 940–1020) was the greatest of the Persian epic poets and the author of the *Sháhnáma* (Book of Kings), which he began at the age of forty to forty-one and completed at sev. At 80, he attached an ironic ending to the immense poem. For Bunting, see Letter 19n.

two characters] Page 15 (ms 100) of the 4 November canto batch contained two penciled Chinese ideograms that DP had trouble locating in her dictionary. These characters, which do not appear in the published version, were intended for Canto 74 between "in Chi heard Shun's music" and "babao, or the hawk's wing" (lines 491 and 495 in the printed text). EP's typescript, along with typed copies by Mary Rudge containing DP's attempts at reproducing the ideograms, is at Beinecke.

roomful of W.L.'s] DP owned several paintings by Wyndham Lewis that she had either bought directly from him or inherited from her mother, Olivia Shakespear. See also Letter 19n.

report from Cornell to Moore] See Letter 60n.

one from you Nov. 24.] Letter 54.

Villa Raggio
Cerisola
Rapallo
Dec 19 1945.

Dearest.

I have no news from you yourself since the Base Censor MSS arrived – There was only one batch sent thus? The numbering is confused & doesn't all follow on. Anyway what I recd has been typed, Greek'd & Chinese'd – & sent to Jas. [Laughlin] & T.S.E. [Eliot]. I have an idea Basil's arabic was "allah" – but you are more probably right – & if you think it was "Firdausi" . . . I have asked T.S.E. to see if he can trail down Basil to find out.

I couldn't track two characters: one in a seal – & the other one at top of same page: but copied them as well as I could from yours.

I am hoping that by now you are in a more tolerable conditions – My own comfortable bed & roomful of W.L.'s etc: seems to reproach me so: the food I feel I earn by marketting & cooking! Yr. Ma fairly tiresome – very carnivore – specially voracious: eats more than I do.

Prices always higher: 40 & 50. lire gone up to 70 & 80. for fruit – & so on, never mind. I certainly was not intended for an old woman's companion-cook!

Ina [Benatti] as usual an angel: She is much distressed abt you. She is making us some ravioli & a tart for Xmas – same as for her own family. I have been able to give her some things to square-up. I showed Elfriede [Bacigalupo] the report from Cornell to Moore. I thought it right she should see it. I do trust you like C. [Cornell] & that he is showing some understanding.

Here post – one from you Nov. 24. saying C. had been in & Miss Mapel. Sorry [Frank] Bacon has gone.

You can write to others than myself? I wrote to Viola [Jordan] some while ago, when you asked: to Bacon & Mrs. also. Macleish & others seem to be trying to get my passport put straight. I am quite intent on getting over to be with you. Its just silly, my living this life, & so dam far away from you. I must see you & be near you, & you can say so, please, to anybody. Moore busy on this job. Do hope you aren't missing army rations.

Please get it into yr. head that I'm coming over as soon as I can. (when that will be . . .?) I shall have Isabel in my room at 12/5 with Sigᵃ Corradi to look after her and Ina. She has always said or taken for granted that I was going to lug her along: but myself is all I can manage: & she hasn't enough to live on in the States + the fare. This time I am just ignoring it – & coming – alone. She's much too weak in body and head now. I can arrange a supplement to what the bly. [bloody] Govt lets her have (i.e. 2,300 lire p. month.) about ½. enough to just live on – A Telegram just in from Moore saying you are "receiving medical treatment." That's a comfort.

All my love

what the bly. Govt lets her have] Isabel received a pension from the U.S. Mint in Philadelphia, where her husband Homer had worked. See Letter 20n.

Telegram] On 17 December 1945 A. V. Moore cabled DP from London: "HUSBAND RECEIVING MEDICAL TREATMENT ADRESS GALLINGER HOSPITAL WASHINGTON DU [D.C.] YOU RITE IMIRESS [IMPRESS] ON HIN JOUR [YOUR] WISH TO VISIT HIM AT UNDE [ONCE] AM WORRYING FOR PASSPORT MOORE=" (OP).

Léger] Fernand Léger (1881–1955), French painter at the forefront of modern art in Paris in the 1920s. EP knew him, had his paintings reproduced in *The Little Review*, and wrote of him in "D'Artagnan Twenty Years After" (1937) (Cookson 452–60).

Davas family] The concierge's family at the Pounds' Paris apartment, 72 bis, rue Notre Dame des Champs, in the 1920s.

63 Notes. In pencil on a thin sheet of white paper with U.S. Great Seal watermark, one side. No envelope. Although filed with the EP-DP correspondence, this letter may actually have been written to Olga and Mary Rudge; it appears not to have been mailed (Lilly).

"Eccelin sunk] A recollection of lines from Robert Browning's early long poem, *Sordello* (1840) Book III:

> "And now
> "What glory may engird Sordello's brow
> "Through this? A month since at Oliero slunk
> "All that was Ecelin into a monk."

In the poem, which takes place at the time of conflicts between the Guelphs and the Ghibellines (ca. 1200), the Italian leader Ecelin da Romano, lord of Vicenza, has been exiled from his city and is wasting away in Oliero's convent. Browning stresses the contrast between Ecelin's former turbulence and his present enforced idleness. Ecelin is the father of Palma, whom the troubadour Sordello loves, and this is the "Eccelin" whom EP mentions in Canto 29. His son, Ezzelino (or Ecelin) III (1194–1259), was the Ghibelline leader whom Dante placed in the seventh circle of hell among the Violent against their Neighbors, and whom EP in his Italian Canto 72 makes to rage against usurers and betrayers of Italy. The sister of Ezzelino III was Cunizza da Romano (Browning's Palma) (ca. 1198-ca. 1279), who in the ninth canto of the *Paradiso* prophesies to Dante in the Sphere of Venus. EP celebrates Cunizza's unfettered sexuality and her freeing of family slaves in his Cantos 6 and 29. Early in 1945, while drafting material for further Italian cantos, he again drew on Cunizza's erotic and visionary associations. Although these sequences were never published, EP recalled them at the DTC and incorporated some of the Cunizza material into *The Pisan Cantos*.

Allusions to Browning's *Sordello* abound in EP's early "Three Cantos" (1917) and survive in condensed form in the opening of the final version of Canto 2: "Hang it all, Robert Browning, / there can be but the one 'Sordello.'" EP quoted a lengthy passage from *Sordello* in *ABC of Reading* (1934) for its "limpidity of narration" (191). He wrote the French critic René Taupin in 1928: "überhaupt ich stamm aus Browning. Pourquoi nier son père?" ("above all I derive from Browning. Why deny one's father?") (Paige 218).

64 Notes. In black ink on five small sheets from a writing-block, one side each except for the final sheet (both sides); envelope addressed to EP at Gallinger Hospital, postmarked "Rapallo 23.12.45," stamped by the Italian censor, and redirected in an unknown hand to "St Elizabeth Hosp." (Lilly)

Letter to yr. Ma] EP's letter to Isabel, dated 22 November 1945 and signed "yr. obstreperous offspring," is printed in Carpenter 708–9.

Old Ma Riess] See Letter 55n.

A letter from Miss Ida] Ida B. Mapel wrote DP on 4 December 1945 to assure her of the wisdom of EP's

letter from the kid [Omar] from Paris: hating a performance of 'La Tosca' & going to Purcell's 'Dido & Aeneas.' Léger (no address) in U.S.A. Davas family delighted to have our news.

Always D

P.S. Yrs. just come – of Nov. 24.

63 EZRA TO ?DOROTHY

Gallinger [Hospital]
[Washington, D.C.]
20 Dec [1945]

Dearets [sic].

Snow meltin' beyond steam heat & birds chirrpin. Thank god you two are together – at least I suppose you are – no mail yet from Italy since I got here.

"Eccelin sunk (or ?shrunk)
In Olaro convent to monk"

(somewhere in R. B's "Sordello." Toward the end, I think, or in last book.

64 DOROTHY TO EZRA

Villa Raggio
Cerisola
Rapallo
Dec 22 1945

Dearest Ming.

Am hoping you'll get a good feed at Xmas . . . Letter to yr. Ma, talking of fried chicken & ice cream was the greatest success: She is convinced you are living on the "fat of the land" – of which we don't see much here – but we are eating quite reasonably, barring prices – Hope Viola [Jordan] sends the coffee: and hoping it arrives. This letter is mostly Xmas greetings -

Ma Majerna has given me this & two other writing blocks. The gentleman with the dachs [dachshunds] – name unknown – stopped me yesterday & had a long pleasant chat about you – & sent his saluti & auguri [greetings and good wishes]. I took Omar in to yr. haircutter – & had such a flood . . . Confucius was good, yes: had I a bible in the house? He found so much comfort in the Old Testament. The Majernas en bloc say they never forget you – + tanti saluti.

Old Ma Riess is a brick. I go on Sundays from 3–6 to look after her while the servant (& illegitimate baby) are out walking. The child howls – but Ma R. is so very deaf now! Ina [Benatti], Nerina [Pagliettini, Ina's daughter], so many questions for news of you, & sympathies . . . real sympathy. Ina seriously said you mattered, as such a great man, whereas, she regretted, but her husband didn't – She gave Omar a cooking lesson:

plea of mental incompetence: "Boil this down and accept its essence for the moment. Call it temporary arrangement. It is a way out of the dilemma—for the Justice Department" (Lilly).

telegram from A.V.M.] See Letter 62n.

Chute back] Father Desmond Chute. See Letter 40n.

I told Omar all about Mary] This was the first time Omar had heard of Olga and Mary Rudge.

Antheil & T. on Harmony.] See Letter 54n.

65 *Notes. In black ink on four small sheets from a writing-block, one side each except for postscripts on back of pages two and four; envelope addressed to EP at Gallinger Hospital, postmarked "Rapallo 28.12.45," stamped by the Italian censor, and redirected in an unknown hand to "St. Eliz. Hosp." (Lilly).*

since about May 3] The date that EP was captured in 1945.

"twisted rhombs ..."] From section IX of EP's *Homage to Sextus Propertius*, composed in 1917 and published in full in *Quia Pauper Amavi* (1919):

> The twisted rhombs ceased their clamour of accompaniment;
> The scorched laurel lay in the fire-dust;
> The moon still declined to descend out of heaven,
>
> But the black ominous owl hoot was audible.
> And one raft bears our fates
>   on the veiled lake toward Avernus
> Sails spread on cerulean waters, I would shed tears for two;
> I shall live, if she continue in life,
>   If she dies, I shall go with her.
> Great Zeus, save the woman,
>   or she will sit before your feet in a veil,
>   and tell out the long list of her troubles.
>   (*Personae* 218)

Seamen's] Unidentified. He is mentioned in letters of Kate Isherwood to DP (Lilly). See also Letters 88 and 99.

"Rasselas"] *Rasselas* (1759) by Samuel Johnson (1709–1784), an episodic work about the title character's search for happiness. It resembles Voltaire's *Candide*, published in the same year. In a letter of 4 February 1946 to Olga Rudge's brother, EP signed himself, "Ezra (Candide)" (OR Papers, Beinecke).

Aramando] See Letter 13n.

Gulizia] Dr. Mario Gulizia. See Letter 57n.

he adored her! & was already speaking a few sentences. A letter from Miss Ida [Mapel] yesterday – A telegram from A.V.M. [Moore] giving me this address for you. I want to know what sort of a doctor you've struck – if its discreet to ask – or answer! Chute back here – going much the stronger for all his troubles.

I told Omar all about Mary when he was here: I thought it better, as so many now know: & I found him quite capable of understanding it – That was, I felt, enough for one visit. He took away a copy of Antheil & T. on Harmony, – Hated La Tosca, in Paris: was due next night to hear Dido & Aeneas, Purcell.

Seems to <u>pay attention</u> to what I say! which is always surprising! He is determined "to write" – but realizes he must have experience to write on. The psychology is at present a deep interest. He whistled me ever so many bits from symphonies etc. wh. I have not heard in years: & true ear, too.

re clothing – were you allowed to take over yr. own, such as it was? & now, what do you wear?

All my love

Yours always

D.

Have now had three remittances from Lloyd's—A.V.M. sure is earning his keep! [John] Drummond & [Ronald] Duncan saw A.V.M. & are arranging abt. publication here & in U.S.A.

65 DOROTHY TO EZRA

Villa Raggio
Cerisola
Rapallo
Xmas day 1945.

Dearest Ming.

Hope you are having some Xmas food! Ina [Benatti] made us ravioli & some cakes – same as for her own family: down below brought us up a plateful of nuts, figs etc. Yr. Ma made a 'real' rice pudding (i.e. milk, & too much sugar) & a cake. We are stuffed to the gills – Omar left us a little coffee.

I have just finished a second pair of knee stockings, from the St. Ambrogio sheep – An awful wet spell: very chilly. Am wearing yr. yellowbelly which I had renovated for you. Tell me about yr. clothing? Been spending the p.m. filing my letters since about May 3. One come up to O.P. [Omar Pound] from a pal – into wh. I am making inquiries – Sympathies about you to him but "I have rarely been moved by words more than these . . ." quoting "twisted rhombs . . . to tell out the long list of her troubles." Did I tell you Omar helped a lot with the cooking here! Meat twice – <u>not</u> as Isabel thought . . . I <u>was</u> amused! & fresh sardines. . . . & refused to have his potatoes pounded up – saying it made them "greasy"—a very entertaining ten days in a somewhat dreary waste. Ma

Document 15 Notes. This memo (FBI document 100–34099–417) contains several office notations and blacked-out lines which do not affect the text and which we have not reproduced. "SAC" means Special Agent in Charge.

Riess very valuable morally to me. Has made me a bag for wools etc. of a most lovely old piece of crimson velvet, lined with persian red & gold ~~embroidered~~ woven silk.

I wonder where you are. Still Gallinger? Do you manage any fresh air or relaxation?

A bloke called Seamen's called: had met you (here I think) about 10. yrs ago — a very interesting afternoon's talk.

Am reading "Rasselas." 18th cent. pleasant & slow and mot juste often but not quite heavy enough to oust one's other thoughts.

dearest — always D.

very kind few words from Aramando in street . . . Gulizia really charming: Ive had a long talk at the pub. corner — I have always seen him before with yr Ma buzzing. He seems to have several ideas in common with you.

We have just picked abt 15.K. of oranges off our one tree!

DOCUMENT 15 MEMO FROM FBI DIRECTOR, J. EDGAR HOOVER

FEDERAL BUREAU OF INVESTIGATION
UNITED STATES DEPARTMENT OF JUSTICE

To: Communications Section   DECEMBER 27, 1945 URGENT

Transmit the following message to: SAC, NEW YORK
                                      BOSTON
                                      NEWARK
                                      WASHINGTON FIELD

DOCTOR EZRA POUND, TREASON. REBULET DECEMBER TWELVE LAST, DEPARTMENT HAS AUTHORIZED DISCONTINUANCE OF INVESTIGATION PENDING FURTHER COURT ACTION AS TO POUND'S SANITY. YOU WILL BE ADVISED IF INVESTIGATION DESIRED AT LATER DATE.

HOOVER

66 Notes. In black ink on a small sheet from a writing-block, both sides; no extant envelope (Lilly).

"Canzone de li Ucelli"] See Letter 37n.

Cantos, 20. pages sent] See Letters 45n and 59n.

67 Notes. In black ink on four small sheets from a writing-block, one side each; envelope addressed to EP at Gallinger Hospital, postmarked "Rapallo 29.12.45," stamped by the Italian censor, and redirected in an unknown hand to "St Elizabeth Hosp." (Lilly).

ruling on bail] A document of eight typed pages, "Memorandum of Law on Application for Bail," prepared by Julien Cornell as EP's attorney and submitted to the court on 27 November 1945, along with a supporting affidavit. It contains a summary of the indictment and the legal provisions for the crime of treason, and argues that "this court has ample precedent for admitting to bail Ezra Pound, who has been charged with a crime hardly more heinous than piracy [an 1813 case that Cornell cites], and not only appears to be insane at the present time as a result of previous imprisonment, but may very likely be rendered permanently insane, and may lose his life, if imprisonment continues" (Lilly; printed in full in Cornell 149–53).

"Rassalas"] See Letter 65n.

Gerhardt's 'Uccelli'] See Letters 37n and 66.

my Doctor-friend] Dr. Mario Casonato, to whom DP sent a copy of EP's *Guido Cavalcanti Rime* (1932). DP met him on the journey back from her first visit to the DTC on 3 October 1945, not "Nov. 3," as she mistakenly says here. See Letter 18n.

the cantos you sent me] See Letters 45n and 59n.

He has sold Townsman] Ronald Duncan sold the magazine *Townsman* in 1944, and Volume 21 (July 1944) became an agricultural magazine called *The Scythe*, still edited by Duncan, its final number published in April 1946. For his play, *This Way to the Tomb*, see Letters 7n, 10n, and 41n.

> Villa Raggio
> Cerisola
> Rap. [Rapallo]
> Dec 28 1945

Dear Jas.

I am enclosing the music, "Canzone de li Ucelli" by Francesco da Milano – & arranged by Gerhard Münch – This goes in the Cantos: you will find the place mentioned in the M.S.S.

> Good Luck for 1946.

> Affecty D.P.

Hope you have recd Cantos, 20. pages sent registered post on Dec. 19. D.

67 DOROTHY TO EZRA

> Villa Raggio
> Cerisola
> Rapallo
> Dec 29 1945.

Dearest.

Nothing yet from you since yr. first letters to me & Isabel. A letter today from Moore: enclosing a long ruling on bail in the U.S. laws.

Will you please apply to the Hospital Authorities for the purpose of obtaining permission for me to visit you. It might hurry up things a little. I want so badly to be near you & see you: I am sure it would be good for you, & give you something to hold on to.

Have just read "Rassalas" – a gentle charming work: a little like Candide – without the french touch of course – Also some Conrad which wears extremely well. Also a Cookbook from Ma Riess! but its too full of eggs and sich although supposed to be war-time cookery. I have found a copy of Gerhardt's 'Uccelli' in Townsman, & sent it on to ~~him~~ Jas [Laughlin]. T.S.E. [Eliot] has had a copy already that Olga [Rudge] found.

This a.m. such a charming letter from my Doctor-friend in Massa. I had just wrapped up a G. Cav. for him! having inscribed the date when I met him on the road, after leaving you on Nov. 3. Laughlin reports to A.V.M. [Moore] that you are getting good care at the Hospital: whereby I conclude he has visited you? I have now sent him typescript of all the cantos you sent me – + the "Uccelli."

A long letter from Bunny [Duncan], Rose Marie [Duncan] is able to write letters, to draw & paint, & sew. May or June however is the earliest she will be let out. R's play a gt. success. He has sold Townsman – it is still going, mostly agricultural, called "The Scythe."

Lets hope for a better Year in 1946, with things cleared up & ourselves together again. Omar too wants a home.

> Always yours

> D.

In black ink on four small sheets from a writing-block, one side each, except for postscripts on back of the final page; envelope addressed to EP at Gallinger Hospital, postmarked "Rapallo 2.1.46," stamped by the Italian censor, and redirected in an unknown hand to "St Elizabeth Hosp." (Lilly)

Phyllis Bottome] See Letter 46n.

a "poem"?] DP's poem "No yaller dog" in Letter 38.

Nassano] Giambattista Nassano. See Letter 11n.

the Dean] Hewlett Johnson (1874–1966), dean of Canterbury (1931–1963), known as the "Red Dean" because of his political and social beliefs. He contributed to Ronald Duncan's *Townsman*, wrote *Social Credit and the War on Poverty* (London: Stanley Nott, 1935), and served as President of the Manchester Chapter of the Douglas Social Credit Association. In *Guide to Kulchur* (1938) EP wrote that "the venerable Dean of C., disgusted with the utter and crapulous lack of fervour in episcopal circles, finds comfort with communists" (330).

"you from N. Eng.? barked the 10th district"] This memory of Congressman George H. Tinkham occurs towards the end of Canto 76 (line 293). DP saw it on typescript page "31 (ms 134)" in the batch of canto material that EP had sent her in Letter 45. See also Letter 59n. For Tinkham, see Letter 29n.

Muratore] Possibly Ludovico Antonio Muratori (1672–1750), Italian scholar who edited collections of historical documents and wrote on church history. For "Baci" (Ruggero Massimo Bacigalupo, Elfriede's husband), see Letter 10n.

Villa Raggio
Cerisola
Rapallo.
Jan. I. 1946.

Dearest Ming.

Here's hoping! for a better year — All my love.

I had a sympathetic letter from Phyllis Bottome: they had dined with T.S.E. [Eliot] who had talked much of us both. It seems she & Omar knew each other! He has evidently moved around a bit, seeking to know our friends. Did you ever get a letter of mine with a "poem"? written after my first visit to DTC? It wasn't very successful . . ma [oh, well] . .

Yr. ma says a psychiatrist will be good for you: "he needs a change of ideas"! meaning that she's bored to death with yr. (inherited!) persistence. She is getting fairly silly now: but has just made a cake for New Year. Are the cherry trees up or cut down in Wash.? do ask — I met Nassano yesty. in the street near Nerina's [Pagliettini]: he looked pretty well . . has only been out about a month.

Our old acquaintance, the Dean, has invented a rack for washing dishes & drying—, says he had had to do dishes himself in these times, & had thought-out this help — This in an Italian paper: fame!

I am studying the new Cantos rather more carefully: didn't have time until the [Chinese] Characters were finished. One of my favourite lines is "you from N. Eng? barked the 10th district" seems firstrate! Wish you could get in touch with him. I wrote twice for you.

All my love

D.

Glory-be. There is now gaz to cook with, twice a day. Such a relief — Have just seen Elfriede [Bacigalupo]—so many good wishes from them.

I have returned the two vols. of Muratore to Baci. He asked rather anxiously one day — so Olga [Rudge] found them for me.

D.

69 Notes. In weak pencil on a sheet of ruled paper, one side; envelope addressed to DP at Villa Raggio, signed by EP under the flap, and postmarked "Washington, D.C. Jan 3 1946." Enclosed was a clipping from the Washington, D.C. Times-Herald*:*

Woman 'Saved' From 'Possum

Several anxious moments were experienced by Mrs. Evane MacCammon yesterday while police, summoned by phone, rushed to her home in the 1300 block Michigan Ave. NE.

Mrs. MacCammon let her terrier, Tiny, out for its early morning romp when she saw (she reported excitedly to police) "- a horrible thing with a long face and a long tail on my back steps."

Mystified but skeptical Pvts. Donald E. Allen and John W. Zeiss of No. 12 Precinct, loosened up their holsters and, in general, prepared to do battle.

But the police didn't have to resort to their weapons; a rapid search through the bushes in Mrs. MacCammon's back yard and a very scared 'possum was discovered.

Jokes and stories about possums ("Possum" was EP's nickname for T. S. Eliot) were a staple with EP and DP.

True Jhonnie] Many folk songs have titles similar to this. Sabine Baring Gould's collection, *Folk Songs of the West Country* (Newton Abbot, 1974), has words and music for a song called "Constant Johnny," a dialogue between two lovers, taken down in Halwell in 1889. The first verse runs:

Constant Johnny I do love thee,

There's none other I do adore,

'Tis your deceitful heart,

Causes me to feel this smart,

O Johnny, O Johnny I'll ne'er see thee more.

(30–31)

The lovers are later reconciled, and the song ends happily. Miss Florence Schmidt gave a recital in London in 1910 of Italian, French, and English songs, including "My Johnny Was a Shoemaker," about a shoemaker turned sailor who will "come back and marry me." EP's translations of some of the other songs were printed in a programme sold at the recital.

olibanum poem] DP's poem "No yaller dog" in Letter 38.

70 Notes. In black ink on four small sheets from a writing-tablet, one side each; no extant envelope (Lilly).

letter from you] Letter 56.

Letter also from Agnes] Agnes Bedford wrote DP on 17 December 1945 (Lilly).

Telegram] On 27 December 1945, A. V. Moore sent DP a night letter telegram from London, received 4 January 1946: "ADJUDICATED MENTALLY UNFITATO TO DEFEND HIMSELF HIS CONDITION GOOD AS USUAL SENT HOSPITAL ARIAL CANCELLED BELIEVE CAUGHT [COURT] WILL EVENTUALLY DISMISS CHARGES. MOORE" (OP). On 21 December 1945, Judge Bolitha J. Laws read in court a "Report of Psychiatric Examination" submitted to him by four psychiatrists: Joseph L. Gilbert, Marion R. King, Wendell Muncie, and Winfred Overholser. They unanimously concluded that EP was "insane and mentally unfit for trial, and is in need of care in a mental hospital" (Cornell 37). Judge Laws ordered EP to be transferred from Gallinger Hospital to St. Elizabeths Hospital. Later, the Department of Justice requested a jury trial, and on 13 February 1946 a sanity hearing was held, during which the four doctors testified concerning EP's mental state. After a few minutes of deliberation, the jury returned a verdict of "unsound mind," and Judge Laws ordered EP to be confined at St. Elizabeths, where he spent the next 121/2 years before the indictment was dismissed. At first he was placed in a cell in Howard Hall, a separate penal building surrounded by a dry moat and reserved for the criminally insane. It had been built after the hospital's original construction of 1855. EP was later moved from the "hell-hole," as he called it, to a more comfortable ward.

69 EZRA TO DOROTHY

[St. Elizabeths Hospital]
[Washington, D.C.]
[3 January 1946]

Dearest

It   is   35   years   since
you   sang   True   Jhonnie.
~~that is what~~

                              E

O thank you for olibanum poem
Dearest Dearest have patience.
buon anno [Happy New Year].
E.

how is mother?

70 DOROTHY TO EZRA

Villa Raggio
Cerisola
Rapallo.
Jan 5 1946.

Dearest.

A letter from you yesty, dated infirmary Nov. 29. Posts extra slow over Xmas.

I saw [Edgardo] Rossaro last week: he is terribly down. Pep [Giuseppe Soldato] is in the mountains & well.

I gather you are able to write & receive letters? not only mine -

Letter also from Agnes: near the end of her tether: her ma out of her mind – no nurse available. Asks shall we all survive these strains. I wrote saying I wasn't going to be smothered if I could help it.

Telegram this a.m. from A.V.M. [Moore] saying 'trial cancelled' & ~~that~~ 'sent hospital' – I conclude that is still Gallinger. Re coffee parcels: three or four have been sent off to yr. Ma – but none have arrived: they say v. few arrive: much stealing. I have already sent you & Unkle George [Tinkham] re chq. I repeat: dated June 28. 1940 (£20.) Answer from Jenkintown [Bank] Feb. 13. 1941. signed Demster. I wonder whether D.T.C. has forwarded any of my letters to you: after Nov. 11 when I saw you, ~~I have written several~~ wrote several to you there, before I knew you had gone . . . the latter on arrival here of Omar on 20th Nov. who had stopped off at D.T.C. to see you and found you'd gone. Nobody ever let me know where you were—only due to child [Omar]. . . Letter from Beulah Patterson, Big Timber Montana. Her brother Tom is in Wash: but she doesn't give his address. She puts forth certain ideas abt yr. situation that had occurred to me, which I am hinting at to A.V.M. Yr. broadcasts reached them at 4 a.m.

Beulah Patterson] For Beulah Patterson and the other Pound relatives, see Letters 37n, 47n, and Pound family chart (p. 000).

On Usury] In his essay "On Usury" (1625), Francis Bacon, after weighing the advantages and disadvantages of interest lending, proposes that there be "two rates of usury, the one free and general for all, the other under licence only to certain persons and in certain places of merchandising." The first rate, intended for the common borrower, should be set at "five in the hundred." The second rate should be restricted to larger transactions between lenders and merchants and set at 8 or 9 percent. It is better, Bacon concludes, "to mitigate usury by declaration than to suffer it to rage by connivance" (*The Essays,* ed. John Pitcher [London: Penguin, 1985], pp. 185–86). As far back as 1912, DP was enjoying Bacon's essays.

71 Notes. In pencil on a sheet of ruled paper, one side; envelope signed by EP under the flap, addressed to DP at Villa Raggio, and postmarked "Washington, D.C. Jan 11 1946" (Lilly).

your list 18th Oct.] See Letters 30 and 31. DP added a notation beneath EP's two ideograms in Letter 71: "(p 412) I.i."

Olson] Charles Olson (1910–1970), American poet and critic, worked for the wartime Roosevelt administration, later taught at Black Mountain College in North Carolina, and is best known for *The Maximus Poems* (1960, 1968). Olson visited EP at St. Elizabeths regularly during the first months of his incarceration. He had submitted a poem, "A Lustrum for You, E.P.," to New Directions, and in replying James Laughlin suggested that he visit EP: "You won't get a word in edgewise but you'll like it, I think" (Seelye xv–xvi). Olson recorded his impressions of EP during his first visit on 4 January 1946: "His eagerness and vigor as he came swiftly forward into the waiting room. The openness in his eyes. And shyness at looking too long at me, turning away, toward window. Still working at his forehead with his thumb, index and middle finger, occasionally as he did so much in court. I marked his emotion most when he spoke of Mary [Rudge] and Omar, his loneliness and worry about them" (Seelye 36). EP talked of the DTC, Mussolini, Brooks Adams, his wish to meet Stalin, and other matters. Distaste for EP's racial and political views eventually made Olson give up his visits.

& their radio was muzzy, out of order. She has planned a letter to you: if she can do anything to "lend ~~you~~ him courage, though I do not think he lacks that." Her mother still going & plays bits on her piano.

Am reading Bacon's Essays: On Usury – he admits 5%.

Must go to catch the out-post.

All my love

D.

Are you really fairly comfortably looked after? I should so like to know, & food? & reading matter?

71 EZRA TO DOROTHY

St Elizabeth Hospital
Wash. DC.
Sunday
Jan.

first sunday. [6 January 1946]

Mao.

    dearest mao.

              not on your list
                18th
                       Oct.

[3802]

[3802]

Olson gt comfort. Hope they let him come back. only solid.

    Miss Ida [Mapel] fix'd coat lining.

        love
        ever
        E.

72 Notes. In black ink on four small sheets from a writing-block, one side each except for page four (both sides); no extant envelope (Lilly).

Lester States Esq] Lester E. States, at this time Second Vice President, had for years handled EP's and DP's accounts at the Chase National Bank in New York. The two hundred dollars that DP received may have come from EP himself, as he suggests in Letter 94. EP had had Julien Cornell cable two hundred dollars to DP and one hundred dollars to Mary Rudge on 20 December 1945 (Cornell's correspondence, Lilly).

Ma Riess] In Discretions, Mary de Rachewiltz describes working for Ma Riess: "I was to put her books in order, read out loud to her and play bezique. I also answered the doorbell, made tea and sometimes prepared a very light supper for her. She was plagued by severe arthritis" (259). See also Letter 55n.

Riverendo] Father Desmond Chute. See Letters 40n and 76n.

indiarubber ball] Unidentified.

Dina howked yr. ma out of bed] Dina was an occasional housemaid. "Howk": "to scoop or dig out." EP found the word in the Scottish poet Gavin Douglas and used it in various works, including the Confucian Classic Anthology: "South lakes full of flickering fish, [. . .] Howk 'em up with a landing scoop" (90).

Villa Raggio
Cerisola
Rapallo.
Jan 8. 1946.

Dearest Mao.

Yr. ma retired to bed these three days owing to the bitter weather: means a good deal of running around, but, on the other hand, I eat by myself in peace! Marie (an ex-maid) comes twice a week, wh. helps a lot.

Today I got Italian lire to the tune of $200 from Chase [Bank]. Nobody more surprised than myself! I wrote *ages* ago, when feeling desperate, to send me at once—but had quite forgotten. I am acknowledging this to Lester States Esq, 11 Broad St NY. Trust Dept: and at the same time have written, that I wish $300, three hundred dollars, to be at yr. disposal – giving him Gallinger address: but saying you will write to him as soon as you receive this letter, saying where you are and how you would like the cash sent.

I don't know whether this will work – but I'm trying anyway. Also I wish to know what I have lying around there – for him to let me know.

No news of Omar: but I suppose I shall get a letter now that the Xmas post scramble is over.

Elfriede [Bacigalupo] called up here, as yr. Ma has such a pain & sore place on her toe – – – – chilblain! Elfr. so thankful you are at least in hospital, & hopes things are going better for you. They are all so good and faithful to you.

Have just recd also a first letter from Miss Ida [Mapel], with a charming calendar: I had had later letters before this one.

Ma Riess wants me to tell you, Mary [Rudge] is working for her: that she is very quiet & discreet, & businesslike – most competent – &, at least in England, would be able to get a large salary as Secretary to some public man – the languages etc. She is also being made use of by Riverendo.

Ma R. knows about her—everybody in fact ... & Ma. R. "she's not stolen her wits" – ! It seems the indiarubber ball also has an illegitimate son – but I don't know what age – so we are all populating the world for the next wars.

Please, tell me what you can, about yr. comforts – food, warmth? clothing? and take all the relaxation & fresh air offered – You've been through altogether too much. Hope you receive my letters. I write at least once a week.

Always yours

D.

Dina howked yr. ma out of bed today! good work! & Ina [Benatti] up to tea -

73 Notes. Sloping pencil scrawl on a sheet of ruled paper, one side; mailed to A. V. Moore in London and stamped received at Shakespear & Parkyn on "25 Jan. 1946," with a note in Moore's hand: "Posted Washington 12 Jan 1946." Moore's airmail envelope is addressed to DP at Villa Raggio, postmarked "London 25 Jan 1946," and stamped by the Italian censor. DP penciled on back of Letter 73, "recd 11 Feb '46" (Lilly).

her birthday] Isabel turned eighty-six on 13 January 1946.

74 Notes. In black ink on four small sheets from a writing-block, one side each; envelope addressed to EP at "St. Elizabeth's Hospital" and stamped by the Italian censor; postmark torn off (Lilly).

Olivia's wrist-watch] DP's mother had a small round gold watch with a Victorian chain. Other small items of gold that DP owned she had to sell off to pay for food, including the band from Olivia's walking stick.

Bride] Bride Scratton wrote DP from Cambridge, England, on 23 December 1945 to say that she had learned of the psychiatrists' report on EP's mental state, adding that his long confinement "was like trapping an eagle in a hen coop" (Lilly). See also Letter 18n.

My lynxes] The extract from Canto 79 that EP had sent DP as a birthday gift. See Letter 24n.

"the Golden Gates of Samarkand"] The English poet James Elroy Flecker (1884–1915) wrote a volume of poems, *The Golden Journey to Samarkand* (1913), and a posthumously published oriental phantasy and play, *Hassan: The Story of Hassan of Bagdad and How He Came to Make the Golden Journey to Samarkand* (1922).

my p-port] On 11 January 1946 DP received from Julien Cornell a copy of a letter to him from Ruth B. Shipley, chief of the Passport Division in the Department of State, saying that the American consul general at Genoa was being authorized to issue DP a passport for travel to the United States, provided that she had not lost her citizenship and that she make a new application (Lilly).

Truman ...] DP may be reporting a remark by Isabel.

Overholser] Dr. Winfred Overholser (1892–1964), a noted psychiatrist, became superintendent at St. Elizabeths Hospital in 1937 after serving as commissioner of the Massachusetts Department for Mental Diseases. He was one of three doctors chosen by the government to report on EP's mental state in 1945. Convinced that court-appointed psychiatrists should put aside legal partisanship and try to arrive at agreement on a defendant's condition, he worked hard to establish a unanimous opinion on EP. Over the years he consistently maintained, despite dissent from some of his doctors, that EP was of unsound mind and unfit to stand trial, and he saw to it that EP's privileges at St. Elizabeths were increased. After EP and DP returned to Italy in 1958, he kept in touch. Here, DP notices the coincidence with the name of Willis Overholser, the American money historian whom EP admired. See Document 7n and Letter 43n.

Mairet] Philip Mairet (1886–1975) served in an ambulance unit in World War I and was imprisoned in Britain as a conscientious objector. Later he was Secretary of the British Adlerian Society and became editor of the New English Weekly after A.R. Orage's death in 1934, continuing until 1949. Social Credit interested him, and after World War II he joined the Soil Association, concerning himself with Christian and ecological issues. We have been unable to locate any essay by Ronald Duncan on "EP's cultural influence," but a two-part essay on EP by Reginald Snell in the New English Weekly may have been written with Duncan's assistance (see Letter 108n). See also Documents 3–5n.

73 EZRA TO DOROTHY

St Elizabeths Hospital
Washington DC.
[12 January 1946]

A. V.M. [Moore] for D.P.

Dear D.

Please everybody write a <u>LOT</u> to me & not expect answers: – Moore tell Ron. [Duncan] – & all.

via London probably quicker than direct from Rap. [Rapallo]

Love to mother for her birthday.

E

74 DOROTHY TO EZRA

Villa Raggio
Cerisola
Rap. [Rapallo]
Jan 13 1946.

Mao!

Yr. Ma's birthday, which luckily I remembered – & offered her at 8.30 am. a tray with nuts, figs, biscuits, soap, some good writing-paper & so on – Created such a twitter all the morning! She gave me back at Xmas, Olivia's wrist-watch – I am so pleased to have it.

OP. [Omar Pound] sent two p.c. photos of himself – one with glasses on – mine – and the other, oh! very pretty without, which of course she likes best – O.K. Just heard from Ronnie [Duncan], he has had letter from you – That's alright. Also I have had a sweet letter from Bride, on reading things about you in papers. I have given her yr. address – & when I answered, enclosed a copy of My lynxes, as I somehow had an extra one: I think she'll 'see' it – She speaks of "the Golden Gates of Samarkand" & says "love is the only eternal thing."

Via various channels it seems likely I may get my p-port, & if so, shall go on & on through the forest – & if I don't faint by the way – I am hoping to fetch up chez toi some time. If by air, one suitcase – if by boat – wh. heaven forbid, I could bring yours as well? Isabel is ½ way towards <u>her</u> p-port – & the idea is she should get escort (competent) later, in spring, & go to an Old Lady's Home. She is writing about this to somebody. I am not going to set up house with her ever again – (put the accents where you like.)

I sent you details of that cheque £20 stg., June 28. 1940 – letter answered ~~January~~ Feb. 13 '41. I am told Truman[?] is a very high up one. I see yr. doc: is Overholser: a pleasant-sounding name. Am enclosing a letter from [Henry] Swabey, wh. can be deciphered with patience. Mairet has asked Ronnie to write on "EP.'s cultural influence" – wh. he will ~~be~~ do. ~~done.~~

Mao Mao.   Yours D.

75 Notes. Sloping pencil scrawl on a sheet of ruled paper, one side; envelope signed by EP under the flap, addressed to DP at Villa Raggio, and postmarked "Washington, D.C. Jan 16 1946" (Lilly).

good news] EP enclosed a clipping from the photo section of the *Washington, D.C. Times-Herald* (14 January 1946), 16, featuring a tiger and its newborn cubs and captioned "Mitt the Proud Pappy": "If tigers smoked cigars, Kala Nag would be passing them out to fellow zoo mates in Miami, Fla. The 650-pound Royal Bengal tiger, believed to be the largest in captivity, gives out with a Madison Square Garden handshake after viewing his triplets for the first time. The kids don't seem too interested in anything at the moment—except for the whereabouts of their mother."

76 Notes. In black ink on four small sheets from a writing-block, one side each; envelope addressed to EP at St. Elizabeths, postmarked "Rapallo 16.1.46," and stamped by the Italian censor (Lilly).

brief letter of Dec. 8.] Letter 58.

yr. Ma had a longer one] Possibly EP's letter to Isabel of 10 December 1945, printed in Carpenter 723.

Hy. Adams on Gallatin] See Letter 58n.

a life of Tom Paine] W. E. Woodward, Tom Paine: America's Godfather, 1737–1809 (1945). Sgt. Durbin L. Horner's review in the Saturday Review of Literature (7 July 1945) concludes: "Mr. Woodward has emerged as an indisputable champion of Paine, that earlier champion of the underdog. He says: 'Paine should be in the Hall of Fame, of course, with Washington, Jefferson, John Adams and other founders of the republic, but his name was voted down. Theodore Roosevelt characterized him as a "filthy little atheist," a three-word phrase with not one word correct, for he was not filthy, nor little, not an atheist'" (12). For Woodward, see Letter 24n.

"1 x 1"] E. E. Cummings's volume of poems, 1 x 1, was published in 1944 by Henry Holt and Co. It was received favorably by critics and earned him the Shelley Memorial Award for 1944 from the Poetry Society of America. See also Letter 34n.

the old lady] Ma Riess. See Letters 55n and 72n.

Mairet] Philip Mairet. See Letter 74n.

Gill's letters] In Discretions, Mary de Rachewiltz recalls that Father Desmond Chute "was editing Eric Gill's letters and asked me to do the typing. The handwriting of the originals was exceptionally elegant; one saw his preoccupation with beautiful lettering" (258). Eric Gill (1882–1940), English sculptor, typographer, and wood engraver with a particular interest in religious art, had been a close friend of Desmond Chute for many years. More than forty of Gill's letters to Chute were printed, together with a drawing of Gill by Chute, in Letters of Eric Gill, ed. Walter Shewring (London: Jonathan Cape, 1947); in the preface Shewring thanks Chute, "who in extremely difficult conditions transmitted from Italy an invaluable group of letters and a most admirable portrait" (14). In 1920 EP cited Gill as an example of "sentimentalisation about religious subjects" and contrasted him with the sculptor Jacob Epstein (Poetry and Prose 4:25). See Letter 40n.

```
sliz    St
        E
        l
        i
        z
        a
        beth's Hospital
        Washington [D.C.]
        14 Jan [1946]
```

Mao

Some good news @ last.

~~Om's addr~~

76 DOROTHY TO EZRA

Villa Raggio
Cerisola
Rapallo.
Jan 16. '46

Dearest Mao.

So glad to get yr. brief letter of Dec. 8. yesterday. Also yr. Ma had a longer one – It always pleases her if you write more to her than to me! So continue! Thankful to hear you are getting some form of rest cure: you surely need it.

A letter from Ronnie [Duncan], very pleased at having had a letter in yr. own hand-writing. Hy. Adams on Gallatin sounds interesting. W. E. Woodward has done a life of Tom Paine, wh. will be worth reading – also I see the comrade had a new vol out "I x I" – these details found in Sat. Rev. July 7. '45. "Theodore R. characterized T.P. a 'filthy little atheist,' a three-word phrase with not one word correct. . . ."

Had the good luck to meet Mary [Rudge] on Sunday: chez Ma Riess: She is help-ing look after the old lady, when ~~her~~ the maid can't be there. I was so thankful for the encounter, senza l'altra [without the other one, i.e., Olga Rudge]. Also I had a message for Olga, wh. was useful. She's [Mary] a large healthy object! Ma. R. says so competent, & likes her so much – I expect there's some charm; but we only had ten minutes.

Oh, yes, it was the new St. Eliz. address for them: & news that Mairet has asked Ronnie [Duncan] to write an essay on "EP's cultural influence." R. delighted to give it 'em good & hot. This was I believe due to [Reverend Desmond] Chute, who wrote Mairet a longish letter full of good friendship towards you – I visited Rev: at Xmas-time, (for yr. Ma partly) & we had a very long & amiable talk.

77 Notes. *In black ink on five small sheets from a writing-block, one side each; envelope addressed to EP at St. Elizabeths, postmark torn off (Lilly).*

I spent Friday in Genova] 18 January 1946.

vice consul] Sofia P. Kearney (1906–1990), born in Puerto Rico, earned a degree from the University of Barcelona (1931). She served in the U.S. consular service in Barcelona, Milan, Lisbon, Tangier, and Rome, before being appointed administrative assistant and vice consul at Genoa on 25 May 1945. Herman Moss had been transferred to Geneva, Switzerland, on 25 October. See Letter 28n.

release my Eng. money] On 10 January 1946 A. V. Moore wrote DP that the Trading with the Enemy Department felt that in view of the uncertainty of her American citizenship and the delay of the U.S. State Department, they "would be prepared to accept an official request by the British Consul to release your funds." Moore added that he had cabled DP the day before, urging her to present herself to the British Consul "as an Allied National or Stateless Person" (OP). On 15 January 1946 Lester Schnare, U.S. consul-general in Genoa, wrote to Shakespear & Parkyn to help with the release of some of DP's funds in the hands of the Custodian for Enemy Property in London. See also Letter 47n.

Goldring] Agnes Bedford wrote DP from Essex on 7 January 1946 (Lilly), mentioning Douglas Goldring (1887–1960)—English writer, publisher, and assistant to Ford Madox Ford on *The English Review*—and his book, South Lodge: Reminiscences of Violet Hunt, Ford Madox Ford and the English Review Circle (London: Constable, 1943). Detailed and realistic, though tinged with nostalgia, Goldring's book did much to revive the neglected reputations of Ford and his companion, Violet Hunt (1866–1942), a journalist and novelist who had grown up in the Pre-Raphaelite circle. Before World War I, she and Ford entertained EP and other writers and artists at South Lodge, Hunt's modest villa in Campden Hill Road, Kensington. At first suspicious of EP's arrogant style, Goldring soon recognized his essential kindness. His comments in *South Lodge* are balanced: "It is sad to think that Ezra has now [become] Mussolini's 'Lord Haw-Haw.' All the same, I will not hear or say a word against him" (63). In 1915 EP told John Quinn that Goldring was "clever, he knows the publishing ropes, he is competent for all sort of jobs about a paper, he has written good short stories and a few nice poems" (*Pound/Quinn* 32). EP wrote Eileen Lane Kinney from St. Elizabeths on 28 April 1946: "Weeping over Goldring's memoir 'South Lodge.'" He said it brought back his "jeunesse, 1908–1920 à Londres. An honest book in a flurried world" (Tulsa, Paige). For Ford, see Letter 14n.

poluphlosbios] From the Iliad I.34. EP wrote W. H. D. Rouse, the translator of Homer, in 1935:

> Para thina poluphloisboio thalasses: the turn of the wave and the scutter of receding pebbles. Years' work to get that. Best I have been able to do is cross cut in *Mauberley*, led up to:
>
> > . . . imaginary
> > *Audition of the phantasmal sea-surge*
>
> which is totally different, and a different movement of the water, and inferior. (Paige 274–75)

Even before *Hugh Selwyn Mauberley* (1920), EP had used Homer's onomatopoeia in "Stele," the sixth poem of "Moeurs Contemporaines" (1918): "Now, quenched as the brand of Meleagar, / he lies by the poluphloisboious sea-coast" (Personae 179). The word occurs again in Canto 74 when EP recalls the water of Lake Garda, near which Mussolini's Salò Republic had been set up: "in diminutive poluphloisboios / in the stillness outlasting all wars" (lines 84–85).

G. Cav.] Guido Cavalcanti Rime (1932). See Letters 2n, 18n, 67n, and Document 6n.

Nov. 20 just come: also one Dec. 16] Letters 51 and 61.

Hickok] Guy Hickok. See Letter 61n.

bothered overmuch by psych....] The psychiatrists examining EP.

Mary is typing a lot of Gill's letters for publication she will have told you, for Rev. So she is getting a little civilization -

Excuse handwriting worse than usual: we are in a <u>bitter</u> spell – Isabel in bed – not ill – just frozen.

So much love

Oh! Ming!

D.

Isabel thinks you "have been so comfortable" since you got back to the States. Extraordinary mental activity.

77 DOROTHY TO EZRA

Villa Raggio
Cerisola
Rap. [Rapallo]
Jan 20. 1946.

Dearest Ming.

Yr. Ma I believe sent a letter yesty. She writes worse than ever now, being both cold & wobbly -

I spent Friday in Genova: one of those days I had always heard tell of: snowing & an icy wind: but I was O.K. in furcoat & the furkin inside! Consulate perfectly amiable: vice consul now a woman, ½ Irish ½ Spanish, whom I liked very much indeed. thank goodness no sign of Moss! She took my application & photos etc: etc: & I shall presumably get my new passport sometime before I die.

I said I wanted to join you "as soon as possible." I also got a letter which I expect to ~~lb~~ will release my Eng. money. Took it to Brit-Consulate & so forth – Greatly preferable atmosphere at U.S.A.

They say there's no civil air service at all as yet: vedremo [we'll see]. I am jealous that you have had yr. first airtrip without me! sorry for the circumstances.

Letter from Agnes [Bedford]: saying may be yr. utterances were indiscreet "but that it had any treasonable intent I shall never believe" – says she is trying to collect herself to write you – She has had an awful time with her Ma gone crazy – no – silly. Mentions a book of two years ago by Goldring about Ford & Violet – full of friendly & appreciative recollections of E – "I will not hear or say a word against him" (Goldring says.) Your friends seem very solid ones – not undeservedly!

I spent Friday night at 12/5 [via Marsala] & took a holiday until Sat. 4. pm. Such a relief. Corradi's fed me & I saw Ina [Benatti]. There was a heavy sea rolling in – & I woke often & listened to it: a lovely noise: I had forgotten how beautiful & poluphlosbios (spelling?) – also torrents of rain – & is that word for heavy sea? or only little wavelets? all kinds, I guess.

I hope the rest-cure is helping you – you had after all done a lot of work, added to all the rest – I had a charming letter from my Dr. friend [Mario Casonato] at Massa: I told you? thanking me, very soberly, for the G. Cav. saying he was off to attend an Italo-

78 Notes. In black ink on a large sheet of white paper, both sides; no extant envelope (OP).

B.] Bim, DP's nickname for Omar.

teach you music] The U.S. Army set up a winter university program at Biarritz to help prepare selected troops for college on the GI Bill of Rights. Omar took courses in psychology and the history of music.

Genova on Friday] 18 January 1946.

vice-consul] Sofia P. Kearney. See Letter 77n.

Two letters yesty from dad] Letters 51 and 61.

old girl-friend] Katharine Proctor Saint. See Letters 56n and 61n.

Faut que je descende ...] "Must go down to see Elfriede [Bacigalupo] to give her news of you and friends. Awfully cold – old lady [Isabel] in bed – so I eat alone and in silence at least!"

Laughlin to T.S.E.] Probably James Laughlin's letter to T. S. Eliot of 23 December 1945 on developments in EP's case, the wisdom of the insanity plea, plans for publishing EP's Confucius and the new cantos, and ideas for rehabilitating his reputation once the legal difficulties were past (Lilly).

American agricultural conference in Firenze – & hoped to read it with calma on his return.

Here yours re. flight, of Nov. 20 just come: also one Dec. 16. I am writing D.T.C. to forward to you at St. Eliz. – So thankful for these letters. -

I have just written D.T.C. to forward – & to John [Drummond] to find Hickok in Rome.

How I regret we didnt have that flight together – Ma! [oh, well!]

I am using all my patience: am plugging along through Consul's etc. to get to be near you – I am hoping to get into friendly relations with Mary [Rudge] – via Ma Riess: but must go very carefully.

I keep hoping you are well fed, & not bothered overmuch by psych. . . . (spelling?)

Yr. Ma pretty well, but v. cold spell rather rough.

Ming Mao!

Yours D.

Love.

78 DOROTHY TO OMAR POUND

Villa Raggio
Cerisola
Rapallo.
Jan 22 .46

Dearest B.

Two letters just come from you – & two large Red X envelopes: Thanks. Bitter cold & snowing. I am glad you are to be in France for a bit – to get yr. french more firmly fixed – I am v. curious to hear about the 'how' they teach you music – I went into Genova on Friday: icy wind & bitter. Application for p.port taken, photos etc: & I think they are giving it to me – in time: anyway amiable: vice-consul a pleasant female. Then I got a letter from Consul to A. V.M. [Moore] which I took round to Brit. Con. & that ought to release my money in England. I feel things are progressing a little. You'll probably never get several of my letters sent to Bremen – so I don't know where we are as to news. Two letters yesty from dad: Nov. 20. & Dec. 16 respectively. The former recounting what a marvellous flight they'd had – Venice, Bruxelles London Azores Bermuda, the other letter saying, Patience: and then telling of an old girl-friend (Granma knew who) who arrived to save his soul, complete with Bible. Is it credible!? She later I will say "sent some chocolate-covered biscuits." I think he is pretty worn-out, whatever state his mind is in -

Mon très cher
M Le Bavardeur [Chatterbox]
A Toi toujours
ta MUM
DP.

79 Notes. In black ink on three large white sheets, one side each; envelope addressed to EP at St. Elizabeths and postmarked "Rapallo 24.1.46" (Lilly).

Two letters from you] Letters 51 and 61.

a Dr's memoirs] Unidentified.

Chase Bank just sent me $200] See Letter 72n.

Gais & the hospital] In Discretions, Mary de Rachewiltz describes her upbringing in Gais and her work as a secretary in a German military hospital at Cortina in the Dolomites during World War II.

U.S. Univ. at Biarritz] See Letter 78n.

Am enclosing an old letter] DP's Letter 57.

Faut que je descende voir Elfriede, donner nouvelles de toi et les amis. Un froid épouvantable — La Vieille au lit — donc, je mange seule et au moins en silence!

I will write again, quite soon — copy of a long letter from Laughlin to T.S.E. most interesting — & encourageing.

Yrs DP

dad at St. Elizabeth's Hospital Wash:

79 DOROTHY TO EZRA

V. Raggio
Cerisola
Rap. [Rapallo]
Jan 23 1946.

Dearest Ming.

Two letters from you: yr. flight ~~to~~ viâ London, Bermuda & Azores — Old Lady all of a chatter — & then a later one, telling of "well now, to think of Katharine Proctor [Saint]" . . . & more twitter: O.K. Nice story (old Chestnut?) in a Dr's memoirs, of a flood of bibles arriving in camp: *not* appreciated: so the little Cockney puts 'em all in a row & has rifle practice: now, sez he, you can each send one home with the bullet mark, to show how the Bible saved yr. life" . . . . . .

Chase Bank just sent me $200 wh. I had written for. I told them also to let you have $300: very un-business-like method: may work: write & ask them ~~if~~ whether it does: & give them yr. address — please: I told them I was telling you to do this.

Excessively cold. I met Mary [Rudge] again last Sunday: she poured out tea for us chez Ma Riess: they get on 1st rate together. M. [Mary] very happy there. I shan't be able to see her again, as she has to go back to No. 60 [Olga Rudge's home].

I like her: she has an awful prim jeune fille bien élevée [well-bred young lady] manner, that is unpleasant: but I think it melts. I am reading & correcting her m.s.s. re Gais & the hospital etc: mostly interesting. She was apparently asked whether she wished to meet me! — & (wisely!) said yes. I believe she wants to go back to Gais: feeling she has nothing to do here: also Ma Riess says some people look askance at her here . . . . "instead of being *more* kind to her." She has put her hair up: & looks charming: she's looking very business & nice & neat. Her face will always be a little wide: but anyway that's a good fault so to say.

From Omar: he has gone to U.S. Univ. at Biarritz until March 15.!! to study "musical criticism": he is equally sceptical with myself on this score: but says he will at least hear some music. He writes you I gather? He's a good child. Did I tell you? He lent me *all* his savings while he was here — as I was very low. I shall shortly be able to refund, I hope. I went to Genova last week (I told you?) Got a letter from U.S. Consul to A. V.M. [Moore] wh. I took to Brit: [British Consulate] wh. ought to release my money quite soon. Anyway I have enough now for quite a while here.

I am really hoping I can help Mary a little: 'morally' I mean: I think she feels lonely here — but it all depends on how free or independent she is from No. 60. I am going

80 Notes. Sloping pencil scrawl on the reverse of an undated typed letter to EP from E. E. Cummings on vacation in Tucson, Arizona; no extant envelope (Lilly).

send these letters] EP means the E. E. Cummings letter that he used to write Letter 80, as well as a letter to him from Viola Jordan. DP received these from Ronald Duncan on 25 February 1946 and acknowledged them to EP in Letter 100.

hers of 22 Nov.] DP's Letters 52 and 53.

Bunting or Nancy] Basil Bunting, Nancy Cunard. See Letters 19n and 44n, respectively.

81 Notes. Typed with black ribbon on a sheet of Cornell's legal stationery, one side; envelope addressed to EP at St. Elizabeths and postmarked "New York, N.Y. Jan 26 1946." Enclosed was a newspaper clipping captioned "Pound Sanity Hearing Postponed Indefinitely" (Lilly).

thick batch of Cantos] See Letters 45n and 59n.

Porteous] Hugh Gordon Porteus (b. 1906), English critic and commercial artist, a friend and admirer of Wyndham Lewis, whom he met in 1930. He reviewed Lewis's works in the *Criterion* and other journals and wrote *Wyndham Lewis: A Discursive Exposition* (1932). He was knowledgeable about Chinese ideograms, and Faber and Faber published his *Background to Chinese Art* in 1935.

The hearing] EP's sanity hearing took place, after postponements, on 13 February 1946. See Letter 70n. On 25 January 1946 Cornell wrote DP of the progress of the case and of the doctors' opinion that EP would not need "to remain very long in a hospital." Cornell predicted, incorrectly as it turned out, that "after a few months the case will be dropped and he will be set free" (Lilly).

carefully. I always send up any letters or papers concerning you—but refuse personal contact.

Please take all the rest you can: tell me any odds & ends re your life there: Glad its warm. [Edgardo] Rossaro yesty in the street: so thankful to have news of yr. whereabouts – & so very sweet & charming in his wishes for your safety. Ina [Benatti] & Co. always ask for news – & send greetings: & I let Elfriede [Bacigalupo] know all I can. They are all good friends of yours.

All my love D.

Am enclosing an old letter that I gave Omar when he left in case he had yr. address in U.S.A. before me.

80 EZRA TO RONALD DUNCAN

St Elizabeth's Hospital
Washington DC
24 Jan [1946]

Dear Ron

Please send these letters to Dorothy – after reading them. nothing from her since hers of 22 Nov. Om's [Omar] address still with papers not sent from other hospital [Gallinger]. Olga's [Rudge] to Cornell, dated 6 Dec. came yesterday.

Any news of Bunting or Nancy or anyone.

maybe they could write me via you. have you any later news from them?

_____yrs E.P.

81 JULIEN CORNELL TO EZRA (WITH MESSAGE FROM DOROTHY)

Julien Cornell, Attorney
15 William Street
New York 5, N.Y.
January 25, 1946.

Dear Mr. Pound:

I have received a letter from your wife in which she asked that I give you the following message which she included in her letter to me because she did not have your address:

> "Can you get a message through to EP? I have no address.
>
> I want him to know that Omar was here for ten days, and the greatest possible comfort to me and full of filial piety towards both of us.
>
> That I now have received some money.
>
> That the thick batch of Cantos has arrived, is being typed neatly, and that I am

82 Notes. Sloping pencil scrawl on a sheet of ruled paper, one side; envelope signed by EP under the flap, addressed to DP at Villa Raggio, postmarked "Washington, D.C. Jan 30 1946," and stamped received in Rapallo "1.4.46" (Lilly).

olibanum poem] DP's poem "No yaller dog" in Letter 38. EP had already thanked her for it in Letter 69.

83 Notes. This letter appears in facsimile in Cornell (75).

clarifying the Chinese characters in it for Porteous or somebody in London, and so much enjoying that little work for him. Am dispatching to London immediately."

I have written to Mrs. Pound giving her your address, also the latest information about the progress of the case. The hearing, as you know, is scheduled for next Wednesday and I will see you in court that morning.

Sincerely yours,

[signed] Julien Cornell

JC:CW

82 EZRA TO DOROTHY

St Elizabeths Hospital
[Washington, D.C.]
Domenica [Sunday]
End Jan [27 January 1946]

Mao

it is long long long.

thank her for olibanum poem

E

83 EZRA TO JULIEN CORNELL

Dungeon
[St. Elizabeths Hospital]
[Washington, D.C.]
Domenica [Sunday]
end of Jan. [27 January 1946]

mental torture
constitution a religion
a world lost
grey mist barrier impassible
   ignorance absolute
         anonyme
futility of might have been
coherent areas
     constantly
      invaded
aiuto [help]

Pound

84 Notes. In black ink on five small sheets from a writing-block, one side each, with final postscript on back of page five; envelope addressed to EP at St. Elizabeths and postmarked "Rapallo 31.1.46." Though dated 29 January, this letter may have been begun on 28 January and concluded on 30 January (Lilly).

brief letter today from you] Letter 69.

one from Miss Ida] Ida B. Mapel wrote DP on 29 December 1945 that "E looks better and is much less nervous, than when I saw him the first time. He said yesterday to tell you he was 'pleasant.' His attendants all speak with pleasure of him, they all seem to do everything he wishes." She added, "St. Elizabeths is a big place with extensive grounds. Food good. They have cows, gardens, etc. etc." (Lilly).

"True Johnnie"] See Letter 69n.

Tecla Monti] Rolando Monti's sister. See Letters 43n and 151n.

called by Brit. poleece] DP made notes of this interview on five small sheets of paper, which some years later she placed in an envelope, noting, "I don't like to destroy." The only part of these notes that DP omitted from Letter 84 is as follows:

> Police: What are yr pol[itical] ideas?
> DP: gave up pol. at 16. [. . .]
> Police: What languages do I know. [No answer.]
> DP: refs. Elfr [Elfriede Bacigalupo] & D. Chute -
>   the latter seemed to give him a slight jolt.
>   [. . .]
> Police: What happened when my husband was taken away?
> DP: I wasn't there - that p.m. two came & asked
>   questions & took away a book of cuttings.
> Police: as souvenir?
> DP: ossibly.
> DP: I mentioned one had been shot soon afterwards for
>   various murders etc I was told.
> Police: What was the outcome likely to be of my
>   husband's affair.
> DP: I haven't the slightest idea (OP).

V. Raggio
Rap. [Rapallo]
Jan 29. 46.

Dearest Ming.

A brief letter today from you, postmarked Jan. 3. 46. Also one from Miss Ida: saying the Hospital has grounds, gardens & cows.

We have a tin of peanut butter! From the sister (in Red X) of that tall Pole. She is charming: more of her anon. Curiously - Sunday I saw "True Johnnie" in a list of gramophone disks chez Ma Riess. She really is a great comfort to me: but very deaf now.

I visited Desmond Macredy [Chute] two afternoons ago: to witness my signature to a codicil, to my will (H.T.T's [Henry Tudor Tucker] money) & he, very shyly, asked if I would send you his love when I wrote: he has asked to see various letters about yr. condition etc: which I have let him have. He is truly sympathetic, & I am glad to have had talks with him (twice.)

I have had a long pile from Chase BK. I gather that there is about $3,000 there: its either $2,900 or $3,100, I don't make out which: only I don't think its both! letter is on its way to [A. V.] Moore, wh. ought to release in England. Omar, bright lad, has got himself for a term into Biarritz Am. Univ. for music & psychology. Very cockahoop: says its not so easy! & anyway hopes to hear some music.

Yes. I have quite a lot of patience: & propose exercising it near you, as soon as possible.

Go to Genova tomorrow. OP's [Omar] new address:-
Co 'C' 1st BN. Student Det.
B.A.U. A.P.O. 268.
No: he doesn't put

~~U.S. Army.~~

Found in a book lent by Ma Riess two playing cards: 8. hearts, & underneath five of spades. Tecla Monti, who knows, says both very lucky.

My love

Oh Mao.

D.

29th. In Genova yesterday - called by Brit. poleece. I felt very calm & took my time answering - They wished to know how I had passed the last 20 years here. My political opinions (1), what I thought of yours - all very silly.

(1) None

(2) economic not political says I -

& that an U.S. citizen (not 'subject') has right of free speech wherever he is - so I thought you had - "I am an artist, not interested in politics." O? We didn't know - painting? Yes. sculpture? No.

The Brits are an unpleasant lot, except ones friends!

Mao mao.

85 Notes. In pencil on a sheet of ruled paper, one side, sent via A. V. Moore in London (Lilly). Moore sent it on to DP in a letter dated 13 February 1946, adding: "The letter he mentions from Omar I re-directed to him at Washington on 11th January. Omar's letters from Bremen always took 2 or 3 weeks to reach London - hence the delay." DP marked Moore's letter in pencil, "recd 25 Feb 46 & ansd" (OP).

yours & yrs via Cornell] Letters 55 and 81, respectively.

Ta S'eu] *Confucio. Ta S'eu* (1942). For EP's translations of Confucius, see Document 7n.

86 Notes. In pencil on a sheet of ruled paper, both sides; envelope addressed to DP at Villa Raggio, postmarked "Washington, D.C. Feb 5 1946," and marked by DP in pencil on back, "OP to buy 1000 Radicals." At Lilly this envelope is associated, probably erroneously, with EP's Letter 89 (Lilly).

Yrs. 19 Dec] Letter 62.

Possum's "4 tets"] James Laughlin wrote T. S. Eliot on 23 December 1945: "Ezra speaks of you, as always, with the greatest affection and is eager to read the *Quartets*, which I am sending down to him" (Lilly). Eliot's major verse sequence, *Four Quartets*, was published in New York in 1943 and in London in 1944, after its four poems, "Burnt Norton," "East Coker," "The Dry Salvages," and "Little Gidding," had appeared individually between 1940 and 1942.

"Some do not"] *Some Do Not* (1924) and *No More Parades* (1925) are respectively the first and second of four novels by Ford Madox Ford collected under the title *Parade's End.* The sequence, which also includes *A Man Could Stand Up* (1926) and *The Last Post* (1928), follows Christopher Tietjens from his pre-1914 world of Tory certitude to his career as an officer in France, where he suffers a partial loss of memory. Tormented by a cruel wife, he bears his sufferings with almost superhuman stoicism and falls in love with a young suffragette. After the war, the two share a cottage with Tietjens's brother, Mark, and Mark's wife. In a letter to Olga Rudge of 23 March 1946, EP compared his own fragile mental state with "Tietjens loss of memory" (OR Papers, Beinecke).

EP was full of renewed enthusiasm for Ford and told Charles Olson that *Some Do Not* "did me more good than anything has, to restore me, except Katherine [Proctor Saint]" (Seelye 59). See also Introduction.

some introd. 1000] The first 1,000 Chinese characters. The ideograms on which all others are based are called radicals.

She's feeling very calm! except for that perpetual mosquito yr. Ma. She's older - & sillier, but still sometimes makes corn bread.

D.

The young Brit. called a couple of the questions "awkward." I said, no not the least "awkward" but difficult to answer in very few words.

D

85 EZRA TO DOROTHY

[St. Elizabeths Hospital]
[Washington, D.C.]
31 Jan [1946]

<u>A.V.M. Please forward to D.P.</u>
Something apparently postponed - Letter from Omar London post mark - 11 Jan - (re Biaritz).
also yours & yrs via Cornell - after Om. [Omar] at Rap. [Rapallo].

put him onto ideogram - did you give him a Ta S'eu??

---

still no news Basil [Bunting], Nancy [Cunard], Vera & G. [Münch].

Mao

E

86 EZRA TO DOROTHY

St Eliz
[Washington, D.C.]
31 Jan [and 1 February 1946]

O Mao
Yrs. 19 Dec. real letter. hope now steady stream.
Bearding[?] Possum's "4 tets" for 1st time oggi [today] - old Fordie a rock - much better than I thought. "Some do Not," platform. (less in 2nd vol. Parades, in fact almost not.) see that Om. [Omar] has @ least Ta Seu - & he shd <u>buy</u> some introd. 1000

or radicals, if <u>posble.</u>

[11304]

yrs. 22 Dec] Letter 64.

"save going hence."] Cf. *King Lear*, V.ii.9:

> Men must endure
> Their going hence even as their coming hither.
> Ripeness is all.

vice consul in Rio] Charles Edward Eaton, born in North Carolina in 1916, is a poet, fiction writer, and art critic who knew Robert Frost, William Carlos Williams, and other noted writers. While a graduate student at Harvard, he attended a lecture that EP gave during his 1939 visit to the United States. From 1942 to 1946 Eaton served as American vice-consul in Rio de Janeiro and founded the Cultural Publication Program, through which American authors and critics appeared in translation in a leading Brazilian newspaper. Eaton wrote to EP on 26 January 1946 asking to publish four of his poems in an anthology of American poetry to be translated into Portuguese by contemporary poets of Brazil. He hoped to use "The Garden," "In a Station of the Metro," "Ité," and "Be in me as the eternal moods" (Lilly). EP was happy to cooperate, but it is not certain that the volume ever appeared. Over the years Eaton's poetry and fiction, which show the influence of his experiences in Brazil and Puerto Rico, have won numerous awards. EP liked his volume of verse, *The Greenhouse in the Garden* (1955), and recommended it to Robert Lowell.

87 Notes. In black ink on five small sheets from a writing-block, one side each except for final paragraph on the reverse of page one; envelope addressed to EP at St. Elizabeths and postmarked "Rapallo 4.2.46" (Lilly).

yr. friend Viola] Viola Jordan's letter from which DP quotes is dated 28 December 1945 (Lilly).

Alice Bacon] Frank "Baldy" Bacon's wife. See Letter 37n.

Pan-Arab League] A movement in the Middle East, emerging from World War I, in which the Arabic-speaking countries of the region, then under British, French, and Ottoman rule, sought to unite on the basis of a common language and a desire to resist all forms of colonialism and, later, Zionist pressures.

Palotai] Vilmos Palotai was cellist in the New Hungarian Quartet, with Sándor Vegh (first violin), László Halmos (second violin), and Denes Koromzay (viola). They performed in Rapallo concerts in the 1930s; EP declared that "they make a QUARTET spelling the whole word in capitals" (*Poetry and Prose* 7:245). In 1938 the quartet, under Zoltan Székely (first violin), won worldwide renown and continued to perform for several years after the war.

Edie] Edie M. Wood. See Letter 39n.

Eva] Eva Ducat (1878–1975), pianist friend of Olivia Shakespear's in London, wrote *Another Way of Music* (1928) and coauthored adventure stories for children. For a time she acted as an informal musical agent for W. B. Yeats. She once told Omar that she had heard DP's father, Hope Shakespear, sing and that he had a fine tenor voice.

Dickie] Ruth Dickie. See Letter 22n.

Vers mis au bas ...] Lines placed beneath a portrait of Mr. [Benjamin] Franklin:

> Glory of the New World of Humanity,
> This kind and truthful Sage leads and enlightens;
> Like Mentor reborn, he hides from the rabble's eyes,
> Beneath the form of man, his Divinity.

"Brief Hour of Francois Villon"] John Erskine (1879–1951) wrote *The Brief Hour of François Villon* (1937), a florid, romanticized novel about the French poet's life and women.

I Feb. yrs. 22 Dec. just come now I hope regular flow. great comfort that yr. letters have started to arrive - Told "don't worry"

Perhaps you cd. @ last read some of the Guido C. [Cavalcanti] - I know more about it now - also some of Shx. sonnets (i.e. stray lines) "save going hence."

U.S. vice consul in Rio wants permit to print Portagoose translation of 4 poem - but is old name, mebbe tradition exists

love

mao

E

87 DOROTHY TO EZRA

V. Raggio
Cerisola
Rapallo.
Feb 2 '46.

Dearest.

Have had letters from yr. friend Viola ("something in the nature of gems") & from Alice Bacon. Am answering the latter. No coffee yet from V. [Viola]. I hear many parcels arrive rifled: especially sugar & coffee don't get to destination: pazienza as usual. I lost mine one day & without thinking said "Oh damn philadelphia" & your ma was hurt, indignant - & didn't speak to me for two or 3. hours. She is incredibly silly! & jumps cheeping from tree to tree more now than ever. I never know who or what she's after.

Viola says "I do not know the authors you mention, Brooks, Adams or Kitson but if they are communistic as perhaps Chas. Beard's 'The Republic' might be it would not be interesting to anybody over here except the communists themselves." (I mentioned B, A, & K: thinking the daughter might have a curiosity.)

What can one do with ignorance? I mean these people may be O.K. in other ways - but you can't do any thing —— There's at last a train through from Genoa to Zoagli - two days ago. The big bridges at Recco & Sori look v. Jap: all huge tree trunks criss-crossed - really fine.

There's been a large poster up 'What Truman says' quoting the poor 'miti' [meek] shall inherit the 'earth,' & more from same place. The large Pole in the bus to Genova:- the English are so cruel - & repeated it three times. Inquiries of a kindly nature after you, & "please my regards to him."

I had rather fun one day: I was in G. [Genova] and a letter came from Egypt (the first) and was there a questioning & who did I know there. I refused all the gambits: & that day & next: Isabel talked of nothing but what was the climate like? Where do they go for holidays? & spoke of everybody she had ever heard of in Egypt - - - The news in it, was lots of grandchildren: his three all married - & was on his old job during the late hostilities: that he often heard the Voice [EP] - (I asked had he benefitted?) & that there is afoot v. strongly the Pan-Arab League: linked to the Brit. Empire - that the place is reeking with money. so!

88 Notes. In black ink on four small sheets from a writing-block, one side each except for postscript on back of page one; envelope addressed to EP at St. Elizabeths and postmarked "Rapallo 7.2.46" (Lilly).

Kate] Kate Isherwood had been interned by the Germans. See Letter 13n.

Gordon] Isabel Gordon, a longtime British resident of Rapallo. In 1933 she was listed as subscribing to the concerts held there. The "old one" may be Miss LaTouche, another British resident. See also Letters 95 and 131.

see they return] An allusion to EP's poem "The Return" (1912):

> See they return; ah, see the tentative
> Movements, and the slow feet,
> The trouble in the pace and the uncertain
> Wavering!

The gradual return of British and Americans who had spent the war away from Rapallo inspired this thought in DP.

J. Erskine] See Letter 87n.

Mary is returning to Gais] In *Discretions*, Mary de Rachewiltz discusses the books that DP gave her: "Dorothy sent me three books of Babbo's [Father's] almost completely decayed; she apologized for the condition they were in, they had been buried in a garden [at Villa Andraea] during the war" (265). She explains why she wanted to leave Sant'Ambrogio: "I did not feel like being a financial burden to [Olga Rudge]; my company did not cheer her up, and I was of no use to anyone" (265).

man who knew you] DP's diary for 1 and 4 February 1946 reads, "caffè with S," probably Seamens. See also Letters 65 and 99.

yr. last brief letter] Letter 69.

yr. m.s.s. of Kung] EP's English translations *Ta Hsio: The Great Digest* and *Chung Yung: The Unwobbling Pivot*, completed at the DTC (see Letter 46n). For Confucius, see Document 7n.

I am asking a dutch friend to get news of Palotai & the Quartette.

Neither Edie nor Eva have ever written to me: & Dickie writes with much acidity
. . . of the poor starving peoples of Europe having to be fed and so on & on.

All my love

How goes it?   D.

Vers mis au bas du Portrait de M. Franklin.

Honneur du nouveau Monde de l'Humanité,
Ce Sage aimable & vrai les guide & les éclaire;
Comme un autre Mentor, il cache à l'oeil vulgaire,
Sous les traits d'un Mortel, une Divinité.

(from a book on printing.) Nouveau Cara[c]tère d'Ecriture gravé à Paris pour M.
Franklin, par S. P. Fournier le jeune, 1781. book Ma Riess showed me. I go to her Sun-
days 3—6 pm & she gives me picture books or whatever - so as not to talk all the time!
Wise old thing!!

Am reading aloud to yr. Ma John Erskine's "Brief Hour of François Villon," which
might be worse - but not much - & she finds it so pathetic.

88 DOROTHY TO EZRA

V. Raggio
Cerisola
Rapallo.
Feb. 5. 1946.

Mao mao.

Just been to visit the Majerna family: Dante's wife is "expecting" & I had a ball of
wool. . . the Signora always much interested in yr. welfare . . they are finding times terribly difficult. Dante having a fit of dispair. Prices don't seem to come down any, as yet.

A letter from poor old Kate: she is coming back - & the Gordon & the old one are
all going to live together at S. Michele. If somebody could write a really bitter satire on
see they return.

I read for ½ hr. every evening in bed - & find Conrad very good, as somebody, I forget who, once said to me . . . such a relief - no women! Am reading F. Villon to yr. Ma
by J. Erskine: readable aloud anyhow: she finds it so pathetic.

Mary is returning to Gais I hear from Ma Riess: who will miss her very much. I left
a package of ~~your~~ books by you for her: such duplicates as I was able to find. I haven't
had time to make her acquaintance properly: & it wouldn't have helped her any, for her
mother [Olga Rudge] to know I was interested - the latter very bitter last time I unhap-
pyly ran into her. Did I tell you the man who knew you about ten years ago is here &
asked what news I had. I have sat in the caffè twice with him - I like him a lot - and a lit-

8

9 Notes. In pencil on a sheet of ruled paper, one side; envelope signed by EP under the flap, addressed to DP at Villa Raggio, postmarked "Washington, D.C. Feb 11 1946." At Lilly, this envelope is placed with Letter 90, but it may well belong with Letter 89. See also Letters 85n and 90n (Lilly).

Hers of Dec 19 & 20.] Letter 62 and probably Letter 64 (22 December 1945), respectively.

tle intelligent male society does me good. Yr. Ma is very silly - & I feel my wits going to dryrot. Ten days since yr. last brief letter. One by same post from Miss Ida [Mapel]: She has been very noble in writing, & I thank her. Weather milder: but we had a bitter spell. Isabel had to stay in bed.

I am so hoping that you are comfortable - & recovering to some extent: do you stay in bed? can you work?

A.V. M. [Moore] writes on <u>21. Jan</u> that yr. m.s.s. of Kung reached him that am. He also sent me a copy of yr. letter to S. & P. [Shakespear & Parkyn] about it: he sent it to T.S.E. immediately.

Did I say Omar has wangled himself into Am. Univ. at Biarritz for a couple of months' study - music. He had written to you. He may now really get french fixed in his head. I think the nomadic tendency must be strong.

All my love   D.

These unimportant scribbles don't bore you? Tell me? They are chiefly to say I'm always thinking of you - - - D.

89 EZRA TO DOROTHY

St. Elizabeths
[Washington, D.C.]
6 Feb [1946]

O Mao

he wd like to write her a letter, she feels very close ce soir.

hers of Dec 19 & 20. & Isabels of 22. have come. Miss Ida [Mapel] brought choco-late tablets - & for the rest allee samee.

mao - E

go on writing to me. I dont know how you can get transport - praps via England?

90 Notes. In pencil on a sheet of ruled paper, one side, with DP's pencil jotting, "recd March 11 46"; envelope signed by EP under the flap, addressed to DP at Villa Raggio, postmarked "Washington, D.C. Feb 12 1946," stamped by the Italian censor, and annotated by DP with ideograms matching those in Letter 90. This envelope is empty and unassociated at Lilly but probably belongs with Letter 90. See Letter 89n (Lilly).

9164] DP wrote "under 'Odes' p 299.III" beneath ideogram 9164 and "not found" beside ideograms 1377 and 7879. The latter two may relate to EP's draft translations of the Minor or Smaller Odes of Part Two of the Confucian anthology, on which he was working at this time.

Bennett] Arnold Bennett (1867–1931) wrote, among his many novels, *Imperial Palace* (1930), about the life of a luxury hotel, from the laundry maid to the magnates who own it, and the political and financial intrigues behind the business. In the past EP had disapproved of Bennett, lumping him with Shaw, Wells, and other Edwardians and calling him "nickel cash-register Bennett" (Paige 296), a glance at the kind of commercial-mindedness that EP satirized in the character of Mr. Nixon in *Hugh Selwyn Mauberley* (1920). EP's view changed dramatically after he read *Imperial Palace* and *The Old Wives' Tale* (1908) at St. Elizabeths. On 17 March 1946 he wrote Olga Rudge: "Bennett a gt. novelist - as good as the french - my damn snobbery deprived me of knowin it in 1910" (OR Papers, Beinecke). See also Introduction.

91 Notes. In pencil on four small sheets from a writing-block, one side each; envelope addressed to EP at St. Elizabeths and postmarked "Genova 11.2.46" (Lilly).

St Elizabeths
[Washington, D.C.]
Feb 8 or 9 [1946]

O Mao

@ least
consolation.   for

[9164]

[1377]

[7879]

& just had a shower.
got Bennetts Imperial Palace
- what else.?
　　　love to you & mother
　　　　　　　E

91 DOROTHY TO EZRA

In Genova
Feb 11 46
Oh Mao Mao.

She may be able to come soon. I get my p.port as soon as I show my ticket <u>paid</u>!! There is a sailing on Feb 25 - which may have room - Takes 18 days - However - - - Life here become so unnerving with Isabel - whom I refuse to escort. Its a responsibility I won't take - I have only enough energy for myself & she has nowhere to go on arrival - & I can't stand it any longer.

I shall cable to [Julien] Cornell if, when, date is fixed - Should be <u>glad</u> to see you again!! Hope yr. patience is in good order. Talk here all elections now - I don't understand the first thing about it - Lots of nice kats out this a.m. as its very fine. Motor bus to G. [Genoa] & return p.m. Also a few very inconvenient trains -

　　　Yours D.

92 Notes. In black ink on three small sheets from a writing-block, one side each; no extant envelope (Lilly).

Two today at last ...] EP's Letters 73 and 71, respectively, the latter inquiring about a Chinese ideogram.

from Miss Ida, good woman, & from Julien] DP had just received Ida B. Mapel's letter of 7 December 1945 (Lilly), as well as Julien Cornell's of 25 January 1946, in which he discusses EP's case and the insanity plea (see Introduction and Letter 81n).

I wrote to you yesterday] Letter 91.

I am interviewing shipping] In late January 1946, American Export Lines (U.S. War Shipping Administration) notified DP that her name could be put on a waiting list for future sailings.

the bloke ...] All unidentified.

93 Notes. In pencil on five small sheets from a writing-block, one side each except for a brief insertion on back of page two; no extant envelope (OP).

Mrs. Hoover] Harriet Hoover, a friend of Isabel's, who lived outside New York.

Henry Millar] Henry Miller (1891–1980), American novelist and painter who settled in Paris in 1930 and wrote *Tropic of Cancer* (1934) and *Tropic of Capricorn* (1939), which Omar recalls reading in the army. Although EP had mixed feelings about Miller's work, he told T. S. Eliot in 1935: "Hen. Miller having done presumably the only book a man cd. read for pleasure and if not out Ulyssesing Joyce at least being infinitely more part of permanent literature than such 1/2 masted slime as the weakminded, Woolf female, etc." (Paige 272). EP recognized and promoted the genius of James Joyce (1882–1941) as soon as he read *A Portrait of the Artist as a Young Man* in manuscript in 1914. From 1917 through 1921 he received the typed installments of *Ulysses* as Joyce produced them, and dispatched them to *The Little Review*, of which he was for a time foreign editor. He wrote Joyce in late 1918: "Dorothy is among your constant readers, and so far as ascertainable from close scrutiny, has never jibbed [at] any remarks by Telemachus Daedalus or other protagonists. She has a growing affection for [Leopold] Bloom" (*Pound/Joyce* 148).

send you mine] DP's poem "No yaller dog," which she included with Letter 38. EP thanked her for it in Letter 69.

92 DOROTHY TO EZRA

Villa Raggio.
Cerisola
Rapallo.
Feb 12 1946

Dearest Ming.

Two today at last - one via A.V.M. [Moore] Jan 12. from Wash - The other Jan 11. Also letters from Miss Ida, good woman, & from Julien. I couldn't find that Chinese Character: it eluded me - & I can't hunt now as the Dict. is mostly transported to v. Marsala - and we have the workmen here, remaking all the bombed ceilings - fearful mess: noise, confusion - Naturally Isabel could go to No. 12. v. Marsala - but as that would be very convenient for me . . . oh! dear no! So I say nothing. I wrote to you yesterday from Genova. My passport will be handed me when I show passage ticket paid & dated. I am interviewing shipping. Air seems hopelessly difficult - One is held up in Lisbon for a week or more anyhow - I shall bring a few clothes for you - a suit & shirts probably. Am gradually transferring pictures etc. to 12/5. [Via Marsala] as we have to leave here anyway - as they want it -

Letter from Omar also. Studying music, and history of, & psychology - & has begun another poem. He has written to you. He is at Biarritz Am. Univ. but alas only for two months. I think he is finding it very stimulating indeed & says there are a good few intelligents of 20 & 21. years. This all sounds O.K.

The bloke who used to be around with "the philosopher" & the wife with the plaits inquired & sent saluti [greetings] to you.

All my love D

93 DOROTHY TO OMAR POUND

V. Raggio
Rapallo
Feb 13. 46

Dearest B [Bim, Omar's nickname].

Yes. I'm trying always to get to U.S.A. to be near dad. I can't stand this any more - We had a parcel from Mrs. Hoover today - mostly eats, most acceptable - After gorging on v. rich cheese, & at the same time hot chocolate, the Old Woman [Isabel] talked like a blue streak for over ½ hr. quite without stopping: I timed it on the clock - She is the greediest person I ever sat with! In fact I'm just fed to the gills.

Henry Millar of certain interest - one is enough, & he has no form. Read J. Joyce's Ulysses - That is a demonic book, of real value - Its a very terrible work - but has all the greatness due to tremendous form, inside its frame (24. hrs of Dublin.) Chatter is no good -

Have you sent yr. poem to dad yet? Its coming on, I think - Try to vary the rhythm - & be careful not to jingle. I am incapable of writing, myself - so excuse! If I have time to copy I'll try to send you mine - which I dont put forward as anything but an emotion

good letter from Julien] For Julien Cornell's letter to DP, see Introduction and Letters 81n and 92n.

"her convex, obstinate forehead"] From Joseph Conrad's story "Because of the Dollars," in *Within the Tides* (London: Dent, 1915): "What I noticed under the superficial aspect of vapid sweetness was her convex, obstinate forehead, and her small, red, pretty, ungenerous mouth" (176).

Isabella Johnson] Olivia Shakespear, DP's mother, was a first cousin of the poet and critic Lionel Johnson (1867–1902) and a close friend of his sister, Isabella Johnson.

94 Notes. In pencil on a sheet of ruled paper, one side, with postscript on back; envelope signed by EP under the flap, addressed to DP at Villa Raggio, and postmarked "Washington, D.C. Feb 16 1946." DP penciled on back of the letter, "recd M. [March] 20" (Lilly).

2 letters (Jan 5 & 8)] DP's Letters 70 and 72.

Granger Kerr?] Mary Elizabeth Grainger Kerr (1864-ca. 1950), born in Dundee, Scotland, and educated privately, was a contralto who excelled in oratorio, songs, and lecture-recitals. She had a special interest in modern music and in English and Hebridean folk songs, and she gave recitals around the world. She sang leading roles in classical and modern music, including Elgar's *The Kingdom* and Delius's *A Mass of Life*. EP knew her in London before World War I and through her met other singers and musicians. She corresponded with EP and DP until 1949.

Ranieri] Prince Ranieri di San Faustino. See Document 6n and Letter 35n.

Beulah @ 4 a.m.] In Letter 70 DP reported that Beulah Patterson, a relative of EP's, had heard his broadcasts at 4 A.M. in Montana. Beulah's brother, Charles Thomas Busha, was a lawyer in Washington, D.C. See Letter 47n.

that 200] two hundred dollars that DP thought Chase Bank had sent her. See Letter 72n.

Bennett's "Imperial Palace."] Arnold Bennett's *Imperial Palace* (1930), about a luxury hotel (see Letter 90n). EP is alluding to Omar's earlier training in hotel management.

Jas brought 74–84 Canto mss] On 14 February 1946, the day after EP's sanity hearing, James Laughlin delivered a clean typescript of Cantos 74–84, made from EP's DTC typescript and used in the preparation of the New Directions edition of *The Pisan Cantos* (1948). Charles Olson saw EP the same day and wrote: "He came in with his bounce back, carrying the Pisa Cantos in his hand which Laughlin had delivered to him this morning. He had already corrected the typed copies of Cantos 74 and 75 (1 page job with music) and wanted me to either send them on or put them in JL's hands if he were still in town. Which he was. And which I did later in the afternoon" (Seelye 72).

- as I have no technique. I sent it as a letter to dad: he thanks me, but hasn't given me any "OK."!

A good letter from Julien. Saw Elfriede [Bacigalupo] today, as my nerves had gone - She says when you go back to Bremen write her re Richard & his brother. When, if, I get to the U.S. we'll know better how finance & many other problems are likely to pan out - including, & importantly, yr. reading & music -

Rereading J Conrad - v.g. much of it - ("~~that~~ her convex, obstinate forehead" - image of Isabel!) I think it would make a beautiful gravestone remark! I'm sorry - She's too much for me any longer.

You can't get any more time at B.A. [Biarritz American] Univ?? I feel I ought to be writing to yr. boss about it - but who is he, & a letter out of the blue isn't much use?

A nice letter requesting news of you & me, from Gran's cousin Isabella Johnson - near Woking - A very good friend & a downright person - made smocks for me as a tiny child. Sister to Lionel poet. I've answered.

Your exhausted but always affecte.

MUM.

A second parcel today from N.Y. with coffee - altogether we call it a day -

94 EZRA TO DOROTHY

St Eliz

[Washington, D.C.]

14 Feb [1946]

MAO.

2 letters (Jan 5 & 8) - after door locked yester - so oggi [today] real Valentine.

Poor Agnes [Bedford] - what about Granger Kerr? Wd you go via England?

Tell Ranieri air lines - air bases - low rates - his future - Rome - majorca - azores etc. Dont understand how Beulah @ 4 a.m. ['a' underlined twice]

Anything re/ money - via [Julien] Cornell. mebbe that 200 was from me not from Chase - if in excess & yrs. coming regular, pass it on to Mary [Rudge]. I dunno how they make out, but apparently they do.

reading Bennett's "Imperial Palace." was it that that started the egregious Omar? food abundant.

love

Love to mother. Saluti a tutti [greetings to all] & [Ma] Reiss, [Edgardo] Rossaro, Pep [Soldato]. Beulah brother cd. call - but only 15 minutes & unhandy to get to.

P.S. Jas brought 74—84 Canto mss for Valentine

95 Notes. In black ink on four small sheets from a writing-block, one side each except for closing lines on back of page four and postscript on back of page one; envelope addressed to EP at St. Elizabeths and postmarked "Rapallo 16.2.46" (Lilly).

Mrs. Hoover] See Letter 93n.

Miss Gordon & LaTouche] See Letter 88n.

Old Mrs. Hazlett] A British resident of Rapallo.

Villa Raggio
Cerisola
Rapallo.
Feb 15 1946

Dearest Mao.

Wonders never cease - I was awakened in the night by the woof and squeak of a train! It is now running from Genova to Rome over wooden bridges.

We have just received a parcel each. Mine from Viola [Jordan], with coffee, raisins & dried peaches etc. The other from Mrs. Hoover, with milk in powder, meat, cocoa, cheese - & so on. All most acceptable. One letter from Omar from Biarritz Univ: with two verses of a poem. I wish he could have more time there: its only two months.

Yr. barber was inquiring after you - The wops are now beginning to understand they've lost the war - the miseria [destitution] & unemployment awful. Ina [Benatti] goes about with a tragic face, I do my best to give her little gifts - USA. food or some such . . but she's proud - & I judge her straights [sic] because she accepted a small bottle of oil yesterday . . . Man in Post Off: inquiring also, very kindly, after you: said he saw my letters were now addressed to a hospital!! What a village.

Am expecting Kate [Isherwood] back any day. She also penniless or thereabouts: Miss Gordon & LaTouche are in the house at S. Michele. We are in an awful mess here: all the ceilings being remade: dust incredible -

A short notice today in Italian paper about yr. being as crazy as a coon! I daresay the psychiatrists do find yr. reactions unusual - abnormal - Ought to be v. interesting to them. Am feeling v. grumpy: I caught an orful cold on my chest in the autobus from Genova.

Old Mrs. Hazlett writes that her daughter also is in an insane asylum - & sorrows with Isabel: adding that at least I. [Isabel] has a d-in-law & Omar. She little knows! (& what a sudden violent dislike Omar took to her, IWP. it was really quite funny!)

Baci [Ruggero Massimo Bacigalupo] himself handed me a buttonhole of Daphne in flower yesterday! A v. small purply plum colour & a most delicious scent. a very beguiling people -

My love to you - & here's wishing we may meet again soon.

D.

somebody used the word buggar to me recently: like a breath of home air, after this rifeened atmosphere.

96 Notes. In pencil on a sheet of ruled paper, both sides; Chinese ode draft in pencil on a half sheet of the same paper, one side; envelope signed by EP under the flap, addressed to DP at Villa Raggio, and postmarked "Washington, D.C. Feb 18 1946." DP penciled on back of the letter, "recd M [March] 20. 46," and next to each ideogram, "not found" (Lilly).

on Basil's door] The name "Firdausi" in Basil Bunting's Persian script, which EP planned to use in Canto 77. DP had discussed the inscription in Letter 62, which EP acknowledged in Letter 86. He may have been reminded again of "Firdausi" while going through the retyped pages of the Pisan Cantos, which James Laughlin had just brought him (see Letter 94).

Ditalevy] A local Italian photographer named Diotalzevi.

Granger-Kerr] Mary Elizabeth Grainger Kerr. See Letter 94n.

Gladys Hines] Gladys Hynes drew the elaborate initials for EP's *A Draft of the Cantos 17–27* (1928). See Letter 48n.

Georgie] Bertha Georgie Hyde-Lees (1892–1968), born and educated in England, married W. B. Yeats in 1917 and helped him with automatic writing and other psychic experiments. During the years 1910–1914 she was DP's best friend, and they remained close after DP's marriage to EP in 1914.

ENCLOSURE] A clipping from the *Washington, D.C. Times-Herald* 15 February 1946, 5, featuring a photo of T/Sgt. Walter H. Lutman holding "'Butch,' four months old leopard cub, at the National Airport. Lutman, who arrived here yesterday from the Orient, plans to take him home to Columbus, Ohio." EP jotted on the clipping: "O Yes & looks rather like Uncl George [Tinkham]."

Cocteau] Jean Cocteau. Ronald Duncan, who wrote to EP on 29 January 1946 of his visit to Paris (Lilly) and describes it in *How to Make Enemies* (London: Rupert Hart-Davis, 1968), 89–96, adapted two of Cocteau's plays for the English stage, *The Typewriter* (1947) and *The Eagle Has Two Heads* (1948). For Cocteau, see Letter 39n.

Brancus'] Constantin Brancusi (1876–1957), Romanian sculptor of abstract and pure forms, whom EP met in Paris. EP admired his art and his quest for perfection and liked to quote his epigrammatic remarks. In 1921 in a special issue of *The Little Review* EP described Brancusi's work as an ongoing effort to get "all the forms into one form; this is as long as any Buddhist's contemplation of the universe or as any mediaeval saint's contemplation of the divine love" (*LE* 442). In 1931 he declared, "I am pro-Brancusi, I see damn little else in sculpture now making" (*Poetry and Prose* 5:268).

Berard] Christian Bérard (1902–1949), French painter influenced by Surrealism who achieved distinction as a stage designer for the Ballets Russes de Monte Carlo and other productions. He collaborated with Jean Cocteau for the stage and the cinema. Duncan discussed various theater projects with Bérard, including the decor for the French production of *This Way to the Tomb*.

Mound over grown ...] An early draft translation of poem XII of Book 3 ("Airs of Pei"), Part One, of the *Classic Anthology Defined by Confucius*, where EP's final version reads:

> Mao Mount's vine-joints show their age,
> Uncles and nobles, how many days?
> Why delay here with no allies;
> Why delay here in lack of supplies?
> Fox furs worn thru, without transport,
> Uncles and nobles, sorry sport!
> We be the rump of Li with tattered tails,
> a lost horde amid fears,
> and your embroidered collars
> cover your ears. (17–18)

St Eliz.
[Washington, D.C.]
15 Feb [1946]
MAO -

Mebbe it is still there on Basil's door. ed. Ditalevy could photograph it.

Nancy C. [Cunard] may have had publisher - or some bank address -

Did Omar try to find Vera & G [Münch]?

Granger-Kerr? poor Agnes [Bedford]. That makes about the list

I like simple news about people. I wonder if Gladys Hines went to Oireland -
Georgie of course dont write

           & so on.

        L   ENCLOSURE:

         O   one leopard cub

          V

           E

              E.   also one

[7534]

Ron [Duncan] been to Paris, seen Cocteau, Brancus' & Berard. (? - whoever that is).
Brancus in 3 coats - no heat.   Rose Marie [Duncan] s[t]ill in hosp. - his letter 29
Jan only ~~16~~ 17 days to get here. will you send him Vera's [Münch] address.

[Separate half sheet]
very rough - only one line finished.

[7534]

Mound over grown
Time's measure shown
  in the tree joints,
Lords, elders, how many days
    for yr leisure?
Waiting for ~~supplies?~~?
   allies?
For supplies?
   Are you? how long?
Tatter'd in fox coats
no new cars,
    none ~~none~~ not from the East
& you are not on the level with us.

We are the rump of Li
with tatter'd tails,
Lords, & our elders,
  a scatter'd horde amid fears
& yr. embroider'd collars
   cover yr. ears.

Shi III.12

     15 Feb

rough - not finish'd yet.

97 Notes. In pencil on two sheets of ruled paper, one side each except for brief postscript on back of the second sheet; no extant envelope (OP). For the ideograms in this letter, see Letter 42n.

don't try to make me THINK] EP's letters in this period make it clear that he felt himself unable to perform strenuous mental activities, such as judging, critiquing, and making decisions. In a letter dated 22 January 1946 from Biarritz, Omar had sought his opinion on two poems he had written (OP).

Highest psych authority] The psychiatrists' testimony at the sanity hearing of 13 February 1946. See Letters 70n and 81n.

Cocteau & Brancus] For Ronald Duncan's visit to Jean Cocteau and Constantin Brancusi in Paris, see Letter 96n. For Cocteau, see also Letter 39n.

Frobenius] Leo Frobenius. See Letter 48n.

St Elizabeths Hospital
Wash D.C.
[mid-February 1946]

Dear Kid.

Fer Xrizake don't try to make me THINK. I want 5 years' sleep. They tell me the Highest psych authority was unanimous - but how the jury found it out (in 4 hours & ½) beats me. The persecutin' atty. seemed to be tellin' 'em that even if I did think I was godamighty, it was O.K. as I was probably more intelligent - however the jury must have been <u>MORE</u> intelligent than I am.

Ron [Duncan] has been seeing Cocteau & Brancus -

go on writin' AT Lenght [*sic*] - but don't expect mental effort from this end - or opinions -

go <u>back</u> to what I once knew. and read Frobenius. did D. [Dorothy] tell you to buy the set of <u>Erlebte</u>.

chin yrs
E.

re/ yrs from Biarritz

98 Notes. In pencil on three small sheets from a writing-block, one side each, with postscripts on back of pages two and three; envelope addressed to EP at St. Elizabeths and postmarked "Rapallo 22.2.46" (Lilly).

R. Ben: T:] The newspaper clipping about a Royal Bengal tiger enclosed in EP's Letter 75.

HD.] Hilda Doolittle (1886–1961), born in Bethlehem, Pennsylvania, moved with her family to Upper Darby outside Philadelphia in 1895. She enrolled in Bryn Mawr College in 1905 but withdrew the following year for personal and academic reasons. At this time she and EP were close friends and for a time considered themselves engaged. In 1911 she went to Europe and, except for short visits to America, remained there for the rest of her life, residing in London and Switzerland with her companion, Bryher (Annie Winifred Ellerman). With EP and Richard Aldington (whom she married and later divorced), "H.D." was a leading Imagist poet in London before World War I; later she published the long poems, *Trilogy* (1944–1946) and *Helen in Egypt* (1961). She also wrote prose memoirs and fiction, including *Tribute to Freud* (part of which appeared in 1945–1946) and the posthumously published *HERmione, Asphodel,* and *End to Torment,* her memoir of EP. In 1946 she was scheduled to teach at Bryn Mawr, but a nervous breakdown resulting from the stress of war (she had remained in London during the bombing) caused her to cancel the engagement, and she spent time recovering in a Swiss clinic. In September 1946 H.D. wrote Norman Holmes Pearson that she had been ill with "cerebral meningitis" precipitated by fears that Bryher would commit suicide during the Blitz (H.D. Papers, Beinecke). See also Letters 109n, 118, and 119n.

tigercubs in Rome] During the 1930s DP visited the zoo in Rome with EP in order to draw animals, especially felines.

[Villa Raggio]
[Cerisola]
[Rapallo]
20 Feb 46

O Dearest Mao.

Forgive pencil - Am in bed, now recovering from a sharp attack of fever & an appalling cold all over my front - BUT I've got yr. Ma shifted to 12/5 [Via Marsala] - I had arranged everything the two previous days & felt v. ill - & on the morning to move her I had to stay in bed - She walked around my room talking & waving her hands, but Rosina [a maid] finally got her off.

Next day yours came with that so furry & disarming R. Ben: T [Royal Bengal Tiger]: the young look perfect devils! They gave me much help! Ina [Benatti] seemed pleased with them too!

Are you having some eye provè [tests]? I do hope to goodness you are not being worried to death. Proctor female [Katharine Proctor Saint] writes Isabel that HD. is in same institute as yrself. Good letter from O [Omar] from Biarritz & three poems. He seems to have taken the bit between his teeth - & to be rushing along the road of Kultch furiously - & full of excitement.

(Oh such an awful mess; dust, confusion with the ceilings being hammered down -) Oh well, that R.B.T. arrived in the nick of time -

Yours always   D -

Dina [a housemaid] to the rescue, doing everything for me. reported, that yr. Ma is very contented at 12/5 [Via Marsala]. She has about six people buzzing round her running commissions fetching & carrying - ecc ecc. So she's more or less back to the state of ringing that there little bell - which I naturally never paid any attention to -

D

It was tigercubs in Rome wasn't it? who swore so horribly at us & so unreasonably!

99 Notes. In pencil on a sheet of ruled paper, one side; envelope addressed to DP at Villa Raggio and postmarked "Washington, D.C. Feb 26 1946." DP penciled on back of the letter, "recd March 25 46" (Lilly).

Vicari] Giambattista Vicari, born in Ravenna in 1909, was a journalist and critic who in 1942 issued EP's *Carta da Visita* through Edizioni di Lettere d'Oggi, which he directed in Rome. He was managing editor of Cornelio di Marzio's newspaper, *Il Meridiano di Roma*, which published numerous articles by EP between 1938 and 1943. Vicari wrote *Il libro dei sogni* (1942) and *Il Cortile* (1943), a novel of which DP translated a substantial part in Washington, D.C. (Lilly). In 1942 EP wrote: "Una sensibilità vera informa i suoi scritti" ("A real sensitivity informs his writings") (*Poetry and Prose* 8:178). His later work included studies of world humorists, and after the war he published a review called *Il caffè*. In 1959 he issued EP's *Versi Prosaici* through Biblioteca Minima.

old Montanari] Filippo Montanari, father of Saturno Montanari (1918–1941), a young Italian poet whom EP admired for the lyrical directness of his melancholy pastoral verse. He was killed in action in Albania. EP published a short eulogy (signed "Nemo") in *Il Meridiano di Roma* (8 June 1941); and an unused passage in EP's pencil drafts of *The Pisan Cantos* links him with Rudolph Dolmetsch, another young artist killed in the war (ms page [309], Beinecke). (See also Letter 47n.) Filippo learned of EP's enthusiasm for his son's verse through Giambattista Vicari, a fellow citizen of Ravenna, and in April 1941 a correspondence began that continued on and off for many years (Beinecke). In 1950 EP received from Filippo several of Saturno's unpublished poems and printed four of these, with his own English translations, in *Imagi* in 1951. The translations were reprinted, and a fifth added, in *Translations* (446–48).

Natalie] Natalie Clifford Barney. Her famous Paris address was 20 rue Jacob. See Letter 17n.

ASS Sieman] Unidentified. See also Letters 65 and 88.

Cherry Bim] Popular song "Ciribiribin." See Letter 54n.

4 blokes climbed out] The *Washington, D.C. Times-Herald*, 25 November 1945, 1, reported the jailbreak: "Five prisoners, all described as dangerous and possibly armed, hacksawed their way to freedom from the District Jail yesterday afternoon in one of the smoothest and most mysterious jail breaks in the city's history. All escaped from a window aperture 15 feet above the floor of the recreation room while a stool-pigeon futilely tried to attract the attention of the two guards assigned to watch the 29 inmates of Cell Block No. 1 during a recreation period [...] The 24 other prisoners in the room at the time refused the chance for escape but helped their fellows by talking and singing loudly and otherwise trying to cover the sounds of sawing." Later that day, one of the five escapees turned himself in. Two guards were suspended, and an investigation was set up to see if the prisoners had had inside help.

100 Notes. In black ink on two small sheets from a writing-block, one side each, sent via A. V. Moore in London, who airmailed it to EP on 12 March 1946; no extant envelope (Lilly).

letter from eec & one from Viola] See EP's Letter 80 to Ronald Duncan, containing letters from E. E. Cummings and Viola Jordan, which he asked Duncan to forward to DP.

one with tiger & cubs] A newspaper clipping in Letter 75.

St Elizabeths
[Washington, D.C.]
21 F. [February 1946]

O Mao.

She might get news of Vicari by writing to him @ the publishing house. I forget the name - & old Montanari @ Post office, Ravenna.

Will try Natalie, but forget the number rue Jacob. one window here view of Potomac sunset - flat, dull as Main @ Francoforte - with that ASS Sieman tryin' to kid himself it was like the Seine - also if I stand on my own window sill another bit.

I long for Pisan paradise./ & the jail was Cherry Bim till ~~the~~ 4 blokes climbed out & rest of us then confined to cells - no assembly hall - (Gallinger [Hospital] quiet & human) - oh well. less melancholia here than wd Xpect - spose its digestive - considerab cheered by a little milk of magnesia.

Wd. like to see London - wd you or Omar go that way? & know what -

& SO ON

O Mao!!!

E.

she write 2 a week

100 DOROTHY TO EZRA

[Villa Raggio]
[Cerisola]
[Rapallo]
Feb. 25. 46.

Dearest Ming.

So I am not started on ~~this~~ today's ship - Seems one of those periods of baulking. First I had the 'flu - very lightly by luck - & anyway thereby got Isabel out of this place. Then its been endless small things: today I hoped for Corradi, to come & take a truck-load of stuff- -ma [well] - Here gazman came testyfying to his affection for you. A letter from eec & one from Viola forwarded to me by Ronnie. I keep on writing to you: where the letters are, the lord knows: I have received the one with tiger & cubs - Thanks: Anyway I have parked Isabel [at] 12/5. [Via Marsala]. Next move, is to be re-vaccinated before setting foot on a ship. Am always demanding to go: shall get over some day. If I can tomorrow, I shall cable you I am OK - ~~that~~ I've extracted some more cash from Lloyd's [Bank] - & am paying a little more than half yr. Ma's en-pension [food and lodging] at 12/5 but have enough for my fare now.

Rotten life so far from you.

All my love   D.

101 Notes. Pencil scrawl on the front of a handwritten letter from William Carlos Williams to EP, dated 21 February 1946; no extant envelope (Lilly).

yr. of 23 Jan.] Letter 79.

102 Notes. In pencil on a sheet of ruled paper, one side; envelope signed by EP under the flap, addressed to DP at Villa Raggio, and postmarked "Washington, D.C. Feb 27 1946" (Lilly).

yrs 23 Jan.] Letter 79, in which DP mentioned Mary Rudge's "jeune fille bien élevée [well-bred young lady] manner." She also discussed two hundred dollars that she thought Chase Bank had sent her.

N. Cox] Nancy Cox-McCormack. See Letter 44n.

Dear Walter] Walter Morse Rummel (1887–1953), American concert pianist and noted performer of Debussy, wrote concert songs, edited rare early music, and arranged works by Bach and Vivaldi for piano. He and EP were well acquainted by 1910 and worked together to put EP's original poems and Provençal translations to music. In 1912 Rummel married Thérèse Chaigneau, pianist in a distinguished chamber group, whom he eventually divorced; later he was involved professionally and romantically with the dancer Isadora Duncan. In 1917 he wrote the incidental music for W. B. Yeats's *The Dreaming of the Bones*. Throughout the 1920s and 1930s his reputation as a pianist increased throughout Europe. He performed in France during the German occupation and became a German citizen in August 1944. *Time* magazine for 24 December 1945 indicates how he had gotten into "tepid water": "Samuel F. B. Morse's grandson, Pianist Walter Morse Rummel, was blacklisted in the American zone in Germany as an ex-Nazi stooge. Born in Berlin to the daughter of the telegraph inventor's second wife, he had lived in the U.S. as a child, returned to Germany at 17, taken German citizenship in 1944. His mother once taught the Bible to President-to-be Teddy Roosevelt" (45). EP refers to "dear Walter" in Canto 80: "Debussy preferred his playing / that also was an era (Mr. W. Rummel)" (lines 10–11).

103 Notes. RCA Radiogram, stamped received in Washington, D.C., "1946 FEB 27 PM 9 12," and marked in pencil on the envelope, "West side notified. HH [Howard Hall]" (Lilly). Ronald Duncan had written DP on 16 February 1946 (received 25 February) that EP had not heard from her since 22 November, and suggested that she cable him (Lilly).

101 EZRA TO DOROTHY

[St. Elizabeths Hospital]
[Washington, D.C.]
25 Feb. [1946]

O Mao.

gt. day. lot of letters come after a dearth. incl. yr. of 23 Jan. - good & long. - re the young.

saluti [greetings] to [Edgardo] Rosaro [*sic*] & all

102 EZRA TO DOROTHY

S Liz
[Washington, D.C.]
26 F./27 F. [February 1946]

O Mao

re. yrs 23 Jan

That j.f.b. elé manner prob. useful if not <u>necessary</u> in present chronology - moeurs [customs, manners] etc. Make sure S. Ambrog. [Sant'Ambrogio, Olga's house] rent is paid. - you presumably had 200 from ME whatever Chase loosend up on. - cd. give it Mary [Rudge], IF no longer needed, cento alla volta [a hundred at a time], as I sent her only 100 - or may be better only cento once. re. sense of just division - but I thought you & Isabel were short @ the time - & was pool not fountain, helas! -

Can you send me some addresses - or if address bks are @ 60 [Sant'Ambrogio] ask M. [Mary] to. I mean in U.S. N. Cox or whomever.

Dear Walter is in tepid water, don't think it is grave or really hot.

Jas [Laughlin] thinks Basil [Bunting] was on a trawler - O hell. I thought it was ground work @ air base. I spose [A. V.] Moore cd. ask @ Admiralty.

several quite humble supporters - very touching. A.M. smell of coffee to[o] weak to damage the nerves.

o Mao   E

103 DOROTHY TO EZRA [TELEGRAM]

RAPALLO VIA RCA
[received] 1946 FEB 27 PM 9 12

EZRA POUND SAINTELISABETH HOSPITAL WASHN
AM WELL WRITING YOU FREQUENTLY DOROTHY POUND.

104 Notes. In black ink on four sheets from a writing-block, one side each except for the last sheet (both sides); envelope addressed to EP at St. Elizabeths and postmarked "Rapallo 1.3.46" (Lilly).

Yrs to hand of Jan 31st] Letters 85 and 86, both dated 31 January 1946 and enclosed together.

I sent a cable this a.m.] Letter 103.

portogoose translations] See Letter 86.

Possum's 4 tets??] T. S. Eliot's *Four Quartets.* See Letter 86.

that Chinese Ch.] See EP's Letter 71.

G. Parodi] Giorgio Parodi. See Letter 2n.

letter from Agnes] Agnes Bedford wrote DP from Essex on 18 February 1946, received 26 February (Lilly).

[Rapallo]
Feb. 27. 46.

Dearest Mao.

Yrs to hand of Jan 31st. saying my letters were arriving - I sent a cable this a.m. to you, as I had a letter from Ronnie [Duncan] two days or so ago saying you were not getting any from me: have of course no idea where the hitch comes. Here the blessèd Ina [Benatti] came up: she has sold some things for us, & is getting lots of odds & ends free. Yr. Ma reported to have an enormous appetite, & to be fairly content in 12/5 [Via Marsala]. I haven't been strong enough yet to stand the strain of stairs, salita [hill path] and the flood. Also I loathe the idea of her being in my beloved studio! It doesn't really matter at all. Tomorrow I hope to get vaccinated - was last done in '29! I got another sum from England today & now have enough for my fare & leave a reserve for Isabel. I had a letter recently from Olga [Rudge], wh. quite prevents my offering her any help: its her funeral. Mary [Rudge] has fled to Gais, I should think very wisely, ruining her nerves and prospects staying at 60.

I hope the portogoose translations get printed. I still like Shxp. sonnets! Last summer read them for ideogram. Some of them go straight into characters all through, must be a lovely lot, in many I didn't see any ideogram. Can't read anything at the moment: moving out all the furniture - and all Isabel's truck as well as mine - She says don't send any more to 12/5 and at the same time a list a yard long of things she can't do without.

I'll write to Omar re Chinese. I asked him to get news of Gerhardt & V. [Münch] but there's no post in Germany from city to city between civilians ecc. ecc. Italians can't write to Germany, except military.

What is Possum's 4 tets??

The trains are now running Geneva[sic]-Rome - & I see long merce-electric [goods trains]. Prices all sky-high. Potatoes 50.l [lire] a kg. so that meat is nearly as cheap, oil less - & the stuffs I hear are a good deal less -

Yr. Ma has had four parcels from U.S.A. - one of books heaven help us! Haven't yet heard what. One of tea anyhow.

Oh what a dull letter: too much house confusion and the workmen have shortcircuited the light, so I have only candle after 7.pm. The faithful Dina [a housemaid] has devoted herself to me during my attack of 'flu. Can't someone be found to look for that Chinese Ch. in Congressional Lib - Jap dept? It beat me quite.

Anyway
all my love
Yours D.

A note from G. Parodi: who called, but we didn't meet sending you his remembrances. A letter from Agnes - also has had 'flu - Her ma is quite dotty now.

Am enclosing one from Bride [Scratton].

105 Notes. In pencil on a sheet of ruled paper, one side, with "Love to Mother" on the reverse; envelope signed by EP under the flap, addressed to DP at Villa Raggio, postmarked "Washington, D.C. Mar 4 1946," stamped received in Rapallo "6.4.46," and marked by DP in black ink, "poem." DP jotted "not done" beside the ideograms in the letter (Lilly).

draft] A draft translation of the sixth strophe of the first poem, Book I, Part Three ("The Greater Odes"), in the *Classic Anthology Defined by Confucius*, where EP's final version reads:

> Mindful what manes stand here to preside;
> what insight to what action is conjoint,
> long may we drink the cup of fellowship,
> Yin's pride in mind, always to show the point,
> a tub of water wherein to note
> thy face. Had Yin not lost the full assembly's vote
> He had long held to drink with the Most High,
> yet mistook fate for mere facility. (149)

A different rendering of some of these lines appears in Tseng's commentary in *Ta Hsio: The Great Digest*, the translation of the Testament of Confucius that EP completed at the DTC:

> The *Odes* say:
> *Until the Yin had lost the assembly. . .*
> *They could offer the cup and drink with*
> *The Most Highest.*
> —Shi King, III, i, i, 6.

We can measure our regard for equity by the Yin. High destiny is not easy. Right action gains the people and that gives one the state. Lose the people, you lose the state. (Confucius 71)

DOCUMENT 16 FBI OFFICE MEMO

Office Memorandum   UNITED STATES GOVERNMENT

TO   :   Mr. D. M. Ladd   DATE: March 4, 1946

FROM   :   J. C. Strickland

SUBJECT :   DR. EZRA POUND

TREASON

On March 2, 1946, Mr. Donald Anderson of the Criminal Division telephonically advised Supervisor [blacked out] that since Pound has been declared incompetent by District Court jury, no further prosecutive action can be taken against him at this time. The indictment will remain outstanding, however, and in the event Pound should be declared sane at some future time, he will then be brought to trial.

ACTION

There is attached a letter to the Washington Field Office, the office of origin in this case, suggesting that the case be placed in closed status.

105 EZRA TO DOROTHY

St. Elizabeths Hospital
Washington, D.C.
[4 March 1946]

6th strophe

[11587]   [7984]

[11618]

                                          draft

Shalt'ou not think on thy 1st (first) ancestor
whose spirit hovers o'er this altar's ~~now stone~~ face

pouring down light,
         True insight's cynosure
~~from whom the current of felicity~~

106 Notes. In black ink on two half sheets of graph-ruled paper, both sides; envelope addressed to EP at St. Elizabeths and postmarked "Rapallo 6.3.46" (Lilly).

Grainger-Kerr] Mary Elizabeth Grainger Kerr. See Letter 94n.

my cable] Letter 103.

Even so Shang, e're lost the people's voice
Fate's boon companion in the holy cup;
from whom the current of felicity?

Even so Shang, e're lost the people's voice
held up the cup to heaven
                in altar rites
& solid bore its weight,
Make him thy tub of cry[s]tal water clear
whereon the face of warning may appear:
Learn that high destiny is nothing light.
Love to Mother.

106 DOROTHY TO EZRA

                    Villa Raggio
                    Cerisola.
                    Rapallo.
                    March 4. [and 5] 1946.

Dearest Ming.

A spell of bitter March cold upon us: but the peach & plum blossoms lovely. Finally forced myself to visit yr. Ma at my Studio [12/5 Via Marsala] - precious queer it looks too! She has huddled in an enormous quantity of furniture: half of which I don't want .... & is already asking what are the prices at pensions: on inquiry I find 600.lre per day up to 1200 p.day are the sort of amounts -

A letter from [Giorgio] Parodi asking for yr. address, & very kindly saying can he help me anyway: I've said I want a berth on the next ship! if he knows anybody in the Navigazione. My lack of acquaintances & "pull" is a nuisance in this case. Ina [Benatti] has helped us to sell nearly all the superfluous: She gets a table, a chest-of-drawers & mirror, & lots of odds & ends - I hope its fair: I think so.

I really have no news for you. A letter from poor old Grainger-Kerr - saying yr. ideas always had been ahead of the times: She is quite crippled, on crutches with arthritis -

I do hope my letters are coming in to you now, & that my cable didn't strike you as crazy: (saying I was O.K. & writing often to you.) it was Ronnie's [Duncan] suggestion, as you wrote him you'd had no news from me since Nov. 22. wh. of course horrified & infuriated me.

The optimistic [A. V.] Moore seems to believe I'm already on the high seas - I wish I were.

The old muratore [mason] who is doing the ceilings here hums all the time!! but a very low & placid hum! I feel it rather a relief to see the whole flat here entirely dismantled, & workmen in it: its given the atmosphere quite a jolt!

I have a little time now to read, or do what I want: will study yr. cantos again.

Mardis Gras [5 March]. read some Cantos last p.m. I find them very lovely. A scrap

107 Notes. In pencil on a sheet of white paper, one side; envelope signed by EP under the flap, addressed to DP at Villa Raggio, and postmarked "Washington, D.C. Mar 9 1946." DP marked the back of the letter in pencil, "recd 17 Ap '46" (Lilly).

George Yeats] See Letter 96n.

Chilanti] Felice Chilanti (1914–1982), Italian journalist, writer on economics, and novelist, who edited the biweekly *Domani* (April-August 1941), which was suppressed by Mussolini for its unorthodox views. Chilanti's flat in Rome served as the meeting place for a group of young dissident fascists and antifascists who were critical of Mussolini and his supporters, particularly his son-in-law, Count Galeazzo Ciano, the foreign minister. EP, who was introduced to this group by Odon Por, considered it extreme but admired its sincerity and was dismayed when Chilanti was arrested on suspicion of plotting against Mussolini's government. In Canto 77 he recalls Chilanti's young daughter saying, "'I would do it' (finish off Ciano) 'with a pinch of / insecticide'" (lines 180–81). Chilanti's memoir of EP was translated by David Anderson as "Ezra Pound Among the Seditious in the 1940's," *Paideuma* 6 (1977): 235–50.

Adriano] Possibly Adriano Ungaro. See Document 6n.

PORC Odon] Odon Por (b. 1883), Hungarian-born economist who lived in Italy, was sympathetic to Social Credit, and wrote on the guild and corporate structure of fascist Italy. His correspondence with EP, which began in 1934, helped shape EP's hopes for Mussolini's economic programs, and EP considered Por the most alert and intelligent economist in Italy. Por wrote for several influential fascist reviews, and EP translated his "Systems of Compensation" for the *British Union Quarterly* (July/September 1937). He also translated his *Politica economico-sociale in Italia anno XVII-XVIII* (1940) under the title *Italy's Policy of Social Economics 1939/1940*, published in Italy in 1941. Por offered EP twenty-five hundred lire, on behalf of the Fascist Confederation of Industrial Workers, to produce the latter translation (Redman 208), which EP refers to in Canto 78 as "Odon's neat little volume" (line 161). See also Letter 2n.

Yrs. 28 Jan re Genova etc] Letter 84, dated 29 January 1946 but probably begun 28 January.

Mrs Rhys] Ma Riess. See Letter 55n.

108 Notes. In black ink on a half sheet of graph-ruled paper, both sides; no extant envelope (Lilly).

letter from Swabey] Henry Swabey wrote DP from Essex on 28 February 1946 (Lilly).

N.E.W. has two articles] Reginald Snell's essay in two parts in the *New English Weekly*, "Ezra Pound: A Reminder" (14 and 21 February 1946), with which Ronald Duncan may have helped (see Letter 74n). Snell summarizes EP's career and the events following his capture in great detail. He concludes the second installment by alluding to EP's expatriate status and the widespread mood of reprisal fostered by recent war crimes tribunals:

> I leave it to others to consider the peculiar spiritual dangers to which an expatriate is subjected—the effect on both American and English writers of transatlantic visits, of short or long duration, during the last 150 years is a fascinating and not unimportant theme. So many human beings are being done to death every day, in so many countries, in so many ways, for so many reasons, with (or more mercifully without) formal judicial proceedings, that it may seem invidious to single out one particular American, a difficult customer at that, who has in any case experienced his years of success. But this man's services to literature (as a practitioner and still more as a teacher of verse writing) are of an order which is not common. Possibly there is nothing that any of us can do; possibly our action must be confined to remembering the good that may be remembered of him. (184)

Fack] Hugo Fack published a supportive piece, "Ezra Pound—Poet and Money Reformer: Traitor or Patriot?", in his Gesellite organ, *Freedom and Plenty* 16, no. 2 (February 1946). EP told Charles Olson that this was the "best defense" of him so far (Seelye 68). For Fack, see Letter 37n.

last I got from you] Probably Letters 85 and 86.

in It. paper says that in Uzbekistan it has been made possible to cultivate cotton, naturally coloured. It doesn't say what colours -

Hoping to see you again someday. Its a rotten waste of my life staying here without either you or Omar. I'd like to make a home for the two of you - somewhere - Japan? I suppose is out of the question at present -

Always yours

Mao! D.

107 EZRA TO DOROTHY

St Elizabeths
[Washington, D.C.]
6 Marzo [March 1946]

Mao

Dont know if this will catch you - afraid transport v. difficult. Can you send my regards to George Yeats - she must have met people here.

Also wd. like to know what come of Chilanti & Adriano, even if you have to ask that PORC Odon. Yrs. 28 Jan re Genova etc. come. lot of blackbirds & finally a KAT not yet conquisted - but in its stand-off, proper dignity in enlarged court.

Love to mother, regards to Mrs Rhys etc.

Mao

108 DOROTHY TO EZRA

Villa Raggio
Cerisola
Rapallo.
March 9 1946.
Dearest.

No news of interest: a letter from Swabey: N.E.W. has two articles on you which I shall see in time. He says Fack has also published.

I hope you are now getting my letters. ~~Your~~ The last I got from you said they had just begun to arrive -

I am still worrying the Navigation for a passage - & [Giorgio] Parodi has started on them for me! I want to get out of this place, as well as wanting to be with you. Old Woman [Isabel] very far from amiable these days: She is in considerable comfort in my Studio [12/5 Via Marsala], with the family running round her all the time - and good cooking. Lots of peach & plum blossom, smelling very delicious in whiffs. Spring is an ambiguous season. Shall I get over in time to see the Japanese cherry blossom?

Have also just been successfully vaccinated: a necessary formality it seems. it didn't bother me at all - only itched a bit.

Always yours

D.

109 Notes. In pencil on both sides of a thin sheet of white paper previously used for an undated note to EP from James Laughlin; envelope signed by EP under the flap, addressed to DP at Villa Raggio, and postmarked "Washington, D.C. Mar 14 1946." DP jotted in pencil on the letter, "recd 17 Ap. 46" (Lilly).

Eileen] Eileen Lane Kinney, a friend of Constantin Brancusi's from Paris days. They traveled to Romania together in 1922, around the time that Brancusi produced *Eileen*, a white stone portrait of a woman's head with chignon (Musée National d'Art Moderne, Paris). She left Paris in 1939 and was living in Washington, D.C., when she wrote EP on 27 February 1946 to remind him that they had danced together at the Bal Bullier years before, with DP and John Rodker present, and to tell him news of Brancusi (Lilly). She visited EP several times, brought him treats and volumes of Verlaine and Rimbaud, and received letters from him, one of which reads: "Do come see me. I can't hold two sides of an idea together. But can live on memory if someone BRINGS it!" (quoted in Wilhelm 261). Kinney translated André Maurois's biographies of Dwight D. Eisenhower (1945) and George Washington (1946).

Aragon] Louis Aragon (1897–1982), French Surrealist poet and novelist who joined the French communist party. EP printed E. E. Cummings's translation of Aragon's "The Red Front" in *Active Anthology* (1933) and thought it "probably the best lyric poem in favour of a political movement that has appeared since Burns's 'A Man's a Man for a' That'" (*Poetry and Prose* 6:21).

enclosure] EP enclosed a letter that Viola Jordan had received from the Office of the President of Bryn Mawr College, dated 6 March 1946, explaining that H.D. (Hilda Doolittle) would not be coming to the United States as expected: "We held the letter which you [Jordan] sent a week or two ago thinking Mrs. Aldington [H.D's married name] would arrive at Bryn Mawr around the first of March. I thought you would want to know that we have now had a cable from her that she will not be able to come to this country because of travel difficulties. I have forwarded the letter to her in England." EP penciled a note to DP on the back of this letter: "This may mean only that H.D. don't <u>want</u> to lecture - but I doubt if she has sense enough to <u>not</u> want - she <u>was</u> xpected. O Mao - note on conditions of transport - adverse" (Lilly). For H.D's mental breakdown in 1946, see Letter 98n.

Olson back in Wash.] Charles Olson. See Letter 71n.

Ronnie hunting for translation] Writing to EP from Hampstead in February 1946, Ronald Duncan said that his successful play, *This Way to the Tomb*, was being considered for production in Italy and that he needed a translator. He hoped that EP, if he would not do it himself, could suggest someone. EP drafted a reply on 1 March 1946: "yr best translators wd/b bros/ in law Carlo Izzo & Aldo Camerino - if they will do any <u>Work</u>. [. . .] you ev. hv. <u>no</u> idea of my present fragmentary state" (OP).

24 E 47] The New York boardinghouse run by EP's Aunt Frank. See Letter 61n.

110 Notes. In black ink on a half sheet of graph-ruled paper folded double and written on four sides, stamped at Shakespear & Parkyn, "RECEIVED 20 Mar 1946"; typed envelope addressed to EP at St. Elizabeths and postmarked "London 20 Mch 1946." DP sent Letter 110 via A. V. Moore, who airmailed it to EP (Lilly).

your letter dated Feb. 8] Letter 90, which included ideograms signifying the Confucian odes.

Cousin Isabella Johnson] See Letter 93n.

Buchan's life of Caesar Augustus] *Augustus* (1937) by John Buchan, First Baron Tweedsmuir (1875–1940), Scottish author, statesman, and governor general of Canada (1935–1940), best known for the adventure novels, *The Thirty-Nine Steps* (1915) and *Greenmantle* (1916). In 1934–1935 EP carried on a vigorous correspondence with him about economics and the corruption in British and American politics. He reviewed Buchan's *Oliver Cromwell* (1934) in the *New English Weekly* for 6 June 1935, saying that Buchan had failed to write the kind of history that "would do its utmost to use past ascertainable fact as enlightenment to present, all too oppressive, problems" (*Poetry and Prose* 6:296). Buchan wrote EP in October 1934 that "I do not differ from you <u>except in</u> opinion (and in that I differ violently). But opinion does not seriously matter. I greatly admire your vigour and courage and often unholy insight" (*Poetry and Prose* 10:263).

109 EZRA TO DOROTHY

S. Eliz.
[Washington, D.C.]
10 Marzo [March 1946]

O Mao.

rather a good day. Eileen have came again with masses of chocolate & a copy of Verlaine - more use than the Aragon she brought last sunday -

Dont be depressed by enclosure but I hear it is very hard to get transport -

15 minutes allowed to visitors - now what else - Olson back in Wash. Ronnie hunting for translator for play.

Love Mao -

E.

love to mother

Mother will die of envy to know I got a bag of salt wafers from canteen - rather like those @ 24 E 47.

110 DOROTHY TO EZRA

Villa Raggio
Cerisola
Rapallo.
March 13. 1946.

Dearest Ming.

I got your letter dated Feb. 8. day before yesty: Went to hunt up Ch. dictionary yesty.! I made out you were reading, or learning by heart the Odes for consolation. The other characters I couldn't trail down. Nothing like them inside three sides of a square. I hope yr. copy of Odes is good-sized print. Corraggio [courage]. A most charming letter from Cousin Isabella Johnson: aged 83. but still able to walk well, & work in the garden! She says she still misses Olivia [Shakespear], who "was such good company."

Am reading some more Conrad: an excellent story-teller: also Buchan's life of Caesar Augustus. Stodgy, but interests me mildly. Buchan has a proper English view of Virgil - seems to prefer Horace to Properzio, & so on. Anyway I have at last got Agrippa, Maecenas & Tiberius sorted as to date.

Felugo's greetings to you, & the newspaper people often ask for news.

We have sold everything (furniture) now, except what yr. Ma is living with - mostly thanks to the blessed Ina [Benatti]. Yr. Ma had a precious queer letter from Kathrine Procter [Proctor] Saint. She must be a terrible woman! She says she took you the Bible: & that 'we' "renewed our profession of faith" also they are praying for the three of us over here. (I suppose Olga's out? as a R.C.?!) also a lot of quite nearly incomprehensible remarks abt. HD. wh. yr. Ma has I think interpreted all wrong.

Anyway, no matter!

Yours D.

Gulizias greetings also.

Properzio] Sextus Propertius (ca. 50-ca. 16 B.C.), Roman poet. EP began publishing his translations from Propertius in *Canzoni* (1911) and brought out the complete *Homage to Sextus Propertius* in 1919. See also Letter 65n.

Felugo's greetings] Perhaps Emanuele Felugo (b. 1882), a resident of Rapallo.

remarks about HD.] Hilda Doolittle. See Letters 98n and 109n.

Gulizias greetings] Dr. Mario Gulizia. See Letter 57n.

111 Notes. In pencil on back of page two of an undated, typed two-page letter to EP from Johnny Reid of Toronto, Canada; envelope signed by EP under the flap, addressed to DP at Villa Raggio, postmarked "Washington D.C. Mar 16 1946" (Lilly).

poems enclosured] These poems by Johnny Reid have not survived. Reid (1915–1985) was a Canadian journalist, writer, and friend of Wyndham Lewis and Marshall McLuhan. He studied music in Toronto and went to London to write. He admired EP's work and visited Rapallo in 1937. In 1941–1942 he arranged to publish articles by Lewis in *Saturday Night: The Canadian Weekly*, for which he worked. His letter to EP (see above) contains a comment about Lewis's stay in Toronto during the recent war—"he settled in a hotel here in the red light district. I doubt if he ever knew it was the r/l district"—which caused EP to scribble in the margin: "??!" Reid thanks EP for "not only the ABC of putting words together (unobtainable elsewhere) but the many personal favours (the trousers were thrown out only a few years back)" (Lilly).

Reeves B.] G. Reeves Butchart (b. 1905), former wife of Montgomery Butchart (b. ca. 1902), the historian of money. Canadian and a British subject, he went to the United States at the age of fourteen and later taught at the University of Pittsburgh and the University of Michigan. He and Reeves divorced in the 1930s. EP valued his anthology, *Money: Selected Passages Presenting the Concepts of Money in the English Tradition 1640–1935* (London: Stanley Nott, 1935). In the preface Butchart thanks EP, "who first aroused my interest in economics and whose suggestions have been a constant provocation to clarity" (5). Butchart also published *To-morrow's Money* (1936), a collection of writings by C. H. Douglas, Arthur Kitson, Frederick Soddy, and others. In *Guide to Kulchur* EP wrote: "Perhaps the first scholarly effort of New Economy in England in our decades was Butchart's collection on 'Money,' in his second effort he put together Seven Men none of whom took the trouble to understand any of the other six" (172–73). To John Buchan EP declared that *Money* would "kill the bastards who use one term to cover three different meanings in LICENCED and hired economics (prof/ships etc.)" (*Poetry and Prose* 10:261). Butchart was associate editor of Ronald Duncan's magazine *Townsman*. EP actively corresponded with both Butcharts in the 1930s (Beinecke).

H. Miller] Henry Miller. See Letter 93n.

peppier pts of H.J.] Henry James (1843–1916). In a special Henry James number of *The Little Review* in 1918, EP paid tribute to the late expatriate and master of nuance: "In his books he showed race against race, immutable; the essential Americanness, or Englishness or Frenchness [...] Peace comes of communication. No man of our time has so laboured to create means of communication as did the late Henry James" (*LE* 298).

112 Notes. In black ink on a half sheet of graph-ruled paper folded double and written on four sides; blue envelope addressed to EP at St. Elizabeths and postmarked "Rapallo 18.3.46" (Lilly).

letter from Miss Ida] Ida B. Mapel wrote DP on 6 February 1946 that she had seen EP the day before: "he weighs 162 lbs. now, which he told me is right for him. He wears civilian clothes. Has a new suit—blue with a narrow stripe—tan (dark) shoes—had a shirt—of a pale tan [...] a two toned necktie of light & dark blue. I told him he looked '<u>nice</u>' and got his thanks" (Lilly). The suit was a present from Caresse Crosby, who also visited EP.

reread "Timon"] Shakespeare's play. Wyndham Lewis's ("W.L.'s") first separate publication was a folder of

111 EZRA TO DOROTHY

[St. Elizabeths Hospital]
[Washington, D.C.]

13 Marzo [March 1946]

Mao -

this better'n might have xpectd. & ~~his~~ poems enclosured to me with it not bad.

Wondr whats come of Reeves B. - you might write her. As you kno I hav no addresses.

Omar is readin' H. Miller hadn't you better putt him onto Maupassant or Flaubert or even the peppier pts of H.J. good foto of the kid [Omar] recd.

love mao E

heard agen from the kumrad [E. E. Cummings]

112 DOROTHY TO EZRA

V. Raggio
Cerisola
Rapallo.
March 16 [and 17] 1946.

Dearest.

I have made one active struggle to get over - better luck next time - I was telegraphed there was a berth in two days time - impossible - my usual physical fatigue- -endless formalities - I am very regretful that I failed - letter from Miss Ida, saying you've a suit & shoes & shirts.

I said I had reread "Timon"? my older impression of it quite different! Possibly due to W.L.'s. I gather you can have reading matter?

Some more cash from Lloyds come through.

Nerina's [Pagliettini] baby expected early in April. I have made inquiries if there is any hereditary inclination to twins! She really is one of the dearest people I know. Says if she "hurries up" (!) ("sbriga") will I wait until its over: also Ina's [Benatti] brother, the butcher, young second wife is about a fortnight behind - & so on - Will finish this a little later -

Saw one swallow just now, very early.

A fellow Confucian visited me today, asking news of you - I think the Kung has left its impression in several hearts.

Now I must go to old Ma Riess - sunday tea [17 March]: & a little intelligent conversation: she doesn't last long now, & when she is tired, she says so, & we retire into our respective books - until the servant returns about 6. pm. Sensible old thing!

Mao Mao

Yours D.

Vorticist drawings and designs, *Timon of Athens* (1913), based on the play. EP regarded Lewis's series as a "great work" on the the motif "of intelligence baffled and shut in by circumjacent stupidity. It is an emotional *motif*. Mr. Lewis's painting is nearly always emotional" (*Gaudier-Brzeska* 93). In his 1943 radio talk "Communist Millionaires," EP discussed Shakespeare's play in terms of money and usury: "'Banish your dotage, banish usury / that makes the Senate ugly,' remarked the stage character, Alcibiades, in Shakespeare's Timon of Athens, Act. III, scene 5. Shakespeare is not my favorite author, but he occasionally bungs a nail on the head" (Doob 357).

cash from Lloyds] On 12 March 1946 DP received a cable from A. V. Moore in London: "RELEASE OF FUNDS ARRANGED YOU WRITE INSTRUCT LLOYDS BANK TO MAKE PAYMENT OF CORNELLS FEES AND EXPENSES AND ANY OTHER PAYMENTS YOY [*sic*] NOW REQUIRE MOORE=" (OP).

113 Notes. In black ink on a half sheet of graph-ruled paper folded double and written on four sides; blue envelope addressed to EP at St. Elizabeths and postmarked "Rapallo 20.3.46" (Lilly).

octet] Omar and Cpl. Harold Mann wrote an octet with tenor solo, piano, and drum, "The Triumph of Faith," which they performed on 28 February 1946 at a concert of student music at the Biarritz American University. The text used was part of the same poem DP quoted in Letter 36. The last section ends:

> Bring me a mantle of lusty red
> to dictate, to dictate,
> 'midst coarse fanfares,
> the triumphant song of Falsehood.

Hamilton Coll.] In 1954 Omar graduated from Hamilton College, where EP had received his Ph.B. in 1905.

114 Notes. In black ink on a sheet of graph-ruled paper folded double and written on four sides; postscript on a half sheet of the same paper, one side; blue envelope addressed to EP at St. Elizabeths, postmark torn off (Lilly).

just returned unopened] Evidently DP's Letter 49.

two from you] Letters 94 and 96 (the latter enclosing a newspaper clipping about a leopard cub and a draft translation of a Chinese ode). DP also received EP's Letter 89 (6 February 1946) while writing this letter.

Basil's Firdawsi] Basil Bunting. See Letters 19n and 62n.

Moore telegraphed] See Letter 112n.

long letter from him recently] Probably Julien Cornell's letter to DP of 25 January 1946, quoted in Introduction and Letter 81n.

kind letter from Fack] Hugo Fack wrote DP on 12 February on his *Freedom and Plenty* letterhead, enclosing his article on EP, received by DP on 20 March (Lilly). See Letters 37n and 108n.

"How is it far if you think of it"] This Confucian question occurs three times in parts of *The Pisan Cantos* that DP had read in typescript (twice in Canto 77, once in Canto 79). *The Analects* record that in response to a poet's cliché ("The flowers of the prunus japonica deflect and turn, do I not think of you dwelling afar?") Confucius quipped: "It is not the thought, how can there be distance in that?" (*Confucius* 233). DP uses it here to reply to EP's remark in Letter 89: "she [DP] feels very close ce soir."

Villa Raggio
Cerisola
Rapallo.
M [March] 18. 46

Dearest.

A long, floody, letter from Omar today, from Biarritz. He has written the words, & a friend the music - for an octet of male voices with piano.!! That child seems to be making a <u>dash</u> at producing something. I don't think its just ambitious self-advertising he's after. The Univ. produced it at students' concert of original works.

He's dashing also at philosophies & seems to think Truth an interesting subject matter. He has also found "a wine called 'Muscat,' subtle & very delicate - good." & mentions a french omelette.

He has been hearing various symphonies, & other music, & one of the Brandenburgs took his fancy. Now I <u>know</u> he is musical!

Its all a tremendous "uprush" evidently. I hope he won't bust. He's <u>also</u> rereading his Chaucer.

I wrote you two days ago - nothing much. Nice letter fr. Miss Ida [Mapel]. She's been so good about writing.

Yr Ma received a parcel today of food from Mrs. Hoover. She was like a schoolboy over it! Tea, coffee, milk, chiefly, & some soap - one piece of which I attracted for Nerina's [Pagliettini] future child, as fine soap is not to be had here.

Yours D.

Omar throws off the idea, what do I think of his going to Hamilton Coll.

114 DOROTHY TO EZRA

Villa Raggio
Cerisola.
Rapallo.
March 23 1946.

Dearest Ming.

The p.office insists on sending my mail also to 12/5 [Via Marsala]: however, the Corradi family extracts mine, so it doesn't have to go through Isabel's curious hands! There were two from you: containing one pleasant cub & ch. poem. One of my letters to you at D.T.C. just returned unopened.

I will try something about Basil's Firdawsi - if I can ascertain who is there.

I have written you I heard from MEG [Mary Elizabeth Grainger Kerr]. She is quite crippled with arthritis - apparently Omar & she correspond, at long intervals.

Agnes [Bedford] still struggling with an idiotic mother. Her last letter nevertheless had that Bedfordian tang . . . ! wh. made me laugh.

Am so glad to hear poor old Brancusi is still going. I forgot like a fool to give Omar

his address. Beulah [Patterson] didn't send me her brother's address - but I sent her yours.

Re Vera & G [Gerhart Münch]: Omar has their address: but soldiers can't communicate with civilians or Germans - & he wld have to find an american friend in their city to write to - and he told me there is no post in Germany between cities - only inside the towns. (Am trying another means - more likely to help.) He found it possible to see Elfriede's [Bacigalupo] brothers as they live close to his Hq. Also he has been absent at Biarritz. I'll mention them to him again.

In yr. Ch. poem [Letter 94] I see three lines anyway, that might be the finished ones!

I will go out to [Edgardo] Rossaro one day soon. Had a long talk in the middle of the road with Aldo, the waiter - on his byke. He was very understanding - "Tell him 'Aldo' sends his greetings & auguri [best wishes]" - Indeed I will.

Nearly everyday somebody of that level asks after you. Also a wide, middleaged man who lives somewhere up this salita [hill path] - whom I can't trace, sent saluti [greetings].

I will get Mary's [Rudge] exact address tomorrow from Ma Riess & send her 5,000 lire. BUT I shall tell her not to tell her mother. I can't be bothered. . . . & I will explain how its from you.

Of course the dollars were those from you. My cash in England is now loosed - two days ago: [A. V.] Moore telegraphed. I am in communication with [Julien] Cornell, at longish intervals. Had a long letter from him recently: all v. interesting. Am now greatly rested, by being alone, & not having that perpetual cooking & spese [shopping]. Ina [Benatti] gives me a square meal about once a week! & I'm doing very happyly.

No. I am not trying England, its not yet as simple as all that. I went all over the Casa del Popolo yesty. with a friend - its empty, & a good deal knocked about - I went onto the roof also: there is a caretaker. I believe they speechyfy there sometimes.

A Most kind letter from Fack, & his article: I have asked him to send a copy to OP [Omar], might catch that exuberant young man's eye.

Begging yr. pardon, which you always granted me; I believe my instinct served me well in that matter.

Always with all my

love

D.

P.S.

midday March 23rd '46. Just seen five swallows, duly arrived - two sat on the tip of the cypress outside this garden. . . I've never seen a swallow on a <u>tree</u> before.

PS. re Casa del Popolo: they have put cardboard capitals about a ¼ way up the lavagna [slate] pillars in the big hall, with ditto arches of very slight span in between.

Yrs of Feb.6. just turned up. "How is it far if you think of it" I daresay I'll be here about another month:. . . . I've got somebody here worrying to get that p.port <u>before</u> I pay for my ticket. Don't be troubled. I'll get over presently, & meanwhile am being helped - of wh. more anon -

115 Notes. In pencil on one side of a sheet of white paper, with EP's jotting on the reverse, "Pound to Pound"; envelope signed by EP under the flap, addressed to DP at Villa Raggio, and postmarked "Washington, D.C. Mar 25 1946" (Lilly).

Miss Ida] DP stayed with Ida B. and Adah Lee Mapel on her arrival in Washington, D.C., in July 1946.

Ron's play] *This Way to the Tomb.* See Letters 7n and 10n.

good book by Olson] *Call Me Ishmael,* an expanded version of Charles Olson's 1933 Wesleyan University M.A. thesis on Herman Melville. At EP's suggestion, he sent the manuscript to T. S. Eliot at Faber and Faber, who rejected it. It was published in New York by Reynal & Hitchcock in 1947. EP remarked, "I read it with joy—made it unnecessary to read Melville" (Seelye 138n). See also Letter 71n.

116 Notes. In black ink on a sheet of graph-ruled paper folded double and written on four sides; no extant envelope (Lilly).

Yrs. of Feb 21st] Letter 99.

Natalie's no:] Natalie Clifford Barney. See Letters 17n and 99n.

Vicari] Giambattista Vicari. See Letter 99n.

Miss Clerk!] Florence Clerk. See Letter 40n.

Conrad, about a Russian] Joseph Conrad, *Under Western Eyes* (1911).

Yeats-Brown] Francis C. C. Yeats-Brown (1886–1944) was born in Genoa where his father, who lived in Portofino, was British consul general. He served in the Indian army before World War I, was captured by the Turks in 1915, escaped, retired from the military in 1925, and worked on the *Spectator* (1926–1928). His books about India include *Bengal Lancer* (1930), on his career in the 17th Lancers and on Hindu religion, and *Lancer at Large* (1936), about his military career and his visits to the Buddha's birthplace and other holy sites, interwoven with observations on the Indians and the British. In *European Jungle* (1939) he attacked the British press, big business, the Treaty of Versailles, and Russian communism; praised Mussolini; and argued that Hitler was misrepresented in the foreign press. He also discussed "the Jewish problem" and contended that Jews dominated business and government in Europe. In 1939 EP wrote Yeats-Brown that he liked "the Italian and Jew chapters" (Beinecke).

115 EZRA TO DOROTHY

S. Elizabeths
[Washington, D.C.]
24 Mz [March 1946]

O Mao.

Seems long time since I had letter from you. You thinkin'; & Miss Ida [Mapel] thinkin'; you are comin' & me doubting you get transport. I spose you'd cable if you were really starting.

Wrote Isabel that I wd/ write her instead of you while in doubt.

copy of Ron's [Duncan] play arrived - Good book by Olson, in typescript. Dont want to read much save novels - naturally I have no news.

Mao   E.

116 DOROTHY TO EZRA

better address:-
Via Marsala 12/5.
Rapallo.
March 26 1946.

Dearest Ming.

Yrs. of Feb 21st postmarked 26. arrived yesterday. You must ask Olga [Rudge] for Natalie's no: rue Jacob: yr. address books are not here - also she had better write Vicari - for same reason. If I have occasion to write to her abt. anything I will tell her what you want.

Today more like spring, blossom nearly over, & swallows have been seen. I am due to tea chez Miss Clerk! "I've no sugar: you must bring yr. own!" "O.K. I don't take it in tea." "I can give you milk." "No. I don't take it." "Oh! then I need not open a can!" "Not for me" - Same old Miss C. as ever. Am v. curious to see whether her curiosity or her egotism gets the best!

I read a little - at the moment I struck an old Conrad, about a Russian: but couldn't stand it in these days. The sea ones are the relief.

I dispatched some money from you to Mary [Rudge], & will send some more when I know the first is safely arrived. Ma Riess gives me news of her: She is very happy in Gais - & wants to buy sheep!

Nerina's [Pagliettini] time very near. I found a small ivory baby's hairbrush of mine - which has amused her - a little good white wool - & have given her my old white Mackenzie-woven shawl - which has my initials on it - the P. anyway will do for hers.

Omar writes he sent you his poems. I don't know that you will feel up to criticizing them for him - but if you can? it would guide his enthusiasm a bit. I have said a little, but you know the kind of way I can criticize, & I don't know if its any use to anybody but you.

Happened upon [Edgardo] Rossaro yesty., in the street. He hears from Pep [Giuseppe Soldato], who is still in the mountains in Piemonte with his sister, & well: no

117 Notes. In black ink on a sheet of graph-ruled paper folded double and written on three sides; blue envelope addressed to EP at St. Elizabeths and postmarked "Rapallo 28.3.46" (Lilly).

Yrs. yesterday from Bill] Probably EP's Letter 101, written in the margins of a letter from William Carlos Williams.

tea with Miss Clerk!] Florence Clerk. See Letter 40n.

Latouche & Miss Gordon] See Letters 88n and 95n.

details - & R. himself had been away - but I got no news from him, & only gave him yr. news, & he will remember you to Pep when he writes. Old gent minus his dachshund also asked after you - and at P. Off. I ran into the masculine one of that lame pair of females. The fluffy one, naturally, died of heart. This one also exclaimed when she heard where you were, ma era sempre tanto buono! [but he was always such a good man] her saluti [greetings].

Am also reading Yeats-Brown The Bengal Lancer at Large i.e. wandering over India in the footsteps of the Lord Buddha - but it tastes very queer after Kung [Confucius].

Always yours

D.

Here La Nuora [daughter-in-law] & I removed the family portraits to safety in her flat below, out of the way of the workmen.

117 DOROTHY TO EZRA

> Villa Raggio
> but address to 12/5 [via Marsala]
> [Rapallo]
> March 28 1946.

Dearest Ming.

Yrs. yesterday from Bill. I also had a note from him in answer to one of mine - pretty rough - Went duly to tea with Miss Clerk! my word! Blue-streaked for 1½. hrs abt her own adventures - (not all un-interesting -) never asked about you - only had I been moved out of the flat? & being the richest English woman in Rapallo, gave me three little bits of dry bread with a small quantity of jam on them - & said there were some biscuits in the drawer - but didn't produce 'em! So that's done!

Better luck yesterday. Kate [Isherwood] is back, & I went out to S. Michele & had tea with them (a real tea) i.e Latouche & Miss Gordan. Kate sends you much love. She is really much developed or steadied, or something - & seems well, apart from her back. She didn't have such a bad time in Germany.

Don't worry yourself at all about my getting transport. I am beginning to see the end of the tunnel, & on a chance guess, shall be here another month: I then hope to be able to make the journey in company of a friend, who would also be able to help me on arrival. I can't go into further explanations in a letter, but have much considered the problem & believe I am doing the best I can.

[A. V.] Moore sends me on a letter from Omar from Biarritz who says he has sent you his latest poems. He says he is finding it easier every day to speak french. He & "6/7 of us" have found a small french café, where they go to eat steak & chips & omelette for 4s/– or 5s/– each . . . It sounds healthy enough. I fear now he is back in Bremen he'll find it very dull & routine.

Must now go down to see Yr. Ma. She wrote you yesty.

Always yours

D. Mao.

118 Notes. In pencil on both sides of John Reid's typed letter to EP of 21 March 1946 from Toronto, which relays news of the British literary scene and Wyndham Lewis's recent books (Lilly). EP sent Letter 118 via A. V. Moore in London, who forwarded it in a letter to DP on 16 April 1946 (OP). Enclosed was a photograph of a bearded Ernest Hemingway, which Reid had included. EP sent a similar photo to Olga Rudge on 18 March 1946, remarking, "Hem's beard got me beat" (OR Papers, Beinecke).

AVM's of 20th recd with yrs. of 9th & of 16th] This refers to three of DP's letters: Letter 110, which she sent via A. V. Moore, who forwarded it to EP on 20 March, and Letters 108 and 112.

K. St. wd be 'terrific'] In Letter 110, DP said that Katharine Proctor Saint "must be a terrible woman!"

terrific meningite] For H.D.'s (Hilda Doolittle) health problems, see Letters 98n and 109n.

119 Notes. In pencil on two sheets of white paper, one side each except for concluding line on back of the second sheet; envelope addressed to DP at Villa Raggio, postmarked "Washington, D.C. Apr 5 1946," and marked in pencil by DP, "to OP." DP marked the second sheet, "recd May 2 '46," and forwarded the letter to Omar, using the back of the first sheet to write her own letter to Omar, which we present as Letter 135 (3 May 1946) (Letter, OP; envelope, Lilly).

I answered yrs. 9th & 16th via Moore] See Letter 118.

Johnnie R.] Johnny Reid. See Letter 111n.

Whistler] EP's early admiration for the American expatriate painter and essayist James McNeill Whistler (1834–1903) is recorded in his poem "To Whistler, American," first published in 1912: "You and Abe Lincoln from that mass of dolts / Show us there's chance at least of winning through" (*Personae* 249).

Frobenius] Leo Frobenius. See Letter 48n.

bk. on Melville] Charles Olson's *Call Me Ishmael.* See Letter 115n.

Edith S. & D. Richardson] Edith Sitwell (1887–1964), English poet and critic who edited the verse anthology *Wheels* (1916–1921) and in 1922 gave a controversial reading of her poem sequence *Façade*. EP regarded her and her brothers, Osbert and Sacheverell, as dilettantes and referred to them as "shitwells" in letters to Wyndham Lewis. Lewis, who did several portraits of Edith, satirized the trio in *The Apes of God* (1930). Dorothy M. Richardson (1873–1957), English pioneer of "stream of consciousness," is best known for her novel sequence, *Pilgrimage* (1915–1938), centering on the heroine, Miriam Henderson. Reviewing *The Tunnel* (1919), the fourth in the series, EP said that in earlier installments Richardson "had very clearly perceived certain milieux" but that *The Tunnel* was full of a "dullness too great to be borne. Miss Richardson has, I think, overdone her method, and her 'perfection' has become just a shade too 'punctilious' for the human mind to endure" (*Poetry and Prose* 3:311–12).

In 1946 EP may have been reading Sitwell and Richardson in *Life and Letters*, an English magazine financed by H.D.'s companion, Bryher, and edited by their friend Robert Herring. Viola Jordan in her letter to EP of 16 March 1946 told him that she was going to get him a subscription to *Life and Letters*, which Bryher had been sending her for the past five years. Jordan may have provided EP with back issues, for the September 1945 number contained an excerpt from Sitwell's "Fanfare for Elizabeth" and two stories by Richardson, "Visitor" and "Visit." In 1946 the magazine ran installments of Richardson's "Work in Progress" and concluded its serial publication of H.D.'s memoir of Sigmund Freud, "Writing on the Wall."

H.D. been deadly ill] See Letters 98n, 109n, and 118n.

I must "people" the outer world] Cf. Benedick's speech in *Much Ado about Nothing* II.iii: "The world must be peopled. When I said I would die a bachelor, I did not think I should live till I were married."

Mahomed's coffin] This refers to the legend that Mohammed's coffin was suspended in midair at Medina, alluded to by Samuel Butler (1612–1680) in part three of *Hudibras* (1678):

For Spiritual Men are too *Transcendent,*

That mount their Banks, for *Independent.*

To hang, like *Mahomet,* in *th' Air,*

by air
Please forward to D.P.
[St. Elizabeths Hospital]
[Washington, D.C.]
29 Mx [March 1946]

Mao

AVM's of 20th recd with yrs. of 9th & of 16th. K. St. wd be "terrific" but for such abundant goodwill - I dont say you wd/ understand ONE word of the dialect. H.D. alas has had terrific meningite. sd/ to abound in Eng.

get 'em to send me as much gossip as possible.

119 EZRA TO DOROTHY

S. Elizabeths.
[Washington, D.C.]
30 Mz. [March 1946]

Mao.

I answered yrs. 9th & 16th via Moore. Sorry you are having such strain - want all letters possible. - letters & visits being only things that pierce the wall. Sent also a lot of news from lil Johnnie R. - No reason Omar shdn't start with advantage of Kung [Confucius] - as not Whistler where I started. - want him to have that & the radicals [Chinese ideograms].

ideogram & Odyssey (& Iliad) being the gt. treasures. I seem to have checked, chopped off his flow by not bein able to answer all his queeries re/ style etc. - was too tired when his letters & poems came. Hope he has got mine by now - the essential is Kung & Frobenius & Odyssey (& Iliad)

Bloke here has done good bk. on Melville (save trouble of reading M.) old line survivors like Edith S. & D. Richardson have learned to write.

H.D. been deadly ill. (I think I wrote that.) no news of Nancy [Cunard] or Basil [Bunting]. I must "people" the outer world somehow -

She suspended like Mahomet's coffin. I spose not much time to write.

Mao

E.

She write as often as pos. even if only few lines (I don't want to nag about it - but as Romains sd/ plaisir aux mains [a pleasure for the hands] to handle a letter.)

Mao

& love to mother.

You can forward this to OM [Omar].

Temple odes very obscure.

Or St. *Ignatius* at his Prayer,

By pure geometry.

Romains] Jules Romains (1885–1972), French poet, essayist, playwright, and novelist. EP published essays on him as early as 1913, and at EP's invitation he served as nominal French editor of *The Little Review* (1918–1921). EP included a section on him and his school of "Unanimism," or "crowd feeling," in "A Study in French Poets" in *The Little Review* (February 1918), saying that "the group centering in Romains is the only one which seems to me to have an energy comparable to that of the *Blast* group in London" (*Instigations* 76). EP's phrase "plaisirs aux mains" alludes to a poem, quoted by him in the 1918 essay (74–75), in which Romains complains of not receiving letters: "J'ai du bonheur aux mains quand j'ouvre une enveloppe": "My hands are made glad, opening an envelope" (from "Un de ceux" in *La Vie unanime* [1908]).

Temple odes] Probably "Odes of the Temple and Altar," Part Four of The Classic Anthology Defined by Confucius.

120 Notes. In pencil on two sheets of white paper, one side each except for concluding lines on back of the second sheet; envelope addressed to DP at Villa Raggio and postmarked "Washington, D.C. Apr 4 1946." DP penciled on back of the second sheet, "recd May 2 46" (Lilly).

Possum] T. S. Eliot, a director at Faber and Faber, was as reluctant to publish EP's Confucian translations as he was eager to bring out his cantos, feeling that the public had no interest in Chinese wisdom and having no enthusiasm for it himself.

Egoist or Nott] The magazine *The Egoist* and the London publisher Stanley Nott. See Letter 48n.

fine job by Olson] *Call Me Ishmael.* See Letter 115n.

W.L.] Wyndham Lewis, *America, I Presume* (1940) and *The Vulgar Streak* (1941).

another bloke] Unidentified.

121 Notes. In black ink on a sheet of graph-ruled paper folded double and written on three sides; envelope addressed to EP at St. Elizabeths and postmarked "Rapallo 3.4.46" (Lilly).

Maclean is dead] For Alan McLean and his daughter Jane, see Letter 29n.

Mrs Sayre died] Mrs. Anne Sayre, American friend of Henghes (Heinz Winterfeld Klussmann) (1906–1975), a German-Jewish refugee sculptor whom EP and DP befriended in the 1930s.

Vetta] A casino located on the mountain behind Rapallo.

20 rue Jacob] Natalie Clifford Barney's Paris address. See Letters 17n and 99n.

St Elizabeths Hosp
[Washington, D.C.]
31 Mz [March 1946]

Mao.

Faber apparently is NOT doing the Kung. Possum (no use urging) obviously TIRED more'n usual plus possumbly religious <u>kink</u>. Ron [Duncan] flurried with theatre - I don't know what you wrote [A. V.] Moore months ago. But do make it clear that WHEN there is any money, we <u>need</u>, as ever, an Egoist or Nott.

Kung, Buntn [Bunting], Angold. a fine job by Olson (on Melville) that Faber won't - W.L. was alive in '40, '41 (bound to be still, oggi [today]) as per the 2 bks. sent by Johnnie [Reid] (non sellers with the usual elaborate bait that don't take).

[Henry] Swabey & <u>Bride</u> [Scratton] between 'em might mobilise something. I won't say 5 months LOST.

re the Kung

[10194]

difference of oysters where he is printed
when ready & where not. MAH!!
don't bother Possum - but make it as strong as poss. to Moore. Omar too young to be put under so gt. a burden YET.

Something to print NOT for the Bloomsbury taste. Ron, I think, spoke of another intending pubr [publisher] but not sure wd. be suitable or want, & don't <u>abs.</u> fancy N.E. Wky [*New English Weekly*] pamphlet which wd do for Kung but absolutely useless for the rest - etc.

another bloke has learned a little arabic AT LAST
love to Mother   E.

121 DOROTHY TO EZRA

Villa Raggio
add: V. Marsala 12/5.
[Rapallo]
March 2 [error for April 2] 1946

Oh Ming.

Just heard Nerina [Pagliettini] has produced a son: last night. I went round to Ina [Benatti, Nerina's mother] this a.m. to see if I could arrange with her to be with N. in the afternoons - just these last days - & found Papa shaving, Ina having dashed off to

122 *Notes. In black ink on a half sheet of graph-ruled paper, both sides; blue envelope addressed to EP at St. Elizabeths and postmarked "Rapallo 6.4.46" (Lilly).*

dollars from Jenkintown] Isabel's widow's pension.

all sorts of voting] On 13 March 1946 the Italian government announced a referendum for 2 June to deter-mine whether Italy should remain a monarchy or become a republic, with simultaneous general elections to the Constituent Assembly in Rome. The main parties were the Christian Democrats, Socialists, Republicans, National Democratic Union, and Communists, along with several splinter groups. The results were announced on 18 June, with about 54 percent voting for an Italian republic, while the gen-eral election to the Assembly gave the Christian Democrats 35 percent, the Socialists 20 percent, and the Communists 19 percent. The Christian Democrats won in Rome, Naples, and Venice; the Socialists in Milan; and the Communists in Genoa, Florence, and Bologna.

Yr. letter just come] Letter 82.

N.'s. Also saw her husband, in the municipio [town hall] where I had to go for a little job - looking very unshaven & a little shaken I thought. I hear all is well. I was with Nerina yesty. afternoon, until her cognata [sister-in-law] turned up.

Another item via Miss Gordon, that Maclean is dead - Jane living with an uncle. ?a Maclean or her mother's wafty brother? Also, from Miss Clerk, that Mrs. Sayre died about three weeks ago in hospital.

The burning local question, to be or not to be a Casinòh. They are already playing up at the Vetta, & the V. naturally objects to one being started down here - Anyhow, all ~~those~~ that hopeless ground along by the Excelsior [hotel] has been dug up, & laid out with flowers & bushes: really very smart.

Surely it was 20 rue Jacob? Yr. daughter [Mary Rudge] has yet to learn. . . . I sent the money (5,000 lire) as you wished to her. Have had an answer, thanking me - no land for sale & she wouldn't ~~thi~~ dream of ~~using~~ spending yr. money for anything else - & has sent it back to her Mother [Olga Rudge]. So I am awaiting some kind of explosion. I wrote quite simply to Mary, repeating what you said to me. If it comes back to me, I'll give it to Isabel!

Ciaò   Ciaò

various jobs to do - & lunching chez the little dutch woman: she's <u>very</u> dull! but she keeps yr. Ma company quite often, wh. is very useful to me, & she owes us lots of meals!

Yours always -

I wear the little Arabic ring, which you left behind -

D.

Do tell me what you think of Omar's pomes!

122 DOROTHY TO EZRA

Villa Raggio
add: v. Marsala 12/5.
[Rapallo]
~~March~~ April 5 1946.

Dearest.

I have just seen Nerina [Pagliettini] & the baby for a few minutes. Everybody was scared to death two days ago, as she had such high fever. . . but its gone now: the infant is huge, & a terrific personality already at three days! N. couldn't speak, more than a syllable, but she's very happy, because all the rest of the family have girls only! I have been feeling quite shaken over all this.

Call by the Chiavari BK [Bank] - dollars from Jenkintown for Isabel to be arranged about.

I have looked through the daily paper with a view to sending you clippings but I really can't find anything worth the trouble. The soi-disant, temporary, Govt. is made up of five parties: there is all sorts of voting for candidates going on - I don't believe there's

123 Notes. In pencil on a sheet of white paper, both sides, with a separate half sheet ("p. 3") of ruled paper, one side; envelope signed by EP under the flap, addressed to DP at Villa Raggio, postmarked "Washington, D.C. Apr 10 1946," and stamped received in Rapallo "14.5.46." DP marked the separate half sheet, "recd from EP 15 May 46 for OP," and forwarded it to Omar (Lilly; separate half sheet, OP).

several letters all @ once] DP's Letters 87, 91, and possibly 88.

"The Lute of Gassir"] This African tale, collected by Leo Frobenius, focuses the theme of the ideal city in Canto 74: "and with one day's reading a man may have the key in his hands / Lute of Gassir. Hooo Fasa" (lines 92–93). The tale tells of Gassire, a prince of the kingdom of Wagadu, who, in order that his lute might acquire heart and sing with feeling, takes the instrument into battle and brings it back covered with the gore of his fallen sons. In Canto 74 EP recalls Wagadu, several times destroyed and rebuilt: "Four times Wagadu stood there in all her splendour. Four times Wagadu disappeared and was lost to human sight: once through vanity, once through falsehood, once through greed and once through dissension. [. . .] Should Wagadu ever be found for the fourth time, then she will live so forcefully in the minds of men that she will never be lost again, so forcefully that vanity, falsehood, greed and dissension will never be able to harm her. Hooh! Dierra, Agada, Ganna, Silla! Hooh! Fasa!" (Leo Frobenius and Douglas C. Fox, *African Genesis* [New York: Stockpole Sons, 1937], 97–98). See also Letters 8n and 48n.

as to Viola] Viola Jordan. See Letters 37n and 87.

Sadakichi] Carl Sadakichi Hartmann (1869–1944), Japanese-American author of *Confucius: A Drama in Two Acts* (privately printed in 1923) and other plays about major religious figures. He also wrote poetry, educational works, and books on art. On 15 October 1924 EP wrote his father: "Ole Sadakichi Hartmann has sent me a copy of his *Confucius*, a sort of play. Badly written, but I think rather beautiful and interesting" (Tulsa, Paige). EP said of him in *Guide to Kulchur*: "Sadakichi has lived. Has so lived that if one hadn't been oneself it wd. have been worth while to have been Sadakichi. This is a tribute I can pay to few men" (310). EP praised him again in Canto 80.

Harvard 'Wake'] *Harvard Wake*, no. 5 (Spring 1946). Cummings contributed a play in blank verse, *Santa Claus (A Morality)*; a prose fable, "The Old Man who said 'Why?'"«MDNM»; and a poem. The issue contains essays and appreciations by key figures, including William Carlos Williams, Marianne Moore, and Allen Tate. EP wrote Cummings on 29 March, "as to Eimi - I think I sd/ so 20 or 19 years ago i.e. - what the laudatory are @ in *Wake*" (*Pound/Cummings* 176). See also Letters 34n, 47n, and 76n.

anybody in the country who has the faintest idea where to go politically: here I'm told about 1/3 population is Communist. I suppose the Allies want a Right Govt.

Yr. letter just come, very late, saying its long - A qui le dis-tu? [you're telling me!]. Nothing yet from Omar since his (presumed) return to Bremen.

Postage abroad now 15. lire! so that's all the good 225. lire to the $ does one!

Yours always

D.

123 EZRA TO DOROTHY

S. Eliz
[Washington, D.C.]
7 Ap. [1946]

Dear Coz

"Travel broadens the mind." - when there is <u>NO</u> common idiom - may split it.

Got several letters all @ once 3 or 4 days ago. Sorry <u>you</u> are so uncomfortable wdn't condemn worst enemy to 18 day sea - still remember discomforts of a 14 day -

AND

so

on.

For Om. [Omar] there is the "The Lute of Gassir" in the Frobenius. Translation as learning technique of writing if he insists. Ideogram. Homer Il. & Odd. [Iliad & Odyssey]. Frob. - basis culture - He told me to write Port Com. [Command] so I have had nowt since his one or 2 from Biaritz [sic].

as to Viola - well there is MUCH deeper iggurence than hern, & thazzzat -

Saluti a Tutti [greetings to all]. I spose the posts are slow & not much gossip. - Sada-kichi died last year. Nice note from a bloke who met him once. - Harvard 'Wake' done good issue on cummings.

Love   Mao   E.

& love to mother.

vide p.~~2~~ 3 sep. sheet

[Separate half-sheet]   ◯

3

of course I dont know what, if anything he has read - my crit. etc. -

I dont want him to spend more than 1 hour a day reading so long as he can observe <u>fluid</u> outer world, instead of book fix'd & static. 10% of time @ his age enough for the printed page.

124 Notes. In black ink on a half sheet of graph-ruled paper, both sides, with the poem on one side of a separate half sheet of the same paper; blue envelope addressed to EP at St. Elizabeths and postmarked "Rapallo 8.4.46" (Lilly).

Yrs. yesty] Letter 105 contained a Chinese ode draft with the line "True insight's cynosure." EP deleted this word from the final version of the ode but used it in poem number III ("Caesar's Wife") of Book 4, Part One: "'Surely of dames this is the cynosure, / the pride of ladies and the land's allure!'" (*Classic Anthology* 22). Meaning "center of attraction or interest," the word occurs in EP's 1943 radio talk "Complexity": "the French were NOT the world's star, the cynosure, best admired model when it come to colonial empire" (Doob 234).

Basil] Basil Bunting. See Letter 19n. DP's remarks here about Bunting and Nancy Cox suggest that she has received EP's Letter 102.

Nancy Cox] Nancy Cox-McCormack (see Letter 44n). DP's letter to her, sent to a New York address on 10 December 1945, was returned, "Inconnu (Unknown)":

> You'll have heard the newspapers about E.? As an old-&-tried friend, please believe me, if you don't believe it anyway of yourself, that there has been no traitor in E.
>
> The broadcasts were on strict conditions that he say nothing against his conscience or his duties as an Am. citizen. He was trying to educate (a fatal error) - teaching Adams, Jefferson, Brooks Adams, etc. etc. & always rubbing in ~~the~~ certain points in the Constitution.
>
> I am told he is very ill now. They won't give me a passport, but my solicitors in London are trying to get me permission to visit him. I have been (am) tied here, looking after Ma in Law - aged 85. doing all the work.
>
> Do you remember a certain small child?! He [Omar] is now 19. & a volunteer in the U.S. Army - in Bremen. I had him here for ten days just recently, after six years - He is really very good & sweet, & seems to have high grade artistic tastes.
>
> I saw EP. twice only at the Camp here in Italy - & that after five months incommunicado - He has managed latterly to do some more Cantos & revised his translation of Confucius.
>
> Now I have no address: pretty awful. If you can find one, please write him a few words for auld lang syne. (OP)

1084] DP uses this ideogram in the sense of "sincerely." EP defines it at the start of *Ta Hsio: The Great Digest*: "'Sincerity.' The precise definition of the word, pictorially the sun's lance coming to rest on the precise spot verbally. The righthand half of this compound means: to perfect, bring to focus" (*Confucius* 20). The ideogram also appears in Canto 76.

V. Raggio.
Rapallo.
Ap. 7. 46.

Dearest.

Your letters have the knack of arriving just in time. Yrs. yesty. enclosing a draft of another Ch. poem.

I'm not sure of the meaning of 'cynosure' - Kate [Isherwood] has a dictionary, wh. probably won't be right.

Yrs to yr. Ma, on Viola's [Jordan] letter. We had one parcel from V. but not two? perhaps she sent one to Olga [Rudge]? I wrote thanking her from Isabel & myself, at once. It was the first we received. Naturally neither Mary [Rudge] nor Olga will accept the money from you. I did my best. I.W.P. [Isabel] & self <u>were</u> v. short & I was thankful. I ~~got~~ changed some Eng. notes I had, & sold my gold chain, & was down to my last two thousand [lire] so you can imagine! Then AVM [Moore] got me some through. I'll ask Moore in my next letter if Basil [Bunting] can be located.

I wrote to Nancy Cox, but the letter has just come back - Also one I wrote to Uncle George [Tinkham].

Am enclosing a 'poem' I wrote early this a.m.

Always yours

D.

[1084]

[Separate page]

A Letter. April 7. 1946.

"My heart is cold
It must be so"
    and I went down,
My own hammering with terror,
    down, down,
As though a hand pushed me under
Until I touched bottom.
I was blind in that green opacity
Breathless for two nights, two days
While the sun beat upon my
        body, burnt my eyes
Up there on the bench those two hours.
        The god has passed.
Because of your manhood
    I am enriched with
"happiness for ever & ever"
So there be peace between us
And a new serenity.

125 Notes. In black ink on a half sheet of graph-ruled paper, both sides; envelope addressed to EP at St. Elizabeths and postmarked "Rapallo 13.4.46" (Lilly).

Jenkintown BK:] Isabel's widow's pension.

R.N. nephew] Christopher Roscoe, back from the Royal Navy, joined Shakespear & Parkyn as a solicitor, where his uncle, William Roscoe, was senior partner after Mr. Parkyn retired. The two Roscoes were distantly related to William Roscoe, the historian who wrote *The Life and Pontificate of Leo the Tenth* (1805), a copy of which EP annotated heavily (HRHRC).

Woodward Life of Tom Paine] See Letters 24n and 76n.

126 Notes. In pencil on a sheet of white paper, one side, marked by DP in pencil, "recd abt 17 May"; no extant envelope. No enclosure about H.D. (Hilda Doolittle) has survived (Lilly).

One from Agnes] Agnes Bedford wrote EP on 8 April 1946 (Lilly).

Vicari & Montanari] See Letter 99n.

Mencken] H. L. Mencken. See Letter 54n. He visited EP on 13 April 1946 and, as EP wrote Olga Rudge the next day, "said nobody who knew me thought I had been @ anything nefarious traiterous etc - but he didn't xpect much immediate effect of <u>that</u>" (OR Papers, Beinecke). On 15 April, Mencken wrote Winfred Overholser, superintendent of St. Elizabeths, to thank him for his courtesy and to report that he had found EP "in good spirits and relatively clear in mind." He enclosed a check and asked that it be credited to EP's account (Jackanicz 198).

Milky novel by Mary Borden] Mary Borden, Lady Spears (1886–1968), wrote over twenty-five novels. "Milky novel" alludes to "Elsie, the contented cow," the famous Borden milk advertisement; EP cracked this joke about the author's name as early as 1917.

Villa Raggio
Rapallo.
Ap. 12. 1946

Dearest.

Am enclosing one of about 15. Ch. paintings that Ma Riess has given me for you. I told her you were still chewing on Chinese, & she said the characters might help you: anyway here's one, but I don't suppose its much use to you without the dictionary!

Its very springlike, & I am feeling pretty slack: seem to have been busy these last days doing nothing: putting away fur coat - running messages for yr. Ma etc. Her money has come from Jenkintown BK [Bank]: and I've opened an acc/- for her at Chiavari BK - so that's fixed, & off my mind. I am told that before sailing one has to be vetted by the Consulate's Doctor: that Baci's [Bacigalupo] certificate is of no value. Have just written to find out the truth, & so it goes: endless. Sh. & P. [Shakespear & Parkyn] have reinforced themselves with a R.N. nephew -

Am just going out to see Kate [Isherwood]: she is solid sort of company, & not filled with nonsensical theories; she is much calmer & <u>very</u> solid nowadays! Miss Gordon, also much softened! there's Kate's dawg, & a thieving ½ grown Kat to add to the Coʸ [Company]. It tipped over a 70. lire can of condensed milk, & drank & wasted: K. in such a rage!

Always yours   D.

Did I say there is a Woodward Life of Tom Paine?

[1084]

126 EZRA TO DOROTHY

St. Elizabeths
[Washington, D.C.]
17 Ap [1946]

Mao

Cheerful letter from Jas. [Laughlin]. One from Agnes, her mother dead. - I keep wanting news of Vicari & Montanari. [Prince] Ranieri ought to go into U.S. Airways. Did I say Mencken got here @ last with a mass of books & chocolates? Wot else. Lady in Bronx zoo adouci'd [tamed] a black leopard - but still rather young. - photos gone on with paper that gets lent around. Milky novel by Mary Borden - wot ells?

Saluti a [greetings to Giorgio] Parodi etc.

I enc. a "buildup" of HD

Mao

E

127 Notes. In black ink on a sheet of graph-ruled paper folded double and written on three sides; blue envelope addressed to EP at St. Elizabeths and postmarked "Rapallo 19.4.46" (Lilly).

Four of yours] Letters 107, 109, 111, and probably 115.

the Rossetti] Probably Dante Gabriel Rossetti's (1828–1882) *The Early Italian Poets* (1861), later issued in a new arrangement as *Dante and His Circle, With the Italian Poets Preceding Him (1100–1200–1300)* (1874; London: Ellis and Elvey, 1892), containing Dante Alighieri's *La Vita Nuova*, sonnets, canzoni, and ballate; and works by Guido Cavalcanti, Cino da Pistoia, and many other poets, organized so as to highlight their lives and interactions.

Ronnie] EP mentions Ronald Duncan's search for an Italian translator of *This Way to the Tomb* in Letter 109n.

Millar] Henry Miller. See Letter 93n.

James Hylton] James Hilton. See Letter 46n.

costs 700 or 800 lire] Because sending a telegram from Italy was so costly, DP planned to cable Julien Cornell once she knew her date of sailing and to have him pass the message on to EP and Ida B. Mapel. Probably a reply to EP's Letter 115.

Villa Raggio.
[Rapallo]
Ap 17. 46.

Dearest.

Four of yours by today's post! Evidently a ship in: as Isabel has had two packages from U.S.A. friends - containing the most beeootiful undies - of which she stood in dire need! (I had given her some of mine last winter -)

Nice, grateful letter from Little Johnny [Reid]. Good lad - but a trial at times!

Re transport: things looking up a trifle today: letter from Consulate re a sailing some-time. Its all the contingent actions bother me so - But maybe, some how . . . . . I have passed a week in a black despair (—partly spring weather -) and am now working it off in another "poem," not yet finished - Wisteria & all sorts of delicious smelling flowers out along the roads.

I lunched & tea'd with Kate [Isherwood] & Co. yesty. & gave Kate a Chinese lesson, which I believe interested her. Am back to La Vita Nuova: but have only the Rossetti - senza italiano [without the Italian]. Am trying to remember [Chinese] characters by putting them in alongside: there's also some G. Cav. [Guido Cavalcanti] in the same little volume. I find the point of view less incomprehensible than 30. yrs ago- -

What does Ronnie want to be translated into ?Murrican?

I know Omar is going in for Millar. I told him one was enough: but it seemed to have started up something in his head. Have had a short letter from him today: so its been a good day for me!

Novel by James Hylton not bad: Am going over R.L.S. [Robert Louis Stevenson]. He is better than I remembered, though always of a certain lightness in weight.

I sent in my last letter a Chinese picture from Ma Riess - & have some more for you.

Saluti [greetings] to you from a squat old man with a yellow face & chinese eyes - Known him by sight for 100. years.

Here's hoping

D.

I should cable Cornell to let you & Miss Ida know - costs 700 or 800 lire nowadays! Tomorrow I must go see the flower carpets in the churches.

128 Notes. In pencil on two sheets of white paper, both sides (first sheet) and one side (second sheet), marked by DP "recd about May 17"; envelope signed by EP under the flap, addressed to DP at Villa Raggio, postmarked "Washington, D.C. Apr 25 1946," and stamped received in Rapallo "18.5.46." Enclosed was a newspaper photo of "Fritzie," a circus bear on roller skates (Lilly).

Eileen] Eileen Lane Kinney. See Letter 109n.

Brancusi] Constantin Brancusi. See Letter 96n.

Mary Reynolds] Mary Louise Reynolds (1891–1950) settled in Paris in 1920 on her war widow's pension and met Cocteau, Dali, Brancusi, and Breton, and became a benefactor to many artists. She studied bookbinding with Pierre Legrain and used Surrealist motifs in her bindings. For many years she was an intimate companion of Marcel Duchamp. She was active in the French Resistance, and in the fall of 1942 she arranged for her escape from occupied France, traveling from Paris to Lyons by train and camion and thence on foot over the Pyrenees into Spain; she reached New York via Lisbon in April 1943. Her friend Janet Flanner, who was Paris correspondent for the *New Yorker*, published a three-part article, "The Escape of Mrs. Jeffries," giving a detailed pseudonymous account of Reynolds's adventures (22 May, 29 May, 5 June 1943). Reynolds died of cancer in the American Hospital in Neuilly, with Duchamp at her bedside. The Mary Reynolds Collection at the Art Institute of Chicago contains books, monographs, and catalogs relating to Surrealism and Dadaism, as well as examples of her bookbinding.

K. Cannel] Kathleen Biggar Eaton Cannell (1891–1974), a Canadian-American trained as a dancer. She and her husband, the poet Skipwith Cannell, knew EP in Paris and London before World War I. In 1921 she divorced Cannell but stayed on in France until 1944. She was fashion editor for the *New York Times* (1931–1941) and in later years wrote on ballet for the *Christian Science Monitor*. Her memoirs are entitled *Jam Yesterday* (1945).

Dame Una P. Hennesy] Una Pope-Hennessy (1876–1949) wrote *Charles Dickens* (1946), which Edmund Wilson reviewed, along with a book by Vera McWilliams on Lafcadio Hearn, in the *New Yorker* (13 April 1946), noting that since both authors "see the world as more or less concentric to their subjects, they cannot entirely see around these subjects or set them in relation to the world; and their narratives are fluid and formless, a succession of houses lived in, children born and brought up, work sold and salaries drawn, relationships formed and dissolved" (114).

Britten opera] EP had seen a leaflet for the Glyndebourne (not "Gielgud") Opera, which planned to present Benjamin Britten's *The Rape of Lucretia*, with libretto by Ronald Duncan, in July 1946. Scheduled artists included Kathleen Ferrier, Peter Pears, and Aksel Schiotz; John Piper was to design the scenery and costumes.

Hargrave] John Hargrave. See Letter 26n.

Morrison] Chinese-English dictionary. See Letter 19n.

Nasano's] Giambattista Nassano. See Letter 11n.

Mme Andrea] Paolina Andraea, at whose villa EP stored some of his books in 1944. See Letter 5n.

S. Eliz
[Washington, D.C.]
Pascua [Easter]
21. [and 22 April 1946]

Mao

Cheerful letter from Om. [Omar]. Moral restored by some caviar sandwiches due to Eileen - who had been phoning to Brancusi who stayed in Paris all thru.

Nooz items: several yrs late: Mary Reynolds walked over Pyrenees, having stayed in Paris rather long. (Idem K. Cannel whom you may or not remember i.e. stayed long).

K.P. [Katharine Proctor] Saint still sending scriptural etc. - Eileen going to send me envelope big enough to hold Easter card that Isabel can understand. Viola's [Jordan] ~~younge~~ eldest having got job ((@ fabulous salary) with firm that makes cards (sale price of this design to be 15 cents as is accepted fer commerce - (no you can't i.e. reply to yr? what can? vide verso.)

& wot ells??

Brancus apparently scandalized @ extravagance of intercontinental phone call. Branc. said Paris beautiful - paper here last sunday full of photos of Paris april under snow.

Branc. been very ill. E. [Eileen] thinks due to that "new" studio - (damp, poor or no heat etc) but says the original one was caving in due to underground stream. & so on.

Dame Una P. Hennesy been doin an apparently dull bk. on Dickens, (this item from N. Yorker) not inside inf [information].

Britten opera (Ron's libretto) being done @ Gielgud or whatever its called. Hargrave active.

Buona pascua [Happy Easter]

Love Mao E. [insert doodled initial]

Miss Ida pretty regular - but dont supply items fer weekly news letter. was in during week. I miss [Charles] Olson etc.

As far as I make out both Miss Ida [Mapel] & Eileen see no one or fewer & fewer - New spritely inmate, here, opines time lag is increasin.

22 Ap. Have you remembered that the english-chinese vols. of Morrison were @ Nasano's - flat not ice-house? don't know that need do anything. Also you have said no more re/ Mme Andrea. There were big cantos & I think some Cavalcanti there with the other stuff.

Mao

129 Notes. *In black ink with pencil additions on a sheet of graph-ruled paper folded double and written on three sides; blue envelope addressed to EP at St. Elizabeths and postmarked "Rapallo 24.4.46" (Lilly).*

letter from you viâ A. VM.] Letter 118.

Louisa & Mary] From her newly released U.K. funds, DP provided twenty pounds apiece to Louisa Crook, the Shakespears' housemaid in London, and Mary Spackman, their cook.

Morgenthau's memoirs] Henry Morgenthau (1856–1946), American banker, served as ambassador to Turkey (1913–1916) and wrote *Secrets of the Bosphorus* (1918), about the intrigues of the German and Ottoman diplomatic officials. His son, Henry Morgenthau, Jr., was secretary of the Treasury under FDR and a target for some of EP's fiercest criticism. See also Letter 13n.

Casino] See Letter 121.

letter from Bedford] Agnes Bedford wrote DP on 8 April 1946 (Lilly).

address
Via Marsala 12/5.
Rapallo.
Apr. 22 '46

Dearest Ming.

A letter from you viâ A.V.M. [Moore] yesterday, written on back of Little Johnnie's [Reid] and an astonishing picture of Hem [Hemingway] - Of local gossip I haven't much: the second wife of the butcher, Ina's [Benatti] brother, has produced a female: Ina called up at 4.a.m. Easter Sunday - having just got Nerina's [Pagliettini] case in good order! Every time her maschio [baby boy] grunts in his sleep, his fond father switches on the light to know what is the matter with it. . . . She made me laugh!

Letters from Louisa & Mary to A.V.M. & myself re the little present I sent them each: both very graceful & charming. Mary proposes getting new spectacles -

The Moll girl just married - her young man fled to U.S.A. but has got back again. I'm also told the Colli girl is to be married - I have had three lunches out di seguito [in succession] over Easter! Such a pleasant change of cooking: with Corradis, with Ma Riess - &, just imagine, with Miss Clerk!! She lunches always at the Canali - we then went back to her house & I read a book on the terrazza & then we had a huge tea: She must be greatly changed by adversity! She has lent me a book of Old Morgenthau's memoirs "Secrets of the Bosphorus." (ambassador during 1914. war.)

I am trying to memorize one Ch. Ch. [Chinese character] per day - and meanwhile not ~~get~~ forget yesterday's.

Lots of pleasant flowers in bloom & smelling sweet. The Casino is now in full swing. They are using the gardens that side of the footbridge as car-park. Sunday I hear there were over 2,000 people had admittance - & yesterday still more - (Easter holiday.) Entrance 300. lire & you have to show a carta d'identità [identity card]. All the gardens dug & replanted: & yesty. a Corso Floreale [flower parade] - the ~~bits~~ cars I saw of no special ~~value~~ interest - Also a regatta.

A short letter from Bedford. Her ma finally died - & B. very pleased at a letter from you - She has had a bad time with the old woman. I am wondering what she'll do & whether she has a cent to her name.

Much love
dearest Mao
D.

Just taken yr. Ma for a walk - she can only go with my arm and a stick - & hardly any distance.

130 Notes. In pencil on a sheet of white paper folded double and written on four sides; envelope signed by EP under the flap, addressed to DP at Villa Raggio, postmarked "Washington, D.C. Apr 29 1946," and stamped received in Rapallo "18.5.46" (Lilly).

Keynes gone] John Maynard Keynes (1883–1946), British economist who advocated government large-scale economic planning and spending to promote employment, and wrote *Treatise on Money* (1930), *General Theory of Employment, Interest, and Money* (1936), and other works. EP's dislike of Keynes, whom he regarded as a Bloomsbury dilettante, went back to 1920 when EP tried and failed to interest him in Major Douglas's Social Credit. Until Keynes publicly admitted the value of Douglas, declared EP in *ABC of Economics* (1933), "I shall be compelled either to regard him as a saphead or to believe that his writings arise from motives lying deeper in the hinterland of his consciousness than courtesy can permit me to penetrate" (Cookson 262). Nevertheless, Keynes's ideas were fundamental to Britain's postwar welfare legislation as adapted by William Henry Beveridge and others. T. S. Eliot wrote a memorial tribute to Keynes ("a great statesman and a great man") in the *New English Weekly*, 16 May 1946: 47–48.

Hugh] EP enclosed two pages torn from *Newsweek* for 22 April 1946 (47–48), concerning Hugh Dalton, Britain's new chancellor of the exchequer, his background and personal style, and his recently announced budget (see also Letter 137n). There are pencil marks next to the sentence: "He reduced the inheritance tax on small estates, and for business he promised abolition of the excess-profits tax" (47). See also Letter 8n.

Mencken been in] H. L. Mencken. See Letters 54n and 126n.

yrs. of 28 Marzo] Letter 117.

Bill Wms] William Carlos Williams. See Letter 47n.

Susan's "art"] Susan Jordan, daughter of Viola Jordan (née Baxter), worked for Norcross Greeting Cards and provided an Easter card that EP planned to send to Isabel. See Letter 128.

Ida] Ida B. Mapel wrote EP on 25 April 1946: "Shall see you next Tuesday sans doute. [. . .] Also please receive one sock!! darned" (Lilly). The Mapels had invited DP to stay with them on her arrival in Washington. See also Letter 9n.

Em. Hough] Emerson Hough (1857–1923), Iowa-born journalist and author of popular historical and frontier romances, including *The Mississippi Bubble* (1902). "Mississippi Bubble" was the popular term for the scheme of John Law (1671–1729), a Scottish financier and banker in France, to exploit the territories of Louisiana. In 1717–1718 he organized the Mississippi Company. Frenzied stock speculation caused the "bubble" to burst, and many investors were ruined. EP refers to the scheme in Canto 65.

131 Notes. In black ink with pencil additions on a sheet of graph-ruled paper folded double and written on four sides; blue envelope addressed to EP at St. Elizabeths and postmarked "Rapallo 29.4.46" (Lilly).

fateful days] Mussolini and other Italian fascists were captured and executed by partisan forces in late April 1945; American troops entered Genoa on 27 April; EP was taken away on 3 May.

"Domenica"] The Sunday supplement, *La Domenica* (Rome), for 21 April 1946, carried "Colazione con EP: poesia e rognoni" ("Breakfast with EP: Poetry and Kidneys"), by Bruno Fonzi (b. 1914), a fiction writer and translator of Mark Twain, Hemingway, and other authors. Fonzi's mildly sarcastic piece portra«MDUL»«MDNM»ys EP as an aging, pampered poet out of his depth in economic matters, and describes DP as a "very gentle, pretty Englishwoman."

kind letter from Miss Ida] Ida B. Mapel wrote DP on 22 March 1946 (Lilly).

"long" porter] Unidentified.

S. Eliz
[Washington, D.C.]
26 Ap [1946] AM [and P.M.]

Mao.

Another of these stretches when mail dont seem to come in. (vide p. 2)

Keynes gone, one less cock-shy - Dunno if Hugh too much for him. No news - save tremendous noise of workmen removin floor mouldings in laudible desire for sanitation, etc. I told you Mencken been in.

V. little Ital. news in papers here. Hardly worth sending this - may hold it on chance of letter @ noon.

[page two]   P.M.

delay justified by arrival of yrs. of 28 Marzo [March]. re Kate e gli scorpioni [Kate Isherwood and the scorpions], also one from Bill Wms.

Will write mother as soon as I get envelope big enough for Susan's "art" - Viola's name was Baxter in 1904. Saluti a [greetings to] Kate e tutti [and all].

Miss Ida with needless zeal sending darned sock by post after repeated injunctions not to bother. - I take it you have by now her invitation etc.

Love Mao   E

Fluffy 'novel' about John Law date 1902 by Em. Hough - covered with lace & rapiers. lable 'Mississippi Bubble' - got as far as demise of Louis XIV.

131 DOROTHY TO EZRA

12/5 v. Marsala
Rapallo.
Apr. 27 46.

Dearest Ming

Anniversary of fateful days - Some of the worst in both our lives, I guess. An article in "Domenica" of Apr. 21. by one Bruno Fonzi, whom I can't the least remember. "Colazione con EP" & sub-entitled "poesia & rognoni," with some queerish remarks abt. yr. humble servant! I will send it on by the next letter - I couldn't get a second copy.

Apr. 25th here a holiday: May 1st is to be holiday as in times past. I saw five camions full of red-shirted young fisters go through - etc: etc: I don't at all like the atmosphere, & shall be glad when I can leave. Its no place to be in now, until for another year or two: quite chaotic - very possibly will be communistic at the elections.

A letter, did I say? from Consulate, asking my signature, if I want to go over ... some sailings during May. The dawdle & delay is very unnerving: anyhow thank heavens I have some money. Such a kind letter from Miss Ida - to go straight to them until they can find me a room or whatever. Will you tell them how much I appreciate their good-

Irish Theaytre in Leeds] Founded as the Irish Literary Theatre by W. B. Yeats with the help of Lady Gregory, the Dublin-based Abbey Theatre group played in Leeds at the Albert Hall in April 1906. Maire O'Neill was the stage name of Molly Allgood (1887–1952), who had a famous romance with the playwright and Abbey director, J. M. Synge, and played, among other important roles, Pegeen Mike in Synge's *The Playboy of the Western World* (1907). She was engaged to Synge when he died in 1909.

Reeves B.] Reeves Butchart, former wife of Montgomery Butchart. See Letter 111n.

132 Notes. In pencil on a torn scrap of white paper, both sides; envelope signed by EP under the flap, addressed to DP at Villa Raggio, postmarked "Washington, D.C. May 3 1946," and stamped received in Rapallo "27.5.46." DP marked the letter, "recd 28 May." Enclosures: a clipping from the photo section of the Washington, D.C. Times-Herald *1 May 1946, 16, captioned "Meet the People" and featuring two lion cubs making their debut at the Fleishhacker Zoo in San Francisco. A second clipping, from page 17 of the same paper, shows a somnolent possum which a policeman holds by the tail, and is captioned: "Pvt. L. M. Daniels holds the 'possum which was caught by the combined efforts of three policeman yesterday. The culprit slunk into a corner of the Fifth precinct and promptly went to sleep." Below the caption, headed "No Cell for Him!", EP wrote, "& not only" (Lilly).*

ness towards me (& to you.) Omar is trying to get over too. I have given him their address. Bless the child - he's started on the russian alphabet!

I wish to goodness we could all be in Wash: - wasting the latter years of our, anyway, lives in this fashion. I am doing my best to keep alive: but Villa Raggio company & such-like aren't much fun!

Am really beginning to remember some Radicals [Chinese ideograms]. My brilliant memory not now chock-full of potatoes & beans.

Younger sister of the "long" porter full of memories of yr. paying the Kids into the cinema - giving her bread & butter one day! She has married a U.S.A. man on a ship & goes to Brooklyn shortly!! probably before me - as she is a "war Bride" - Moll- girl ditto. Wish I were composed of different balance of glands! Its, I suppose, the usual-all-my-life, opposition of sun & moon, - delay. Oh! Apollo! help!

All my love — D.

Letters from poor old MEG. [Mary Elizabeth Grainger Kerr] very crippled - & Agnes [Bedford], whose Mother is dead at last: She (A.B.) must have been through an awful time.

Kate [Isherwood] is quite a comfort to me - Long reminisce with Miss Gordon re Irish Theaytre in Leeds. Was W.B.Y. in love with Maire O'neil? & so on! I felt as though I had been re-incarnated at least three times since then! Very queer impression.

D.

I have no address to find Reeves B.

132 EZRA TO DOROTHY

S. Eliz.
[Washington, D.C.]
I Maggio [May 1946]

O Mao

There really is some news oggi [today]. Vide enc.

E

Also P.S. the Possum.

133 Notes. In black ink on a sheet of graph-ruled paper folded double and written on four sides; no extant envelope (Lilly).

A date not likely to be forgotten] EP was taken away on 3 May 1945. Anita was the woman who lived on the ground floor of the house, No. 60, occupied by Olga Rudge in Sant'Ambrogio.

Two letters from you yesty] Letters 119 and 120. DP forwarded Letter 119 to Omar, using the back to write Letter 135 to him.

Jarvis Reade ...] Harold Vincent Jervis-Read (b. 1883), English composer who set poems by Francis Thompson, T. Sturge Moore, and others for chorus and orchestra and wrote *The Arrant Artist* (1939), on the philosophy and aesthetics of music. Roger Quilter (1877–1953), an English song composer who had been a student with Percy Grainger in Frankfurt, set many English poems for voice and composed works for children. William Wallace (1860–1940) was a Scottish opthalmologist, composer, and writer on music who based symphonic poems on Dante, Goethe, and Rossetti. He provided translations of Nietzsche for Delius's *A Mass of Life*, first performed by Thomas Beecham at the Queen's Hall in London on 7 June 1909, with Mary Elizabeth Grainger Kerr singing a leading role. In 1910 the first performance of Wallace's symphonic poem *Villon* was given in London.

old Yellow-Belly] In her letter to DP of 8 April 1946, Agnes Bedford refers to DP's friend, "davey," who had written books and lived at Little Easton, ten miles from Bedford's family cottage in Essex. We have not identified this person.

Zola's "L'Assommoir"] *L'Assommoir* (The Dram-Shop), a novel published by Emile Zola (1840–1902) in 1877, of which there were at least two«MDUL»«MDNM» translations into Italian, *Lo scannatojo* (1879) and *L'Assommuàr* (1880). It deals with the effects of alcoholism.

Morganthau's 'Bosphorus'] See Letter 129n. Mustafà Kemàl (1881–1938), who took the name of Kemàl Atatürk ("Father-of-the-Turks"), had a brilliant military and political career, mostly against the Western powers, in Tripolitania (1911–1912), at Gallipoli (1915), and in Palestine (1917), before serving four terms as president of the Turkish republic (1923–1938). He is regarded as the founder of modern Turkey. In 1928 EP declared: "There is in American public life today no man as enlightened as Mustapha Kemal Pasha" (*Poetry and Prose* 5:17).

H.T.T.'s affairs.] Olivia Shakespear's brother, Henry Tudor Tucker, died in 1943.

babbling "of green fields"] The death of Falstaff in Shakespeare's *Henry V* II.iii: "For after I saw him fumble with the sheets, and play with flowers, and smile upon his finger's end, I knew there was but one way; for his nose was as sharp as a pen, and 'a babbled of green fields."

old Eden's book] Rev. Frederic Eden, an old friend of Olivia Shakespear's, wrote *A Garden in Venice* (1903) and *The Nile Without a Dragoman* (1871). Olivia dedicated her last novel, *Uncle Hilary* (1910), "To my friend Frederic Eden."

Via Marsala 12/5
Rapallo.
May 3rd. '46

Dearest.

A date not likely to be forgotten. All my love. I shan't ever forget returning late to No. 60 & seeing Anita & the two men on the doorstep, waiting. Well, thank heaven you're still there to write to. Two letters from you yesty. One of which I will forward to Omar, as you ask. I think he is immersed in Army duties

—he has written very little, & shortly, to me, but I keep on writing to him about once a week, & mentioning books or whatever for his further reference. He seems to remember, & absorb what I say! So I am careful to ~~say~~ speak of what matters.

Re the publishing - I haven't written more than a couple of times to that slow-belly Possum [T. S. Eliot] as A.V.M. [Moore] is always in communication with him. I can't tell just yet what money there will be (and what conditions in England are??) - I must wait until I see a little more clearly: I hear writing-paper an awful price over there.

Most likely the Kung [Confucius] doesn't suit Possum. I still go along with the Chinese - every day—but haven't got several books I should like. . . . I daren't touch the question of books which are up at No. 60. Shouldn't be surprised (but its only a surmise?) if she [Olga Rudge] got over before myself! I have an idea she is thinking of it? All this on least possible foundation. Omar is hoping for leave to England in four or 5. weeks.

Letter from [Mary Elizabeth] Grainger-Kerr. Jarvis Reade died suddenly of cerebral hemorage. Roger Quilter expected to tea - Her old belovèd Dr. Wallace dead: but she says she is too much out of the world now to have any news.

Bedford's mother dead - oh I told you. She can't trail down old Yellow-Belly, who lives ten miles away: but hears he has written another book.

Red flag flying on the factory chimney up by tennis courts, on May 1st. & various speeches I believe. Very likely to be a communist govt. I hear: but I don't talk with anybody on politics; & its all chaotic, with the worst wop vices on top, as far as I make out.

Am deep in Zola's "L'Assommoir" (in Italian). Its very interesting: terrific amount of detail, wh. seems to me to rather over-balance. . . . I've never read any Z. When young I was told to read Balzac, as Zola was too horrible. Its no worse than Balzac - & I suspect much better written? Am stuffed up, with Morganthau's 'Bosphorus.' A long book of the war 1914—18 years there - and no mention of Mustafa Kemal anywhere!! Even when he, Morganthau, goes to see the fighting at Dardanelles - not a nice book.

I'll write A.V.M. [Moore] re publishing in my next to him: posted to him only yesterday; a pile of papers, signed re transfer of my address to c/o S. & P. [Shakespear & Parkyn] later on there will be to sign re H.T.T.'s affairs.

I found Isabel in bed yesty: babbling "of green fields" about teaching Omar "the beauty & loveliness of life" & that he ought to read old Eden's book on the Garden in V. I found it best to retire speechless, onto the terrazza! She does stay in bed every once in a while - but she's a tough 'un!

Am just off "to spend a nice day in the country" as Kate [Isherwood] calls it! i.e. lunch & garden & tea.

Always yours D.

134 Notes. In pencil on two sheets of ruled paper, one side each; no extant envelope (OP).

Sorry you can't come] Omar, who had hoped to get emergency furlough, cabled EP from Bremen on 9 April 1946: "ENDEAVORING VISIT WASHINGTON STOP HAVE REQUESTED INVESTI-GATION BY RED CROSS LOVE=OMAR" (OP). Samuel A. Silk, first assistant physician at St. Elizabeths, wrote Omar on 27 April to say that EP was "making a satisfactory hospital adjustment" and that there was no need for alarm (OP).

Ford's preface] Ford Madox Ford's preface to his *Collected Poems* (1913; London: Martin Secker, 1916), first published in two parts in *Poetry* (August-September 1913). In it he describes his efforts "to register my own times in terms of my own time" (13) and to discover a living poetic idiom to replace the derivative rhetoricizing of the Victorians. "It is the duty of the poet to reflect his own day as it appears to him, as it has impressed itself upon him" (26). In his obituary on Ford (1939), EP said of the preface: "It advocated the prose value of verse-writing, and it, along with his verse, had more in it for my generation than all the groping (most worthily) after 'quantity' (i.e., quantitative metric) of the late Laureate Robert Bridges or the useful, but monotonous, in their day unduly neglected, as more recently unduly touted, metrical labours of G. Manley Hopkins" (Cookson 461).

ces sales (b)Russes!!] One of Henri Gaudier-Brzeska's (1891–1915) notebooks contained a pen portrait, "Sale Russe qui peut la vodka" (*Gaudier-Brzeska* 41). EP often used phrases like "horrible Russians" and "terrible bolshies" (*Poetry and Prose* 5:198) to mock European preconceptions or to convey his own sense of Russia as chaotic and barbarous. See also Letter 136n.

yr / former project] A career in hotel management. See also 10n.

Frobenius] Leo Frobenius. See Letters 48n and 123n.

135 Notes. In black ink on back of the first page of EP's Letter 119; no extant envelope (OP).

S. Elizabeths Hos.
[Washington, D.C.]
3 Maggio [May 1946]

Dear OM

Sorry you can't come. If in London you might get the Confucius printed. Steer Ronnie [Duncan] to Wyndham [Lewis] who has no ethos but who has <u>not</u> mental paralysis - Possum's [T. S. Eliot] cant be helped & shdn't be joggled - he has sense of duty - W.L. has pity & sentiment (don't tell him I said so.)

Study Ford's preface to his collected poems instead of Xpectin me to criticize in & from my present state -

Benedictions.

E.

Navy or Air Force ought to trace Basil [Bunting] (best Eng. poet of his decade, as [J. P.] Angold shd have been of his -)

As to yr. earlier letter. I take it you meant your going to Hamilton [College]: Having started with Ronnie & Possum I take it you cd stand atmosphere of rural beanery about two weeks. esp. as old men who <u>had</u> some culture 40 years ago are now dead. & Time lag increasing. might as well go to Oxford & be done with it - a vulgar boiler factory with scientific (or pseudo) gadgets wd be terra incognita - you might learn something I cdn't tell you in 1/20th of the time.

As also learnin hrooshun - new territory - ces sales (h)Russes [these beastly Russians]!! - I think Hamilton wd stifle smother. etc. even if you are goin' to be a culchurhound & have abandoned yr/ former project - where also <u>is</u> time lag local. - none of 'em re have read Frobenius etc.

Benedictions

Sorry you can't get here.

L. EP.

Via Marsala 12/5
Rapallo.
May 3. 46.

Dearest Omar.

As per over, am forwarding. dad quite right re Kung [Confucius] being v. important, and the Ch. [Chinese] radicals. I am having yet another go at them, now that I have a little time to spare: the essence of the Kung being that one must put order in oneself, one's own thoughts, & then one can begin to understand, (& help) other people. <u>Order</u> <u>any</u> <u>where</u> spreads an influence like the rings of water from a stone thrown in: <u>and</u>, do we need it in these days!

136 Notes. In pencil on two sheets of ruled paper, one side each; envelope addressed to DP at Villa Raggio, postmarked "Washington, D.C. May 7 1946," and stamped received in Rapallo "27.5.46." DP penciled on back of the second sheet, "recd 28th May" (Lilly).

Letr. from Om] See EP's Letter 134n to Omar for several of the details mentioned here.

P. Bottome & spouse] The author Phyllis Bottome (see Letter 46n) and her husband, A. E. Forbes Dennis. They knew the Roosevelts, and on 6 March 1935 Forbes Dennis wrote Eleanor Roosevelt from Rapallo, urging her to give serious consideration to the Social Credit ideas of Major C. H. Douglas and to allow EP to send occasional reports on the progress of Social Credit "to you or the President direct" (FDR Library, Hyde Park). Mrs. Roosevelt's secretary replied on 15 June 1935 that the president "fears that the credit system is not practical under present conditions" (Beinecke).

Cantos 52–71] See Letter 24n.

Good letter from Stella] Stella Bowen. See Letter 48n.

Miss Adah Lee] Adah Lee Mapel, Ida's sister, visited EP on 30 April 1946 and brought him a peanut butter sandwich. Many years before, she had heard George Santayana lecture at Radcliffe College and at the Sorbonne. See Letters 9n and 19n.

ces sales hRusses - Excideuil] Excideuil, a town in southern France with an impressive castle and many troubadour associations, figures in EP's Cantos 29 and 80. He visited it during his 1912 walking tour and returned with DP in the summer of 1919. It is not clear how "ces sales hRusses" (see Letter 134n) connects with Excideuil, but EP may be linking Russian political purges with the Roman Catholic Church's persecution of the Albigenses, a religious group of southern France in the twelfth and thirteenth centuries. The Albigenses, who accepted a Manichaean dualism of good and evil, were declared heretics by the Church; some hundreds of worshipers were put to death in Montségur in 1244. EP believed that Eleusinian elements in the religion of the Albigenses—elements present also in the art of the troubadours—were the true source of the Church's opposition.

It is worth noting also that on 5 August 1919 DP wrote her mother from Rocamadour, forty-five miles south of Excideuil: "We struck a dozen or so of Russian soldiers singing <u>magnificently</u> in a café on Sunday evening" (Grover, reproduced on the final unnumbered page).

her two re Miss Clark] Probably DP's Letters 116 and 117 in which she relates the ordeal of tea with Florence Clerk.

Mrs Burton Harrison] Constance Cary Harrison (1843–1920), Virginia-born author of novels depicting American social life, including *Sweet Bells Out of Tune* (1893), illustrated by Charles Dana Gibson (1867–1944), creator of the Gibson Girl. She also wrote under the name of Mrs. Burton Norvell Harrison.

Goldring's South Lodge] Douglas Goldring. See Letter 77n.

137 Notes. In pencil on a sheet of white paper, one side; envelope addressed to DP at Villa Raggio, postmarked "Washington, D.C. May 14 1946," and stamped received in Pegli (a port town near Genoa) "1.6.46." Enclosures: a typed letter from W. A. Lyly of Toronto to John Reid, dated 6 May 1946, attesting to Lyly's and other Torontonians' admiration for EP; and a newspaper clipping about Hugh Dalton (see below) (Lilly).

Eileen Tut-n-khamen'd] Eileen Lane Kinney excavated a *Manchester Guardian* for 10 April 1946 containing an article on Hugh Dalton's Budget Day speech as chancellor of the exchequer. Headed "A Nonchalant

Found Isabel taking her day-in-bed yesterday. She was babbling about Omar's learning about "the beauty & loveliness of life." Her suggestions as to what you should <u>read</u>, to attain this state of mind - sent me onto the terrace, before I strangled her!! I later retired in good order to Ina's [Benatti] for an hour!

Pass- & trans-port still in suspension.

Your MUM

136 EZRA TO DOROTHY

S. Eliz
[Washington, D.C.]
4 Mag [May 1946]

Mao

Letr. from Om [Omar] - saying can't get here. possibly going London. Tell him to see as many people as posbl. P. Bottome & spouse in yester. forget his name. can't tell anyone much in ½ hour - Time allowd 'out of town' visitors. Also if people hadn't read Cantos 52–71 how can one tell 'em subsequent - full of bonne volonté [goodwill].

Good letter from Stella re her memorial [?]panntry etc.

Did I say Miss Adah Lee had been to Santayana lectures, pre-diluvian—how small the woild.

No news of Basil [Bunting] or Nancy C. [Cunard]. Have gi'en Om enough program (Ford's preface, Frobenius etc.) to fill 1/2 year of non-university time. O.K. that he learn rhooshun - ces sales hRusses [these beastly Russians] - Excideuil.

& so forth - he had her two re Miss Clark etc. et ceterarrrr.

Old novel 1893 by Mrs Burton Harrison. D. Gibson illustrates, to follow Goldring's South Lodge - the period before.

137 EZRA TO DOROTHY

S. Eliz.
[Washington, D.C.]
9 Maggio [May 1946]

Mao.

Her optimism re/ passage - slacks off tendency to write - also I keep waitin' for letters to answer. Eileen Tut-n-khamen'd a Manchester Guardian, vide <u>enc</u>. i dunno if it was coincidence - guess you dont want a full page unabridged (M. Guard.) of all the spitch.

lungs seat of righteousness

liver   "   "   benevolence

Chancellor," the piece dwelt on Dalton's hand gestures and style of oratory during his two-hour speech before Parliament (see also Letter 130n). On 5 May 1946 EP wrote to Eileen, quipping, "I hv. NEVER before had a copy of the Manchester Guardian in my hands [. . .] Guardian marrrvelous. Unique copy shd be preserved in amber. Not since Tut's tomb was open'd" (Tulsa, Paige). For Kinney, see Letter 109n.

several items pro & con] Unidentified.

Mencken heard from] H. L. Mencken wrote EP from Baltimore on 6 May 1946, saying that he had enjoyed his April visit at St. Elizabeths and adding that he had always disliked Ford Madox Ford as a person and as a writer (Lilly). See Letters 54n and 126n.

138 Notes. In black ink on a sheet of graph-ruled paper folded double and written on four sides; no extant envelope. No enclosure has come to light (Lilly).

It. King] Vittorio Emanuele III abdicated on 9 May 1946 in favor of Umberto II, who was himself forced into exile a month later, largely due to a referendum demanding an Italian republic in place of the monarchy. See also Letter 122n.

letter yesty. from Miss Ida] Ida B. Mapel wrote DP on 5 April 1946: "I saw Ezra this week and he looks well—is having time outdoors as the weather is suitable" (Lilly).

KAT you mentioned] See Letter 107.

"Mr. Polly"] H. G. Wells (1866–1946), *The History of Mr. Polly* (1910); *Kipps, the Story of a Simple Soul* (1905).

the two W.L.'s] Two books by Wyndham Lewis that EP mentions in Letter 120. DP's remarks here about Moore, Bunting, and Angold reply to EP's comments in that letter.

Roscoe junior] Christopher Roscoe. See Letter 125n.

Dunning] Ralph Cheever Dunning (1878–1930), expatriate American poet who lived in Paris from 1905 on and published a drama, *Hyllus* (London, 1910), and volumes of verse, *Rococo* (Paris, 1926) and *Windfalls* (Paris, 1929). EP, who considered Dunning's neo-Victorian style a relief from faddish experimentation and mechanical vers libre, published him in *The Exile* (1927–1928) and *Profile* (1932) and promoted him in *Poetry* in 1925: "In Dunning's metric there are marvels of precision. Time and again the phrase is so worn, so familiar at the start; and then the dénouement—the unexpected, the perfectly clear, living speech; unspoiled by the scansion" (*Poetry and Prose* 4:368). James Joyce was horrified in 1927 when EP pronounced his recent poems old-fashioned but lavished praise on Dunning's verse, which Joyce considered "drivel" (*Pound/Joyce* 230). By 1938 EP could admit that much of Dunning's verse was "bad": "My point being that the kind of badness was instructive, and belonged with the quality" (*Poetry and Prose* 7:303). In *A Moveable Feast* (1964), Ernest Hemingway paints a comic picture of EP's concern in Paris for the reclusive, opium-addicted Dunning.

Zola] See Letter 133n.

Madge] Edith Madge, an English missionary who taught music in India, China, and Kashmir most of her life. She was the daughter of Canon Madge, librarian at Winchester Cathedral from 1879.

good deal of mail oggi [today] but not from her [DP] -

several items pro & con recd. California Press et al. slowly discovering part of the facts. Mencken heard from. Miss Ida [Mapel] darned a sock.

                    & so on.

                  Mao   E.

Love to mother.

138 DOROTHY TO EZRA

                    Villa Raggio
                    Rapallo.
                    May 10. '46

Dearest Ming.

Very summery today - Roses all busting out into good smell: syringa & heliotrope also. Yr. Ma making a housegown from an Indian printed curtain: The It. King has abdicated - in favour of Umberto, who is today Umb. II. Just met [Dr.] Gulizia who always asks news of you. Enclosed may entertain you. A letter yesty. from Miss Ida who had just seen you. I am very thankful you have time out of doors - hope the KAT you mentioned is visible & approachable! Am not in contact with any animals here - frogs at night rather pleasant - & birds in early a.m.

I saw Nerina [Pagliettini] yesty: she has become that maternal. . . and seems most happy. Ina [Benatti] says her husband is such a <u>good</u> man. Ma Riess going fairly strong: she is a very intelligent old thing, & really a comfort. Also she lends me books - Isabel's taste in reading matter entirely baffles her! The itch for information, - suitable-to-be-passed-on-in-conversation she can't understand!

Am reading some Wells novels: he really writes very well at times - always without any feeling of "style" - quite curious: but his psycology is very neatly given out - I found "Mr. Polly" most interesting, better than Kipps. Some of D. H. Lawrence's Letters, but they bore me - Some ditto by Kath. Mansfield - seems to me of no value whatever - to the public. I shouldn't be reading such things if I had anything newer - I hope to read the two W.L's you speak of, some time - I have written [A. V.] Moore yr. remarks re a publishing-&-magazine or somesuch . . . Roscoe junior is hunting Basilio [Bunting], as he, R., was in Navy- -I have my doubts as to whether it will be the slightest use, or of interest to anybody, to publish Basil unless there is new stuff; the [J. P.] Angold I don't remember. You know how it was with the Dunning. We'd better look to the Young I think!

Omar is an amusing card: I wrote him that if & when he made me a Mother-in-Law, I expressly wished it understood, she was never in any way to feel responsible for me. . . . (after a fit of fury with Isabel!) & he answers "Don't worry about being a Ma-in-Law yet, for a long while, as I have no intention of creating that sort of trouble for some while. . at least, not until I am earning my own living & not sponging off the Family Fortunes," & adds "All my best love, especially to Dad if you see him soon" - All of which I had to <u>skip</u> when I read his letter to I.W.P.

139 Notes. In pencil on a sheet of white paper, one side; envelope addressed to DP at Villa Raggio, postmarked "Washington, D.C. May 16 1946," and stamped received in Rapallo "19.6.46" (Lilly).

(chines picture)] The ideogram is for Soo-Chow, a town in China, possibly the merchant's home. DP had sent this picture as a gift from Ma Riess in Letter 125.

ground-hawg] EP enclosed a clipping from the Washington, D.C. *Times Herald*, 13 May 1946, 12, captioned "Not Tobacco Road—but Kenvir," featuring a photo of Alice Mapier, a coal miner's daughter, feeding her pet groundhog. The article, "Honeysuckle Vines Can't Hide Mud, Filth and Outdoor Privies," by Frank M. Smith, concerned living conditions in Kenvir, a Kentucky coal-mining town.

Woodward "T. Paine"] W. E. Woodward's *Life of Tom Paine*. See Letter 76n.

novels from J.C.] On 3 May 1946, Julien Cornell, EP's attorney, bought fifteen novels at a secondhand bookstore and had them sent to EP by railway express.

Bennett] Arnold Bennett. See Letter 90n. For Ford Madox Ford, see Letters 14n and 86n.

Rather scrappy, this - nothing very much to write. Am taking a rest from the Zola. Its detailed & heavy, might be rather different in french.

Always yours   D.

Oh! I forgot. A letter from Madge! from Kashmir, where she spent the war, teaching music in a school for English boys - speaking of ~~your~~ "his Melodiousness," & assuring me of her friendship in spite of 'time & space.' I have answered in affectionate tone.

139 EZRA TO DOROTHY

S. Eliz
[Washington, D.C.]
13 or 14 Maggio [May 1946]

Mao -

Thank ma Ries for the merchant (chines picture) naturally I cant read what he is selling, not tea.

[9523]

out of garden - whether its 'baccy I can't say.

was a ground-hawg in todays T. Herald but it has gone to other ward - so I doubt if I shall get it to enclose - greetings to Kate [Isherwood], etc. love to mother. Yes, saw notice of Woodward "T. Paine." Lot of novels from J.C. - Bennett better than I thought. Ford remarkable - weekly papers the destruction of human good sense. [Charles] Olson got hold of some good 'small' revs [reviews] - etc. hope you wont have too awful a state room.

Mao.   E.

P.S. Enc No. I.

140 Notes. In black ink on a sheet of graph-ruled paper folded double and written on three sides; blue envelope addressed to EP at St. Elizabeths and postmarked "Rapallo 16.5.46." Enclosed: a clipping from an Italian newspaper, captioned "Regali dell'ex re" and dated by DP "11 Maggio 46," that comically figures the former Italian king's gift to the nation of his coin collection as a parting tip or gratuity (Lilly).

Dino Compagni] Florentine official (ca. 1255–1324), who, like his contemporary and fellow citizen Dante Alighieri, fell into disfavor after the defeat of his political faction, the White Guelfs. He secretly wrote an important chronicle of the city's political life. His sonnet to Guido Cavalcanti, translated by Dante Gabriel Rossetti and published in *Dante and His Circle* (1874) (see full citation at 127n), reproves Guido for his arrogance as a lover: "And thou but know'st of Love (I think) his name: / Youth holds thy reason in extremities" (141).

letter yesty. from Agnes] In two undated letters to DP, Agnes Bedford described her hand injury, sustained while cleaning up after workmen who were repairing bomb damage (Lilly).

Eileen Crossley] Unidentified. For Eileen Lane Kinney ("Brancusi's Eileen"), see Letter 109n.

"Men & Women in Love"] H. G. Wells's *Stories of Men and Women in Love* (1933) contained *Love and Mr. Lewisham, The Passionate Friends, The Wife of Sir Isaac Harman,* and *The Secret Places of the Heart.*

Via Marsala 12/5
Rapallo.
May 14. 46.

Dearest Ming.

We've been drowned in an awful three-days' deluge: & cold too - better today. I have been occupied in copying out the Radicals [ideograms] to send to Omar, as it seems unlikely he'll find them in Bremen: anyway it may keep him in mind that we both wish him to learn them: I have sent on the first sheet, up to 86th. Naturally to me it seems vastly more important than Russian, but possibly if the Russian-AngloSaxon war breaks out - he may be right, so I am not saying anything to him to discourage, <u>any</u>, activity! I found a sequence in the Radicals of 8. or 9., that I am trying to turn into a poem! I am so thankful of a little leisure, in wh. to turn over certain things in my mind: my "mind" isn't too bright, but rather (a trifle) improved from the last couple of years.

Have done two other pomes: not fit to send at present. I certainly know <u>nothing</u> of the métier.

Am going on with the Dante-Cavalcanti & putting Ch. Ch. [Chinese Characters] of simple words in the margin. I can't learn the Ch. just in a string, its too dull! I am finding bits I understand & like immensely; also one of Dino Compagni to Cav [Cavalcanti].

Had nearly illegible letter yesty. from Agnes - written with her left hand, her right in plaster of paris - but she doesn't say what happened to it. <u>Poor</u> Bedford! No other letters for the moment. Yr. ma heard from one of her friends, I forget which, that a Eileen Crossley is coming over & will come to see her: is this the Eileen you mention as having brought chocolates (bless her!) and if so, is it Brancusi's Eileen? I can't think of anyone else.

Have just finished our "omnibus" of H. G. Wells "Men & Women in Love." He was very busy trying to work out his ideas - & two of the four novels are really very interesting: complete lack of style I should say? but le mot juste sometimes, & several excellent points re women.

Consular letter arrived here: there is a place for me on an animal called the "Marine Carp" about June 16.

So perhaps I shall really get off this time, & see you again before so very long: I must now write to [A. V.] Moore etc.

Yours D.

Oh Ming! Ming!

141 Notes. In pencil on a sheet of white paper, one side, with postscript on reverse; light blue envelope with a blue thirty-cent U.S. airmail stamp, addressed to DP at Villa Raggio, postmarked "Washington, D.C. May 22 1946," and stamped received in Rapallo "30.5.46." DP penciled on back of the letter, "recd May 31. 46" (Lilly).

Mrs Studer] Clara Studer lived in Elmhurst, New York, with her husband, Alfredo, an engraver. Her letters to EP from 1946 show that she was interested in Social Credit, Hugo Fack, and money reform, and agreed with EP's views (Lilly). The Studers visited EP at St. Elizabeths, and DP sent Clara several of his economic pamphlets, including *Oro e lavoro* (see Letter 46n), in which the Studers took a special interest. In later years she and her husband retired to Italy, and she continued to write to EP and DP about economic and ecological matters. In a letter to EP of 16 May 1946, Clara enclosed an airmail stamp for his use (Lilly).

Fordie's "Last Post"] Ford Madox Ford's *The Last Post* (1928), the final novel of his World War I tetralogy, *Parade's End*, which EP mentions he is reading in Letter 86. A lyrical, melancholy work, *The Last Post* concludes the story of Christopher Tietjens and his family via a series of interwoven interior monologues. Set in a rural cottage and its grounds, the book evidently put EP in mind of Ronald Duncan's account of his experiment in communal farming, *Journal of a Husbandman* (1944). See Letter 7n.

air field] Bolling Field, the air force base to which EP had been flown from Rome, could be seen and heard from the grounds of St. Elizabeths Hospital.

bk on Bismark] Juljan Klaczko (1828–1906), *Two Chancellors: Prince Gortchakoff and Prince Bismarck*, translated from French into English in versions by Mrs. Tait and by Frank P. Ward (both 1876). Otto von Bismarck (1815–1898), the Prussian statesman, used cunning diplomacy and war to acquire the long-disputed duchies of Schleswig and Holstein at the base of the Jutland peninsula. Lord John Russell (1792–1878), as British prime minister and as foreign secretary, was deeply involved in the "Schleswig-Holstein Question."

142 Notes. In black ink on a smallish sheet of white paper folded double and written on four sides, with a further half sheet of the same paper, both sides; envelope addressed to EP at St. Elizabeths and postmarked "Rapallo 21.6.47" [sic], evidently an error for "21.5.46" (see also Letter 144). Letter 142 is written on old-fashioned writing paper with "Via Marsala 12–5" written at the top in Isabel's hand; the envelope is of a heavy white paper, unlike the kind used by DP. Having returned to her studio at Via Marsala where Isabel had been staying prior to her accident, DP evidently used some of Isabel's stationery (Lilly).

Three letters from you] Letters 123, 128, and 130 (enclosing an article about Hugh Dalton).

Mrs. Clara Studer] See Letter 141n.

Fack] Hugo Fack wrote DP a supportive postcard on 25 April 1946, saying that he had sent a copy of his paper, *Freedom and Plenty*, to Omar (Lilly). For Fack, see Letter 37n.

I rescued all I could find] A reply to EP's inquiry in Letter 128 about books left with Paolina Andraea. See also Letter 5n.

our Castello] The small castle in the bay at the southern end of Rapallo, built in 1550 after a bloody pirate attack on the town. It served as a prison until 1963, when it was turned into a museum and art gallery. It is a well-known landmark, and DP used it in one of her watercolors, "Hommages—To Vorticism," exhibited in London in 1974 ("Vorticism and Its Allies").

re ch. poem] The manuscript that DP discusses has not come to light. Her references to flame, plants, and the phrase "Lady of our delight" may point to poem XVII of Book 3 ("Airs of Pei") in Part One of *The Classic Anthology Defined by Confucius*. In EP's final version, the poem is called "The Appointment Manqué" and contains the lines:

> Lady of azure thought, supple and tall,
> I wait by nook, by angle in the wall,
> love and see naught; shift foot and scratch my poll.
>
> Lady of silken word, in clarity
> gavest a reed whereon red flower flamed less
> than thy delightfulness. (20)

141 EZRA TO DOROTHY

S. Liz.
[Washington, D.C.]
20 Mag [May] 1946

Mao -

Stamp due to Mrs Studer who had recd 'Oro' etc. -

~~Will hold this~~. Noticed something moving rather rapidly yester - & saw no propeller - doing "barrel roll" - (i.e. side ways not loop). a.m. paper says jet planes @ 550 miles per hour.

Eileen [Kinney] brought Fordie's "Last Post." forerunning Ronnie's agriculture.

Dunno as there is really any sense in using posta aeria for this - other than commemoratin' the "jets" & usin' the stamp. The air field is in sight of orspital so a good deal of audible swish etc. - also got a bk on Bismark starting most of mess @ Schleswig Holstein & J. Russel (prime swine) in 1863.

Love Mao E.

& greetings to mother.

Keep waitin yr news - nacherly. E

142 DOROTHY TO EZRA

Via Marsala 12–5
Rapallo
May 20 1946.

Dearest.

Yes. Yes. a 48. hours- -Yr. Ma sat onto the floor instead of a stool, & has broken her hip - Baci [Bacigalupo] has put her in the hospital. She was quite cheerful this a.m. no pain <u>except</u> when she moves: no fever. I saw the Xray photo this a.m. & Oliva the surgeon - so nice & gentle & kind with her: I shall in time find out but I am nearly sure he attended the Old Man [Homer Pound]. Anyway there is the large stalwart masseur who came to Homer (Joseph, I think) who said yr. Ma looked younger than I did!! I was very exhausted, after having sat up all night with her, & run round getting her carried to Hosp. etc. etc: Baci as usual kindness itself & all helpful. They sent up for me 10.30 p.m. I was dead asleep. So now. . ."its an ill wind". . . I am once more in my own Studio [12/5 Via Marsala] - since yesterday - & the Corradis take me on to feed instead of I.W.P. [Isabel]. She didn't look at all like dying today - Everybody is visiting her - & [Father Desmond] Chute bringing her custard & wine. . . . Three letters from you the day before all this, wh. I haven't had a moment to answer - I <u>can't</u> remember: did I write you that I am hoping to sail on June 16.?

Omar has a changed address but still in Bremen - He has sent it you. I don't know quite what he is up to . . . . very-oyster since Biarritz! Olga [Rudge] wrote me. . . . she has some idea also of "getting off to Washington." Its no concern of mine: I'd rather

not travel on the same boat! but the gods will arrange it, their own way. I burn incense - & have all the Ch. dict. safely here: 4. white & 3. brown vols. as now bound. I feel it our greatest treasure.

A letter from Mrs. Clara Studer offering any help to me - even to a visit. I sent her Oro & Lavoro at [Henry] Swabey's request. A good p.c. from Fack. A lot of people seem very kind to me - I have a fear that I should disappoint them in person - so hopelessly English! I rescued all I could find at Villa Andraea. All the books, including large cantos, had been hidden by the servants in the rubbish heap - She herself had an awful time: a week in prison, with horrors, in our Castello: followed by great illness, at the Verdi hospital - then the once I saw her, she was still at Verdi, but helping. Later she went to her son in Como - On the whole, you seem to gather more news than I do. Thanks for clipping re Hugh D [Dalton].

I am afraid to communicate with certain people - I mean post - perhaps this is excessive. Mail always comes in gusts. Here its all elections & my heavens TALK, reds, white blue pink yellow green .... an awful amount of paper wasted on the walls. I believe much feeling ... and the women to vote. A most hopeless-feeling messy chaos.

re ch. poem. Do you think its <u>ivy</u>?? Could it be mosses? no - I don't believe in yr ivy. Flame? ivy never turns in colour. Dictionary only produces following

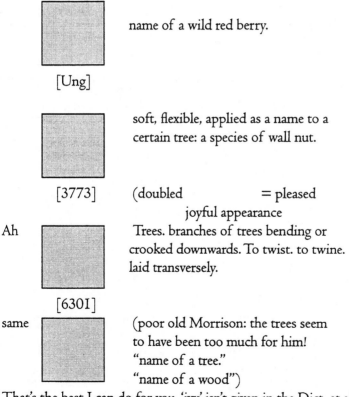

name of a wild red berry.

[Ung]

soft, flexible, applied as a name to a certain tree: a species of wall nut.

[3773]   (doubled   = pleased
                joyful appearance

Ah   Trees. branches of trees bending or
       crooked downwards. To twist. to twine.
       laid transversely.

[6301]

same   (poor old Morrison: the trees seem
       to have been too much for him!
       "name of a tree."
       "name of a wood")

That's the best I can do for you. 'ivy' isn't given in the Dict. at all.

                    Ever yours D.
"Lady of our delight" is too near- -Dantescan?

143 Notes. In pencil on a sheet of white paper, one side; envelope signed by EP under the flap, addressed to DP at Villa Raggio, postmarked "Washington, D.C. May 24 1946" (Lilly).

Om is goin in for] In Letter 127 (17 April 1946), to which Letter 143 replies, DP comments that Omar is "going in for" the novelist Henry Miller. See also Letters 93 and 111.

<u>*what*</u> *costs 700*] A transatlantic cable from Italy. See Letter 127.

scarsegging] Based on the Italian *scarseggiare,* "to be in short supply."

Rosamund Mathers] Rosamond Crowdy Mathers translated French authors. She was the wife of Edward ("Bill") Powys Mathers (1892–1939), a poet who published adaptations of J. C. Mardrus's French translation of the Arabian Nights and, as "Torquemada," composed crossword puzzles for the *London Times*. In reply to a letter from EP, Rosamond wrote from London on 14 May 1946, recalling the early days in London when EP would appear with "flaunting hair and beard and velvet jacket." She added: "Bill never forgot your generosity and value as his critic" (Lilly).

re. O.P.] Omar had sent EP some poems to critique.

144 Notes. In black ink on a half sheet of graph-ruled paper, both sides; blue envelope addressed to EP at St. Elizabeths and postmarked "Rapallo 25.6.47" [sic], evidently an error for "25.5.46" (Lilly).

the Consolato] DP's passport was issued on 6 June 1946 and signed by Lester L. Schnare, the U.S. consul general in Genoa. It was only the eleventh passport to be issued after the reopening of that office, and was amended by Sofia Kearney, the U.S. Vice Consul (see Letter 77n), to cover DP's journey to the United States, and void after 6 July, the date the *Marine Carp* was due to dock in New York.

143 EZRA TO DOROTHY

S. Liz.
[Washington, D.C.]
21 M. [May 1946]

M
A   if she wd write the KEY words clearly & leave the illegible
O   unimport. etc. he dont know what she sz/ Om is goin in for
(her Ap. 17) nor <u>what</u> costs 700.

Cd/ think if he knew how much money she is allowed to get <u>out</u> of Eng. & what exchange is (real & legit.) & costs of which what.

butter & pepper & paper scarsegging <u>here</u> - lovely letter from Rosamund Mathers, - "Bill" died in '39.

re. O.P. I cant judge etc. writing in formative stage - more work to ~~diagnose~~ one page of such than to compose 600 page book.

MAO.

Om. sez they wont giv him leave further than London.

144 DOROTHY TO EZRA

12/5 v. Marsala
[Rapallo]
May 23. 1946.

Dearest Ming.

Went into the Consolato this a.m. I seem all set to sail June 16. on that Marine Carp! Its about 14. days – We stop in at Palermo: about 500. people I hear. The woman who is more or less vice-consul, anyway most active, is really very kind & helpful & answered all sorts of odds & ends of questions most patiently.

Genova smothered in voting posters. I suspect there will be a lot of feeling in the matter.

I have at length evacuated Villa Raggio – really and finally – a great relief – a horrible atmosphere – and latterly fair discomfort. Isabel seems very well indeed, apart her hip. She's always in a state of indignation about something or other – food – flies – or whatnot. The food is quite decent. [Father Desmond] Chute visits her, which I am told has favourably impressed the nuns!

Poppies by the roadside in flower – communist symbol. Roses etc: along the walls most gorgeous, & sweet.

Am tired & must go to Hospital – I go twice a day for a short time only – as I have nothing to say to Isabel whatever!

Yours D.

Civilian mail open into Germany. Have written Vera [Münch].

145 Notes. In pencil on a sheet of white paper, both sides; envelope signed by EP under the flap, addressed to DP at Villa Raggio, and postmarked "Washington, D.C. May 25 1946" (Lilly).

hers 5 Ap.] EP refers to several of DP's letters here. In Letter 124, dated 7 April 1946, DP enclosed her poem about touching "bottom" ("A Letter") and noted that she had sold her gold chain. In Letters 121 (2 April) and 122 (5 April), she gave news of Nerina Pagliettini's new baby boy. Letter 122 mentioned the exchange rate of 225 lire to the dollar.

Rodker publishing] John Rodker was a director, with Martin Freud (Freud's son) and Barbara Low, of the Imago Publishing Co. in London, which printed the writings of Freud and related works such as Hans Sachs's *Freud: Master and Friend* (1945). Rodker had written EP about his publishing work on 12 May 1946 (Charles Olson Papers, Connecticut). See also Letter 48n.

O. R. Agresti] Olivia Rossetti Agresti (1875–1961), daughter of the pre-Raphaelite William Michael Rossetti, translated Cesare Longobardi's book on land reclamation in Italy (1936) and wrote *After Mussolini What?* (New York: Italian Historical Society, 1937), on the corporate state and the League of Nations sanctions against Italy. Her translation of EP's *What Is Money For?*, "A che serve il danaro?", appeared in *Meridiano di Roma* in 1941. From 1921 to 1943 she worked for the Italian Association of Joint Stock Companies and edited its monthly journal. She was sympathetic to Mussolini's aims and helped develop propaganda for the Italian Ministry of Popular Culture. She lived in Rome much of her life, and EP saw her often when he was there to record his broadcasts. Mary de Rachewiltz recalls: "There was deep friendship between them, and she was one of the people he was most at ease with. [. . .] There was great serenity and tolerance in her, except when she spoke of Roosevelt" (*Discretions* 165). She and EP corresponded actively while he was at St. Elizabeths. At the start of Canto 76 he quotes her as saying of Mussolini: "'Will' [. . .] 'break his political / but not economic system.'"

2nd Confucius] Probably EP's Italian translation of the second Confucian classic, Chiung Iung: L'asse che non vacilla (The Unwobbling Pivot) (1945). He issued his Italian version of the first of the classics (with Chinese text) as Confucio. Ta S'eu. Dai Gaku. Studio integrale (1942). See also Document 7n.

S. Eliz
[Washington, D.C.]
23 Mag. [May 1946]

Mao.

Sorry she feelin low — as per hers 5 Ap. Hope she hit bottom* (re <u>her</u> poem, vide verso) & is startin to ~~asee~~ rise. Complimenti to Nerina [Pagliettini] — but say shd have been doublets or plus. She [DP] not always CLEAR, — I spose the sale of chain ref/ time when my 200 1st <u>arrived</u>, not since? Anyhow exc. [exchange] @ 225 is definite (official exc? — pension $3–$4 a day. is it edible) but not how much she can get from London — or if enough to take flat in Roma or wot-t-ell. London don't sound much catch — & this country is expensive, etc. (Rome not been bombed) — no use my tryin to think as have ~~not~~ no data. Anyhow — can't even tell if all friends have mental paralysis re KUNG [Confucius] or not — several active. Rodker publishing with some Freud from Vienna (s. or gd.s [son or grandson] or ?) — oh well she be clear when possible & I cant judge anything. Pope has a white enamel typewriter — otherwise no Ital. news.

Oh yes, good letter from O. R. Agresti, 36 v. Cino Menotti. if she (the Ag.) cd/ ascertain whether the 2nd Confucius circulates etc? — apart from that & Ta Seu most of the rest is out of date. Might find Reeves [Butchart] via New Eng Weekly 15 Regents Pk. Ter. N.W.1.

*re p. I. that refs. poem. that sink down — bad feelin as per canto.
nothing more from Om. [Omar] save change of address.

Love   Mao   E

& to mother.

(not writ)
DP _____ not D.P.
now [⊖] in current print — for Displaced Person.

146 Notes. In pencil on a sheet of white paper, both sides; envelope signed by EP under the flap, addressed to DP at Villa Raggio, postmarked "Washington, D.C. May 28 1946," and stamped received in Rapallo "18.6.46." DP jotted in purple pencil next to each of the ideograms, "not found," and added at the bottom of page one, "?'links-' RLS. [Robert Louis Stevenson] grass on sand" (Lilly).

condolences to I.W.P.] Although EP had not yet received DP's Letter 142 with its news of Isabel's broken hip, he had just had a letter from Julien Cornell, dated 22 May 1946, quoting Olga Rudge's cabled message about the accident (Lilly).

S. Eliz
[Washington, D.C.]
25 Mag [May 1946]

M   if she has time fer Ch. she stick, <u>stick</u>
A   STICK to the radicals [ideograms] – not 5 minutes to other
O   till she <u>knows</u> 'em – <u>Write</u>
      'em out, & send 'em to <u>Om</u> [Omar].

    I cd. teach Ch. much quicker than I learned – prob. quicker than any has learned it in occident. After <u>rads</u>, the pronouns & prep. & commonest <u>advs</u> but ALWAYS dissecting the compounds into components.   MAO.

Prayer

[1092]

I err'd, I pay, I awaken
Wasps be not stroked by men
Nor hawk for wren twice mistaken
let me not be engulph'd in
the multitude of my family's calamaties [*sic*],
nor nest twice on a sand-storm.*

_____

*litterally,
prob. grass on windy
shifting dune.   [7065]

she can look up

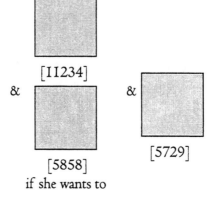

[11234]

&   &   [5729]

[5858]
if she wants to

         mao   E

condolences to I.W.P.

147 Notes. In black ink on a half sheet of graph-ruled paper, both sides; blue envelope addressed to EP at St. Elizabeths and postmarked "Rapallo 31.5.46" (Lilly).

Two from you] Letters 132 (enclosing clippings) and 136.

girl's Easter card painting] Viola Jordan's daughter, Susan. See Letters 128 and 130.

Isabel's leg] Isabel had broken her hip. See Letter 142.

Sunday is the voting] See Letter 122n.

'sortes Virgilianae'] "Virgilian lots," the custom of opening Virgil or another venerable author at random and encountering a line that will foretell the future. Iranians use the poet Hafiz.

<u>also</u>

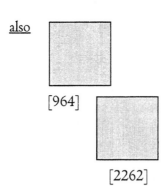

[964]

[2262]

147 DOROTHY TO EZRA

Via Marsala 12/5
Rapallo.
May 29 1946

Oh Mao.

Two from you lately: one containing two nice cubs & a possum – also a very neatly-written one to Isabel with the girl's Easter card painting – a certain amount of technique. Isabel's leg is O.K. She has no pain except when it is necessary to move her a little – & looks better otherwise than I have seen her in a long time. The food quite good at hospital – & I take her extra fruit or somesuch most days.

Weather here impossible: no warmth – no sun – might be April in England.

Sunday is the voting – & I am arranging to be able to stay at home for a couple of days, should things be rough – I think they well may be.

I cabled [Julien] Cornell I was sailing – (unberufen! [touch wood!]) & asked him to inform you & Miss Ida [Mapel].

I expect Omar has had his leave to London by now – in which case he will also have heard from A.V.M. [Moore]

Raining again.

I must go to Hospital now – Kate [Isherwood] has given me a dear little stubby book of Chinese patterns, designs I should imagine for clothing materials etc: I take a 'sortes Virgilianae' in it every day! Rather amusing!

Always Yours   D.

148 *Notes. In black ink on a sheet of graph-ruled paper folded double and written on four sides; blue envelope addressed to EP at St. Elizabeths and postmarked "Rapallo 1.6.46." Clipping enclosed: "Paolo Zappa assolto [acquitted]," from Nuova Stampa, dated by DP "14.5.46" (Lilly). See Letter 36n for Zappa.*

Ritchies] Unidentified.

HTT's collection] Henry Tudor Tucker, DP's uncle, owned drawings of "Dorelia" by Augustus John (1878–1961), an early Wyndham Lewis, Japanese prints, engravings by Dürer, etchings by Whistler, and other works. William Roscoe, the senior partner at Shakespear & Parkyn, was an amateur painter himself, and chose two drawings of "Dorelia," one of which is now in the Tate Gallery.

Sansoni] Luigi Sansoni, violinist who took part in Rapallo concerts in the mid-1930s.

"Nothing matters . . .] DP had seen this twice in canto extracts that EP had sent from the DTC: "nothing matters but the quality / of the affection" (Canto 76, lines 158–59); "nothing counts save the quality of the affection" (Canto 77, line 67).

Via Marsala 12/5
Rapallo.
May 31st. 1946.

Dearest.

I wrote you a very scrappy letter two days ago: the weather was awful! Two nights ago I felt a long earthquake shiver: reported today – one Italy, one Swiss. I am arranging to stay at home for the couple of days of this voting – there may be rites [riots?].

I happened to see the Rome Express, wagon-lits, go through yesterday p.m. all covered with Communist posters. They, all parties, are still putting up posters in the town even today – (voting 2nd June).

Yr. ma is going on very well at the Hospital: & is well looked after – Baci [Bacigalupo] goes in, as a friend – & lots of people. Olga [Rudge] goes frequently. Unfortunately I ran into her there this a.m. She called me into the corridor & made a scene: calling me very ugly names in her most venemous manner. I didn't answer – but left her abruptly. I hope to heavens I get off on 16th – for a multitude of other reasons as well. This place is vile nowadays avvilita [degraded] – & vicious – atmosphere most repulsive. I believe Japan is the place to head for! – Certainly not back here for ages – London possibly?

A little chinese each day: a visit to poor old Kate [Isherwood], I see Ina [Benatti] fairly often: Nerina [Pagliettini] now too absorbed in her baby to be much use to me. Am reading various odds & ends – all unimportant.

I do hope to see you again before very long! Meanwhile the gods be with you. They have been good to me in several ways lately.

The Ritchies out here for a few weeks to inspect their property: not very friendly. Basil [Bunting] can't be traced unless we can give his date of birth & the ship he served on – Somebody will hear abt. him I suppose, in time.

I have offered some of HTT's collection [of] drawings on loan to Roscoe (Sh. & Parkyn) & he has chosen two John drawings & seems delighted. I said I hated pictures stacked in the cellar!

Love Oh Ming   D.

Sansoni in the street – sent saluti [greetings] & always [Edgardo] Rossaro.

You said a wise & great thing, when you said "Nothing matters but the quality of the affection" (do I quote correctly?) & one might say also Pretty lucky too – !

D

149 Notes. In black ink on a sheet of graph-ruled paper folded double and written on four sides; blue envelope addressed to EP at St. Elizabeths and postmarked "Rapallo 4.6.46" (Lilly).

Voting today] See Letter 122n.

"La festa dell'ascensione . . .] "The Feast of the Ascension comes to us with an abundance of sporting events." Easter Sunday was on 21 April in 1946 and Ascension Day on 23 May.

Yr. airmail letter] Letter 141.

two John drawings] See Letter 148n.

Chinese "sortes"] See Letter 147n.

yr. "ivy" poem] See Letter 142.

a messy bolge] "Bolgia," Dante's term for one of the pouches or pockets of Hell. Cantos 18–30 of the Inferno describe Dante's tour of the Eighth Circle, called "Malebolge" ("Evil-Pouches"), with its ten pockets where the various forms of fraud are punished. DP had lately been reading Dante and his contemporaries; see Letters 127, 140, and 150.

Via Marsala 12/5
[Rapallo]
June 2 1946

Dearest

Voting today. Awful weather — one of those storms that make one believe in all sorts of horrors!! Two nights ago a long earthquake shock under my bed . . . reported duly in newspaper next day. (I told you this?)

Following amused me:- "La Festa dell'*ascensione* si presenta ricca di avvenimenti sportivi": sort of high jump or what-not??

Yr. airmail letter came very quickly.

I have heard of Omar being in London from [William] Roscoe & MEG [Mary Elizabeth Grainger Kerr]. R. [Roscoe] has been loaned two John drawings of H.T.T.'s which he will enjoy. OP & MEG seem to be good friends — Can't remember what I have written & what only thought to write you.

My Chinese "sortes," daily, continue to amuse me no end. Water sign & a journey the day I heard (later in the day) from Navigation! — & various others such.

Am stuck (no wonder!) in my poem based on a sequence of Ch. Ch. [Chinese Characters] I found in the radicals. I got a good half done — the end too difficult! I keep on worrying about yr. "ivy" poem.

"As the red berries cling to the branch"

You got mine? in which I gave you the dictionary for the tree-feather-feather-etc:

I think I like
best

[6301]

"May happiness uphold thy house"

but its a queer simile anyway — which is what.
As the berries flame on the southern bough. (nasty joggling sound)

I must be crazy to be sorting you out thus!!

Oh! well! I am praying all the gods in earth & sky to get me over to you shortly. Am not worrying about the ship — Am long past that. Voting day: the sortes comes on "power-authority."

one you had marked
as it happens.

[6193]

150 Notes. In black ink on a half sheet of graph-ruled paper, both sides; blue envelope addressed to EP at St. Elizabeths, sent registered mail, postmarked "Rapallo 8.6.46," stamped received in New York "Reg'y Div Jul 8 1946" and in Washington, D.C. "Reg. Div. Jul 9 1946" (Lilly).

purgatorio — Binyon] Laurence Binyon's translation of Dante's *Divina Commedia.* See Letter 16n.

How I want to get away from here: this land turns evil — its such a messy bolge. Ma!
[well!] such a lot of things to talk ~~to~~ with you about — Meanwhile Yours ever D.

After all, such as I am, you have considerably made me — "educated" all my finer
sensibilities — for which I thank you.

Is this any good?

> Let fly our dreams
> Because across the light
> with goodness & pity
> We wove a truth
> Intangible. (unalterable?)

D.

150 DOROTHY TO EZRA

Via Marsala 12/5
Rapallo.
[8 June 1946]

Dearest Ming.

I felt it in my bones! The "Marine Carp" is postponed: now supposed to sail 23.
June. instead of 16th.

Kate [Isherwood] will be glad anyhow! She is in despair at my leaving — having no
friends at all here, or anybody to sfogare [unburden] to.

Yr. Ma doing very well in hospital — another six weeks or two months probably —
Its cheaper there than in a pension for her.

Have reread the purgatorio — Binyon. There are beautiful things — that's not news —
but I don't think its a "woman's book" — Its so hard (diamondy -) not sentimental — I
see what a comfort it may be — I somehow feel the G. Cav. [Cavalcanti] more human!

Very hot, all of a sudden. I want to catch the P. Off open -

so a rivederci -

I am coming — when the gods permit. Am now beginning to look forward to seeing
something entirely new to me.

dearest

Yours D.

151 Notes. In black ink on a half sheet of graph-ruled paper folded double and written on three sides; blue envelope addressed to EP at St. Elizabeths and postmarked "Rapallo 13.6.46" (Lilly).

Possum has gone over] T. S. Eliot was in the United States in June and July 1946, attending to business affairs and visiting family members whom he had not seen since before the war. He saw EP at St. Elizabeths but missed DP's arrival in Washington by one day. Eliot wrote her from Cambridge, Massachusetts, on 10 July 1946, that he hoped EP could be moved to a private sanatorium as soon as possible (Lilly).

The Croce's shop ruins] Several shops and the church in Rapallo were damaged by straying bombers, mostly British, that meant to hit the port of Genoa some miles up the coast. The Croce's dry goods shop in the main street, Via Mazzini, was close to EP and DP's former apartment in Via Marsala.

Monti's shop] Luigi Monti (1875–1935) owned a shop called "Ars Umbra" in Via Mazzini that sold handicrafts. Luigi was a writer whom EP praised in Guide to Kulchur (91). His son, Rolando Monti, was a painter (see Letter 43n). Tecla, Rolando's sister, also painted, and ran "Ars Umbra" after Luigi's death.

152 Notes. In black ink on a sheet of graph-ruled paper folded double and written on four sides; light green envelope addressed to EP at St. Elizabeths and postmarked "Rapallo 21.6.46" (Lilly).

sorry I haven't written clearly] In Letter 143, EP complained of not being able to read DP's handwriting.

sale of the chain] See Letters 124 and 145.

the Ch. prayer] In EP's Letter 146.

151 DOROTHY TO EZRA

Via Marsala 12/5
[Rapallo]
June 12. 1946.

Dearest.

Nothing from you recently. I am still hoping to get away on 23rd June. The planets really seem very queer! I have heard from three friends in London that Omar was there – but nothing from himself – possibly he's written to N.Y. I also hear Possum has gone over.

Isabel going on well: received a package lately with various foods and two pair of stockings – the latter at the wrong moment! Her only idea of my arrival in U.S.A. is to go see her aged & decrepit friends & "have some conversation." Thanks.

The Corradis feed me well – rather a lot of pasta, & not quite enough vegetables, but the former excellent – from parenti [relatives] in the interior.

The Croce's shop ruins now being sorted out. The house above the Monti's shop also begun on. The church nearly finished. [Father Desmond] Chute v.g. to yr. Ma. We were amused, because he left a packet of brioches in her room instead of the fruit parcel – & when he returned, to rectify his mistake, she had already eaten half the quantity of brioches! I go twice a day & take her fruit, generally.

I fear Ina [Benatti] & Co. are terribly hard up. I have given her as much clothing as I can of mine, & she can probably bargain some of it against food – I believe Vittorio [Benatti] is out of a job -

Talk with [Dr. Mario] Gulizia – who says to me, You go away, & <u>never</u> come back here to Italy. I told him that was my feeling at present.

due to I.W.P. [Isabel]

Hoping – – – – !

Yours en attendant [in the meantime]

D.

152 DOROTHY TO EZRA

Via Marsala 12/5
Rapallo.
June 19 1946.

Oh dear Mao!

I am so sorry I haven't written clearly – my handwriting has become very shaky these last months. 700 lire = cost of a very brief cable to Cornell (airmail letter to U.S.A. 60. or so lire it. [italian]). I have asked Lloyd's to send me £50. stg. a month: but there may be some delay in getting it over to U.S.A. The sale of the chain was just <u>previous</u> to the arrival of the money from you, not since.

153 Notes. In purple pencil on three sheets of graph-ruled paper folded double and written on four sides each, except for the last sheet (on three); light-green envelope addressed to EP at St. Elizabeths and postmarked "New York, N.Y. Jul 6 1946." The pages of the letter were wet at some point, and the text is difficult to read; the envelope was not affected by moisture (Lilly).

S.S. Marine Carp] An official list of instructions for passengers describes the *Marine Carp* as a "piroscafo di soccorso" or "relief ship" (Lilly). More than 450 passengers were aboard. DP was on the sea from 23 June until 6 July.

Signora Bondi] Wife of the station master in Rapallo.

C. di Savoia] EP traveled from New York to Genoa on the super-express Italian liner, *Conte di Savoia* when he returned from his visit to the U.S. in 1939.

Ovidian lands now behind me — & in front?] Ovid (43 B.C.–A.D. 18), exiled for political reasons from Rome to Tomis (now Constanta in Romania on the Black Sea), looked back on his tribulations and forward to nothing in the *Tristia* (Sorrows).

Travel broadens the mind] A motto EP used often (see Letter 123).

Tomorrow am due at Genova Consulate for all the formalities – before sailing: due to go leave June 23 – Here you can't even start to find a flat until you have paid down about thirty thousand lire. wh. you never see again.

Exchange 900. lit [lire italian] to I.Stg.
Cherries 80. lire a kilo –
a restaurant meal about lit. 500—(humble)
butter 60 or 70 lire Kg.
Sugar 1500 lit a Kg.
Gaz etc: all terrific – increased.
Shoes 5,000. a pr.
and housing problem fearful.
Apricots 80 lire a Kg.
Plums less ~~because~~ there is no sugar to preserve them.

Thanking you for the Ch. prayer: very nice. Here Vittorio [Benatti] blew in, on a visit to his relatives the Corradis. He is out of a job. Its all very desperate and dreadful for the ones who are the least [bit] honest, & wish to work honestly -

My love -

D.

Lunch time & packings to do ad infinitum. Yr. ma clouée [confined] in the hospital for another month they say, but she is otherwise very well indeed & pleased with a letter from you by this same mail.

She, i.e. myself, hasn't been down so far into the depths again! & had several good moments -

I have sent Om. [Omar] the Radicals [ideograms] up to, I think, 156 or so – but haven't had time to finish -

Kate [Isherwood] up to tea – I gave her a copy of yr. Chinese "prayer" – She liked it immensely. She left me nearly in tears. Oh! well!

D.

153 DOROTHY TO EZRA

[S.S. Marine Carp]
Palermo – on our way –
June 25 1946

Dearest Ming

Gawd! What a life! I went ashore yesterday p.m. with Signora Bondi from Rapallo – but it is no use posting to you from here – I posted & telegraphed back to Italy. Sicily after breakfast looking more lovely—that pale pinky brown, & misty into the sea, but with heavy shadows. My old sketches from here are quite true in colour, "una mattina tutto limpida" [a very clear morning] says the uneducated maid at that pension. A lot of damage – & in the harbour several islands which turn out to be iron wreckage. We had

an awful passage on Sunday p.m. All the emigrant class seasick. I myself was well & at our table of 14. only me & one other girl managed dinner! but I had to lie down, as one could hardly stand up. Felt very tired day after – but we are having 24. or more hours peacefully here, & can make up! Its an awful crowd. My cabinful pretty decent (8. of us & one v. small wash basin). They have just strung strings all across to hang up their washing. No – No. Its not the C. di Savoia – but we get fair food, abundant, & real ice cream. I have a very kindly steward who pats me on the shoulder – (not one of the negroes). One real Lady on board! who knows ambassadors etc. but is perfectly natural & unaffected about it. We have spoken of Dante & religion – & one old man – who has travelled much – finds the church (RC) no use to him – says he goes to a funeral if necessary – but otherwise. I expounded a brief word of Kung [Confucius] & he [?]smiled slowly, & agreed – but don't seem to know ~~much~~ anything about Kung or any thing else – (business I suppose?) He wears a grey woollen cap, might have been knitted by Martha Washington! & this a.m. he broke his only pair of glasses, and here illness aboard – ??quarantine?? Hell! I am keeping this as a kind of diary. D.

I don't know, Wed?
[26 June]

Anyhow Palermo left last p.m. & now a.m. nothing in sight except a vast wobbly sea, handsome indigo, & a few clouds. Just had a sort of waffle – with maple syrup – I rather think Am. food will suit me if I don't eat too much. The Ovidian lands now behind me – & in front? Anyhow a good store of memories. If one is made up as a sort of recipiente [container] for actions forming memories – then I do pretty well! Even though Palermo is in ruins – I hadn't time to go see as we were forbidden to go ashore the second day. Beautiful weather any how – we left Genova under stars & stripes – flying nothing now. Nothing to write about except one's interior thoughts. These People seem terrible stupid. What a devastating emptyness! we haven't sighted even a seagull – & this is still the Inland Sea! I dont wonder the Argonauts & Ulysses were considered great travellers – & speak of "contrary winds" etc. Travel broadens the mind – Just had boat drill -
Well well well. Love

Thursday.
[27 June]

I repeat, Gawd what a life – The children appear to be in hundreds. I got up early as the only chance of a clear deck to walk up & down a bit – Have made up to old Martha Wash – He's quite fun – he stammers something awful at moments! He has strong binoculars wh. he lends me.

Today lots of movimento [traffic]. Two schools of porpoises, three ships, passing Majorca – & we were dealt out cigarettes & chocolate. Fancy these things being of interest!

Don't seem to be enough brains here to make a decent pair of humans! I suppose all things come to an end??

Yours D.

Friday –
[28 June]

Another week! Its been beastly since Gib. [Gibraltar] wh. we passed at mezzanotte [midnight] – I didnt see it – I saw Majorca earlier. I have stuck it out on deck – but 1/2 the ship load is ill & I don't count it a pleasant pastime. Excuse the butter! I had a breakfast roll in my bag – I am sure you can't read all this. Old Martha W. spoke up & said he'd spank me if I didn't eat something at lunch time! so I tumbled into the diningroom & got some biscuits (Eng) crackers (U.S.A.) wh. have probably saved me – D.

Sunday.
[30 June]

Sea flat – thank heaven. Had a good breakfast. Yesty: only item was 3 birds. I have burnt an awful scarlet! I didn't put on any cream, as I never burn like that – but it was a rather rough, & very nasty, (you know) day & I lay on deck – never thought about it. Am wearing the family impermeabile [raincoat]. The boat is very—dirty. The coal black – I shall arrive a disgrace. Signora Bondi (station-master's wife) is proving a good pal. She's a lively intelligent little woman, & is going to a job in a bank in N.Y. The Real Am. Lady is very pleasant – I painted, "then you studied all the lives of the painters?" No – bad memory – but I studied their pictures – Typical! "How odd"! Oh my aunt!

Filthy sea all yesterday & last night. Today better & I've eaten a good breakfast. Perhaps I shall really be seeing you again, before too long – Seems incredible. I shall post this as soon as possible on landing – its none of it of any importance, but may while away some of yr. time – IF you can read it. Up to present I have been able to remain incog. though I doubt if anybody on board would ever have heard of you – The groups are sorted out now, Swedenborgian like to like. Orders last p.m. at about 10. ocl. by loudspeaker, for those on Sun Deck to ab[b]andonare [leave] immediately – There has been a lot of promiscuous lovemaking I hear. Then three persons were called by name, to the Master's Office—funny elderly gull with white topnot waving.

Getting very hot. Yesty. saw two birds, 1 ship, 2 whales, 1 flying fish, lovely sunset. Nothing herein of any immediate importance – Yours D.

154 Notes. Western Union telegram, sent from New York City at 1:57 P.M. on 6 July 1946 and received in Washington, D.C., at 3:49 P.M. the same day.

JAS] DP was met on arrival by James Laughlin and stayed at his home in Norfolk, Connecticut, on Sunday, 7 July. See Introduction for DP's first days in the States.

155 Notes. In black ink on a half sheet of graph-ruled paper, both sides; no extant envelope (OP).

Mr. Laughlin] See Introduction for DP's letter to James Laughlin describing her first visit to EP.

letter just recd from T.S.E.] T. S. Eliot. See Letter 151n.

galleys of Confucius] EP's Confucius. *The Unwobbling Pivot & The Great Digest* was published by New Directions in 1947.

154 DOROTHY TO EZRA [TELEGRAM]

NEW YORK, NY
6 [July 1946]
157P[M]

EZRA POUND=

STELIZABETH HOSPITAL=

SAFELY ARRIVED SPENDING SUNDAY COUNTRY WITH JAS SEEING COR-
NELL MONDAY THEN COMING WASHINGTON LOVE=

DOROTHY.

JAS.

155 DOROTHY TO ARTHUR VALENTINE MOORE

c/o Miss Mapel.
[3301 P Street N.W.]
Washington D.C.
[11 July 1946]

Dear A.V.M.

Just a hurried word that I landed last Sat. (today Jy 11 .46) OK, that Mr. Laughlin
met me & took me to his home for the Sunday – & Monday I spent mostly with [Julien]
Cornell: Tuesday I came here by plane: very thrilling! 1.hr 20.m. only.

I am being helped all along: I saw EP. yesterday for <u>one hour</u> special – & today for
15 minutes – the usual visiting time (three days a week). He evidently must be got out
into some kind of less prison-y sanatorium: his own wish . . . . & a letter just recd from
T.S.E. saying the same: T.S.E. & I managed to miss each other. He saw EP.

I corrected at Laughlin's the galleys of Confucius.

EP. well physically: very nervous – & no wonder. His head good on just one subject
during 15. minutes.

More anon. Cornell very solid I believe. I want OP. [Omar] badly to help me run
around.

Yr. large batch of paper for Brit. Consul here. I will attend to these next week.

Its very very sticky & hot!

Sincerely

Dorothy Pound

Appendixes

Notes. Typed carbon, with EP's ink corrections, on four sheets of white paper, one side each, and marked by him "copy" in ink on page one; no signature. The first page is initialed: "5–7-45 F.L.A. Rapallo" and "EPB 6–12–45" (Beinecke). "F.L.A." was Frank Lawrence Amprim, the FBI special agent assigned to EP's case (see Letter 2n). "EPB" was Elisabeth Prender Buchanan, an attorney who had joined the Department of Justice in 1930. Amprim obtained the document from No. 60, Sant'Ambrogio, on 7 May 1945 and sent it on to Washington, D.C., as evidence in the case. The text of EP's letter to Biddle has been printed, with minor differences of wording and punctuation, in various places, including Heymann 136–38.

Attourney General Biddle] Francis Beverley Biddle (1886–1968), U.S. attorney general (1941–1945) and descendant of Nicholas Biddle (1786–1844), financier and president of the Second National Bank of the United States, whom EP criticized in *ABC of Economics* (1933) and in his radio talks. The "bank war," in which Martin Van Buren fought for an independent Treasury against the banking interests defended by Biddle, is a subject of Cantos 34 and 37. In Canto 88 EP refers to "Geryon's prize pup, Nicholas Biddle" (line 193).

under indictment for treason] On 26 July 1943, a federal grand jury in Washington, D.C., returned indictments against eight Americans who had been Axis broadcasters: Jane Anderson, Robert Henry Best, Douglas Chandler, Edward L. Delaney, Constance Drexel, Frederick W. Kaltenbach, Max O. Koischwitz, and EP. All except EP had broadcast from Berlin. A new indictment was returned against EP on 26 November 1945, after his return to the United States.

"The Organum of Confucius"] Amprim's memo to J. Edgar Hoover of 10 July 1945 lists radio scripts prepared by EP that Amprim had obtained. Among these is one titled "The Confucian Organ," broadcast on 17 August 1942 (FBI document 100–34099–235). Another memo indicates that this talk was beamed to the United States and the United Kingdom and adds a brief summary: "Equal basis. Philosophical basis of Confucius (and by implication of totalitarian and Axis ethics)" (document 100–34099–309). Copies of the radio script (titled "Confucian Organum") are at Beinecke.

free speech over the radio] In June 1940, *Townsman* published EP's epigram: "Free speech without freedom of radio is a mere goldfish in a bowl" (*Poetry and Prose* 8:38). EP modified this in Canto 74: "free speech without free radio speech is as zero" (line 42).

Arthur Kitson's] Arthur Kitson (1860–1937), writer on banking and money (see Document 6n). He and other money reformers and Social Crediters, such as A. R. Orage, criticized the Cunliffe Committee—appointed in 1918 and led by Lord Walter Cunliffe (1855–1920), governor of the Bank of England (1913–1918)—for its conclusion that Britain should return without delay to a gold standard at prewar par, a measure that Kitson regarded as a prelude to depression and war. In November 1929 the British government set up a committee of economists and businessmen under the chairmanship of Hugh Pattison, Baron Macmillan (1873–1952), to inquire into banking, finance, credit, and other factors of domestic and world economy. Their report (1931) dealt with many issues, including the need for expanded purchasing power and a managed economy, and strongly urged that Britain depart from the gold standard. Nine weeks later, the Bank of England suspended gold payments. EP told Senator Bronson Cutting in 1932 that "I only read [the report] a few weeks ago because I supposed it wd. be BUNK, and it was. Interest mainly in old [John Swanwick, Baron] Bradbury's final note of dissent" (*Pound/Cutting* 72). The Macmillan Committee is mentioned in Canto 46.

Brooks Adams] See Document 7n.

APPENDIX I

Ezra Pount to Attorney General Francis Biddle

E. Pound   copy
12 v. Marsala
Rapallo [Italy]
Aug. 4. 1943

To Attourney General Biddle
Attourney General of the U.S.A.
Washington, D.C.

I understand that I am under indictment for treason. I have done my best to get an authentic report of your statement to this effect. And I wish to place the following facts before you.

I do not believe that the simple fact of speaking over the radio, wherever placed, can in itself constitute treason. I think that must depend on what is said, and on the motives for speaking.

I obtained the concession to speak over Rome radio ~~after~~ with the following proviso. Namely that nothing should be asked of me contrary to my conscience ~~and~~ or contrary to my duties as an american citizen. I obtained a declaration ~~of belief~~ on their part ~~in~~ of a belief in "the free expression of opinion by those qualified to have an opinion."

The legal mind of the Attourney General will understand the interest inherent in this distinction, as from unqualified right of expression.

This declaration was made several times in the announcement of my speeches; with the declaration ~~Nothing will be~~ "He will not be asked to say anything contrary to his conscience, or contrary to his duties as an american citizen" ("Citizen of the U.S.).

Those conditions have been adhered to. The only time I had an opinion as to what might be interesting as subject matter, I was asked whether I would speak of religion. This seemed to me hardly my subject, though I did transmit on one occasion some passages from Confucius, under the title "The Organum of Confucius."

I have not spoken with regard to THIS war, but in protest against a system which creates one war after another, in series and on system. I have not spoken to the troops, and have not suggested that the troops should mutiny or revolt.

The whole basis of democratic or majority government assumes that the citizens shall be informed of the facts. I have not claimed to know all the facts, but I have claimed to know some of the facts which are an essential part of the total that should be known to the people.

I have for years believed that the American people should be better informed as to Europe, and informed by men who are not tied to a special interest or under definite control.

The freedom of the press has become a farce, as everyone knows that the press is controlled, if not by its titular owners, at least by the advertisers.

Free speech under modern conditions becomes a mockery if it do not include the right of free speech over the radio.

And this point is worth establishing[.] The assumption of the right to punish and take vengeance regardless of the area of jurisdiction is dangerous. I do not mean in a small way; but for the nation.

I returned to America before the war to protest against particular forces then engaged in trying to create war and to make sure that the U.S. should be dragged into it.

Arthur Kitson's testimony before the Cunliffe and MacMillan commissions was insufficiently known. Brooks Adams brought to light several currents in history that should be better known. The course of events following the foundation of the Bank of England should be known, and considered in sequence: the suppression of colonial paper money, especially in Pennsylvania. The similar curves following the Napoleonic wars, and our Civil War and Versailles need more attention.

We have not the right to drift into another error similar to that of the Versailles Treaty.

We have, I think, the right to a moderate expansion including defence of the Carribean [*sic*], the elimination of foreign powers from the American continent, but such expansion should not take place at the cost of deteriorating or ruining the internal structure of the U.S.A. The ruin of markets, the perversion of trade routes, in fact all the matter on which my talks have been based is of importance to the american citizen; whom neither you nor I should betray either in time of war OR of peace.

I may say in passing that I took out a life membership in the American Academy of Social and Political Science in the hope of obtaining fuller discussion of some of these issues, but did not ~~fight~~nd them ready for full and frank expression of certain vital eleme[n]ts in the case, this may in part have been due to their incomprehension of the nature of the case.

At any rate a man's duties increase with his knowledge. A war between the U.S. and Italy is monstrous and should not have occurred. And a peace without justice is no peace but merely a prelude to future wars. Someone must take count of these things. And having taken count must act on his knowledge; ~~adim~~ admitting that his knowledge is partial and his judgement subject to error.

Notes. This memoir was assembled from two letters written by Ramon Arrizabalaga to John Edwards, assistant professor of English at the University of California, Berkeley. The letters, dated 31 January and 13 March 1956, are typed on letterhead of Consumer's Supply Company ("Ramon and Louie") in Fallon, Nevada, and are housed in the Ezra Pound Collection at the University of Tulsa's McFarlin Library Special Collections. Edwards, whose papers make up the bulk of Tulsa's EP collection, was researching a biography of EP in the 1950s and wrote to Arrizabalaga with questions about EP's stay at the Office of the Counter Intelligence Corps (CIC) in Genoa in May 1945. We have omitted nothing of substance in the documents and have made only slight changes in format and punctuation.

Ramon Arrizabalaga] See also Document 6n.

Merriman] George Thorpe Merriman (b. 1915), born in Eau Claire, Wisconsin, graduated from the University of Wisconsin and its law school and served as a law clerk at the Wisconsin Supreme Court from 1939 to 1942. Later he was district attorney for Jefferson County, Wisconsin. Trained in Chicago, he served in the Counter Intelligence Corps from 1942 to 1946. After landing at the Anzio beachhead, Sergeant Merriman moved through Rome, up the coast to Pisa and Viareggio, and eventually joined the Ninety-second Division, heading a subdivision CIC detachment in Lucca and arriving in Genoa at the end of April 1945 along with other Allied troops. He missed EP in Rapallo on 3 May by an hour or two, having been delayed by an erroneous Army Intelligence report that EP was in Portofino, a small resort town on the coast near Rapallo.

Frank L. Amprim] See Letter 2n.

statement that Pound would sign] EP's Sworn Statement (Document 6).

note to his wife] See Letter 2.

Miss Olga Rudge] See Letter 1n.

daughter by his mistress] Mary Rudge. See Letter 10n.

two pictures] These famous photographs have been incorrectly identified in EP scholarship. The photo of EP sitting at a typewriter with a copy of Confucius open beside him, commonly thought to be taken at the DTC, was in fact taken at the CIC in Genoa. Arrizabalaga's copy of the photo, which his daughter has kindly permitted us to reproduce (see p. 000, photo artwork), is stamped on the reverse: "SECRET. 16 May 45. Fifth Army, Genoa area, Italy. Ezra Pound, radio commentator and advisor to Mussolini. He is an American citizen and is indicted by U.S. Government for treason. He continues his work while in custody of 92nd Div., C.I.C. Photo by Lees, 196th Signal Photo Co." The other photo (see p. 000, photo artwork) shows EP being interviewed by a man who is usually identified as Frank L. Amprim but is in fact Ramon Arrizabalaga, as the stamped caption on the back of his copy indicates: "SECRET. 16 May 45. Fifth Army, Genoa area, Italy. On the left is Mr. Ramon Arrizabalaga, C.I.C. Chief Investigator, talking with Ezra Pound, author, radio commentator and advisor to Mussolini. He is an American citizen and is indicted by the U.S. Government for treason. He is in custody of the 92nd Div., C.I.C. Photo by Lees, 196th Signal Photo Co."

Ramon Arrizabalaga's Memoir (1956)

I can't recall whether or not we were given any information relative to Pound while in Africa, preparing our intelligence information for the Italian invasion. Probably it was during our operation in Italy that we were briefed on Pound. Then, that he was an FBI personnel target, but that we were to apprehend and hold him for their disposition. We knew that there were several personnel targets of that nature in Italy, that there were several FBI Agents in the Theatre of operations gathering the necessary information and data, and preparing their cases for use in the event their targets were captured.

The "SHOW" was CIC's [Counter Intelligence Corps] only in the sense that they were to apprehend and turn over or hold for the FBI, certain personnel targets. The actual "SHOW" as such was FBI. CIC assisted and cooperated in apprehending and any other way possible. The 92nd Infantry Division CIC Detachment, of which I was the Special Agent in Charge, or commanding officer, knew where Subject allegedly lived and was on the lookout for him.

The facts are, that we went through Rapallo in great haste, and into Genova as there were many (possible) CIC personnel targets there, and we were a part of an "S Force" (Special Force) composed of an S Force Commander, two companies of troops (for securement and guarding of certain installations etc.), several other intelligence agencies, British, American and Italian, which had a job to do.

On April 30, 1945, we, CIC, entered Genova, and on May 2, I asked Special Agent CIC, George Merriman, to go to Rapallo and arrest or check on Subject, as we had obtained information he was living there. We actually thought that he had fled to Northern Italy. Merriman got waylaid and did not get to Rapallo until the morning of May 3rd.

On the afternoon or evening of May 3rd, we received information from Col. Donald MacWillie, AC of S [assistant chief of staff], G2 [Army Intelligence], 92nd Infantry Division, that a Regimental Commander had in his protective custody an American Citizen, whom he was protecting from the Italian Partisans. The Col. added that it was up to us to determine his status and disposition. I cannot remember which Regiment it was, or the name of the Regimental Commander. The man was Ezra Pound. The Partisans wanted revenge, and Subject was glad to be in custody of Americans.

My CIC Detachment with offices (the whole sixth floor, shared with SCI-Z, a branch of OSS [Office of Strategic Services]) in No. 6 Via Fieschi, had Italian Cara-

binieri Police as guards around the clock, and Pound was quartered and fed there under protective custody for several weeks, and until he was officially turned over to 5th Army Provost Marshal. It would have been difficult to force him to leave us, as he was quite happy there.

The day after his apprehension, Frank L. Amprim, Special Agent of the FBI, with Headquarters in Rome, Italy, arrived, and worked for days getting a statement that Pound would sign. Amprim had been working on the case for about a year or more, as I recall. Amprim (assisted at times by me) would interview Subject, get a statement and Pound would refuse to sign it. We finally had him make some changes or corrections and initial them, and finally, Pound condescended to sign the statement on May 7th, a copy of which I have, with the changes, additions and initials and signature.

We had Subject write a note to his wife and mistress, asking them to turn over to us, various documents, papers, magazines etc., which Amprim wanted. Amprim and I went to Rapallo with the note, and gave the women some coffee, canned corn (the latter they really appreciated) and some other staple foods, and while we sipped their wine and ate their cookies, they produced and turned over to us, the desired material.

I may add that no sooner had the information of Subject's apprehension been received through dissemination, Fourth Corps G2 ordered our G2 to turn Subject [over] to them, and only upon informing them that Frank Amprim of the FBI was in the process of interrogation did they rescind the order. Frank Amprim returned to Rome about May 10th or 12th, stating to me that when Pound's trial would begin, I would have to appear as a witness, which led me to believe at the time, that I might get to the good old U.S.

I made several requests to higher headquarters to be relieved of Ezra Pound, and finally, after some weeks, 5th Army Provost Marshal sent several Jeep loads of MP's to Genova to take him away. It was actually rather a sorry sight to see the big six foot MP's commanded by a Captain, relieve Subject of his shoestrings, belt, necktie and clamp a huge pair of handcuffs to one of his wrists, the other end to an MP's wrist and take him away. We had treated him courteously and he couldn't understand it. He said to me, "I don't understand it." I said, "Mr. Pound, you are no longer under my jurisdiction, and I can't help it." He then said, "Do they know who I am?" I answered, "Yes they do." They took him to Pisa.

Pound appeared to be in good health and particularly good spirits during his stay with CIC in Genova, had no complaints either with regard to food, or lodging. I mentioned to him once, (while Amprim and I were trying to get the statement from him) that I did not like the conditions under which he was living, and that I would like to find a nice small apartment for him, where he could stay, under protective custody, of course, but he would have none of it. He was afraid for his life if he were to be away from us, and he actually felt secure with us. The picture definitely changed when the 5th Army Military Police relieved us of him and took him to Pisa. I would not be surprised if he did have a breakdown after that, as the treatment must have been considerably different.

I might add that at the time Subject was taken into custody by 92nd Div. CIC, his mistress, Miss Olga Rudge, another expatriate American, was with him. She too remained in our custody with him for several days, and was then released. She gave me a printed copy of Pound's version of Confucius, which he mentions in his statement, for

a souvenir. Pound, his wife, Dorothy Pound and Miss Olga Rudge (his mistress) had been living together at Rapallo for some time. The daughter by his mistress, Miss Rudge (whom we later saw and talked with), was living in Northern Italy.

Frank Amprim wrote me on 29 November 1948, and in one paragraph, said, "As we were ready to try him for treason, the government psychiatrist found him mentally incapable of standing trial. He is presently in an institution in Washington. Recently he told reporters that a person couldn't write poetry in the bug house. I guess he hasn't changed much." It might be worthwhile trying to contact Frank Amprim, whose address, in 1948 was:

FRANK L. AMPRIM
Attorney and Counselor at Law
Suite 2–4-6–8 Cahalan Bldg.
Wynadotte, Michigan.

I am enclosing an exact original copy of the statement obtained from Ezra Pound, every page initialed, every change and every page also initialed. Please send it back to me, as I value it highly as a souvenir and don't want to lose it. Am also enclosing two pictures, one of Ezra Pound posing at the typewriter while doing some of his work, and the other, taken while being interviewed by me, while in custody. The pictures were taken by the 196th Signal Photo Co., 92nd Inf. Div., at the direction of Colonel Donald MacWillie, AC of S, G2, 92nd Infantry Division. Please send them back to me when you send me the Statement.

Sincerely yours,
Ramon Arrizabalaga Jr.

APPENDIX II

Glossary of Chinese Ideograms
and Morrison Translations

310]　Chang. To manifest or display, constant, usual, common, frequently.

Letters 30, 31

964]　Chin. To move, to agitate, to shake, to excite, to raise, to rescue, to adjust, to put in order, to repair. To stop, to receive.
Letter 146

1084]　Ching. Without guile, without admixture, of one mind, sincere, true, honest, sincerity, truth.
Letters 21a?, 124, 125

1092]　Ching. To form, to regulate, to stop or cause to desist, to repress, to caution, to warn, to correct.
Letter 146

1377]　Chow. To provide for fully, to supply the wants of, a curve, to perform a circle, to complete; faithful.
Letter 90

2026]　E.　That which by nature is constituted fit, proper, fitting for, suitable to, according with, union, harmony. Business, affair.
Letter 31

2029] E. What is fit, suitable, or proper for man, virtue, goodness, order, right. Persons who form friendships. An acquaintance.
Letter 31

2262] Fe. Square bamboo basket or box. Not, not right, those who do what is illegal, vagabonds, banditti.

Letter 146

3773] Heue. Soft, flexible, applied as a name to a certain tree, a species of walnut.

Letter 142

3799] Heuen. To call to, to call out, to make a clamorous noise.

Letter 28

3802] Heuen. Incessant bewailing. Eminent and conspicuous in moral virtue, authority, to fear.
Letter 71

3810] Heuen. Loud clamorous noise.

Letters 21a, 28, 31

3818] Heuen. Fallacious, false, irregular, clamorous, noisy, the clamor and disturbance made by a great many persons talking at the same time. The name of a plant.
Letters 21a, 28

5729] Keen. The shooting forth of grain, eminent virtue and talents. Proud.

Letter 146

5858]   Keen. The shoulder; to bear on one's shoulder, to sustain, to be competent to, firm (misprinted in Morrison as 8858). Letter 146

6193]   Keuh. Power, authority, temporary or peculiar circumstances, which like authority compels one to deviate from a regular course. To comply with circumstances. Letter 149

6301]   Kew. Trees, or the branches bending or crooked downward, to twist, to twine, laid transversely (misprinted in Morrison as 9301). Letters 142, 149

7065]   Lee. Name of an acrid herb, which seems to fly up into the air.

Letter 146

7534]   Maou. A cow's tail held in the hand to make signals with, a kind of banner in the army. Riding in a particular manner. Letter 96

7879]   Nan. The region of heat and luxuriant vegetation. The region which sustains and cherishes plants and living creatures. The south. Letter 90

7984]   Neen. To ponder, to consider, to read in a singing tone, the thoughts.

Letter 105

9019] Seuen. From a *house* or *covering* in which winds revolve and cause to circulate the material principles in nature, to revolve and extend to every place, to spread out, to expand, to proclaim to, to declare to, to summon. A high degree of intelligence.
Letters 28, 31

9164] Seuen. Verse, poetry, an ode, composition which may be sung or chanted, "The Odes."

Letter 90

9523] Soo. A certain medicinal plant, cheerful, joyous, happy; to desist, to take, to resuscitate, to agitate. Also, *Soo-chow,* a famous and populous district in Keang-nan.
Letter 139

10194] Tih. Having found what one wanted, to be successful in doing something, to obtain what one wanted, to attain the end proposed.
Letter 120

11234] Tsze. To sustain, or bear the duties devolving on one.

Letter 146

11304] Tzse. A female able to bear, to bear, to produce, to cherish, to love, to promise a woman in marriage. Letters, a letter or written character of any kind.
Letter 86

75th
Radical,
Muh] Ung. The name of a wild red berry.

Letter 142

11587] Wan.　To draw a line, to paint a picture or representation of a thing, an assemblage of colors, fine composition. The veins, lines, or grain of wood or of stone, marks or spots on skins. The ripple on the surface of water, any thing ornamental, it includes every excellence and virtue. Letters, literature, literary men; civil officers.
Letter 105

11618] Wang.　A king, sovereign, royal, a title of honor, applied to deceased ancestors, to dependent princes of the empire, and to the emperor's uncles and brothers.
Letter 105

11632] We. From *a run-away* and *heart*. To escape from the memory, to forget, to be lost, to be disregarded, the mind absent.
Letters 21a, 28, 31

Works, Libraries, and Collections Cited

Abbreviations in **bold type** are those used in the notes to the letters in this volume. This list contains libraries, collections, and works frequently cited but does not, except in a few instances, include items cited only once or infrequently; ordinarily, such works are incorporated directly into the notes following the letters. Notes to the Introduction are self-contained at the end of that section.

LIBRARIES AND PRIVATE COLLECTIONS

Beinecke Rare Book and Manuscript Library, Yale University. (**Beinecke**) Among the Beinecke's Pound-related holdings are the Olga Rudge Papers. (**OR Papers**)

Burke Library, Hamilton College. (**Burke**)

Harry Ransom Humanities Research Center, University of Texas. at Austin. (**HRHRC**)

Houghton Library, Harvard University. (**Houghton**)

Lilly Library, Indiana University. (**Lilly**)

McFarlin Library Special Collections, University of Tulsa. (**Tulsa**) The Ezra Pound Collection at Tulsa contains, among other materials assembled by John Edwards, photocopies of transcriptions of EP letters made by D. D. Paige. (**Tulsa, Paige**)

Private collection of Omar Pound. (**OP**)

PUBLISHED WRITINGS OF EZRA POUND

ABC of Reading. 1934; New York: New Directions, 1960. (**ABC of Reading**)

The Cantos. 13th printing. New York: New Directions, 1995. (**Canto**, followed by canto number and line numbers)

Confucius: The Great Digest, The Unwobbling Pivot, The Analects. 1951; New York: New Directions, 1969. (**Confucius**)

"Ezra Pound Speaking": Radio Speeches of World War II. Ed. Leonard W. Doob. Westport, Conn.: Greenwood Press, 1978. (**Doob**)

Gaudier-Brzeska: A Memoir. New York: New Directions, 1970. (**Gaudier-Brzeska**)

Guide to Kulchur. 1938; New York: New Directions, 1970. (**Guide to Kulchur**)

Instigations. 1920; Freeport, NY: Books for Libraries Press, 1969. (**Instigations**)

Literary Essays. Ed. T. S. Eliot. 1954; New York: New Directions, 1968. (**LE**)

Personae: The Shorter Poems. Ed. Lea Baechler and A. Walton Litz. 1926; rev. ed. New York: New
  Directions, 1990. (**Personae**)

Poetry and Prose Contributions to Periodicals. 10 vols. Ed. Lea Baechler, et al. New York: Garland, 1991.
  (**Poetry and Prose**)

Selected Prose, 1909–1965. Ed. William Cookson. New York: New Directions, 1973. (**Cookson**)

Shih-Ching: The Classic Anthology Defined by Confucius. 1954; Cambridge, Mass.: Harvard University
  Press, 1976. (**Classic Anthology**)

Translations. New York: New Directions, 1963. (**Translations**)

PUBLISHED LETTERS OF EZRA POUND

Selected Letters, 1907–1941. Ed. D. D. Paige. 1950; New York: New Directions, 1971. (**Paige**)

Pound/Cummings: The Correspondence of Ezra Pound and E. E. Cummings. Ed. Barry Ahearn. Ann Arbor:
  University of Michigan Press, 1996. (**Pound/Cummings**)

Ezra Pound and Senator Bronson Cutting: A Political Correspondence, 1930–1935. Ed. E. P. Walkiewicz
  and Hugh Witemeyer. Albuquerque: University of New Mexico Press. (**Pound/Cutting**)

Pound/Joyce: The Letters of Ezra Pound to James Joyce. 1995. Ed. Forrest Read. New York: New Directions, 1970. (**Pound/Joyce**)

Pound/Lewis: The Correspondence of Ezra Pound and Wyndham Lewis. Ed. Timothy Materer. New York:
  New Directions, 1985. (**Pound/Lewis**)

The Selected Letters of Ezra Pound to John Quinn, 1915–1924. Ed. Timothy Materer. Durham, N.C.:
  Duke University Press, 1991. (**Pound/Quinn**)

Pound/Zukofsky: Selected Letters of Ezra Pound and Louis Zukofsky. Ed. Barry Ahearn. New York: New
  Directions, 1987. (**Pound/Zuk**)

BOOKS AND ARTICLES BY OTHERS

Cannistraro Cannistraro, Philip V. *Historical Dictionary of Fascist Italy.* Westport, Conn: Greenwood
  Press, 1982.

Carpenter Carpenter, Humphrey. *A Serious Character: The Life of Ezra Pound.* Boston: Houghton
  Mifflin, 1988.

Cole Cole, John Y., ed. *Books in Action: The Armed Services Editions.* Washington, D.C.: Library of
  Congress, 1984.

Discretions de Rachewiltz, Marry. *Ezra Pound, Father and Teacher: Discretions.* 1971; New York: New
  Directions, 1975.

Grover Grover, Philip, ed. *Ezra Pound: The London Years, 1908–1920.* New York: AMS Press, 1978.

Heymann Heymann, C. David. *Ezra Pound: The Last Rower.* 1976; New York: Seaver Books, 1980.

Jackanicz Jackanicz, Donald W. "Ezra Pound at St. Elizabeths Hospital: The Case File of
  Patient 58,102." *Manuscripts* 43 (Summer 1991): 193–206.

King King, Michael. "Ezra Pound at Pisa: An Interview with John L. Steele." *Texas Quarterly* 49
  (1978): 49–61.

Lenin Lenin, V.I. *Imperialism: The Highest Stage of Capitalism.* New York: International Publishers,
  1939.

Mariani Mariani, Paul. *William Carlos Williams: A New World Naked.* 1981; New York: W.W. Norton, 1990.